The Mitchell Beazley Illustrated Encyclopedia of

WORKING IN WOOD

Tools·Methods·Materials·Classic Constructions

Margaret Morrison

The Mitchell Beazley Illustrated Encyclopedia of

WORKING IN WOOD

Tools·Methods·Materials·Classic Constructions

Ernest Scott

Mitchell Beazley

The Mitchell Beazley Encyclopedia of
Working in Wood
© Reed International Books Limited 1980
Reprinted 1984, 1988, 1992, 1993
All rights reserved.
No part of this work may be reproduced or utilized in any form
by any means, electronic or mechanical, including photocopying,
recording or by any information storage or retrieval system, without
the prior written permission of the publisher.
ISBN 1 85732 017 4
The Mitchell Beazley Encyclopedia of Working in Wood was
first published in Great Britain by Mitchell Beazley,
an imprint of Reed Consumer Books Ltd
Michelin House, 81 Fulham Road, London, SW3 6RB
and Auckland, Melbourne, Singapore and Toronto
Phototypeset by Filmtype Services Limited, Scarborough
Origination by Gilchrist Bros, Leeds
Printed in Hong Kong

Art editor
John Ridgeway

Designers
Ayala Kingsley
Niki Overy
Nick Paul
Val Hill

Production controller
Barry Baker

Executive editor
Lawrence Clarke

Editor
Joanna Chisholm

Consultant editor
Pamela Tubby

Researchers
Louise Egerton
Pam Taaffe

Editorial assistant
Charlotte Kennedy

Contents

The author and publishers wish to acknowledge the contributions made by these specialist mastercraftsmen in the following subject areas:

Carcasses and frames
Mike Farrow
Lecturer in furniture studies at the London College of Furniture and Member of the Society of Industrial Artists and Designers. Served his apprenticeship as a cabinetmaker in his grandfather's workshop.

Classic constructions
John Coles
Lecturer in restoration and conservation studies at the London College of Furniture. Served his apprenticeship to an antique restorer and cabinetmaker. Is a practising restorer as well as a consultant to an international furniture group.

Design
Alan Tilbury
Design consultant and tutor in the School of Furniture and Design at the Royal College of Art.

John Barden
Furniture specialist at the Design Council. Is a practising design consultant.

Materials
Bill Hallworth
Senior lecturer in wood science, technology and timber economics at the London College of Furniture and Associate of the Institute of Wood Science. Practised as an importer in the timber trade and surveyor in timber preservation and is now a consultant to the furniture trade.

Parquetry and marquetry
Ernie Ives
Fellow of the Marquetry Society and Editor of the *Marquetarian*. Practised as a boatbuilder for 12 years and then spent 20 years teaching craft and marquetry.

Restoration
Roger Woods
Fellow of the College of Craft Education and lecturer in furniture subjects at Rycotewood College.

Alan Dyer
Professional restorer; family craftsmen since 1824.

Surface finishes
Bert Burrell
Lecturer in wood finishing and french polishing at the London College of Furniture. Served his apprenticeship as a polisher-improver and has practised as a polisher for 35 years.

Veneering
Ernest Jones
Lecturer in fine craftsmenship and cabinetmaking at Rycotewood College. Served his apprenticeship to a handcraft furnituremaker; has practised as a cabinetmaker and taught cabinetmaking for 37 years.

Woodcarving
Paul Ferguson
Part-time lecturer in woodcarving and gilding at the London College of Furniture. Served his apprenticeship to a Master Carver and now runs his own woodcarving and gilding business.

Woodturning
William Wells
Member of the College of Craft Education. Has practised as a woodworker and furniture designer for 10 years and has spent 20 years teaching both adults and children.

Foreword

Handling wood and sensing its textures and fragrances brings to mind the pleasures of a bygone age, when the woodworking skills of mastercraftsmen were commonplace. In our technological age, as these traditional skills are required less and less in the pursuit of a living, they are coveted more and more for the sheer pleasure inherent in their mastery.

The object of this book is to make the secrets of these skills available to all who seek them. It provides the essential sound basis on which successful woodworking is founded: how to select the most suitable material and best method of working, how to maintain and use the correct tool for the job and how to apply the principles of design and construction.

Working in Wood is divided into six sections: Classic constructions; Design; Tools; Methods; Materials; and Fixtures and fittings. Each section is treated separately and linked by an extensive index. All technical terms are fully explained in the comprehensive glossary.

The **Classic constructions section** introduces the subject of woodworking through some of the finest furniture ever made. Each piece has been selected for its universal appeal and as an example of quality craftsmanship. Even with the development of sophisticated power tools, the principles underlying the best traditional techniques are wholly applicable to fine woodworking today. All the key methods and materials relating to each piece are contained in individual cross-reference panels.

The **Design section** is an analysis of all the problems that need to be resolved before starting any project. The appropriate design tools are illustrated and their uses demonstrated in the context of planning a project.

The **Tools section** is an analysis of all the hand and machine tools required in producing quality work, from the basic kit to specialized fixed power tools. The tools are divided according to their uses, such as sawing, planing, smoothing and chiselling. A complete description is supplied with each tool, and on the same or accompanying pages there are precise instructions on how to work with each.

The **Methods section** is a comprehensive demonstration of all the essential techniques in woodworking: jointing; working manufactured boards; frame- and carcass-making; bending; laminating; woodturning; woodcarving; veneering; finishing surfaces and restoring. Each technique is described through illustrations of the key actions by the specialist craftsman and precise step-by-step text.

The **Materials section** is an extensive study of the most sympathetic of all materials. It provides a complete understanding of wood, from how the tree grows, to how wood is converted and seasoned as well as the considerations to make when selecting and buying timber. More than 50 woods are illustrated in full colour, and there is a detailed table defining the strengths, screwing, nailing and gluing properties and uses of the world's major timbers. Manufactured boards and veneers are also described.

Finally, the **Fixtures and fittings section** is a detailed compendium of all the universal woodworking accessories from intricate cranked and cylinder hinges to space-saving wardrobe rails and cupboard corner fittings.

As the scope of this book is so vast, Ernest Scott has worked in association with a team of specialist mastercraftsmen, each an expert in his chosen branch of woodworking. As a result, *Working in Wood* contains the accumulated knowledge of, literally, hundreds of years of practical experience. That experience is presented in a way that makes *Working in Wood* a unique book. The craftsman best communicates his expertise by demonstrating his skills and describing his actions as he works. This is exactly how *Working in Wood* has been created. Photographers and researchers have been specially commissioned to witness and record the author and the team of specialist mastercraftsmen, each demonstrating their particular craft. In this way their unique knowledge has been captured and passed on.

Classic Constructions

An introduction to the subject of woodworking through some of
the finest and most enduring furniture ever made

The Tudor chest

The chest may be described as the predecessor of all basic furniture forms and for many centuries it fulfilled a unique multipurpose role within the medieval and Tudor home. In this environment it served as table, chair, storage unit and often, owing to the highly mobile way of life, it was a packing case as well.

The earliest chests were crudely constructed from sections of solid timber, which were hollowed out and bound with iron straps to minimize the effects of shrinkage. These dug-out chests were made from the trunks of fallen trees — the contemporary usage of the word "trunk" being a reminder of their origin.

It was not until technology was developed to convert timber into board form in the early fourteenth century that the now familiar chest structures appeared. These early planked chests consisted of six or more boards nailed and pegged together to form a lidded box on to which elaborately scrolled iron strapwork was applied to provide both strength and decoration.

During the latter half of the sixteenth century the chest underwent a fundamental change: the boards used to construct the front and back sections were joined, not edge to edge as before but at right angles to each other, forming a simple H frame. This represented an important technological step as, instead of relying on restraint to control shrinkage, efforts were now being made to construct a form that would be tolerant of timber movement.

As time progressed the two uprights became narrower and longer until they extended well below the central board to form feet. The central board itself gave way to the use of top and bottom rails connected by muntins, within which panels were contained loosely in grooves to enable them to shrink and expand without detriment to the structure as a whole. This form of construction is well demonstrated in the main illustration, which clearly shows the skeletal nature of the framework left by the evolution of the earlier H frames, in which thinner solid panels are contained. This form of construction proved immensely practical — so much so that it formed the basis of all furniture production until the end of the seventeenth century.

The chest was subject to many decorative treatments, of which the most international was the linenfold panel, which may be found on many items of furniture of the late sixteenth and early seventeenth centuries. This style of decoration, attributed to fifteenth-century Flemish architectural carvers, is often said to have been used on chests to denote their contents. However, this presupposes a selective use of the chest in medieval homes, which is contrary to their utilitarian evolution.

Lid in oak made from several narrow boards glued together — a technique that demonstrates the maker's awareness that several narrow boards were more stable than one or two wide boards

Top and bottom front rails in oak, decorated with guilloche carving. This device has been extensively used by furnituremakers in numerous countries over many periods; it is, however, relatively uncommon on furniture of this period

Iron strap hinge — later known as a garnet hinge. This type of hinge would commonly be fixed with iron nails, often driven right through the back and then clenched

Panel in oak with scroll and roundel carving. This panel would be loose fitting within a groove to allow free movement and have its grain direction running vertically

Bearer supporting the lid and providing protection against cupping. Bearers, however, tend to be self-defeating as, unless an allowance for shrinkage is made, they can cause severe splitting

Front rail tenoned into leg stile and secured with draw bore pegs. This technique was widely used to compensate for the inadequacies of available adhesives

Dugout chests were hewn with axe and adze from hardwood trees that were roughly cut to shape. Commonly, these chests were bound with wrought iron straps to protect them from excessive deformation when shrinkage occurred.

The boarded chests of the thirteenth and fourteenth centuries were made from sawn hardwood boards held together by wooden pegs and iron straps. In many cases these straps consisted of elaborate scrolls that incorporated the nail positions as part of the overall design.

This joined chest of the late fifteenth century is an excellent example of an early piece of furniture that had incorporated the then newly-discovered jointing principles. Notice the wide uprights forming stiles that extend well below the centre board.

This arcaded chest of the sixteenth century is evidence of the success of jointed structures. The upright stiles have become narrower, making them less vulnerable to shrinkage and giving them a more leg-like appearance. The arcading is typical.

The early-seventeenth-century mule chest is considered to be the first piece of furniture to contain drawers, or tills as they were first known. This example highlights the refined use of frame and panel construction to form a light, portable storage unit.

Stile extending below the lower rail line to form the foot. This is a common technique in frame and panel construction

Bottom rail tenoned between the stile and grooved to take both the panel and bottom boards

The split-carcassed chest of drawers of the seventeenth century represents the final development of the chest. The elaborate use of applied moulding and split turnings almost completely obliterated the frame and panel construction.

Muntin dividing two panels and providing resistance to racking. The prominence of the muntins in this example has been greatly reduced by the addition of roundel carving

The dresser

The dresser had its beginnings in the medieval period, when, in the large communal halls, a trestle table or board was set aside for the specific purpose of dressing meat. The tables became more utilitarian when open shelves were added for the storage and display of utensils. However, during the Renaissance the communal halls disappeared as a more refined way of life evolved, and the dressing board became transformed into the more respectable and decorative court cupboard. This was simply an arrangement of tiered shelves and closed cupboards. It was not until the late seventeenth century that the dresser, as it is now recognized, made an appearance.

Because of their functional background these items were well suited to the rural way of life, and the basic form of graduated shelves over potboard or cupboard seems to have been simultaneously adopted over most of northern Europe. Many different styles existed but specific claims by some individual areas to a particular type or form were largely unfounded. Certainly, the term Welsh dresser, as most dressers are referred to, holds no significance as to its origin.

As with most country-made articles the dresser may be found in a wide range of woods, because the rural craftsman would have used only those that were indigenous — oak, elm and some of the harder fruit woods being traditionally associated with the dresser. It was not until the availability of improved surface coatings that the use of pine and other softwoods became popular, because these finishes provided some additional protection against the hard use to which the furniture was subjected.

Because of their size, dressers were generally made in two separate sections or carcasses. The top section was constructed with two solid shaped ends between which top and shelf boards were jointed. These were then held as a rigid structure by a planked back and cornice rail. Usually the top rested on the lower section; sometimes it was suspended from or even built into the wall. The construction of the base section varied according to type. However, in general, the construction remained close to the traditional frame and panel principle, where mortised and tenoned frames formed the structure on to and into which side and back panels were grooved and drawers and doors suspended.

The example illustrated is a fine dresser from the early eighteenth century and demonstrates these principles clearly. The addition of mouldings to the front frame and the arched door detail serves to disguise the severity of line associated with this form of construction. Additionally, the arcaded cornice rail and moulding provide proportional balance.

Two-section cornice moulding providing proportional balance

H hinge in brass, sometimes referred to as a parliament hinge

Stile extending below the frame to form the foot – a common feature

Horizontal member designed to show at the side – typical of country- made furniture

Scalloped frieze rail suggesting Flemish influence

Planked back and bottom rebated and grooved into the carcass

Shelf capped with decorative moulding providing safe storage for fragile items

Top carcass side, shaped to provide a graceful line to what would otherwise be a slab-like structure. Scratch beading on the leading edge lightens the appearance

Applied bar moulding, disguising the otherwise angular appearance of the frame and panel structure

Carcass shoe, sometimes permanently fixed to the base section; the top section is dowelled into it

Drawer, with fielded front and lining in pine, suspended on rails between front and back framework

Door lock, in steel with brass face escutcheon, the key serving as a handle

Fielded panel, loose fitting in a groove within the framework

Lower carcass of frame and panel construction, providing a reliable and resilient structure

Peak arched door, a feature of early-eighteenth-century country furniture, in this case enhanced by the fielded and moulded panel

Static panel decorated to provide symmetry to the front

A

B

C

The cornice rail and moulding on the top section often provide a reliable basis for dating.
A. Frog's-back frieze, associated with later dressers.
B. Fretted arch, found in many furniture periods.
C. Scalloped and pierced frieze, associated with early dressers.

D

E

F

G

H

J

K

L

To display china, shelves had a plate restraint (**D, E, F**). These examples also show common shelf-edge treatments. Functional fittings, such as the serpent hinge (**K**) and butterfly hinge (**L**), were often of brass; wooden knobs (**G, H, J**) and iron hinges may also be found.

The combination of storage facilities offered by dressers is varied. Most have closed cupboards and drawers in the base section. Some, however, have an open base shelf, called a potboard, and may include spice drawers, cupboards or clocks in the top section.

The bureau

Towards the end of the seventeenth century written communication began to play a significantly more important role in social and economic life, and in many homes of substance rooms were set aside and furnished especially for this purpose. Thus escritoires and writing tables dominated the libraries and drawing rooms of the period. However, gradually a less formal attitude was adopted and this change was reflected by the innovation of the bureau.

It is generally held that the bureau was directly contrived from the sixteenth-century Bible box as both share the common feature of a sloping fall flap that provides, when opened, a writing surface and, when closed, useful storage and a convenient area from which to read.

Later, the bureau sections became stacked over secondary carcasses containing drawers. These secondary carcasses were themselves raised on stands or stacked in combinations to bring them to writing height. The lower carcasses were often terraced or curved and contained various combinations of drawers and cupboard arrangements. However, the fashion for multiple supporting carcasses quickly passed and the single supporting carcass came into favour. The main bureau illustrated is typical of this early eighteenth-century period. It is finished in walnut veneer applied to an oak substrate and the interior of the upper carcass has been fitted for the storage of writing materials. A feature common to this type of bureau is a slide beneath the pigeon holes providing access to a well or void.

As the century progressed the practicality of the bureau was enhanced by a natural extension of the storage facility by the addition of top carcasses that were often devoted to book storage or fitted to suit a variety of other requirements. This modification consolidated the characteristics of the bureau and the split or double carcass gave way to the single unit that is now common.

The important position that bureaux held among contemporary eighteenth-century furniture is evidenced by the tremendous care with which they were made. The bureau interiors were intricate and delicately treated with subtle adaptations to conceal secret compartments and other facilities such as candle-slides and pen trays. The exterior workmanship was also of the highest quality.

The convenient storage afforded by the bureau led to further interesting adaptations, of which the secretaire drawer was perhaps the most novel and popular as it provided similar facilities but could be more discreetly combined within a wider range of furniture forms.

Split- or double-carcass formation is evidence of the bureau's ancestry

Mid moulding in walnut to disguise the double-carcass formation

Walnut veneer applied to an oak ground (the practice of veneering on cheaper softwoods was established later)

Candle slides incorporated within the drapes

Loper extended to support the flap

Dummy drawer fronts on the face of the upper carcass (drawers in these double-carcass types are relatively uncommon)

Ogee-bracket foot more commonly associated with later mahogany furniture

Lapped dovetail joint in the drawer's corners

Column-fronted drawers
operated by a finger pull from
within a central cupboard are a
common bureau feature.

Veneered slide for access to a
storage well created by the split-
or double-carcass formation

Back flap hinge in brass

Hide or material such as
baize, for softening the
writing surface

Drawer lining in oak,
common to quality
pieces of the eighteenth
century

Walnut veneer (feather or
curl) used in matching pairs

Quadrant moulding inset into
the drawer front, for masking
the drawer's fitting tolerances
and for reducing the visibility of
the carcass members

A. Drop, or pull, handle (1680s).
B. Solid plate handle (1700s).
C. Pierced, or fretted, handle
(1750s).

D. Swan-necked handle (1750s).
E. Octagonal plate or ring
handle (1780s).
F. Stamped plate handle (1780s).

The tambour desk popularized
in America in the 1880s *(top)*
and the universal secretaire
(above) are extensions of the
bureau concept.

An American bureau bookcase
(1750s) shows the bureau as an
item of grandeur rather than one
of function.

The bureau on a stand (1680s)
highlights the bureau's box-like
origin. Note the carrying handles
on the sides.

The tallboy

During the late seventeenth century the craft of cabinetmaking developed fully into a separate trade concerned only with furnituremaking and so became totally distinct from the other woodworking crafts. This was largely due to the wide acceptance of veneering, which had proved so popular that furniture forms were developed to display this art to the full. Carving and panelling disappeared, to be replaced by flat surfaces that showed off the grain pattern and the high polish given to the veneer. Cabinets and chests became raised on stands or stacked one on the other to elevate them to a new prominence in the elegant interiors. These pieces, which are correctly termed clothes presses, have now become colloquially known as "tallboys", of which the mid-eighteenth-century example illustrated is a direct descendant.

With the adoption of veneering came some significant constructional changes, because the frame and panel carcasses of earlier years did not provide the necessary flat unbroken surfaces. Thus evolved the slab constructional form, in which the major components were made from solid sections of wood, joined at the corners by dovetails. From this box-like structure drawers and doors were suspended. This method was ideal for multiple-carcassed stacking furniture and by the mid-eighteenth century the concept had become commonplace. It is still widely employed as the most economic and practical method of creating storage furniture of substantial size.

The illustrated example demonstrates this principle clearly in that the carcasses and associated sub-frames are constructed to interlock, with the top carcass being slightly narrower and shallower than the base section. This allows it to fit snugly within a cover moulding, which also serves as a locating bar. Full advantage has been taken of the sectional and graduated form of the piece by the addition of running mouldings used both to disguise joint lines and to provide proportional balance, as can be seen on the pedimented cornice.

The whole top section of this clothes press has been devoted to the storage of folded linen, with sliding trays running within grooves cut directly in the solid sides. However, later examples can be found with hanging space only or with combinations of both sliding trays and hanging space, in which case they are more correctly referred to as wardrobes. The base section has the conventional arrangement of drawers suspended on drawer rails and runners.

Clothes presses were made in many types of wood, the choice being affected by expanding world trade. However, in most European countries, mahogany and walnut were greatly favoured.

Butt hinge in brass secured with steel screws

Three section cornice moulding

Solid carcass side in Honduras mahogany dovetailed to a faced softwood top and bottom

Scratch bead used to distract the eye from the protruding hinge knuckles

Carved base moulding applied to a softwood sub-frame to form a plinth

Broken pediment with
turned central patera

Detachable cornice sub-frame
located by corner blocks glued
to the carcass top

Lining tray, in oak with
mahogany front, running in
grooves cut into the sides

Panel chamfered to reduce its
thickness where it meets the
frame and secured by beading
within the rebate created by the
face moulding

Pedimented cornice frames were
popular throughout the
eighteenth century. The swan-
necked pediment (*top*) has a
fretted plate above an arched

frieze rail and is typical of later
examples. Separate pediments
and cornices were superseded
by shaped and crested head
rails (*above*).

The radial, or broken, corner
with carved patera was
commonly used to decorate
framed doors in tallboys of the
eighteenth century.

Cock beading was fitted to
protect the face veneers of
drawer fronts. Its projecting
section also disguised the
fitting tolerance.

Cock beading of half-round
edge section

Inset brass escutcheon

Drawer lining in oak with
softwood back

Mahogany curl veneer applied
to a softwood ground

Drawer suspended on
softwood runners housed into
the carcass sides, mortised into
the front rail and grooved to
incorporate a softwood
dustboard

Drawer lock in brass secured
with steel screws

Mahogany curl veneer applied
to a solid ground

Mid moulding attached to the
base carcass, serving as a
locating bar for the top carcass

Swan-necked handle in brass
bolted through the drawer
front

Bracket foot, in mahogany
with rear facing sections in
softwood, secured to the frame
with a glue block

Applied feet were fitted directly
or to a moulded sub-frame.
A. Bun foot (1700s).
B. Bracket foot (1700s).

C. Double ogee foot (1750s).
D. Single ogee foot (1750s).
E. Bracket foot (1780s).
F. Swept bracket foot (1780s).

The drawleaf table

The drawleaf table first appeared in the late sixteenth century. At the time it represented an innovation contrary to the prevailing techniques and principles of furnituremaking as it incorporated a relatively sophisticated extension mechanism not found in other contemporary furniture. Carcass furniture in the sixteenth century, for example, was of basic panel and frame construction with the addition of only a door and drawers, where required, for specific purposes. Tables were also simple, being either of the dormant or gateleg type. Although it had an extending capacity, the latter table was based on a simple, logical design that was not comparable with the imagination and accuracy required to develop the drawleaf table.

The drawleaf table had a central top under which two sliding extension leaves were positioned. These pulled outwards, either at the sides or, more commonly, at the ends. When extended, the central top dropped into the void left by the leaves and so formed a single continuous surface. To make this movement possible, runners (called lopers) that were attached to the leaves passed through guiding bearers and slots in the main frame. When the table was not extended, the main frame concealed the mechanism.

The main illustration shows a drawleaf table typical of the late sixteenth and early seventeenth centuries and it exhibits the rugged characteristics of the oak furniture of that period. An interesting feature of this table is the cleating, or keying, around the central top and leaves. This was done to minimize the possibility of the wood distorting and so fouling the operation of the table. This feature demonstrates the growing understanding of using timber as a precision material.

Drawleaf tables may be found with a variety of leg arrangements, but traditionally they are of the four-legged type with a stout underframe and stretchers, which are necessary to provide resistance to the forces imposed during extension.

The basic form of the drawleaf table has not changed since the sixteenth century and there have been only some minor mechanical improvements. The principle of the drawleaf, however, has been adapted in a variety of ways. The intricate extending tables of the eighteenth century included circular versions in which segments operated individually to increase the diameter. In the nineteenth century, the principle was incorporated not only in tables but also in writing desks in order to increase their writing surface. As a result of the improved extension mechanisms now available, the drawleaf is undergoing a revival in popularity — a fact that is a tribute to the foresight of the sixteenth-century furnituremakers.

Cleating applied to the leaves and central top at right angles to the grain of the central panel. Cleating was used in an attempt to limit the effects of warping. In general, however, these cleats were self defeating and resulted instead in the wood splitting

Timber of quality, for various reasons, has always been prized. The bulbous leg is a fine example of an economic use of wood because, to save excessive waste, applied blocks were glued to the leg in order to increase its diameter where needed on a leg of this type.

The sliding extension leaves of the drawleaf table were held on cantilevered runners passing through the frame and under a centre bearer. The angle of these runners was contrived so as to allow each leaf, when extended, to rise by the thickness of the central top.

Central top in solid oak comprising boards butted together to the required dimension

Centre bearer balancing the table's appearance when closed and providing a restraint for the leaf runners when extended

Moulding carved in tongue-and-dart repeat pattern on lower edge of underframe

Runner on which an extension leaf is suspended

Rail inlaid in ivory and ebony in a geometric design, suggesting the carved strapwork of earlier furniture periods

Gadrooning, or nulling — a common repeat design for carving

Leg with architectural capital, providing proportional balance

Stretcher rail in oak of stout proportions, visually lightened by scratch beading on its face edge

Main body of the bulb carved in stylized leaf pattern. These designs were often based on an oak leaf

Leg in oak with a typical bulbous turning popular during late sixteenth and early seventeenth centuries. These turnings took their shape from the puffed sleeves of contemporary costumes

The sixteenth-century trestle table is an early example of knock-down furniture. The two solid trestles at the ends were joined to a central stretcher by a removable joint, which in most cases was a projected and wedged mortise and tenon, as illustrated (*above*). **The table dormant** has acquired the modern name of the refectory table. Such tables were of considerable size and they often incorporated as many as eight or ten legs. The number of legs and stout underframe give these tables a rigidity for which they have become famous.

The gateleg table

The gateleg table has been one of the most popular and enduring table designs ever introduced.

Gatelegs were first made in the last quarter of the sixteenth century, when the Protestant upsurge throughout Europe brought a plainer style of living, in smaller, more private apartments. This change was reflected in the furniture of the period and created a demand for smaller, more utilitarian pieces that could be quickly adapted to a variety of uses. Of these pieces the gateleg — or, to use the original name, falling or faldyn — table is a fine example. The term gateleg is of much later origin and is derived from the action and construction of the pivoting sub-frame, which is reminiscent of the conventional gate.

The earliest type of gateleg had a single gate and flap. This type, normally of semicircular form, was designed to stand against a wall with the gated side to the rear. This meant that, to be opened to a full circle, the table had to be moved, which was clearly a disadvantage. A more sensible early adaptation was the triangular type, which fitted conveniently into a corner and had the gate and flap to the front.

As gateleg tables gained in popularity these single gated types were superseded by twin gated ones, which were made in a variety of shapes — ovals, rectangles and polygons being popular. The base frames were often of trestle construction and were joined at the feet by a single planked stretcher. As the gateleg principle developed it was incorporated into other structures — the gated centres of eighteenth-century Hepplewhite tables being a fine example of this.

The table illustrated displays all the rugged solidity of a country-made table of the late seventeenth and early eighteenth century. Most tables such as this would have been constructed from hardwoods that were indigenous to the country of origin; oak, elm, beech and walnut may be found in surviving examples. However, yew and some fruit woods may also have been used, as well as other hedgerow timber.

The base frame of the example is constructed with baluster-turned legs and bun or bobbin feet. The legs are well jointed to the table rails at the top and to the stretcher rails at the base, using draw bore mortises and tenons. This table illustrates well the basic construction of all true gatelegs. The gate should hang from the rails and stretchers, and the underframing should be so proportioned that the supports are equally spaced when the top is opened. These open frame structures are pleasingly simple, reliable and rigid and lend themselves to adaptation, as may be seen in surviving examples that incorporate drawers, shelves, cupboards and additional gates.

Plain butt joint with steel back flap hinge. This is a common configuration for tables of this period

Thumb moulding applied to the leading edge to lighten the visual thickness. Traditionally, this moulding did not form a quadrant but the shape of a human thumb when pressed on its side

Gate assembly pivoted between stretcher and top rail by an integral wooden dowel

Gate halved into the rail and stretcher to close flush with the main frame. This avoided the top fouling when closed

Bobbin foot and leg turned in one continuous piece

Turnings are ideal for the decoration of gateleg frames. Some typical turnings associated with these tables are shown (left).
A. Gun barrel turning (1760).
B. Spiral twist turning (1640).
C. Bobbin and reel turning (1650).
D. Baluster turning used in various periods with numerous decorative features. This turning takes its name from the architectural balustrade.

Top in oak formed from glued and butted boards

Arched end rail suggesting the Flemish influence prevailing at the time

Side rail, sometimes made from softwood to conserve timber : joined to leg with a draw bore mortise and tenon. This joint was used extensively by the early furnituremakers to overcome poor adhesives and assembly problems

Stretcher rail with scratch beading lightening this otherwise conspicuous component

To improve the appearance of folding tables the groove and bead joint was used where the top met each flap. This joint preceded the rule joint.

Where legs and stretchers intersect, halving joints are used even though they weaken the table's structure where it is most vulnerable.

The semicircular gateleg table (E) operated with a single gate at the rear and the top folded forwards when closed. The triangular type **(F),** when closed, fitted neatly into the corner of a room. It had only a single gate, but its top folded downwards, covering the front frame when closed. The tilt top table **(G)** had only a single gate, which was pivoted centrally. This enabled the table to fold into a form that was ideal for storage.

The Pembroke table

Pembroke tables take their name from the ninth Earl of Pembroke, who in the mid-eighteenth century is said to have designed a new style of table. The precise definition of a Pembroke table, however, is difficult to establish as the term is now used to describe a variety of tables that in many cases have contrasting appearances, although some features can be identified as being common to all: they are mostly of moderate size, light in structure and contain a drawer or drawers. A more specific generic feature of this family of tables is perhaps the top arrangement of a central section flanked by two rising flaps that are held in the open position by fly support brackets incorporated within the underframing. This design differs very distinctly from drop-leaf and gateleg tables, where the flaps are supported by hinged or pivoted legs.

The most usual form of Pembroke table is that shown in the main illustration. This style of four-legged table was popularized in the late eighteenth century and the example shown emphasizes the delicacy of treatment common to these tables. The carcass contains a single drawer, so a dummy drawer has been designed on the rear frieze rail to give the table a symmetrical appearance. The top is oval in shape with rule joints, which give a pleasing appearance to the hinge detail. In common with most Pembrokes, the legs terminate in castors and are of sufficient section to conceal the side rails and fly support mechanism, which consists of two traversing brackets stoutly pivoted by knuckle joints. These mechanisms occur in opposing pairs or singly, depending on the size and quality of the table. In general all Pembroke tables in the late eighteenth century displayed a scrupulous attention to detail that cabinetmakers in succeeding periods have been at pains to perpetuate.

During the peak of their demand, in the last quarter of the eighteenth century, Pembroke tables provided the leading designers with the ideal medium on which to display the highly stylized decorative treatments popularized by them. Hepplewhite and Sheraton in England and Phyfe in America all produced designs for Pembrokes that succinctly focused their own personal styles. The English craftsman utilized subtle blends of mahoganies and satinwoods in conjunction with classical motifs of marquetry, painted decorations and bandings, while Phyfe exaggerated the graceful lines of the Pembrokes using indigenous timbers such as walnut and mulberry.

Pembroke tables are now in common use in both Europe and America, where numerous versions of the original concept, such as the pedestal breakfast table and the sofa table, may be found.

Mid moulding housed into the legs and applied to the underside of the drawer rail

Drawer front constructed from sectioned softwood with mahogany veneer on the face only

Drawer lining in mahogany with the grain direction of the bottom running across the width

Knob in brass with a stamped face and ring

Crossbanded and inlayed capital, the section of which is sufficient to carry the side rail and fly-support mechanism

Leg tapered on three sides only to give a splayed appearance

Castor in brass secured with steel screws

Dummy drawer to the rear, giving a symmetrical appearance

Rule joint between central top and flap

Floral decoration and motifs executed using a combination of marquetry background and painted foliage with highlights

Astragal moulding worked on the leading edges to lighten the appearance of the top

Crossbanded borders in mahogany with the grain running at right angles to the perimeter

Top in solid mahogany veneered on the face with Honduras mahogany, applied in bookmatched pairs on the centre top and continued on the flaps

The rule joint is used to conceal the otherwise unsightly gap that would be left when a flap is lowered. The geometrics of this joint require the use of a specialized hinge with one flap approximately one-third longer than the other to clear the hollow in the cove of the joint.

Fly support brackets are knuckle jointed and applied to the carcass to maintain the flaps in the open position. They are found in pairs on large, quality pieces.

A. Threaded castor with an astragal cap.
B. Round socket, or cup, castor for turned legs.
C. Square socket, either flush fitting or flanged (*above*).
D. Lion's paw toe castor found on the pedestal-type table.

The breakfast table of the eighteenth century used the same constructional principles as the Pembroke but had an enclosed lower carcass.

The sofa table is not strictly a Pembroke but has similar ancestry. True Pembrokes would have the flap along the side rather than the ends.

The Windsor chair

The success of the Windsor chair has been attributed to its immense practicality and its simplicity of design.

Since its introduction in the early part of the eighteenth century the Windsor chair has undergone numerous minor changes, determined by prevailing fashions. However, its basic form has remained unchanged. The term Windsor chair is generally applied to all chairs that display the simple characteristics of peg or stick construction used in conjunction with a solid saddled seat. Various combinations of back and leg arrangements may be found.

It is generally thought that this type of construction had been used by chairmakers for some time prior to the evolution of the recognizable Windsor. This construction technique provided a degree of flexibility during manufacture as the wedge-fit used for the slats and spindles made assembly similar to the procedures used in the craft of coopering. Tension was provided by compressive force, and stress by the bracing action of the back stretcher sections. This provided the chair with some unique qualities, in that it provided additional strength when forces were imposed and a high tolerance to material deformation.

The materials traditionally associated with chairs of this type have always been those most amenable to the constructional techniques used. In Europe, for example, ash, elm and yew were commonly utilized for the steam-bent sections, whereas for the turned and sculptured members denser woods such as beech, oak and hickory were used, together with a wide variety of fruit wood and hedgerow timbers. For this reason it was common to find an individual chair made in three or more different woods and this added to its charm.

Windsor chairs are found in various countries, each having their own distinctive styles and types. Individual localities have also become associated with particular adaptations and styling; even the craft terminology varied among the diverse clusters of local craftsmen working in proximity to the standing forests from which their woods were taken. The low-back chairs of Philadelphia, where the making of these chairs was centred from the beginning of the eighteenth century, and those of Suffolk are fine examples of this.

In general it is possible to subdivide the Windsor's form into three main categories: the tall, gently curving comb back; the distinctive hoop or bent back; and the low-backed tub. Each type has an infinite number of variations in its own developmental history.

Among contemporary adaptations, some retain the peg construction but most rely on improved adhesives for rigidity, which together with loose upholstery tend to debase the original elegance of the Windsor chair.

Four main types of Windsor chair are shown; within each, a wide variety of turning, splat and rail shapes exists.

A. Mendlesham Windsor (1800s).
B. Gothic Windsor (1750s).
C. Smoker's bow (1850s).
D. American fan back (1780s).

E. Bentwood, or swept, arm and upright (1750s).
F. Turned spindle imitating the leg shape (1730 onwards).
G. Stout baluster arm (1850s).

H. Simple plain-turned H form.
J. Cross- or X-frame stretcher associated with circular seats.
K. The classic crinoline, or cowhorn, stretcher.

The turned sections are reamed with a slight taper and compression fitted (L) or are through wedged into a bored hole (M).

Front legs are traditionally the turned baluster type (N, P). Both these and the cabriole leg (Q) are used with plain legs at the back of the chair.

Bentwood
hoop back
in ash

A B C D

A. Plain baluster splat.
B, C. Pierced splats.
D. Wheel back.

Spindle in beech, providing
tension and rigidity between
the seat arm and back

Pierced back
splat in elm,
tenoned
through the
arm rail

Bentwood, or swept, arm
support in ash, dowelled and
fox-wedged into the ash arm

Saddle seat in elm, shaped with
the adze and scraper into a
flowing contour reminiscent of
the riding saddle

Plain spindle -turned rear legs
in beech

Baluster -turned leg in beech,
demonstrating the instinctive
use of proportion by country
craftsmen

Crinoline stretcher in ash, the
curving shape providing
tension between the legs

The walnut chair

At the end of the seventeenth century European chairs were noted for their tall, slender appearance and graceful proportions. However, the new century brought change and a style of chair emerged that was based on the contemporary proportions, yet possessing greater continuity of line. This new style, attributed to Daniel Marot, a French designer and furnituremaker, represented such a fundamental change in design that its effects influenced other furnituremakers well into the mid-eighteenth century.

In contrast to the previous angular style, the new eighteenth-century chairs were given gently curving backs that undulated in profile and had a central solid support or splat, which replaced the caned panels previously in fashion. Perhaps more important was the innovation of the cabriole leg, the graceful lines of which were in complete harmony with the new taste and which proved so popular that adaptations were to be found in the majority of succeeding furniture periods. It is thought that the cabriole leg was an adaptation of the S-scroll leg and that it represented a revival of the classical use of natural shapes and forms. This is borne out by the fact that in its early use the cabriole leg often terminated in a cloven foot or hoof. As it developed to a more sturdy form, the cabriole leg provided sufficient stability to enable furnituremakers to dispense with supporting stretcher rails to the underframes.

The chair shown in the main illustration is typical of chairs of the early eighteenth century and demonstrates the subtle modification by the English and Dutch craftsmen of the period of Marot's more florid style. This translation successfully blended the elegance of the original French concept with a sturdy practicality. This chair has the rising shape of its crest rail accentuated by C scrolls and hipped rear uprights, around which a vase-shaped splat and scroll-over arms add to the curvilinear design. An interesting feature is its cabriole legs, which terminate in knurl, or whorl, feet. The cabriole leg proved immensely popular and on fine-quality chairs it was used in conjunction with curved seat rails and a carved ornamentation such as shells, husks and acanthus leaves added to the knee and wings.

Early-eighteenth-century chairs were almost exclusively made in walnut and often bore decorative veneers on their flat upright surfaces. Walnut burr was laid on the splats and seat rails, and crossbanded veneer was laid around the flat faces of the back.

The international origins of this style, humoured by solid craftsmanship, give chairs of this period a restrained elegance that is second to none.

A

B

C

D

These backs are all of early-eighteenth-century origin. The French concept was modified by English and Dutch craftsmen. **A.** Florid style of an early design by Marot.

B. Anglo-Dutch variation with a baluster splat.
C. Hipped back of late origin with a vase-shaped splat.
D. Early Georgian adaptation with a pierced splat.

Seats in the early eighteenth century were heavily shaped, often having only one straight side. They were of the drop-in type, in which a beech frame was lap halved together and

then profiled to fit within a rebate cut into the seat rails. The illustration (*above*) of the most popular frame shape at that time shows this treatment clearly.

E F G H J K L

The development of the cabriole leg is illustrated (*above*).
E, F. Scrolls suggesting the later form of cabriole.
G. Early cabriole.
H. Early cabriole with hoof foot.

J. Fully developed cabriole with hipped section and pad foot.
K. Fully developed cabriole with claw and ball foot.
L. Fully developed cabriole with pad foot.

Crest rail with shell-form carving. Because of their double curving shape, these rails are sometimes known as cupid's bows, of which they are reminiscent if held vertically

Carved patera applied over the joint line between the splat and crest rail

Solid central splat of baluster form, faced with walnut burr veneer. The floral marquetry is evidence of Dutch influence

Carved ear suggesting a C scroll formed between it and the patera on the crest rail

Scroll-over, or shepherd's crook, arm, the curving shape of which contributes greatly to the chair's elegance

Rear leg cut and shaped from a single section of wood

Back frame, with face veneered in walnut burr

Splat shoe, providing both strength and tolerance during fitting

Drop-in seat upholstered on to a beech frame

Curving front rail, with face veneered in walnut, shaped to blend in with the legs

Rear leg terminating in a pad foot. Notice the changing section as the leg rises

Cabriole leg with acanthus leaves at the knee and hip. Notice the knurl, or whorl, foot and C scrolls bridging the leg and wings

The balloon-back chair

More than any other item of furniture, the balloon-back chair has increased in popularity through the fashionable interest in antiques. This is perhaps due to the chair's unique decorative quality and the fact that it possesses an elegance that enables it to look equally good whether placed on its own, in pairs, or amongst furniture from other periods.

Although the balloon-back chair reached its peak of demand in Europe and America during the mid-nineteenth century, the term "balloon back" was not coined until the last quarter of the century and it is thought to be of American origin. The chair's style is almost exclusively English and its development may be clearly plotted through the dining- and drawing-room chairs of the early nineteenth century.

The balloon back has its origins in the classical Grecian-style chairs of the late Regency period. These chairs had a very square appearance with a wide crest rail, extending over the upright back legs, and a horizontal rail positioned halfway between the crest rail and seat. During the 1830s these chairs, particularly those made for drawing-room use, had become elaborately covered with scrolls. While the overall construction remained the same, the crest rails had developed a distinctive downward appearance, created by the use of scrolls at either end.

The transition of the fully integrated crest rail and rear legs to form a continuous curve seems to have been made in the late 1830s. These balloon backs had a distinctly flattened crest rail that closely resembled the proportions of their scrolled predecessors. As the century progressed the upward curve of the crest rail became more exaggerated and the rear legs developed an inward curve or waist. The only reminders of their classical origins were the tapering padded seats and the straight, turned front legs. The final modification took place around 1850, when gently curving cabriole legs (in this case sometimes referred to as French legs) were introduced, to provide balance to the exaggerated shape of the back. These legs were normally fielded with a carved hip and were used in conjunction with serpentine-shaped seat rails. The pleasing proportional balance this created is well shown in the main illustration.

By 1860 the balloon back had become a standard pattern with several adaptations to suit a variety of uses. Dining chairs remained relatively plain and were made in quality woods such as rosewood, mahogany and walnut. Drawing-room and bedroom balloon backs, however, had lively curved embellishments to mid- and crest rails and were made in such timbers as walnut, maple and birch.

The early balloon back of the 1840s was based on the Grecian and scroll-top chairs, which started a line of development, ending in the variations of the 1860s.
A. Grecian style chair (1830).
B. Scroll-top chair (1835).
C. Early balloon back (1840).
D. Double C scroll (1865).

Early counterparts of the balloon back had angular tapering seats (**J**) with fluted and turned legs (**E, F**). True balloon backs had a serpentine-shaped seat (**K**) and French legs (**G**). Later variations adopted cane seats (**L**) with turned and splayed (or horned) legs (**H**).

Das Lehnenquerstück ist auf die Hinterfüße aufgedübelt – bei Stühlen dieser Art eine sehr verwundbare Konstruktion.

Das geschnitzte Mittelstück aus Walnußholz wurde mit den hinteren Beinen verzapft. Oft waren die Verzierungen so üppig, daß es leicht brach.

Die aufgepolsterte Sitzfläche enthält Sprungfedern, die dem Polster eine Mitte des 19. Jahrhunderts beliebte, extreme Wölbung geben.

Die Seitenzargen aus Buche wurden mit den Beinen über Schlitz und Zapfen verbunden und sind an der Unterkante leicht gefalzt, damit die Köpfe der Polsternägel nicht zu weit hervorstehen.

Die geschwungene Form der Vorderzarge und eine aufgesetzte Walnuß-Schmuckleiste an ihrer Unterkante sorgen für fließende Übergänge zwischen Rahmen und Stuhlbeinen.

Die Hinterfüße bestehen bis zum Lehnenquerstück aus einem Stück Walnußholz; ihre ›Taillierung‹ unterstreicht die Ballonform der Rückenlehne.

Mit Spitzen, Fransen oder Bändern verdeckte man die Polsternägel.

Das Bein ist am Sitzflächenansatz rechtwinklig, um die Zargenverbindung zu erleichtern, und verjüngt sich nach unten zu einem ovalen Fuß.

Das Vorderbein mündet mit moderatem Schwung in einem angedeuteten Volutenfuß.

Das Cabriole-Bein trägt mit den geschnitzten Verzierungen an Fuß und Knie in hohem Maße zur Eleganz des Stuhls bei.

Design

An analysis of all the problems that need to be
resolved before starting any project

Design tools

Before attempting to make any article, such as a piece of furniture, from wood the main dimensions and method of construction need to be established. For very simple pieces it is possible to work from a free-hand sketch, but usually an accurate drawing either of the whole item or details of its critical dimensions is essential. An effective drawing can be made with very little equipment. The most basic equipment required to make a working drawing is a flat surface, such as a drawing board, to work on and straight-edges, such as a T-square and set square, to draw against.

The drawing board should have a straight edge to guide the T-square and a semi-hard surface that will accept the point of a compass. At its simplest the drawing board is a sheet of smooth card on a table.

The T-square is a straight-edge with a stock firmly fixed at right angles across one end. On some T-squares the straight-edge is tapered on one side. It is better, however, to buy a T-square that is parallel-sided so that the worker can use both edges, making it easier to draw near to the bottom edge of a board. A second advantage of a parallel-sided T-square is that it can be used by both left- and right-handed people. A bevelled edge will improve drawing accuracy as the worker can see the drawing edge and therefore position the T-square with greater precision.

Standard set squares, 30°/60° and 45°, are the most important single instruments and it is therefore worth buying the best available. A large adjustable square is a great advantage when drawing the long lines and angles that are common in furniture drawings. As with all other plastic instruments, buy tinted transparent plastic in preference to plain as it can be seen more easily when covered by scraps of paper and drawings. Clean T-squares, set squares, rules and templates regularly; most can be washed in warm soapy water.

The board and straight-edge can be bought as a single unit. A "parallel motion" straight-edge is fixed to the board and operated on pulley wheels with either tensioned wire or cord guides. A "drawing machine" has a head with two rules set at right angles to each other, which can be adjusted to any angle on the surface of the board.

For best results both pencils and pens must be properly maintained. Avoid dropping any type of pencil as the lead breaks very easily — within the casing as well as at the tip. Sharpen a wood-cased pencil at a shallow, even angle to give a gradual taper and therefore a slower thickening of line as it wears. When using a pen with a tubular nib and plunger it is essential to use the ink recommended by the manufacturer and to wash it out after use. Ink flow is controlled by capillary action. If the ink is too thin it will blot; if it is too thick it will starve the nib.

Avoid a coarse-textured cartridge paper when using a pencil as it will wear the point quicker; this will cause carbon dust to collect on the surface, making it easier to smudge the drawing. Buy a thicker paper if drawing in ink or if intending to make many revisions. Printed graph papers can save constant measuring. They are available printed with different size squares and iso-metric grids and can either be drawn on to direct or be used as a backing to a tracing paper overlay.

Wood-cased pencil

Clutch pencil

Ratchet pencil

Pencil eraser

Nylon-tip pen

Ruling pen

Reservoir pen

Tubular-nib pen

Scalpel

Drop compass

Spring-bow compass

Set square

Adjustable square

Scale rule

T-square

Wood-cased pencil
Leads are graded in hardness (**H**) and blackness (**B**). Grades are numbered, the highest numbers being the hardest and blackest respectively. The blacker the lead the quicker it will wear.

Clutch pencil
The lead is gripped by a set of jaws, released by pressing the pencil's top. Sharpen the lead on fine garnet paper.

Ratchet pencil
The lead is very fine and is released from the top through a controlled feed. It does not require sharpening.

Pencil eraser
The type with a coiled paper casing is the most convenient.

Nylon-tip pen
For rough pen work. The type with a metal casing at the tip will not leave ink on the rule.

Ruling pen
The nib is filled directly from an ink dispenser and can be adjusted, by turning the screw, to a wide range of thicknesses.

Reservoir pen
The pen has an ink reservoir to which nibs for varying line thicknesses can be attached.

Tubular-nib pen
The pen has an ink container with a range of tubular nib and plunger attachments. It can be used at any angle.

Scalpel
A very sharp knife with a detachable blade.

Circle template

Ellipse template

Eraser shield

French curve

Flexible curve

Drawing machine
A pair of parallel arms clamped to the edge of the board allows the drawing edges to be positioned anywhere.

Drop compass
The pin forms a vertical axis, making it easy to draw very small circles.

Spring-bow compass
Used for most circle drawing.

Use trammel heads for very large circles (*see* page 55).

Set square
An adjustable square with wide arms for greater rigidity is useful but expensive. All edges should be smooth and bevelled to allow for greater accuracy.

T-square
Choose a square with parallel sides and bevelled edges.

Scale rule
Used to measure in proportion to produce scaled-down drawings. Choose one with thin scale lines and thin edges for accurate measuring.

French curve
Set of templates used for drawing free curved shapes.

Flexible curve
Used for drawing large flowing

shapes. The curve can be bent to follow any shape. It has a lead core with a plastic sleeve.

Ellipse and circle templates
Especially useful for drawing small ellipses and circles.

Eraser shield
Used to protect areas of the drawing around a line or detail to be erased. Made from thin flexible steel.

Basic design techniques

There are basic drawing tenets, methods and conventions that help to simplify and speed-up the drawing process and to avoid the problems of misreading the final result. Drawing methods relate to an understanding of basic geometrical shapes, proportion and scaled drawings. In order to produce a drawing of manageable size it is necessary to reduce, in exact proportions, the intended dimensions of the object. To do this, a scale rule is ideal. Choose a scale to suit the size of the object being drawn and the amount of detail needed to be shown. Full-size drawings of such details as mouldings are often drawn alongside scaled drawings of the whole subject. The usual scale for individual pieces of furniture is 1:5 in metric or 1:4 in Imperial, and for room layouts 1:20 in metric and 1:24 in Imperial. The scale 1:5 means that 1 centimetre on the scaled drawing represents 5 centimetres on the object.

Of the various methods of laying out a drawing the most universal is known as third-angle projection; the individual face-on views usually shown are one or more of the following: the front, the side and the top. By representing these views pictorially, however, with the three surfaces adjoining each other, the projection can be more easily read and understood. The easiest pictorial projection to draw is an isometric one.

In drawings, there are conventional ways to present and record dimensions, diameters, radii, sections and types of material, so that they can be readily interpreted both by the designer and the intended user of the finished object. For clarity, dimensions are added not to the outline itself but between the extension lines, which are extensions of the object's outlines. Write the figures centrally above the dimension line, omitting the unit of measurement, which can be specified in a title box describing the drawing. All dimensions should be so placed that they are readable from the bottom right-hand corner of the drawing.

Of the many methods and skills that will be acquired with practice, the following should prove useful. When running a pencil along a straight-edge, rotate the pencil slowly to give an even wear and an even thickness of line. One of the main problems when drawing in ink with a pen that is not equipped with a tubular nib is the possibility of the ink being drawn under the straight-edge by capillary action; this invariably results in the ink smudging when the straight-edge is removed. To avoid this, use bevel-edged rules and set squares with the bevel downwards, so that the edge is not resting on the work. If the straight-edge is not bevel edged, angle the pen away slightly to prevent the ink from flowing back under the edge. To avoid smudging when using a T-square on a drawing board, secure two pieces of string so they are held flat and taut across the board, top to bottom. Rest the T-square on the string.

When drawing up large areas of work, cover parts already completed with tracing paper to avoid any smudging. An ink line drawn on tracing paper can be removed easily by scratching with a scalpel; the surface may then need to be lightly burnished with the back of a teaspoon to avoid subsequent lines spreading. Finally, good lighting is essential for accurate drawing. Apart from a general light, an adjustable local light will be needed to highlight the work area.

Basic geometrical shapes

Circle parts.

Finding the centre of a circle.

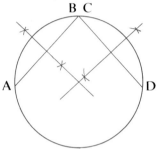

Drawing a hexagon.

Drawing an octagon.

Drawing an equilateral triangle.

Basic geometrical shapes
The circle is the key to a number of geometrical shapes. To find the exact centre of a circle draw a chord AB. Set a compass to over half AB. From A scribe arcs inside and outside the circle. Repeat from B, intersecting the arcs. Join up the points of intersection. Draw a chord CD. Repeat this process. The lines intersect at the centre. To draw a hexagon, first draw a circle with a radius equal to the side length of the required hexagon. With the compass at this setting, step around the circumference six times. Join up the points. To draw an octagon within a square, draw the diagonals of the square. Set a compass to half the length of a diagonal. With the compass point on a corner intersect the adjacent sides. Repeat from each corner and join up the points of intersection. To draw an equilateral triangle, first draw the line AB to the required length. Set a compass to the line length and describe two arcs, one from A and one from B; join up the lines from the point of intersection C. To draw an ellipse, first decide and draw up the major and minor axes, AB and CD, which bisect each other at right angles. Set a compass to AX. From C intersect AB giving points N_1 and N_2. Insert pins at N_1, N_2 and B. Tie string tightly from N_1 to N_2, via B. Remove pin B. Keeping the string taut, draw the ellipse.

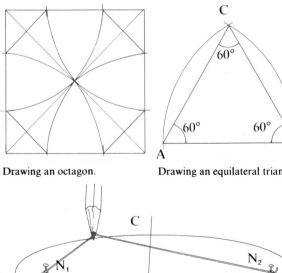

Drawing an ellipse.

Isometric projection

Third-angle projection

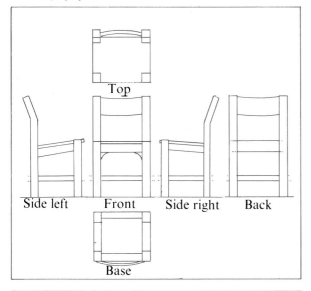

Top

Side left   Front   Side right   Back

Base

Drawing symbols

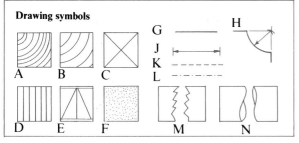

A   B   C

D   E   F   M   N

G
J
K
L
H

Third-angle projection

One of the most straightforward ways of representing a three-dimensional object is to draw the individual views from the front, side and top. The front view (front elevation) is drawn first; the view from the right (side elevation) is drawn on the right of it and the view from the left is drawn on the left; the top view (plan) is drawn above the front view. By following these conventions the drawing will be universally understood. All views should be drawn to the same scale in proportion to the intended dimensions of the object. As many as six views can be drawn; for simple objects, however, front and side elevations should convey all the necessary information to describe the object.

Drawing symbols

For clarification, symbols can distinguish the types of material to be used, such as finished hardwood (**A**), finished softwood (**B**), nominal-sized timber (**C**), multi-ply (**D**), blockboard (**E**), chipboard (**F**). Lines of different thickness are used to clarify parts of the drawing. Use the thinnest lines

Isometric projection

Of the many pictorial methods of presenting a drawing, the isometric projection is one of the most common and most straightforward.
Conventionally all vertical lines are drawn vertically and all other lines are drawn to the side of each vertical at 30° to the horizontal base line. Use a 30°/60° try square with a T-square. The three isometric axes around which all drawings are made are shown on the drawing (*above*). Because of this rigid geometrical method, which does not follow the laws of perspective, the picture will appear distorted. Being mechanically correct, however, it can be used for taking off dimensions. This makes the projection particularly useful for complicated structures.

for initial guide lines and the thickest (**G**) for the main outline. Make a thin line to indicate diameters and radii (**H**) and for dimension lines, drawn between extension lines (**J**). Use thin, short dashes for hidden details (**K**), a chain line as a centre line (**L**), jagged lines for rectangles (**M**) and wavy lines for cylinders (**N**).

Planning a project

A methodical approach to design, following the inception of an idea, is likely to ensure the best solution to the problems of intended use and construction. This design approach can be broken down into basic stages: the brief or analysis of the idea; sketch drawings; scaled drawings; and models and rods (full-size drawings). A cutting list is then made of the required materials.

The brief identifies the intended use and function of the object within its proposed context. It can set limits on the materials and finishes and how they are to be used. It can set visual guidelines; thus, for compatibility with existing furniture or room setting, the intended proportions, positioning and colour can be compared. The brief need only be a short statement clarifying the needs for the object. Even where ideas may seem very clear and the furniture simple, a brief is always useful as a written record, providing a check on progress throughout the project. In the example illustrated the brief would describe the following requirements: a table with fixed top to seat two people; to be used mainly with one side against a wall with seating positions either at the ends or on one side; stable hardwood supporting the structure; veneered top with a durable finish harmonizing with the chairs.

Sketch drawings
The designer's sketchbook translates the written brief into a series of visual solutions. Among the general considerations incorporated will be the material sizes and thicknesses, with appropriate allowance made for joints. It can also include a more precise breakdown of materials required, such as any fixtures to be used and any special tools that may be required. From the various sketches and ideas, one will be selected and developed. Check that the sketch chosen conforms in all aspects with the outline on the original brief. In the example illustrated the following are a few of the considerations that have been made: the size of the top; its height and rail width to give sufficient knee clearance; the leg structure and the method of connecting the rails with joints, knock-down fittings or dowels; the lower shape of the rail; and, finally, how to fix the top.

Table with fixed top to seat two people

1200 mm
600

Seating arrangements

720mm

Set legs in from line of corners of top to avoid being kicked.

Decide on this shape

Difficult to sit at

Try alternative profiles and check width of rail

Turned leg

Leg joint details

Mitred Mortice and Tenon?

Bolt head?

Soften edges

Button fixing to top

Table top lipping

Bolt head sunk in block - hardwood or metal. This will spread the force more evenly down the length of the rail and shoulder.

Scaled drawings

The scaled drawing is the basis for confirming the decisions taken at the sketch stage and for establishing accurate dimensions and proportions. The most straightforward drawing uses third-angle projection to show, respectively, the front, side and top views. A scale of 1:5 (metric) or 1:4 (Imperial) will usually result in an overall drawing of manageable size. An isometric drawing, showing the three views combined, is a useful aid to a fuller appreciation of the design. When designing furniture to fit a particular room, it may also prove helpful to apply the same principles of scaled drawing to the room itself. Cardboard cut-outs of each item of furniture can be moved around a scaled plan of the room to establish the position and suitability of the new piece. The example illustrates an isometric projection.

Models and rods

Full-size drawings against which the work can be laid for checking are known as rods. The drawing is usually a cross-section, either vertical or horizontal, to show the joints more clearly; it can be laid out on lining paper or a sheet of three-ply or thin board. It is especially useful when defining a particularly intricate part of the design, such as the position of the pivot on a folding chair, and for checking the work at progressive stages. For a more complete evaluation of the overall appearance of the object a scaled model, made from stiff card or balsa wood, is helpful. Balsa-model details can be taken direct from the scaled drawings; when using stiff card, take the dimensions from the scaled drawings and redraw the object, making as many surfaces as possible continuous with their adjacent sides for cutting and folding into a three-dimensional form. The example illustrates a rod for the joint in the table leg, drawn using third-angle projection and also as an isometric drawing.

PLAN

SIDE VIEW·L·   FRONT VIEW   SIDE VIEW·R·   TITLE : DINING TABLE LEG
SCALE : FULL SIZE

The cutting list

Using the scaled drawings or rods, the cutting list can be prepared for ordering the wood — either in nominal or finished sizes. Nominal is the size that the boards are cut on the bandsaw or a circular saw. When planed the board's thickness is reduced by at least 3 mm/$\frac{1}{8}$ in. Prepared wood is indicated on the cutting list either as finished sizes or PAR (planed all round). List the names of the parts, the number of pieces of the same size; then, in order, the length, width and thickness, allowing 13 mm/$\frac{1}{2}$ in of waste in length and 6 mm/$\frac{1}{4}$ in in width. Specify the wood required and re-check the total number of parts. The example illustrates the cutting list for the table.

Cutting List	All finished sizes · Units in m·m.				
ITEM	N° OFF	MATERIAL	LENGTH	WIDTH	THICKNESS
Leg Members	4	Pine	735	70	30
Leg Members	4	Pine	735	50	30
Rails	2	Pine	1,052	100	20
Rails	2	Pine	440	100	20
Top	1	Pine	1,212	606	23
Buttons for top	14	Pine	45	35	20
Leg inserts	4	Mahogany	102	20	20
Pellets to cover bolt heads	4	Mahogany	150	20	20
Dowels	24	Beech	40	11 (dia)	
Corner leg braces	4	Large complete with 6 mm/$\frac{1}{4}$" mushroom-headed bolts, washers and wing nuts.				

Storage

Ideally, well-designed storage should be capable of coping with the changing demands of an individual or a family, it should be easily accessible, make economic use of space and protect the items against dust, mildew and extremes of temperature. The main restraints on any design are the size of the items to be stored, the available space for storage, the height to which the items can be lifted and the distance that can be reached to retrieve them. These ideal requirements and restraints should also be considered in the context of the area needed for circulation around other objects or work surfaces and the daily routines in each room.

Storage items can be categorized into those used most frequently, such as food, shirts and toys, and those used only occasionally or seasonally, such as lawn-mowers, winter overcoats and suitcases. Those items used frequently should be easily accessible and those used infrequently should be well protected.

Storage units can be categorized into those that are free-standing and those that are fixed. Apart from individual pieces, free-standing storage can be considered in modular form; unit-size carcasses can be fitted out individually to suit particular requirements and be arranged, rearranged and added to at will. The modular system can also be applied to fixed storage. Manufactured boards fixed from the floor to the ceiling can be used to take adjustable shelves and units. Fixed storage can be built-in or be attached to a wall. Whatever the type of storage, fixtures and fittings can influence the design (*see* pages 256–65).

Key dimensions

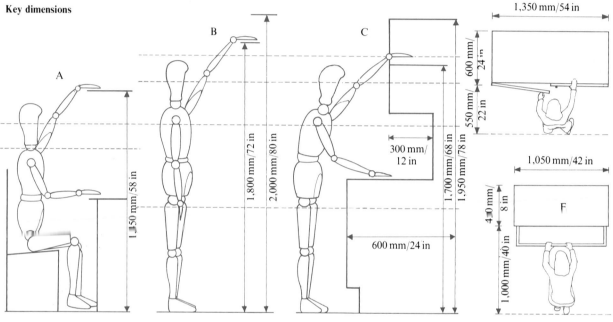

The central zone for storing items most frequently used or heavier items requiring two hands to lift with minimal effort is between 700 mm/28 in and 1,300 mm/52 in. Longer term or lighter weight storage not requiring direct visual access should be stored above or below this zone. The average eye level for an adult when standing is from 1,550 mm/62 in to 1,750 mm/70 in, and when sitting is from 1,100 mm/44 in to 1,250 mm/50 in. Comfortable vertical reach when sitting should be considered (**A**), as should both comfortable reach and full stretch when standing (**B**) and when leaning over a work top (**C**). Allow sufficient area when using a wardrobe (**D**) and a chest of drawers (**E**).

Free-standing modular storage

Drawer fronts

A. Inset drawer front. B. Overlapping drawer front. C. Rebated drawer front.

Drawer fronts
Only when a carcass is well built from well-seasoned timber can each drawer be made so that it is visually framed by the carcass without any gaps appearing between the carcass and the drawer front (**A**). If a less rigid carcass is used or if the carcass is to be positioned on an uneven floor, gaps can appear between the carcass and the drawer. To avoid this, the drawer front can be extended to cover whole or part of the carcass (**B**), or be rebated (**C**).

Door types

A. Double track doors. B. Triple track doors. C. Concertina doors.

Door types

A side-hung door provides best access to a cupboard, but at low level such a door can be impractical and at high level it can be dangerous. Sliding doors do not have these disadvantages; however, access is restricted. Three sliding doors on a double track give access to only one-third of the carcass at one time (**A**); three sliding doors on a triple track give access to two-thirds (**B**). A sliding, pivoting door (**C**) combines the advantages of the side-hung and sliding doors.

Hinging doors

C. Lay-on door, 270° sweep.

B. Lay-on door, 180° sweep.

A. Inset door, 180° sweep.

D. Bottom-hung door.

Hinging doors

A simple butt hinge fixed to a door inset flush into the carcass allows the door to open through 180° (**A**). If the door is not inset flush into the carcass the sweep will be restricted. (Dotted lines show maximum sweeps.) A door fully covering the carcass edges can be hinged to open through 180° (**B**). By moving the pivot point, specialized hinges enable lay-on doors to open when two carcasses are butted side by side (**C**). For bottom-hung doors, the hinge should allow the flap to open flush with the inside of the carcass (**D**).

Fixed modular storage

Tables

Of the many variations in table design, there are four basic types from which all others developed. Each type reflects the distinct requirements of the designer faced with the following key problems. Is the table for regular or infrequent use? How much space is available? How many will use the table at any one time?

The first type is the fixed-top table, such as refectory and coffee tables; it is the simplest to design and construct, whether for regular or infrequent use. The second is the collapsable table, such as trestle and card tables, which resolve the problem of infrequent use. The third and fourth types are the extending tables, the first having visible flaps, such as on gateleg and Pembroke tables, the second having hidden leaves, such as on drawleaf and swivel-top tables.

Whatever the type of table, the considerations of height are applicable to all. The height from the floor ranges from 675 mm/27 in to 725 mm/29 in for tables related to seat heights. The lower height applies to machinist tables, such as those used by typists, the higher to dining tables. The height of tables used while standing, as in the kitchen or workshop, is about 900 mm/36 in. For occasional tables the range can be between 300 mm/12 in and 550 mm/22 in.

Key dimensions

450 mm/18 in
575 mm/23 in
750 mm/30 in

The key dimensions, when deciding the size of the table top and the position of the supporting structure, are a width of 575 mm/23 in per person, allowing for a reasonable amount of elbow room, and a clearance of 300 mm/12 in from the edge towards the centre of the table for the sitter's legs. When seated at a table, the back of the chair is usually about 400 mm/16 in to 450 mm/18 in from the edge of the table; allow, therefore, a minimum of 750 mm/30 in from the edge of the table for circulation. A square table will take four people comfortably. A rectangular table provides greater seating capacity than a square one of the same area. The minimum comfortable width for a rectangular table is 750 mm/30 in. The minimum diameter for a round table — perhaps the most sociable shape — is 1,000 mm/40 in to seat four people. An oval table combines the best qualities of the round and rectangular tables. Leaves or flaps can be added to any of these tables. In each case consider the position of the supporting structure and the problem of the sitter's position in relation to the table legs. (Table-leg positions are indicated by black dots.)

Fixed-top and collapsable tables

Fixed-top and collapsable tables
A fixed top can be almost any size, and it can be supported on free-standing rigid structures or folding structures. The rigid structure can be very simple, consisting of a free-standing leg assembly glued and screwed to a top (**A**) or legs braced to a simple batten support (**B**). The refectory table (**C**) is a long narrow solid-top table. Large tables can be difficult to transport so it is worth considering a detachable top or legs; a hanger bolt and wing nut is the simplest way of fixing removable legs (**D**). A common form of folding table is the card table (**E**). Four irregularly spaced rails act as stops when the table is folded, and a turn catch locks the table against a rail in the upright and folded positions. Different leg assembly is preferable for long tables (**F**). The trestle table is the classic folding table; the two trestles are kept upright with a web strap and are located between two rails fixed the length of the top (**G**). The design is ideally suited to seasonal use.

Visible-flap tables

A

B

C

D

Hidden-leaf tables

A

B

C

D

E

Visible-flap tables

The main disadvantage of visible-flap tables is the restriction on seating when the flap is not in use. However, the folding-leg frame, such as in the gateleg table, offers the greatest extension of area of any type of table. The most usual visible-flap table is the double gateleg (A). A whole range of tops can be used with one or more gates pivoted on the main frame. Instead of gates, the Pembroke table (B) has support brackets pivoted at the sides. These can either comprise one long bracket or two short ones, depending on the size of the flap. The single-flap table has a top that slides in grooves; a fall flap hinged to the edge of the table can be raised and the whole surface slid across so the leg-frame supports both the flap and the top (C). The drop-leaf table has a fixed top housing a slider frame for each flap; the flap is raised and the slider is pulled out to support it (D).

Hidden-leaf tables

The drawleaf table (A) consists of two leaves and a centre bearer supporting a loose top; all are of identical thickness. Runners screwed to the leaves slide between guiding bearers and slots in the main frame. The swivel-top table (B) has a double top hinged along one edge, which is pivoted, allowing it to move through 90°. The most satisfactory shape, when swivelled and opened out, is a square. An alternative to end leaves is to use a centre leaf. The simplest type has a sliding top divided across its width. When both halves are pulled apart, a loose centre leaf, stored below the top or away from the table, is fitted centrally on to the frame (C). In a similar version the centre leaf is in two halves hinged together and pivoted at the sides to cross rails; the complete leaf can be folded up and swung down within the table frame (D). The envelope-top table (E) is a variation of the swivel top. The table has a square lower top pivoted to the frame, allowing it to move through 45°, and an upper top made of four triangular sections which is hinged to the lower top.

Chairs

Traditional chair design and construction demand a high degree of specialist skill, the main problem being that one component rarely meets at a right angle to the next. Modern designs, however, employ straight-sectioned timber, where possible, and timber that has been bent by steaming or laminating for curved work.

Before starting a design there are three key points to consider — stability, durability and comfort. Will the chair fall over when a sitter starts rocking it? Will it stand many years of use and misuse? Are chair arms necessary? Will the type of upholstery be suited to the chair's use? Finally, the visual appearance has to be considered. Will the chair suit the room setting?

Of all these considerations comfort is the one on which chairs are primarily judged. However, comfort is not measured or guaranteed by the amount of soft upholstery. The essentials to comfort are the angles and positions of the individual components and the support given by the completed frame. If they are correct the body muscles should not have to work significantly to maintain a comfortable posture.

A front seat height of 400 mm/16 in to 450 mm/18 in is suggested so the sitter's feet may rest on the floor, with a seat depth not exceeding 460 mm/18½ in if the back is straight across its width, or 420 mm/16¾ in if the back is curved. This will ensure that the front edge of the seat does not exert pressure at the back of the knees, resulting in blood starvation in the legs. The seat should slope back slightly, between 5° and 8° from the horizontal or by about 20 mm/¾ in in height between the front and back legs. This slope will help to hold the natural tilt of the pelvis and lumbar curve of the spine. About 200 mm/8 in above the seat the chair back should be shaped to follow the lumbar curve and then be extended, for a high back, at a 20° to 25° angle to the vertical to support the shoulders. The front edge of the arm rests should be about 200 mm/8 in above the seat and set back by a minimum of 60 mm/2½ in to ensure that the knuckles are not crushed when the chair is pulled up to the table's edge. The amount of upholstery should be kept to a minimum.

The chair dimensions illustrated are the maximum suitable for the "average-sized" person; they should therefore be considered carefully in relation to the worker's specific needs. In particular when designing dining chairs ensure that they relate to the height and structure of the table.

Rigid frame

Top-stacking frame

Side-stacking frame

Stacking chairs

Side-stacking principle

Top-stacking principle

Stacking chairs

The design of most stacking chairs is derived from two basic types — those that stack from the front and those that stack from the top. A front-stacking chair has part of the structure offset to allow one frame to pass over the next. Usually the side frames are constructed in two L shapes, one forming a back leg and floor rail, the other the front leg and seat rail; the two are offset at the join. A top-stacking chair has legs fitted to the outside edges of the seat frame, again slightly offset to give a tolerance for stacking. Both types are usually capable of stacking five or six chairs deep before the stack becomes unstable. By adding arms the chairs will be stronger and more stable when stacked.

Folding chairs

Front-to-back folding principle

Side-to-side folding principle

Folding chairs

The design of most folding chairs is derived from two basic types — those that fold from the front to the back and those that fold from side to side. The deck chair and park chair are typical examples of the first and the "director's" chair is typical of the second. These two basic types can however be combined. The key feature of any design is the positions of the pivot points. One way of assessing the correct positions is to use strips of card pinned at each pivot point. The pivots themselves, whether standard hinges or bolts, will determine the stability and durability of the chair. Make a prototype of the pivots early on in the design process.

Front-to-back folding frame   Side-to-side folding frame   Combination folding frame

Beds

As well as being the most used piece of furniture in a house, a bed can also dominate any planning and layout of a room. Only by disguising it or folding it away can the room take on an independent character. The variations on bed design are thus for the most part centred on the problems of space saving and storage. The three main types of rigid space savers are the stacking bed, the nest of beds and the bunk bed. The bunk bed can be developed by converting the lower bed into a table or a storage unit.

The interrelation of the bed base with the mattress is the key to comfort. The sleeping surface must be horizontal with no sag; ideally it should allow the spine to maintain its natural shape. This is best achieved by increasing the firmness of the mattress from a soft top surface down to a more resistant bottom.

The design of a bed will be limited by the standard sizes available if a proprietary mattress is to be used. It is therefore worth considering making a mattress, using rubber foam or layers of polyurethane foam of varying densities and original-shape recovery rates.

The ideal support

The human spine naturally forms a straight line when viewed from the front and back, and an S shape when viewed from the side. The ideal mattress should hold the spine as close as possible to this shape. A very firm mattress gives better support than an oversoft one.

Circulation and storage area

Circulation and storage area
The minimum circulation space around a bed when bedmaking should be 650 mm/26 in at the sides and 500 mm/20 in at the foot and between twin beds. Allow more space if there is to be a storage area underneath. The dotted lines represent drawers pulled out to their fullest extent. A bed should be easy to move for room cleaning. To ensure that it is unlikely to move accidentally, fit the base with glides and castors, for free movement, or glides with wheels, for movement in one direction.

Bed types
Stacking beds (A) are useful when a room has to double as a bedroom and play or sitting room. Up to four beds can be stacked together with either just the mattress in position on each bed or with each bed fully made up. Each supporting leg on bunk beds (B) can be divided into two to allow the bunks to be separated into two single beds. A double bed (C) can be built from two single beds, connected at the base by a hook. The mattresses are zipped together. This construction makes it easier to move the bed from room to room and gives the opportunity of varying the firmness of the mattresses according to requirements. A nest of beds (D) is an alternative to stacking beds.

A. Stacking beds

B. Bunk beds

Bed bases

A. Slotted-slat base

B. Webbed-slat base

C. Board base

D. Collapsable frame

Bed storage

A. Drawers

B. Lift-up top

C. Linked single beds

D. Nest of beds

Bed bases

The dimensions of the bed base will be restricted if a proprietary mattress is to be used. Examples of standard sizes are 900 mm/36 in, 1,500 mm/60 in and 2,000 mm/80 in in width, and 1,900 mm/76 in and 2,000 mm/80 in in length. Ideally the bed should be 200 mm/8 in longer than the user's standing height. The height of the bed will be a compromise between a comfortable height for sitting (up to 450 mm/18 in) and one for easy bedmaking (600 mm/24 in). The height can affect the appearance of the room — a low bed making a room look much bigger. The base can consist of solid wood or five-ply slats, either slotted and screwed (A) or attached to webbing (B) to allow the slats to flex; a manufactured board drilled over its whole area to ventilate the mattress (C) or a collapsable frame with a tourniquet action for tensioning the canvas base (D).

Bed storage

The base frame can be designed so that it is high enough to accommodate storage units underneath. Drawers can be suspended from or fitted into the base (A). Alternatively, a detached storage box on castors is simpler to make; however this has the disadvantage that the box will not move with the bed. A bed with a lift-up top (B) can have its full base area used for storage. This design, which incorporates spring-loaded hinges, is usually only suitable with lightweight foam mattresses.

Tools

A survey of all the hand and machine tools
required to produce quality work

The tool kit

The basic tool kit

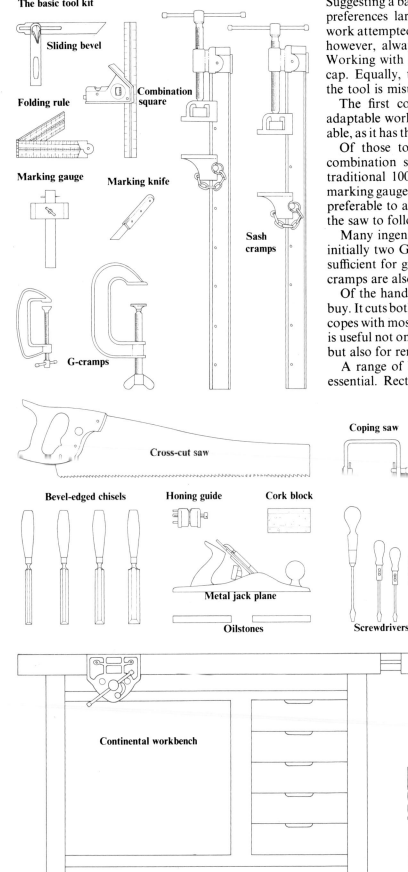

Sliding bevel

Folding rule

Combination square

Marking gauge

Marking knife

Sash cramps

G-cramps

Cross-cut saw

Coping saw

Tenon saw

Bevel-edged chisels

Honing guide

Cork block

Punches

Cross pein hammer

Mallet

Metal jack plane

Oilstones

Screwdrivers

Bradawl

Pincers

Suggesting a basic kit must inevitably involve personal preferences largely dependent on the nature of the work attempted; whatever the tool eventually selected, however, always buy the best quality at the outset. Working with inferior tools is an unnecessary handicap. Equally, the best results cannot be achieved if the tool is misused or not sharpened or maintained.

The first consideration should be a sturdy and adaptable work top. The continental bench is preferable, as it has the facility to hold the wood at both ends.

Of those tools for measuring and marking, the combination square is far more versatile than the traditional 100 mm/4 in try square. Of the gauges a marking gauge is the most essential. A marking knife is preferable to a pencil, making a finer, clearer line for the saw to follow.

Many ingenious holding devices are available, but initially two G-cramps, one large and one small, are sufficient for general work. Two medium-length sash cramps are also indispensable for clamping frames.

Of the handsaws, a cross-cut saw is a sensible first buy. It cuts both with and across the grain. A tenon saw copes with most jointing problems, and the coping saw is useful not only for its normal work of cutting curves but also for removing the waste when dovetailing.

A range of best-quality bevel-edged chisels is also essential. Rectangular section chisels are marginally

Continental workbench

Two-speed power drill

Set of small drills

Flat bits

Countersink bit

stronger, but clumsier. A chisel bevelled on three sides gives a clear view of the area being worked; suggested sizes are 3 mm/⅛ in, 6 mm/¼ in, 13 mm/½ in, 19 mm/¾ in and 25 mm/1 in.

Most planes are designed for specific operations, but a good general choice is a metal jack plane. It will do the work of a jointer plane, such as planing edge joints, and in most cases that of a smoothing plane, such as cleaning up wide surfaces. For smoothing with abrasives a cork block is essential to ensure an even surface. Two oilstones, one medium and one fine, are needed to keep blades in prime condition, together with a honing guide for maintaining the correct bevel.

A bradawl with the blade integrated with the handle and a nail-punch are essentials. Of the screwdrivers choose a long cabinet screwdriver for heavy-gauge screws, a large and a small ratchet screwdriver for general use and a narrow rigid screwdriver for repairing items such as locks.

A cross-pein hammer and a pair of pincers cope with most nailing work. Despite the introduction of so-called unshatterable chisel handles, a wooden mallet will cause less damage than a hammer. A two-speed power drill is the best first-time buy for the basic kit. Select a set of small drills up to 6 mm/¼ in, a countersink bit with a round shank and a set of six flat bits. A second drill will be needed when using accessories.

The follow-up tool kit

The basic tool kit as described will be quite adequate for general work. The additional tools (*illustrated below*) are probably the most useful for extending the range of the original kit. It is important, however, to realize that they are mostly specialist tools. It is therefore essential to consider whether the work justifies the additional cost.

If the intention is to make traditional joints, a mortise gauge will be necessary to set out the double lines of the mortise and tenon joint as well as two mortise chisels (3 mm/⅛ in and 6 mm/¼ in) to lever out the waste. For dovetails a cutting gauge makes a very fine line for accurate working. Use a dovetail saw for very fine joinery work. For large frames a long try square is very effective for checking squareness. Two pairs of cramp heads will provide two extra sash cramps of variable length. A rip saw and panel saw, or a good power jigsaw, will also justify their purchase.

A metal smoothing plane is a good addition to the jack plane. The remaining planes illustrated are all important in their own right, but study their specialized uses and only buy when the need arises. Buy two spokeshaves: one with a flat sole for forming convex curves; the other with a curved sole for concave curves. When finishing hardwood surfaces a cabinet scraper is invaluable if used correctly.

The follow-up tool kit

Steel tape Try square Trammel points Dividers Mortise gauge Cutting gauge Cramp heads

Rip saw Panel saw Power jig saw Dovetail saw

Toothing plane Metal smoothing plane Block plane Shoulder plane Plough plane

Pin hammer

Compass plane Spokeshaves Cabinet scraper

Hand router Mortise chisels Set of small drills Hand drill

The workshop

The workshop should ideally be a space set permanently apart from the rest of the house. A closed door will discourage outside interference and will allow the woodworker to leave work in progress.

The workshop must be warm, well lit and have good ventilation. Windows and a corrugated vinyl transparent roof will provide natural light. Where windows cannot be opened, a ventilator must be installed to provide good air circulation. Beware of naked flames in the workshop and always keep a fire extinguisher close at hand. A basic first aid kit should be readily available in case of injury.

Thoughtful and methodical planning of the work area will continually benefit efficient working, especially if the workshop is kept tidy and the tools are ready to hand.

The most important item in the workshop is the workbench, around which other fixtures and equipment should be arranged. Drawers are useful for keeping pencils, a rule, a steel tape and small oddments. Cupboards will store tools, which should be racked separately to protect them from damage. Each tool should be considered separately when deciding the best place for storage and the method of storage such as clips and magnetic strips. Return each tool to its proper place after a working session. Planes should be laid sole downwards on a piece of lightly oiled felt. Chisels and saws should be fitted with plastic sheaths, wherever possible, to protect their blades. Hand tools should be rubbed over with white spirit and grease occasionally to clean off resin and to prevent rust.

A portable workbench can be folded and neatly hung against the wall from strong hooks. A plastic bin should be kept in the workshop to hold wood shavings, used abrasive paper and other litter.

Store manufactured boards upright on edge against a dry wall and lodge them securely with a wooden batten fixed to the workshop floor.

Overhead fluorescent tubes give shadowless illumination while an angled spotlight over the work area gives an effective concentrated light.

Lay short ends of wood horizontally for easy identification. Stack longer pieces vertically between mild steel rods.

Certain fixed power tools can be connected via a flat belt to a common motor that is built into a specially designed table. The system illustrated shows a planer/thicknesser, a table saw and a spindle moulder; however, any combination of power tools can be included on a table of this type.

Keep all toxic materials, such as thinners and lacquers, in only small quantities. Place all adhesives well away from direct heat.

Store nails, screws, pins, etc., in small separate containers, which must be kept dry. Label them clearly and arrange them methodically for easy access.

Tools placed in cupboards, drawers and under cover are protected from dust and rust. A bag of silicagel will further discourage rust.

Many hand tools can be racked with spring clips, rubber webbing, magnetic strips, hooks, projecting dowel rods or drilled blocks.

Fit power sockets above the work surfaces close to the power tools so their flexes can be short and they will not trail on the workshop floor.

Stout shelving provides extra storage space and is especially useful for portable power tools that are too heavy to hang on the walls.

Cover concrete floors with vinyl sheeting for warmth. A rubber mat or slatted board will provide additional comfort and warmth while working.

Stack sawing trestles one upon the other to leave as much floor space as possible for assembly work and general movement.

The workbench

The main purpose of the workbench is to support the wood being worked. To do this it must be sturdy, especially to withstand diagonal stresses. The top should be absolutely flat and level, made from thick hardwood and supported by four solid legs with a bracing structure. The whole bench must stand at a comfortable height for the individual worker.

The workbench should also accommodate wood of varying proportions and shapes; clamping devices and bench-dogs are therefore built into it. Work-top mortises are either part of the proprietary bench or they can be made. They take metal or nylon bench-dogs, which can be adjusted to the level required. Mortises can also be used to take a holdfast. Those cut into a vertical batten of solid wood, known as a deadman, also take a holdfast that is useful for supporting awkward work such as doors. Alternatively, metal spring-loaded bench-stops can be sunk into the work top.

The woodworker's bench vice, made of cast-iron with wooden jaw facings, is the main clamping device. It can be fitted by the worker. It is usually bolted to the underneath of the bench, close to a leg for maximum stability. The rear jaw is fitted 10 mm/$\frac{3}{8}$ in down from the bench top and is sunk flush into the apron. Some benches have an integral sliding tail vice. Mortises are worked into the tail vice and the front of the bench. By using the tail vice in conjunction with bench-dogs the wood can be gripped at both ends. The tail vice can also hold a deadman. Whatever the vice, it will not withstand heavy hammering.

Jigs act as guides for accurate planing and sawing; they are simple to construct. Amongst the most useful and easily made is the bench-hook, which fits either in a vice or against the bench apron. The shooting board is more practical than the bench-hook for planing thin boards and end grain.

A portable workbench can be used, in addition to or instead of a permanent workbench. Many accessories are available, making it extremely versatile. A pair of sawing stools is invaluable when sawing large pieces.

Woodworker's bench vice
Opening capacity 113–375 mm/ $4\frac{1}{2}$–15 in. For holding the work, usually horizontally. Place the work centrally where possible. When the work is placed in one side only, support the other with waste wood of the same thickness as the work-piece to minimize strain.

Mortise

Portable workbench
This small rigid bench has adjustable legs and a folding structure for neat storage. The two boards can expand to give a larger working surface or can contract to act as vice jaws for holding both parallel and tapered work. The mortises hold the bench-dogs.

Sawing stool
For supporting lengths of wood for sawing and marking. The legs and frame may be softwood but the top must be hardwood. With a pair, one top should be wider than the other for neat stacking. The components can be assembled with brackets.

Bench-hook
Gripped in the vice. Protects the work top and provides a stop for the work to be sawn. It is made from hardwood.

Mitre box
For sawing the work, generally at 45° and 90°, but it can be adapted to any angle. It is made from hardwood.

Shooting board
For planing end grain square. The plane is used flat on its side and is held directly over the blade.

Tool well

Holdfast
For holding work down when the shank is in a work-top mortise and for horizontal holding in a deadman mortise.

Bench apron

Metal spring-loaded bench-stop
Fits flush with the work top. The work is planed against its serrated jaw, which is raised by means of a screw.

Tail vice
For holding the work. It is mounted at one end of the bench and may accommodate mortises to take bench-stops.

Deadman
Is held vertically in the tail vice. Its mortises accommodate the holdfast for holding larger work horizontally.

Bench-dog
Fits securely into a work top mortise by means of a leaf spring. A second bench-dog fits into a tail mortise. The work is

gripped between the two by tightening the vice. They must project to half the thickness of the work. They are made from metal or nylon.

Measuring and marking tools 1

The most ancient units of measurement are those based on the human foot, outstretched arm and hand. Then, around 2500 BC, the Egyptians used calibrated wooden or stone rods based on the cubit (a forearm's length) and later the Romans used a folding bronze foot rule.

Measuring and marking tools must be treated with special care: if edges, blades and surfaces, hinges, locking screws and rivets are damaged the tools lose their accuracy and are therefore of no further value. Always mark cutting lines, joints and anything else requiring accuracy with a sharp knife or a scribing point rather than with a pencil.

The try square is essential for preparing and checking a true edge. On the best try squares the stock end of the steel blade is L shaped.

Of those tools for measuring or marking flat surfaces, a spirit level with a long body is more accurate than a short one. A chalk line and reel can double as a plumb bob for testing vertical surfaces, provided the reel is sufficiently weighty.

Of those tools for marking parallel lines, the cutting gauge, with its cutting edge, is ideal for marking across the grain; a marking gauge when used across the grain will merely scratch the wood.

Retractable tape
Length 900–5,000 mm/
36–192 in. Flexible steel or
fibreglass tape in a case.

Folding rule
Length 300–1,825 mm/
12–72 in. For measuring and
laying out.

Steel rule
Length 150–900 mm/6–36 in.
Made of stainless steel. Can be
used like a straight-edge.

Straight-edge
Length 300–1,825 mm/12–72 in.
For testing straightness and
flatness. A strip of parallel-
sided steel with one bevelled
edge for cutting and scribing.

Spirit level
Length 75–1,825 mm/3–72 in.
Use central vial to check level
of a surface and the two vials
at each end to check for
plumb. The bubble in each vial
should appear centrally.

Sliding bevel
Blade length 190–323 mm/
7½–13 in. For marking or
checking any angle. The slotted
blade is set against a protractor
or the work.

Mitre square
Blade length 150–300 mm/
6–12 in. Set at 45° for mitres.

Try square
Blade length 150–300 mm/
6–12 in. For checking
straightness and squareness of
adjacent surfaces.

Combination square
Blade length 300 mm/12 in.
Combines the functions of the
rule, try square, mitre square
and spirit level. The square
head slides along the steel rule.

Retractable tape · Folding rule · Steel rule · Straightedge

Sliding bevel

Spirit level

Miter square

Combination square

Try square

Chalk line and reel

Trammel heads

Profile gauge

Compass

Dividers

Scriber

Inside calipers

Outside calipers

Marking knife

Marking gauge

Cutting gauge

Mortise gauge

Chalk line and reel
Length 5,000–30,000 mm/
196–1,200 in. For marking
long straight lines by "snapping"
the chalked cord against a surface.
Trammel heads
Length 100 mm/4 in. Two steel
points that, when fixed on a
wooden beam, can scribe a
large circle.
Profile gauge
Length 150 mm/6 in. For
tracing and checking work.
When pressed against a shape
the steel needles slide back to
reproduce the outline.
Compass
Capacity 100–200 mm/4–8 in.
For marking a small circle.
Scriber
Blade 100 mm/4 in. For marking
with and across the grain.
Dividers
Capacity 100–200 mm/4–8 in.
For scribing a circle, stepping
off and measuring.
Inside calipers
Capacity 100–200 mm/4–8 in.
For measuring the inside
diameter of a pipe, tube and
bowl.
Outside calipers
Capacity 100–200 mm/4–8 in.
For measuring the outside
diameter of a cylinder.
Marking knife
Blade 50 mm/2 in. The blade is
ground to a bevelled skew for
marking against a rule or
straight-edge.
Marking gauge
Length 160–240 mm/6¼–9½ in.
For marking a line parallel to
an edge, along the grain or on
end grain. The stock, which
acts as a fence and is locked by
the thumb-screw, is often faced
with brass to protect against
wear. The spur at the end of
the stem marks the line.

Cutting gauge
Length 160–240 mm/6¼–9½ in.
For marking across the grain
parallel to an edge. The flat
blade in the stem, which is
secured by a wedge, can be
removed and sharpened. Also
cuts veneers and cardboard.
Mortise gauge
Length 925 mm/9 in. For
marking both sides of a
mortise and tenon. Two spurs,
the inner one adjustable,
protrude from the sliding stem
to mark parallel lines.

55

Measuring and marking tools 2

Before marking out can begin on any piece of wood, it must have datum lines: one flat side and one edge square to it. Choose the better looking side to be the face side. Plane it flat and level. With the straight-edge, check across the face for flatness — also along its width, its length and from corners to diagonally opposite corners. When the face is true, pencil a loop — the face mark — in the centre, extending the line to the better of the two side edges. Plane this face edge square with the face side and check it along its length with the straight-edge. To square up the remaining surfaces, set the marking gauge to the required width and, from the face edge, mark both sides. Plane to the gauge marks. Set the gauge to the required thickness and gauge both edges from the face side. Plane to the gauge marks. Accurate measuring, marking out and checking are essential. Tools must be carefully set.

Face side

Face edge

Thickness

Width

Setting and using gauges

1. Set stock using a rule.

2. Tap the gauge on the bench.

3. Hold the stock firmly.

Setting and using gauges
Loosen the thumb-screw. Set the distance between stock and spur by pushing the stock away with a rule or pushing it towards the spur with your thumb (**1**). Tighten the thumb-screw and check the setting. If it is incorrect do not loosen the thumb-screw but tap either the stock or the spur end of the stem on the bench (**2**). Recheck and, if correct, tighten the thumb-screw. When using any gauge, keep the stock tight against the work (**3**).

Drawing lines and outlines

Marking parallel to an edge.

Finger gauging.

Making equal subdivisions.

Marking parallel to an edge
Set a combination square to the required distance. Then hold the head tightly against the edge and, with a pencil against the end of the rule, run it along the board.
Finger gauging
To draw a line close to an edge, use the middle finger as a gauge for the pencil.
Making equal subdivisions
To divide up a given width into equal spaces, angle a rule between the two parallel sides until the readings on the rule are easily divisible by the number of spaces required.
Scribing
To shape a board to fit against an irregular surface first rest it at right angles to the surface; then draw a compass along with the point running against the surface.
Using a profile gauge
Use the gauge to duplicate mouldings or turnings. Push the needles fully out on one side. Hold the gauge squarely to the shape and press against it. The gauge will then show the profile of the shape and the negative profile.

Scribing.

Using a profile gauge.

Measuring and checking verticals, horizontals and planes

Using a spirit level.

Using a retractable tape.

Using pinch rods.

Using a plumb bob.

Checking for winding.

Using a spirit level
The air bubble will be central between the datum lines when the surface is level or plumb.

Using a retractable tape
Hook the end of the tape over the work to take an external measurement. For an internal measurement butt the metal hook against the work.

Using a plumb bob
To check if a surface is plumb, hold the string against a rule at the top of the surface and a set distance, such as 75 mm/3 in, away from it. When the bob stops swinging, ask an assistant to check with a second rule that the measurement from the surface to the line is the same at the bottom as at the top.

Using pinch rods
Use two overlapping battens to take a measurement. Put coincident marks on both; then transfer the measurement to the wood to be cut.

Checking for winding
To check whether a board is twisted in its length, known as being "in winding", place a steel rule at each end and sight across the top edges to see if they are parallel. Two parallel battens can be used instead.

Measuring and checking angles

Using a try square.

Measuring internal angles.

1. Reverse the try square.

2. Draw a second line.

3. File blade for correction.

Using a try square
When checking for squareness, always hold the stock of the try square tight against the work otherwise the tool is being used as a straight edge and not as a square.

Measuring internal angles
Walls are rarely square to each other, so always measure and set out the first angle with a sliding bevel.

Checking a try square
With prolonged use or if it is dropped, a try square can become inaccurate. To check it, plane a perfectly straight edge on a board. With the stock of the try square tight against the edge, draw a line along the blade. Reverse the square and check whether the blade is coincident with the line (1). If it is not, draw another line along the blade (2). The blade must be corrected so that it bisects these lines. File along both edges of the blade, working diagonally with a smooth file. (3). Check the try square again. When correct, drawfile to remove the initial file marks. Smooth the edges with an oilstone.

Cramps 1

Cramps are used for holding materials during working and while glue dries. Originally all cramps were made of wood, but these have mostly been superseded by metal and tough plastics. The hand-screw and cam cramp, however, still have wooden jaws.

The G-cramp is the most common general-purpose cramp. It has many variations: miniature cramps; deep-throat or long-reach cramps; and spin-grip cramps, which can be tightened quickly with one hand. The edge cramp, toggle cramp, quick-release cramp and cam cramp have similar uses to the G-cramp.

The problem of clamping mitres and frames has been solved in many ingenious ways. The lightweight mitre cramp, which is in fact a set of four corner cramps, is useful for picture frames, while the heavier metal frame cramp has greater capacity. The versatile web cramp can be adapted as a frame cramp by using four right-angled wooden or metal corners.

A number of bar cramps are needed when any large flat surface such as a table top is being glued. Cramp heads fixed to a batten can be made up to a cramp of any length required.

Fretwork clamp

C-clamp

Edge clamp

Fretwork cramp
Capacity 25–100 mm/1–4 in. A small lightweight steel cramp.
Edge cramp
Capacity 38–75 mm/1½–3 in. Depth 50–112 mm/2–4½ in. For pressure in two directions.
G-cramp
Capacity 50–300 mm/2–12 in. Most varieties have a swivel shoe on the screw end.
Quick-release cramp
Capacity 100–600 mm/4–24 in. For clamping flat surfaces, edge joints and the sides of carcasses and frames.

Toggle cramp
Holding capacity 360 kg/800 lb. Strong steel cramp with trigger release and an optional sliding lower jaw. The upper jaw pivots up to 84° backwards.
Cam cramp
Capacity 200–575 mm/8–23 in. For clamping fine surfaces as its heads are cork faced.
Hand-screw
Capacity 50–300 mm/2–12 in. Steel screws pivot in wooden jaws, which can exert parallel pressure or can be angled for concentrated pressure.

Hand vise

 Web clamp

Frame clamp

Joiners' dog

Miter clamp

Hand vice
Capacity 19 mm/¾ in. For gripping very small work.
Web cramp
Length 3,500–6,000 mm/ 144–240 in. Canvas or nylon webbing tensioned by ratchet mechanism for clamping large, irregular and round shapes.
Joiners' dog
Width 25–75 mm/1–3 in.

Tapered steel staples driven into end grain for holding glued butt joints.
Frame cramp
Capacity 50–100 mm/2–4 in. Holds right-angled joints securely during assembly.
Mitre cramp
Capacity 32 mm/1¼ in. Four corners with strong spring-loaded jaws hold the work.

Quick-release cramp

Cam cramp

Sash cramp

Toggle cramp

T-bar cramp

Hand-screw

Jet cramp

Cramp heads
Can be fitted to a board of any length over 38 mm/1½ in wide and 25 mm/1 in thick. Useful because they are adaptable and easily portable.

Jet cramp
The heads can be fitted to a steel bar of standard section and of any length. Heads can be reversed to apply outward pressure for jacking. Unlike other bar cramps, both heads move along the steel bar and lock by wedge action.

T-bar cramp
Capacity 760–1,985 mm/ 30–78 in. A heavy-duty joiners' cramp. Any bar cramp over 1,525 mm/60 in long will usually be of T-section steel, which resists bending. A lengthening bar can be added.

Sash cramp
Capacity 450–1,370 mm/ 18–54 in. For the assembly of cabinetwork; clamping flat surfaces and edge joints; and clamping carcasses and frames from side to side. Two cramps can be bolted end to end to cover a wider span.

Cramp heads

Cramps 2

Wood can be bruised if it is gripped too hard between the metal jaws of G-cramps and sash cramps. Cramps with wooden or plastic-capped jaws, however, are less damaging. Always place a piece of waste wood between the cramp and the work to spread the pressure. For odd shapes and angles, scraps of carpet can be used instead of waste wood. When gluing up assemblies make sure that the bar or spine of the cramp is aligned with the work; if it is not, the weight of the cramp may pull the work out of square. To prevent cramps from pulling the work out of alignment, always alternate cramps on each side of the work when more than two are being used. For example, when clamping the sides to the top and bottom of a carcass, sash cramps should be placed alternately front and back.

Most cabinetwork requires a number of sash cramps to be used in assembly. Improvised cramps can be made from battens and waste wood.

G-cramp

Always use waste wood to protect the work from the metal jaws. Usually, position with the wing nut towards the ground, leaving the working area free. A swivel shoe on the screw end locates easily on slanting surfaces. The leverage exerted by the screw thread creates great pressure.

Hand-screw

To open and close hold a handle in each hand and revolve both handles. Tighten the inner handle; then apply final pressure with the outer handle, making the jaws parallel or angled. As long as the wooden jaws are kept clean no waste wood is needed to protect the work.

Cam cramp

Move the lower beechwood head up the steel bar until it presses against the work. Lock with the lever, which is worked by cam action.

Jet cramp

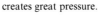

Slide the lower jaw up the steel bar. Lock it by turning the handle clockwise. Release the cramp with a single turn of the cramp handle.

Quick-release cramp

Move both heads into position along the steel bar. The spring-loaded wedges in the heads will automatically lock themselves. Fix in position by tightening the knob on one of the heads. To apply an outward pressure for jacking work apart, remove the heads from the steel bar and reverse them.

Joiners' dog

Drive into end grain to draw the ends of boards together. The tapered steel points leave marks, so the work will need filling or covering.

Hand vice

Grip a hand vice in the bench vice or hold it in the hand. Use when working on metal fittings that are too small to hold by other means.

Web cramp

Slide the webbing around the work and tension it with the steel ratchet. Can be used with metal angles for clamping around corners.

Sash cramp

Adjust the cramp initially by sliding the tail shoe along the steel bar and securing it with a pin through one of the holes in the bar. To move the tail shoe,

tap it along the bar with a mallet. (It is made of cast iron and a hammer may shatter it.) Make final adjustments with the tightening screw at the

other end of the bar. Use for clamping all large constructions together during assembly while the glue dries, checking the pressure is even.

Ensure enough cramps of the right length are available before beginning assembly. Use T-bar cramps in the same way as sash cramps.

Lengthen sash cramps by placing the tail shoes face to face or by removing both tail shoes and bolting the bars tightly together.

The work must be adapted to fit the cramps when even cramps specially devised to hold awkward shapes cannot be used. Glue cramping blocks to

the work with brown paper between. Then clamp the work. When dry, remove the work. Knock off the blocks; then soak or smooth off the paper.

If a number of cramps are to cover the same distance, cut battens roughly to size. Screw a pivoting cleat to each end. Put the battens in place. Tap them

so they slant, pivoting the cleats and making the battens fit tightly. Cleats rigidly screwed to each end of a batten can be used with folding

wedges tapped in to supply pressure. Bore holes in a batten to take a movable tail shoe, locked by a bolt and wing nut for rough adjustment.

At the other end, fix a cleat with one sloping side matching the slope of a wedge. Make fine adjustments by tapping in the wedge.

Mitre cramp

Cramp heads

Place the work against the corner fence, where two sprung jaws will hold them while the glue dries on a mitre joint or while pins are hammered in.

Make a mitre cramp with blocks of wood recessed at the inner corners. Apply pressure with strong cord resting in grooves on the outside. Twist the cord around a stick, rest the stick against the frame to lock the windlass.

Use cramp heads in pairs on a 25 mm/1 in section wooden batten. Bore holes in the batten at regular intervals. Place the cramp heads and batten over the work and lock in position with pegs placed in the holes.

Hand- and backsaws 1

Saws are of three main types, categorized according to the job they do: handsaws for rough cutting and conversion; backsaws for joints and fine work; and special saws for curves and shapes. Handsaws have flexible tempered steel blades; a well-tempered blade when bent from tip to handle should spring back into a perfectly straight line. Backsaws have a brass or steel strip folded over the top of the blade to give rigidity and add weight along the line of the cutting edge.

The basic design of the handsaw was established in the mid-seventeenth century. The English type, incorporating an oval hand-hole and angled grip, became the standard pattern almost everywhere for both hand- and backsaws. A modern alternative to the traditional beechwood handle is one made of polypropylene; this is usually moulded on to a PTFE-coated blade, which reduces friction when cutting.

A saw's teeth are specifically designed to cut either along the grain, as with the rip saw, or across the grain, as with the cross-cut saw. A cross-cut saw will also cut along the grain, but less efficiently than the rip saw. The greater the number of teeth in a given length of blade, the finer and slower the cut. Some woods can be naturally tough; in such cases use a saw with smaller teeth. The number of teeth is expressed as so many points per 25 mm/1 in. Saws also have their teeth set to prevent the blade binding in the kerf or cut.

Rip saw
Blade 600–650 mm/ 24–26 in. 4½ points to 25 mm/1 in. For boards 13 mm/½ in and upwards, when cutting with the grain.

Handsaw parts

Taper ground blade for kerf clearance

Skewback for good balance

Traditional beechwood handle set low for efficient cutting

Backsaw parts

Back edge reinforced with brass or steel for rigidity

Traditional beechwood handle set high for correct balance

Straight parallel blade

Rip saw teeth are set as shown above, with their tips bent over in alternate directions to prevent binding.

Each tooth is filed to form a chisel edge. This enables it to cut the fibres cleanly along the grain of the wood.

The teeth on a cross-cut saw are sloped on their leading edge as well as being filed at an angle and set.

Filed in this way, each tooth is sharply pointed to act as a knife to sever the fibres of the wood.

Half-rip saw
Blade 625 mm/25 in.
6 points to 25 mm/1 in.
For boards of less
than 13 mm/$\frac{1}{2}$ in, when
cutting with the grain.
Is lighter than a rip saw.

Cross-cut saw
Blade 600–650 mm/
24–26 in. 7–8 points
to 25 mm/1 in.
For general cutting
across the grain. Will
also cut with the grain.

Panel saw
Blade 510–550 mm/20–22 in.
10 points to 25 mm/1 in.
Similar to the cross-
cut saw but used on
thinner woods
and man-made boards.

Dovetail saw
Blade 200–250 mm/8–10 in.
18–22 points to 25 mm/1 in.
For very fine joinery
work especially for
cutting joints.

Razor saw
Blade 125 mm/5 in.
Points too numerous
to count. For extremely
delicate work. Replace
blades when blunt.

Bead saw
Blade 100–200 mm/4–8 in.
32 points to 25 mm/1 in.
For fine joinery
work, leaving a
smooth finish.

Tenon saw
Blade 300–350 mm/12–14 in.
12–14 points to 25 mm/1 in.
For general bench
work especially when
cutting joints.

Hand- and backsaws 2

Sawing is a skilful process; mastery is achieved only with constant practice, but attention to the following points will make the work easier. A blunt tool is more difficult to control than a sharp one. A sharp saw needs little pushing; unnecessary force makes it more difficult to follow a line and can cause the saw to buckle. The saw should be well-balanced and should cut smoothly, virtually under its own weight. For efficient cutting, saw with the blade in line with your arm and shoulder; start the cut low down and bring the saw up to the correct cutting angle. Then move the saw up and down in long steady movements.

Saw vertically wherever possible, even if this means that the wood must be gripped out of upright in the vice to bring the cutting line to the required angle. If the saw binds in the wood, rub three drops of oil on the blade. (Avoid oils that will stain the wood.) In extreme cases, drive a narrow wooden wedge into the saw-cut to hold it open. Wipe any resin residue off the blade, using white spirit; then wipe with oil.

If saw teeth are overset, that is alternate teeth are pushed too far over, it will be more difficult to work the saw. This can be corrected by side dressing. (This and other methods of maintaining saws are covered on pages 72–3.) To bring a wandering saw back to the cutting line, twist the blade towards the line, working with the narrow front end of the saw.

Ripping

To saw on only a single stool overhang the board a bit at a time, steadying it with the knee. Saw halfway in from each end of the board.

Hold short lengths in the vice. Secure the wood so that only a little bit projects at a time, otherwise the wood will vibrate, making the cut inaccurate.

If a level higher than the stool is more convenient for ripping, fasten the wood to the bench and hold the saw upright, using both hands.

Place the board across two stools and start sawing at the overhang. Then lift the saw and board back and continue sawing between the stools.

Using a rip saw

Rip saw teeth are specifically designed for cutting along the grain. If used for cross-cutting the rip saw may jump and cause an accident. Should ripping prove difficult, try changing to a half-rip saw or in extreme cases to a cross-cut or even panel saw.

Short boards can be ripped in the vice or on a single stool. Longer work needs supporting on two stools. An angle of 60° between the saw and the work is comfortable when ripping on stools, but in a vice a rip saw should be held horizontally to the work.

Controlling a handsaw

To control a handsaw with accuracy needs experience. A forefinger held along the handle aids control.

The saw must be guided to the cutting line. Steady the blade against the thumb. Start with a few backward cuts.

Using a cross-cut saw

To cut a groove across the grain, the wood fibres must be cut before the waste is removed or they will splinter. This is the principle of a cross-cut saw: the knife-like points of the teeth sever the fibres.

The small teeth of a cross-cut saw make a clean cut with minimal splintering. It will also rip effectively, though it is slower than the rip saw because of its smaller teeth. A panel saw is a smaller version of a cross-cut saw. It too can be used for ripping, although it cuts even slower than a cross-cut saw. When cross-cutting the most suitable angle to hold the saw blade is at 45° to the work.

Using a backsaw

Backsaws are designed for fine accurate work. Their blades are thinner and teeth finer than handsaws. The weight of the steel or brass back enables the saw to cut under its own weight so that force need not be used to make the cut.

Both tenon saws and dovetail saws can cut along or across the grain and for bench work both are used with a bench-hook. The tenon saw is good for cutting thin plywood, giving a cleaner cut than cross-cut saws. The back will not interfere with deep sawing if the saw is held at a shallow angle to the work. The dovetail saw is for similar but finer work to the tenon saw.

Cross-cutting

To saw off a short end hold the board firmly against the bench well and start cutting. Stop just before the end.

To complete the cut change the direction of the saw to prevent the offcut falling and splintering the board.

Alternatively place the board in the well of the bench and support the offcut with the free hand while sawing.

To saw off a long end stand at the end of the bench, rest the board along the well and support the offcut while sawing.

Controlling a backsaw

Begin the saw-cut with one or two backward strokes at the far side of the cutting line. Working the blade in the cut, gradually level out the saw.

Then follow the vertical cutting line. Saw smoothly using the length of the blade. Keep the wood still by holding it against a bench-hook.

For an easier grip, and to avoid obscuring the cutting line with the saw blade, it is often better to work small pieces of wood against the saw.

When cross-cutting on a stool put knee pressure on the board with the cutting line overhanging. This ensures a clear view of the line.

Saws for shaping 1

For a saw to cut round a curve the blade has to be narrow or it will bind in the wood. To cut a tight curve, the blade must be very narrow; however, the narrower the blade the weaker it becomes and this inevitably leads to compromise in the design of saws. The solution that has been used for centuries is to hold the blade in tension in some kind of frame. Frame saws with the blade in the centre of the frame were used by the Romans, and the cantilever principle of the modern bowsaw was known and in use as far back as the thirteenth century. The blade in the bowsaw is held between two uprights, or cheeks, that pivot on either side of a central stretcher rail. The blade is tensioned by pulling the tops of the cheeks towards each other by means of a twisted cord and toggle or, in some bowsaws, by a threaded rod tensioned by wing nuts. Coarse- and fine-toothed blades can be used in the bowsaw and the blade can be swivelled to allow the saw to cut parallel to the edge of the board.

Thick boards, 16 mm/⅝ in and upwards, must be cut by a heavily framed saw such as the bowsaw; however it will not be possible to cut sharp curves. A coping saw with its narrow blade can tackle curves of very small radii, but its use is confined to thin woods and the softer metals. With the coping saw and fretsaw rigidity is determined by the quality of the steel in the frame so do not buy anything less than the best.

The two frameless saws illustrated — the compass saw and the padsaw — have their advantages and disadvantages. Because they are frameless, they can be used in places where other saws would be restricted by their frames. Although the compass saw blade tapers, allowing it to start a fine cut, its overall width is still restricting. On a shallow curve, however, it will cut almost as quickly as a handsaw on a straight line. The compass saw shown is one of a nest of three saws fitting on a single handle with each additional blade reduced in size. The padsaw blade is narrow, but, because it has been thickened to counteract the tendency to buckle, it can become hot and hard work to use.

Continental bowsaw
Blade 300–675 mm/12–27 in.
Depth of cut 150–200 mm/6–8 in.
9 points to 25 mm/1 in.
Two operators can use the saw for cross-cutting.

Compass saw
Blade 125–275 mm/5–11 in.
9 points to 25 mm/1 in.
Three interchangeable blades can be fitted according to the curvature of the cut.

Coping saw parts

Handle

Frame

Swivelling spigot

Threaded spigot

Blade

Blade holder pin

Bowsaw parts

Cord

Toggle

Cheek

Pivot point

Dry stub mortise and tenon

Stretcher rail

Operating handle

Blade

Handle

Padsaw
Blade 125–375 mm/5–15 in.
9 points to 25 mm/1 in.
For cutting holes away from edges; originally for making the straight cuts in keyholes.

Bowsaw
Blade 250–400 mm/10–16 in.
Depth of cut 125–190 mm/5–7½ in.
Coarse- and fine-toothed
blades are available. For
straight cutting or broad curves.

Coping saw
Blade 150 mm/6 in.
Depth of cut 125 mm/5 in.
15–17 points to 25 mm/1 in.
For cutting curves and
removing waste in dovetails.

Fretsaw
Blade 125 mm/5 in.
Depth of cut 275 mm/11 in.
32 points to 25 mm/1 in.
Similar uses to a coping saw
but it has greater depth of cut.

Saws for shaping 2

When using saws for cutting curves, face the work directly and stand with the feet apart. The saw should be introduced at right angles to the work and the blade held in the horizontal position. The bowsaw is operated by its long handle. Both bowsaw and coping saw are used with two hands: one hand wrapped tightly around the other with the fingers astride the blade.

The worker always has three options while sawing shapes: to change the direction of the blade; to switch saws; or to readjust the position of the wood in the vice. Use these options freely, depending on ease of working and how much support the vice is providing. Altering the direction of the blade is quickly done on most frame saws. Place a hand on each side of the blade otherwise the blade will twist and perhaps break. Be prepared to switch to a saw with a wider blade when the opportunity arises; the narrower the blade, the more difficult it is to cut a straight line.

Frequently change the position of the wood so that the point of sawing remains near the vice jaws. If too high the wood will vibrate and the blade may break.

With the bowsaw, cutting is on the push stroke; this comes naturally to most woodworkers. With the coping saw, where the blade can be fitted with the teeth facing towards or away from the handle, cutting on the push stroke tends to compress the frame and loosen the blade, whereas cutting on the pull stroke conserves the blade, however, the cutting line may be obscured because the fibres are raised.

Correct stance

Coping saw

Spigot pins are split and grooved so that when a blade is slid into the split the pin will slot into the groove.

To change a blade compress the frame against the bench to allow the blade pins to pass the spigots.

For an interior cut release one end of the blade. Pass it through a drilled hole, refit the blade and start sawing.

When tightening the handle, after replacing the blade, hold the spigot to prevent the blade twisting and breaking.

To prevent the blade slipping out of line when both hands are on the saw handle, start the cut inside the cutting line.

Finish a cut by adjusting the blade angle in an upward direction. Alternatively, start a fresh cut at the other end.

Bowsaw

To fit a bowsaw blade pass the holding pins through the handle extension into the blade and out the other side.

To tension the blade turn the toggle and cord. When the blade is taut tuck the toggle against the stretcher rail.

To adjust the angle of a bowsaw blade hold the frame steady against the bench while turning both handles.

To cut curves in thick boards use a bowsaw's sturdy frame fitted with a toughened blade. Keep the blade horizontal.

Fretsaw

A fretsaw blade is held, with the aid of wing nuts, by a friction grip. The frame is compressed for blade tension.

A V-shaped block supports the work when fretsawing. Clamp the block level with the bench top and cut within the V.

The fretsaw is usually worked vertically, cutting on the down stroke. The blade teeth face towards the handle.

Compass saw and padsaw

A compass saw blade is slotted for easy changeover. It passes around two screws in the handle, which are then secured.

A padsaw handle is slotted throughout its length. The blade, held by the two screws, can project to any length.

To start an interior cut with a padsaw or compass saw, first bore a hole to accommodate the blade tip.

Power hand saws

Sawing is a common task when working with wood and may be tiring to do by hand. Power saws speed up this work and do it more accurately than a handsaw.

A circular saw makes straight accurate cuts with and across the grain. The size of a circular saw is determined by its blade diameter. A size of 125 mm/5 in to 190 mm/$7\frac{1}{2}$ in is sufficient for most purposes. The maximum depth of cut is approximately one-third the blade diameter. The blade should not be exposed during working: all reputable makes of saw have a fixed upper blade guard and a lower spring-loaded guard, which retracts automatically.

A jigsaw is an extremely versatile tool that will cut up to 63 mm/$2\frac{1}{2}$ in in softwood and 25 mm/1 in in hardwood and particle boards. Its major task is to cut curves but it can also make straight cuts, although it does not have the capacity and speed of a circular saw. Many different blades can be fitted. Variable speed models are available; use a slower speed for cutting round curves and through harder materials.

When using these saws, support the work securely so it cannot move and ensure that the blade will be unobstructed beneath the work. Prevent vibration by making the cut close to the workbench. Start a cut by resting the sole on the workpiece, with the blade clear of the surface and in line with the cutting line. Switch on the saw and allow it to develop full speed before advancing it through the work. Do not push or the motor will overload; jigsaw blades may break. Never force or twist the blade: it may cause kickback. When the cut is complete, turn off the saw and continue to hold it until the blade stops; in partial or blind cuts, let the blade stop before removing it from the cut. For accurate straight cuts, always use a guide fence, either the rip fence supplied with the tool or a home-made T-guide.

Blunt circular saw blades are best resharpened by a professional; jigsaw blades should be discarded.

As with all power tools, never make any adjustments to these saws without first switching off and unplugging the tool. Check the power cable regularly for cuts and wear, and take care in use that the cable is not beneath the work, where it might accidentally be cut.

Jigsaw
Switch lock
On/off switch
Blade locking screw
Blade holder — Sole
Rip fence

Among the different blades available are those for fine cutting wood and man-made boards (**A**) and those just for plywoods and particle boards. Others will rough cut wood only (**B**) while some will also cut soft metals.

A

B

Blade holder

Sole

Blades are bought for specific manufacturers' saws. The teeth cut on the upward stroke, so place the face side of the work downwards.

Before ripping lubricate the fence with candlewax. Set the fence to the required distance from the blade and press it against the side of the work.

Cut a curve free-hand slightly to the waste side of the cutting line. Using a firm grip support the board fully. Do not force the saw.

To cut a circle drive a nail through the centre of the work, invert the fence and slip it over the nail. Then start the cut, using the nail as a pivot.

To begin a plunge cut tilt the saw on its front end with the blade well clear of the work. Switch on and slowly lower the blade through the wood.

Circular saw

A B
D C

A variety of blades is available for different kinds of work. The most useful are those for cross-cutting (**A**), ripping (**B**), and combination cuts (**C**). The planer blade (**D**) gives a smooth finish. A carbide-tipped blade is much harder than an ordinary steel blade.

Blade guard

Blade

Angle adjustment scale

Sole

Rip fence adjustment

Free-hand cutting guide

Rip fence

To fit a blade lower the bottom blade guard. Withdraw the bolt and washer. With the new blade over the spindle hole replace the bolt and tighten.

To cut at any angle between upright and 45 set the saw against the calibrated angle adjustment scale. Check the cut on some waste wood.

To cut wood with minimal splintering rest the saw sole on the work with the blade against the edge. Adjust the blade to project 3 mm/⅛ in.

Stock

Before cross-cutting make a T-guide with an overlong stock. Cut through the stock and the work. The stock can then be used as an exact T-guide.

For sawing across the wood at an angle clamp or pin a temporary fence to the work. The fence must be thin enough to clear the motor.

When ripping use the fence supplied with the saw. Measure from inside the fence to the blade allowing for the set of the saw teeth.

Sharpening and maintaining saws

A sharp saw needs no forcing, but once the teeth become dulled the saw will cut slowly and inaccurately. If it is forced, it may wander from the cutting line, jam in the kerf or buckle. The complete process of renewing the edge on saw teeth is called refitting and it involves three quite separate stages — topping, setting and sharpening. All hand- and backsaw blades can be refitted. The blades of frame saws should be discarded when blunt. Circular blades for power saws should be professionally sharpened.

During each stage of refitting the saw must be held securely along the length of the blade. It can be held in the vice with battens on either side. A special saw-sharpening vice is available which clamps to the bench. The disadvantage with these methods is that the light may not be good enough, the best possible light being required for accurate refitting. A purpose-made saw horse is better. Make the first attempt at refitting on a new saw, because the angles of the teeth will be relatively easy to follow. If it is difficult to keep a saw to

the cutting line, it is likely that the teeth on one side are higher than those on the other. Topping is the remedy.

In topping, the teeth are filed to the same height with a smooth, flat file, which must be held horizontally; make a topping cramp to ensure this. If the file is not held horizontally, the teeth on one side are liable to be filed more than on the other. Each tooth touched by the file will show a bright white spot of new metal. If, after two or three strokes, some teeth are still not showing a white spot, the teeth are too uneven and should be sent to an expert for reshaping.

After topping, the teeth must be set. This involves bending the tips of the teeth alternately to right and left of the blade. The result is that the kerf formed during cutting is wider than the thickness of the blade, giving the blade clearance and reducing friction. The width of the kerf should be no more than one and a half times the thickness of the blade. The teeth should be set to no more than half their depth and to the same side to which they were originally bent. Bending them the

Topping

650 mm/26 in

Clearance for handle

Tapered recess

Saw chop

Slot

Kerf

Swivel arm

Swivel arm

Knee rest

Through tenon

Footrest

A saw requires topping when its teeth are uneven or worn to irregular levels. In the illustrations (*above*) these are greatly exaggerated.

Hardwood block

Wedge

File

Topping cramp.

Topping a saw in a saw horse.

Topping
The tops of the teeth are filed with a smooth, flat file to level them. To ensure the file is held flat, make a topping cramp from a grooved hardwood block. Taper the top of the groove. Hold the file in the groove with a wedge. Some woodworkers prefer a handsaw edge to be slightly rounded in its length to produce a more effective cut for the energy used. This can be done in stages at each topping.

A saw horse holds the saw firmly along the length of its blade and can be set up anywhere in a good light by propping its swivelling arms against a wall. Cut the saw chops long enough to support the longest handsaw blades. Shape the chops at one end to provide clearance for the saw handle. Cut tapered recesses in the outside edges of the chops to fit into the uprights of the saw horse. Line the recesses with abrasive paper to increase friction. Make the frame from two uprights joined by two rails through tenoned at convenient heights to act as a footrest and a kneerest. Attach the swivelling arms to the uprights with screws and washers. Cut the uprights to accommodate the saw chops. Then cut a slot to provide a clearance for backsaw backs. Make a kerf below the slot for handsaw blades.

To top a saw, clamp the saw blade in the saw horse, well projecting from the saw chops. Hold the topping cramp against the saw blade so that the file is flat on the teeth. Run it along until a bright white spot of new metal is visible on every tooth.

other way may break them. The setting must be uniform on each side; for the saw to work true, the teeth on each side must do the same amount of work.

The easiest way to set a saw is to use a proprietary saw set. Professional saw doctors use the thin cross-pein of a hammer to top the teeth on an anvil. This method is quick but demands much experience. Over-setting is a mistake amongst amateurs; this makes the saw inefficient as more effort is needed to cut the wide kerf and more wood than is necessary is wasted as sawdust. If the set is excessive, it can be remedied by side dressing. Lie the saw flat on the bench and run the edge of a lubricated oilstone lightly along the teeth for two or three strokes on both sides. Subsequent sharpening without setting brings the saw back to normal.

In sharpening, the cutting edge or point is renewed on each tooth. A saw can be sharpened two or three times before it needs re-setting, but it should be topped lightly before each sharpening. This has the two-fold effect of ensuring that the teeth remain level through-out and the white spots provide guides for sharpening. The aim in sharpening is to file away the bright white spot left on each tooth by topping. Tapered triangular files are used for sharpening. A file of the correct length must be used depending on the number of points per 25 mm/1 in on the saw. The file must fit correctly in the gullet — the space between the saw teeth. Always discard files when they start losing their cutting edge. Once dulled, control of the file is lost and consequently tooth angles will be inconsistent. The teeth of rip and cross-cut saws are differently shaped, and so must be sharpened accordingly. The teeth of dovetail and tenon saws are more difficult to sharpen as they are so small. Light is all-important, and this emphasizes the value of a portable saw horse.

When a saw is in very bad condition, an extra shaping stage can be introduced after topping. Shaping would only be necessary if the saw had been incorrectly sharpened, repeatedly. It should then be put into the hands of an expert for re-cutting.

Setting

1. Adjust the dial.

2. Place the saw set over one tooth.

Setting

The easiest way to set saw teeth is with a pliers-type saw set. Adjust the dial according to the number of points per 25 mm/1 in (**1**). This controls the amount and depth of set. Place the saw set over one tooth, lining up the plunger squarely with the centre of the tooth and squeeze the handles (**2**). The plunger presses the tooth against the anvil, the bevel of which was set when the dial was adjusted. Set each alternate tooth in turn along one side of the saw, then turn the saw around and set the intermediate teeth on the other side of the blade.

Sharpening

Rip saw teeth.

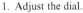

Angle of filing a rip saw.

Cross-cut teeth.

Angle of filing a cross-cut saw.

Sharpening a rip saw.

Choosing the correct file for sharpening		
Saw, type of	Points per 25 mm/1 in	File length
Dovetail	18–22	150 mm/6 in
Tenon	12–14	175 mm/7 in
Panel	10–12	200 mm/8 in
Cross-cut	7–8	225 mm/9 in
Rip	4½–6	250 mm/10 in

Sharpening

Lower the saw in the saw chops so that the teeth and no more than 3 mm/⅛ in of the blade are showing. Select a file of the correct length. Fit a handle to the file. Holding the file at each end, begin filing at the toe end of the saw. Work on every saw tooth that bends away from the worker. To sharpen rip saw teeth, seat the file snugly in the gullet, holding it horizontally and at right angles to the saw. File only on the forward stroke, applying even pressure to adjoining teeth. Remove half the white spot on adjoining teeth. Then turn the saw around and work back again. Sharpen cross-cut, panel and tenon saw teeth in a similar way, but hold the file at an angle of about 65° to the blade and lower the file handle slightly. Sharpen the teeth on a dovetail saw at right angles like rip saw teeth. After sharpening, side dress the saw very lightly to remove any wire edge, using the edge of an oilstone.

Chisels and gouges 1

A chisel has a long narrow blade that is used to cut deep narrow recesses for joints, such as mortises, and shallow recesses for butt hinges; it is also for paring and chamfering. A gouge has a curved blade and is used to cut and smooth grooves and hollows. Cabinetmakers' gouges have blades with parallel sides; carvers' gouges can be parallel or fishtail.

The cutting edge of chisels and gouges is across the end of the blade, the width of which designates the size of the tool. Handles can be made of wood or plastic.

Chisels and gouges are classified by the way in which the handle is fastened to the blade: either by a tang or a socket. A tang is a tapered end inserted into the handle.

A socket chisel has the end of the blade formed into a conical socket, which fits over the handle. A socket chisel is generally used on heavier work than a tang chisel. A heavy-duty chisel can have a shock-absorbent leather washer between the bolster of the blade and the handle to absorb the blows of the mallet.

Chisel blades can be rectangular in section or bevelled to give clearance when cleaning out corners or working in undercut or acute angles, such as dovetail housings. Bevel-edged chisels are lighter and less robust than rectangular-sectioned chisels. Mortise chisels have strong but narrow blades for chopping and levering out waste.

Firmer chisel

Bevel-edged firmer chisel

Drawer lock chisel

Butt chisel

Bevel-edged paring chisel

Firmer chisel
Blade 3–50 mm/$\frac{1}{8}$–2 in wide and rectangular in section. For general work.

Bevel-edged firmer chisel
Blade 6–50 mm/$\frac{1}{4}$–2 in wide. Less rigid than the firmer chisel; preferable for lighter and more specialized work.

Drawer lock chisel
Blade 10–16 mm/$\frac{3}{8}$–$\frac{5}{8}$ in wide. Use with a hammer in close

spaces, e.g. drawer openings. Thickened blade acts as a fulcrum to lever out waste.

Bevel-edged paring chisel
Blade 6–50 mm/$\frac{1}{4}$–2 in wide. The bevel edges give a clearer view of the work.

Butt chisel
Blade 6–50 mm/$\frac{1}{4}$–2 in wide. Short blade for cutting hinge housings. Preferred by many workers as a general chisel.

Chisel and gouge parts

Handle

Ferrule

Tang

Ferrule

Ferrule
Bolster

Leather washer

Leather tip

Grinding bevel

Socket

Cutting edge

Honing bevel

In-cannel gouges have their cutting bevels ground on the inside and are for vertical curved cuts. Out-cannel gouges, with external bevels, are for hollowing out curves.

Gouge blades are made in many different sweeps that all conform to circle radii. Scribing and firmer gouges are commonly available in fewer sweeps than paring gouges.

Scribing gouge

Firmer gouge

Cabinetmakers'
mortise chisel

Paring gouge

Registered
mortise chisel

Lock mortise
chisel

Lock mortise chisel
Blade 10–16 mm/$\frac{3}{8}$–$\frac{5}{8}$ in wide.
For cutting recesses for locks and other stub mortises.

Registered mortise chisel
Blade 6–50 mm/$\frac{1}{4}$–2 in wide.
For heavy work; fitted with a leather washer.

Cabinetmakers' mortise chisel
Blade 6–13 mm/$\frac{1}{4}$–$\frac{1}{2}$ in wide.
Sturdy socket chisel to withstand continual blows.

Paring gouge
Blade 3–38 mm/$\frac{1}{8}$–1$\frac{1}{2}$ in wide.
Sometimes has cranked blade for hand clearance.

Firmer gouge
Blade 3–50 mm/$\frac{1}{8}$–2 in wide.
Out-cannel gouge for convex curves or fluting, bevel down.

Scribing gouge
Blade 3–25 mm/$\frac{1}{8}$–1 in wide.
General purpose in-cannel gouge for concave curves.

Chisels and gouges 2

Vertical paring

Pare with a sharp bevel-edged chisel, exerting force directly from the shoulders with one thumb on the handle, the other thumb guiding the blade to the line. Keep the chisel upright, bevel out. Remove only small amounts of wood at a time.

Horizontal chiselling

1. Hold the chisel bevel up.

2. Remove the waste.

Horizontal chiselling
Saw on the waste side of the squared lines down to the gauged lines on each side. Then from one side chisel to the centre of the housing. Steady one elbow on the bench with the hand holding the chisel near the blade, bevel up (**1**). Pointing the chisel slightly upwards, work down to half the housing depth, removing a little waste at a time (**2**). Reverse the wood and gradually chisel down to the gauged line. Then finish off the first side. Check for flatness. Level the base, using hand pressure only.

Cutting a rectangular recess

1. Cut across the grain.

2. Chop across the waste area.

3. Remove the waste.

Cutting a rectangular recess
Chisel across the grain at one end, just inside the marked line, using a chisel held vertically, bevel inwards, and a mallet (**1**). Then chop on the line. Repeat at the other end. Cut along the grain near the lines, then directly on them. Chop across the wood grain at 6 mm/¼ in intervals (**2**). Level out the waste, working from the centre, bevel down (**3**). Finish with a router.

Cutting a stopped rebate

1. Chop into the waste.

2. Cut vertically.

3. Remove the waste.

Cutting a stopped rebate
Start at the end of the rebate, holding the chisel at an angle, bevel down. Chop into the waste, using a mallet (**1**). Move back about 10 mm/⅜ in at a time. Then chop vertically, close to the line (**2**). Clear out the waste with a slicing action (**3**). Trim the side and bottom of the rebate, adjusting the work in the vice so as to keep the chisel cutting vertically all the time.

Drawer lock chisel

Trimming veneer

The drawer lock chisel can cut recesses and mortises in awkward places. Place the cutting edge in position. Supporting the chisel, strike its steel bar with a hammer as near as possible above the cutting edge. In very small spaces the side of the hammer may be used.

Veneer can be cut with a chisel as well as a knife. Hold the chisel with the bevel against the straight-edge and the blade tilted away, so the cut is made with a pulling motion by the leading edge. Cut mitres in veneer with the chisel held vertically to avoid splitting the wood grain.

Cutting a chamfer with mitred ends

Mark the chamfer in pencil by finger gauging or by using a simple waste-wood gauge (1). (Do not use a marking gauge, which will leave score marks in the wood.) Slice the mitred end in one stroke, holding the chisel, bevel up, and striking the handle with the palm of the hand (2). Then cut the chamfer from the other direction if the direction of the grain allows, working towards the mitre in small steps with the chisel held bevel down. Work with hand pressure, applying a pulling restraint with the other hand (3). Gradually work up to the mitre and down to the limits of the chamfer. Take small chips first to establish the direction of the grain; then, if the grain permits, take longer strokes, aiming to leave a smooth surface to the chamfer so that it will need no more finishing.

1. Mark the chamfer.

2. Slice the mitred end.

3. Cut the chamfer.

Cutting a chamfer with rounded ends

Mark the chamfer in pencil. Begin by cutting the rounded ends. Hold the chisel, bevel down, and cut each end in one stroke, with a scooping cut, down as far as the limits of the chamfer. Then cut the body of the chamfer, working gradually in the same way as for the chamfer with mitred ends.

Cutting a chamfer on end grain

On curved and intricate edges on end grain it is sometimes easier to work a chamfer with a chisel than a spokeshave. Pencil in the chamfer. Work the chisel at an angle, producing a slicing action. Chisel bevel down for concave curves and bevel up for flat surfaces and convex curves.

Out-cannel gouge

Use an out-cannel gouge to pare the edges of convex curves. The radius of the curve must match the sweep of the gouge. Cut away only a little at a time and guide the blade with a finger of one hand.

In-cannel gouge

1. Shape the ends.

3. Lever out the waste.

In-cannel gouge

An in-cannel blade on, for example, a scribing gouge can be used to cut internal curves, such as the finger slots on sliding doors. The curve of the gouge must match the curve to be cut in the wood. Start by shaping the ends, holding the gouge vertically (1). Chop along the grain near the straight lines with a bevel-edged chisel, then cut directly on them. Chop out the waste with a series of 6 mm/¼ in cuts, holding the gouge at an angle and moving it backwards after each cut (2). Lever out the waste with a chisel (3). Cut deeper if necessary, repeating the sequence of cuts with a gouge and a chisel. Level the base of the recess with a small hand router.

Bench planes 1

A plane is a cutting tool for removing shavings to a precisely controlled depth. A bench plane has a flat sole and a wooden or metal body; it is used for reducing the width or thickness of a piece of wood, making it straight, and for smoothing a surface. The bench plane reached an advanced stage of development in Roman times and the modern metal version could be considered a definitive tool.

Although the wooden plane is still in use, the metal plane has a cutting edge that is more quickly and precisely adjusted. Once a plane has been correctly set, the flat sole controls the blade and the depth of cut so

that the worker's full strength can be used for the driving force. It is important therefore to know how a plane is adjusted.

The cap iron prevents the wood tearing by breaking the shaving as soon as it is raised by the blade. The closer the cap iron to the cutting edge the sooner the shaving is broken, although there is greater resistance in the cut. The size of the mouth enables cuts of varying degrees of fineness to be made; a wide mouth allows a thicker shaving to be cut with a deeper set blade. Adjustment of the cap iron, mouth and blade should suit the grain and the required surface finish.

Adjusting a plane

Set the cap iron about 1.5 mm/$\frac{1}{16}$ in back from the cutting edge for a softwood. For a hardwood or a fine finish the gap should be reduced. This is done by realigning and securing the cap iron on to the back of the blade. Ensure a tight fit to prevent shavings wedging between the two

The width of the mouth opening is governed by the position of the frog. For general use, line up the edge of the frog with the top edge of the mouth. For fine work the mouth should be narrower. Remove the cap iron and blade. Slacken the screws that fix the frog and move the frog with its adjustment screw.

The depth of cut is increased by pushing the blade out. This is done by turning the adjustment nut clockwise. Check the setting by holding the plane upside down with the sole level with the eye. The cutting edge should appear as a narrow black line. For fine work the blade should hardly show.

The lateral adjustment lever is used to ensure that the blade protrudes an equal amount across its width. Move the lever from side to side and check the alignment with the plane held upside down. Once the blade is set, take up any slack in the adjustment nut so the blade cannot move.

Metal plane parts

Lever

Lever cap

Cap iron

Toe

Blade or cutting iron

Lateral adjustment lever

Handle

Frog

Heel

Sole
(often corrugated to counter suction)

Adjustment nut

Frog adjustment screw

Lever cap screw

Frog fixing screws

Mouth

Jointer or trying plane
Length 510–600 mm/20–24 in.
For planing long edges and
surfaces straight and square
before jointing.

Jack or fore plane
Length 350–450 mm/14–18 in.
General-purpose plane for
jointing and final smoothing;
also for rough smoothing stock.

Smoothing plane
Length 200–250 mm/8–10 in.
For final smoothing before
sanding, after truing up with
jointer or jack plane.

Locking wheel

Blade or cutting iron

Mouth

Block plane
Length 140–200 mm/5½–8 in.
Used one-handed for end grain
and chamfers. Can be fully
adjustable or non-adjustable.

Wooden plane parts

Wedge

Cap iron

Blade or cutting iron

Handle

Heel

Throat
(the outlet for shavings)

Sole

Adjustments to wooden planes
Depth of cut and lateral
adjustments are made to
wooden planes by tapping the
back of the blade with a
mallet. First loosen the wedge
by striking the toe or
hardwood striking button with
the mallet. Having adjusted the
blade tap the wedge home.

Face

Frog

Mouth

Toe

Bench planes 2

Careful planing smooths the wood and makes surfaces square in preparation for accurate working out and cutting of joints. Always sharpen and adjust a plane before using it. Lie the wood to be planed horizontally on the bench against a bench-stop; if gripped in the vice, planing may be uneven.

Keep a piece of candle on the bench or in the apron pocket and use it to lubricate the sole of the plane. Resin from wood will make planing harder so wipe any residue off the plane sole using white spirit.

To square a piece of wood, begin by planing off the high spots; then take shavings from the whole surface. When planing wide surfaces it is easy to remove too much wood from diagonally opposite corners. Therefore check the shape of the board frequently.

To plane an edge straight, remove shavings from the middle first, then plane the whole edge. The success of all joints depends on accurate planing.

After using a plane, place it on its side on the bench. This will prevent the cutting edge coming into contact with other metal objects and being dulled. Store a plane on its side on a shelf or in its box. Wipe wooden planes with linseed oil occasionally to prevent drying.

The sole of a wooden plane will eventually wear down and the wedge-shaped mouth will widen. To restore the mouth to its original width, recess a piece of hardwood in front of the blade.

Correct stance

At the beginning of a stroke press down on the front of the plane; then press evenly. Finish by pressing at the rear.

Stand with the outer foot braced in front and place the shoulder, hip and plane in a straight line so as to exert full control.

Planing a wide board

Move the plane diagonally across the wood in both directions, with and against the grain, overlapping strokes to cover the whole surface.

Finish by taking fine shavings in parallel strokes down the wood in the direction of the grain. Check the smoothness of the surface by hand.

Checking a surface

To check if a surface is flat use the tilted edge of the plane as a straight-edge. Place the straight-edge diagonally to check against winding.

Alternatively check a planed surface with a steel rule, along the grain, across the grain at intervals and in both directions diagonally.

Planing a narrow edge

Planing square

If an edge is out of square push the plane towards the high edge. If the blade is sharpened to a slight curve it will take a thicker shaving in the centre.

To check if a face is square with one side push the stock of the try square tight against the side of the wood. Hold against the light.

To keep the plane in the centre of a narrow surface place the thumb on the toe and run the fingers as a guide along the side of the wood.

A long plane rides on the high spots, levelling them out until one continuous shaving can be taken along the wood; a short plane follows the contours.

End grain and the edges of thin boards must be supported to prevent the wooden fibres on the edge breaking away. The stop on a shooting board will provide the necessary support. Hold the plane centrally at its point of balance and allow the wood to overhang very slightly. Alternatively, support end grain by gluing or clamping a piece of waste wood to the work-piece before planing, so any splintering will be from the waste wood and not from the work-piece.

To plane end grain to a line first plane a chamfer at one end. Reverse the wood and plane towards the chamfer. Take care on the last strokes.

Planing chamfers

Planing halfway from each side is a good alternative, especially on wide boards. The plane must be sharp, finely set and firmly under control.

Instead of reversing the wood when planing from each side reverse the plane, holding it as shown. Secure the wood firmly against juddering.

For delicate work, such as putting a light chamfer on an edge, use a block plane held at an angle; a larger plane would obscure the work.

Planes for shaping 1

Shaping planes fall into two groups: those that cut grooves, rebates and other shapes, and those that are used for trimming and smoothing shapes and awkward areas that bench planes cannot reach.

Amongst the first group are the plough, combination and multi-plane, which have interchangeable blades of different widths and profiles. The plough plane cuts with the grain; the fence enables the cut to be made a fixed distance from the edge of the work and

the depth gauge limits the depth of cut. The combination plane is similar but has two knife-edge spurs for cross-grain cutting. The multi-plane is the most versatile of these planes.

Amongst the second group of shaping planes are the shoulder, bull-nose and compass planes and the hand router. The blades on the shoulder and bull-nose planes are set at a low angle bevel upwards, enabling them to be used on end grain.

Rebate and fillister plane
Length 250 mm/10 in. For cutting identical rebates once the fence and depth gauge have been set. The blade has a forward position for corners.

Normal blade position

Guide fence

Forward blade position

Sole adjustment nut

Sole locking screw

Flexible sole

Ovolo

Round

Hollow

Compass plane
Length 250 mm/10 in. For planing convex or concave surfaces. Metal versions have a flexible adjustable sole; on wooden ones the curve is fixed.

Scratch stock
For making small mouldings and grooves for inlays. Made from a piece of saw or scraper blade ground to shape and secured in a wooden holder.

Moulding plane
Length 225 mm/9 in. For shaping mouldings and edges. Sole and blade have the same profile. Moulding planes can be used one after the other.

Adjustment nut

Depth gauge

Clamping screw

Cutter clamp

Removable body

Removable nose

Blades or cutting irons

Blade or cutting iron

Shoulder plane
Length 100–200 mm/4–8 in. For trimming shoulders and rebates. Blade extends right across the sole. This plane can also be used on its side.

Bull-nose plane
Length 75–100 mm/3–4 in. For working close up into corners and ends of stopped rebates. Blade is positioned at the toe of the sole.

Side rebate plane
Length 125 mm/5 in. For smoothing and widening side walls of grooves and rebates. Two blades enable plane to be used in either direction.

Hand router
Width 200 mm/8 in. For smoothing and cutting grooves and recesses. Cutters are set at a shallow angle to work with a paring action.

Plough plane
Length 240 mm/9½ in. For cutting grooves and rebates, 3–13 mm/⅛–½ in wide, with the grain. Up to ten different blades are available.

Blade clamping screw

Blade adjustment screw

Depth gauge screw

Blade or cutting iron

Guide fence

Blade or cutting iron

Sliding section

Combination plane
Length 250 mm/10 in. For cutting rebates, grooves and beads 3–13 mm/⅛–½ in wide, and tongues 3–6 mm/⅛–¼ in wide; has 18 different blades.

Spur
Spur

Beading stop

Guide fence

Blade or cutting iron

Sliding section

Beading stop

Guide fence

Fence adjustment screw

Multi-plane
Length 275 mm/11 in. For cutting mouldings; also strips from a board edge, using its slitting knife. The most versatile plane, with 24 blades.

A   B   C   D   E   F   G   H

A. Sash cutter
B. Tonguing cutter
C. Rebate and housing cutter
D. Reeding cutter
E. Beading cutter
F. Fluting cutter
G. Ovolo cutter
H. Slitting knife

Planes for shaping 2

To set a plough, combination or multi-plane, first fit the selected blade, adjusting it for depth of cut; then set the guide fence and the depth gauge. Blades are best set to cut a thicker shaving than a smoothing plane. The sliding section acts as a cramp to hold the blade against the body of the plane. A slot at the top of the blade locates on the shoulder of the adjustment screw. Very narrow blades must be set with the adjustment nut. The guide fence can be set either on the left- or right-hand side of the body; when on the right, however, it will cancel out the use of the depth gauge. The beading stop acts as a fence when cutting a bead on a tongued board, because the guide fence has nothing to bear against. For most operations the beading stop should be removed. Always hold the plane upright and keep the guide fence tight against the wood to prevent the plane from wandering. To make any cuts across the grain, lower the spurs to score the grain ahead of the blade, thereby ensuring a clean cut. Keep the spurs sharp with an oilstone. Lightly oil all the adjustment screw threads occasionally. Rub candlewax on the fence and sole to help the plane run smoothly.

If possible always try to work a compass plane with the grain, holding it square to the wood and not at an angle. The blade is set and adjusted like a bench plane's. The blades on shoulder and bull-nose planes are set at a low angle, bevel upwards, enabling them to cut end grain. A scratch stock blade can be filed to any profile; a used hacksaw blade is ideal as the steel is tempered to just the right degree of hardness.

Combination and multi-planes

Set the guide fence the required distance from the plane body using a rule. Finger-tighten the two adjustment screws on the fence rods.

The depth gauge is a horizontal fence fitted to one side of the body. Use a rule to set the gauge to the required depth for the cut.

Start making all cuts at the far end of the work and take a few short cuts, moving a little farther back with each stroke. In this way, the plane will run in a guide groove that it has cut. Then take continuous shavings the full length of the cut until the depth gauge rests on the wood.

Cut a wide rebate in two stages. Make the first cut on the outside edge to the required depth. Adjust the guide fence and cut the inside part of the rebate to complete the cut. If the inner part were cut first, the depth gauge would have no support when cutting the outside edge.

Cut a narrow rebate using the method shown above. Choose a blade that is very slightly wider than the rebate to cover the rebate fully.

Cut a groove in the same way as a wide or narrow rebate, but adjust the fence accordingly. The guide fence can be set on either side of the plane body.

When cutting a housing the fence cannot be used, because it will be working against end grain, which is not smooth enough for accurate work. Pin or clamp a batten in place of the fence, making allowance for the batten when setting the depth gauge. Lower the spurs. Use the body spur alone for a cross-grain rebate.

When cutting a tongue the depth gauge is not required as the depth of cut is limited by the blade itself, which has an adjustable stop in the centre. Take extra care to set the guide fence so that the tongue will be cut exactly in the position required. Remove the beading stop from the sliding section on the plane.

Shoulder plane

Bull-nose plane

Side rebate plane

When trimming with this plane set the blade for a fine cut. Keep the side, which is square with the base, tight against the side or bottom of the rebate.

Use a bull-nose plane for working rebated corners. It can be an integral tool or, as shown here, a shoulder plane with the nose removed.

Adjust the depth gauge so the tip of the blade just touches the bottom of the work. Remove the nose for working into stopped rebates.

Hand router
Insert the cutter from beneath. To set it, slacken the locking screw on the clamp; then raise or lower the cutter using the adjustment nut **(1)**. Tighten the locking screw. Remove most of the waste with a chisel. Lower the cutter until it rests on the bottom of the recess. Give the adjustment nut another half turn down; lock the cutter and plane at that level **(2)**. Continue, lowering the cutter a half turn at a time until the recess is the required depth.

1. Adjust the cutter.

2. Plane a recess.

Compass plane

This plane is normally used with the grain, holding the blade square to the work, not at an angle. Set the blade when the sole is flat; then adjust the sole curvature.

Hold the plane on the work and turn the adjustment nut until the sole is about the same shape as the work. For convex shapes, the sole should be slightly flatter than the work.

For concave shapes it should have a sharper curvature. To make a concave curve, mark the two extremities and the central depth. Hold a springy lath against the three points

and get an assistant to draw the curve against the lath. Saw down to the line at intervals; remove most of the waste with a chisel, finish shaping to the line with the plane.

Moulding plane
Use a round plane for making hollows and a matching hollow plane for forming rounds and beads. First work a chamfer with a bench plane. Shape with the moulding plane, starting at the front and working back. Then smooth with abrasive paper wrapped around a shaped block of wood. The plane has no guide fence so it requires skill to keep it at the correct angle. Hold it so the fingers of one hand act as a guide fence against the side of the work.

Scratch stock

This plane is home-made to any profile up to about 25 mm/1 in wide. Slot the cutter in a thick piece of wood or between two pieces screwed together. File

the cutting edge square and hone it like a scraper blade. Use only with a forward scraping action with the tool tilted away.

Power hand planes

The power plane takes the hard work out of smoothing large wood surfaces. The revolving cutter block holds two or three blades and is similar to the cutter block on the planer/thicknesser (*see* page 112). The cutter block extends across the full width of the plane sole and determines the maximum width of cut in one movement. The depth of cut can be adjusted in two ways. On some planes the soles are independently adjustable. The rear sole must be set level with the lowest point of the circle described by the blades, and the front sole is raised by the amount equal to the depth of required cut. Other models have a single sole pivoted at one end and this can be raised or lowered to set the depth of cut.

Always place the plane on the work before switching it on. The power plane must be used carefully on boards wider than the width of the sole, otherwise it will cut in a series of grooves the width of the sole, and ridges will be formed between cuts. Adjust the blades to take very shallow cuts on the final strokes and plane slowly for a smooth finish.

The power router is capable of numerous cuts and it has largely superseded the hand router and moulding planes. It cuts grooves, housings, rebates, tenons and a wide variety of edge mouldings. It can also cut a number of joints such as tongued and grooved and dovetail, using a special dovetail template (*see* page 139). It consists of a motor fitted with a chuck that is raised or lowered above a flat sole plate. Bits held in the chuck protrude vertically down through the sole. The motor operates at very high speeds, from 18,000 rpm to 28,000 rpm, so the router leaves a very smooth finish on the work. The bits rotate in a clockwise direction, so the tool has a tendency to twist in that direction. For this reason, always feed the router into the work against the rotation of the bit.

Clamp the work firmly. Switch the tool on and allow it to reach full speed; then lower it or push it towards the work. Move it steadily through the work. Too fast a speed will overload the motor. Too slow a speed may burn the work and damage the cutters. With practice, the sound of the motor is the best guide to the correct rate of feed. Bits with a very wide range of profiles can be fitted into the power router. Some types, with pilot tips, are used for shaping and moulding edges. The pilot tip does not cut, but rides against the edge of the work to act as a guide for the bit.

Power plane

On/off switch
Depth adjustment knob
Guide fence
Rear sole
Blade guard
Front sole
Guide fence lock

The revolving blades between the adjustable soles provide the cutting action. The groove in the front sole acts as a guide when chamfering.

To plane a surface place the tool on the work, switch it on and apply a steady, even pressure. Do not push too hard through the work.

When planing a rebate adjust the fence so it limits the sole to the rebate width. Make a series of shallow cuts to the required depth of the rebate.

For a narrow surface adjust the fence so the cutting area is in the middle of the sole, making it easier to balance the plane on the work.

When planing a chamfer place the groove on the front sole on to the edge of the work. Plane in several passes to the required depth.

Power router

Depth of
cut lock

Depth of
cut adjuster

Sole

Handle

On/off switch

Depth of
cut scale

Chuck

Hole for cutter

Router bits

Router bits can have carbide
tips for longer life. Bits A-C cut
into the thickness of the wood.
Bits D-J have pilot tips for
shaping edges. The straight
cutter (A) is for grooves and
routing. There are also bits for
veining (B), wide, shallow
grooves (C), beading edges (D),
chamfering (E), rebating (F),
rounding edges (G), cutting
coves (H) and ogees (J).

To fit a bit disconnect the
router, loosen the chuck with
the wrench, insert the bit shank
and tighten the chuck. Adjust
the sole for depth of cut.

Freehand routing requires
careful control as varying
wood grain directions as well
as the motion of the bits tend
to take control of the cut.

When cutting near an edge fit
the guide fence. Hold the fence
firmly against the edge of the
work, which must be straight
and smooth.

When cutting away from the
edge pin a batten to the left of
the router to act as a fence,
because of the clockwise
rotation of the bit.

For a wide housing use two
guide battens. Position each so
it allows the router to cut the
outer sides of the housing; then
rout out the centre.

When cutting near a curved
edge remove the straight-edge
plate on the front of the fence.
Rest the V-cut recess in the
fence edge against the work.

When moulding the edge of a
circular board or cutting a
circle, use the fence as a
trammel point by pinning it to
the centre of the work.

To convert the router to a
spindle moulder clamp it upside
down beneath a special
conversion table. Push the
work past the projecting bit.

Shaping and smoothing tools 1

Shaping tools are used for the intermediate processes between preliminary forming and finishing. They are employed extensively to shape and smooth curved work that is inaccessible to planes. Rasps and files, with their bludgeoning abrasive action against wood, are rarely used by cabinetmakers, who feel that wood should be cut and not just worn away. The modern Surform, however, has a blade surface that contains numerous cutting edges, which have a long life even when used on chipboard, plastic laminates and gritty surfaces. It has the added advantage that there is clearance for the dust and shavings to fall away.

A half-round file has a mild action when shaping wood. The round side will smooth the edges of a hole and glasspaper can be wrapped around it for final finishing.

A drawknife is a specialist tool that will remove surplus wood much more quickly than a plane, but it needs experience and a close understanding of grain to produce good-quality work.

A spokeshave is used with a pushing action to smooth narrow sections of curved wood. It produces the same results as a smoothing plane. A metal spokeshave is adjusted much like a plane and it has largely supplanted the older wooden version, which is set by tapping the tanged spokeshave blade through the framework.

A cabinet scraper is a piece of saw steel with two edges turned to form sharp hooks. It removes minute shavings, leaving a cleaner finish than abrasives. A scraper plane does a similar job.

File parts

— Handle
— Ferrule
— Tang
— Heel
— Face
— Edge (cut or safe)
— Point

A   B   C

Single cut file teeth (B) are for precision work. Double cut **(C)** and rasp teeth **(A)** are for fast removal of wood.

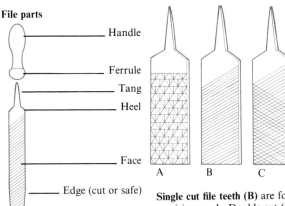

To remove a file handle strike the ferrule of the handle sharply with the "safe" (uncut) edge of another file.

To fix a handle on a file place the tang in the handle. Hold both vertically and strike the handle on the bench.

Surform block plane
Length 140 mm/5½ in.
Use with one hand for numerous roughing-off jobs on wood, man-made boards and laminates.

Surform plane
Length 250 mm/10 in.
Use as a rough plane for fast preliminary shaping of the work.

Surform round file
Length 225 mm/9 in.
For fast removal of wood. Can be used with or without its front handle.

Surform flat file
Length 250 mm/10 in.
Similar to a Surform plane but more flexible. May break fibres if worked across the grain.

Drawknife
For quick rough-shaping before using a plane or a spokeshave.

Spokeshave
Has round sole for concave work, flat for straight and convex work.

Scraper plane
Is a cabinet scraper held in a frame and bowed in the middle. Use with the blade sloping forwards.

Cabinet scraper
For a fine finish on flat hardwood surfaces. Is made from good quality saw steel.

Smooth flat file
Length 100–350 mm/4–14in. For all types of work except curves. Clean frequently with a file card.

Cabinetmakers' half-round file
Length 100–350 mm/4–14 in. Combines features of both round and flat files. Tempered for working only on wood.

Round file
Length 100–350 mm/4–14 in. Obtainable in various degrees of coarseness. For wood carving and for enlarging holes.

File card
For cleaning clogged up dust from file teeth. Consists of fine steel wires bedded upright in a wooden base.

Shaping and smoothing tools 2

To work successfully with shaping and smoothing tools requires skill and careful attention to the direction of the grain. When using these tools, which are all worked with a pushing or pulling action, it is important that the work is held very securely in the vice or with cramps, or is butted against a bench-stop.

A versatile shaping tool is the cabinet scraper. The wire edge, or hook, with which it cuts removes very fine shavings when it is correctly sharpened and used, enabling the cabinet scraper to give a very smooth finish to wood. Unlike an abrasive, it should produce shavings, not dust, which can clog the grain. It can also deal with awkward areas of wood such as knots, burrs and wild grain, both on solid wood and veneers, but be careful not to leave a small hollowed area as it will be evident when polished. Scrape over a wide area so that the hollow cannot be felt by the flat of the hand. Check by holding the work to the light.

The cabinet scraper is not an easy tool to operate, because its cutting edge is so fine and because the control must come entirely from the hands and fingers. It must be held at the correct angle; otherwise it will not cut effectively. The area of the cut is controlled by the pressure of the thumbs, which bow out the blade, varying the curve and localizing the cut. Work in the direction of the wood grain or diagonally across it. This tool can also remove old surface finishes without the aid of solvents. When scraping away a finish, angle the cabinet scraper so that the hook bites between the surface finish and the wood, and work the tool at an angle along the grain. The cabinet scraper will remove gummed paper tape from veneers and excess glue that has been allowed to dry on the surface of veneer or solid wood.

A scraper plane is much easier to operate than the cabinet scraper alone, although it is not possible to achieve such a fine degree of control. It is, however, less hard on the fingers and thumbs.

In contrast to cabinet scrapers, files and rasps are used for much rougher and coarser work. Never smooth with a file or rasp without first fitting a handle, because the tang is very dangerous and it can easily pierce the hand. Always work from short grain to long grain when smoothing surfaces. Surforms can be worked with or against the grain, as the individually formed teeth slice away the wood.

Spokeshaves have rather limited uses and are best operated on narrow, curved shapes. They are rather similar to a smoothing plane, but require more skill to be worked successfully. On a wooden spokeshave there is no cap iron, so the grain will tear if the spokeshave is not always used from short grain to long grain. When smoothing curves with both metal and wooden spokeshaves, always stroke the grain down the curve.

The blade of a drawknife is bevelled like that of a chisel. It can be used for a range of tasks, including rapidly removing wood from an over-wide board, debarking a log and rough shaping of turning stock.

Cabinet scraper

A. Working with a pushing action.

B. Working with a pulling action.

C. Working one-handed.

D. Scraping at the end of a board.

Cabinet scraper
The cabinet scraper can be operated in a variety of ways. The most common method is with a pushing action. Hold the scraper in both hands, and bow the centre slightly outwards by pressing with the thumbs (A). Start with the scraper vertical; then tilt it away until the hook on the edge just bites into the wood — this will be at an angle of about 70°. Push the scraper away taking fine shavings from the surface. If dust, and not shavings, is removed, the scraper needs sharpening. Should the corners of the blade dig into the wood, press more firmly with the thumbs to bow out the blade more.

The scraper can also be operated with a pulling action. Hold the tool in both hands with the thumb of one hand and the fingers of the other bowing the blade (B). Alternatively, hold it in one hand, bowing the blade with pressure from the three middle fingers pushing against the little finger and thumb (C). For the best and most even cut, hold the cabinet scraper at a slight angle across the grain, and push or pull it parallel to the grain. When scraping wood at the end of a board, work the scraper diagonally across the wood (D).

File, rasp and Surform

Using the flat side of a file.

Using the round side of a file.

Cleaning a file.

Using a Surform.

File, rasp and Surform
All of these tools cut on the forward stroke only; lift the tool on the return stroke. The cabinetmakers' half-round file is the most common wood file. The flat side is handy for levelling out recesses after chiselling. Hold it diagonally across the recess and take care that the file's thin edges do not damage the sides of the recess. The flat side can be worked on convex curves. Level out concave curves with the round side of the file. Keep the file teeth clean and free of clogged-up dust by cleaning the file with a file card. Stroke the wires of the card down the file parallel to the teeth. Rasps and rasp planes, such as Surforms, rapidly remove large amounts of wood and are ideal tools for preliminary shaping before filing or planing.

Spokeshave

Shaving concave work.

Shaving convex work.

Using a wooden spokeshave.

Spokeshave
Use a spokeshave to smooth narrow curved pieces. All spokeshaves, whether with a round sole for concave work, a flat sole for convex work or with a wooden frame, are operated in the same way. Use with a pushing action and keep the wrists very flexible. The angle will frequently need to be changed. Control the angle of the tool with the thumbs pressing on the handles. Work from short to long grain, stroking the grain down.

Drawknife

Shaping convex work.

Shaping concave work.

Drawknife
Operate the drawknife with a pulling action. The tool requires skill and experience to work accurately as the depth of cut depends on the angle at which the bevelled blade is presented to the work and all control comes from the wrists. Greater control can be exerted when working concave curves if the bevel is held downwards. For straight and convex cuts, wood can be removed more easily with the bevel upwards. As much heavier chips can be cut than with a plane, it is essential to watch the direction of the grain. Keep the drawknife very sharp.

Grinding and honing 1

Dull tools are unsafe and hard to use. Sight down the blade: a dull edge or one with tiny defects in it reflects the light and shows up as a white line.

New chisels, gouges, planes and shaping tools have a bevel of 25° ground on the cutting edge by the manufacturer. Before the tool can be used, a bevel of 30° must be honed on the oilstone. A smaller angle will cut wood more easily but its fragile edge will break readily; a larger angle will hold its edge longer but will create more resistance. The honing bevel of 30° can be maintained over a number of honing sessions. The grinding bevel of 25° must be restored on the tool only after repeating honing, or if the edge has become chipped. After grinding back to 25°, the edge must be honed again to 30°.

All sharpening stones work in the same way: the particles of the stone remove the softer particles of metal. Coarse particles cut fast, but leave a coarse edge on the tool. Fine particles cut slowly and leave a finer, sharper edge.

Oilstones are used for honing. Most oilstones are composite man-made stones that are of even density throughout their thickness.

Artificial stones are made from abrasive particles, crushed, graded and then bonded together. They are available in coarse, medium and fine grades. Combination stones are available with different grades for each half thickness.

Oilstones must never be used dry — the pores soon choke with metal particles. A lubricant carries away the particles and prevents the tool becoming too hot through friction, which can draw the temper of the cutting edge, shown by the edge turning blue. If this happens, the metal must be ground back to remove all the softened metal. With oilstones, a good, thin machine oil is suitable. (Vegetable oils can clog the pores.) Paraffin can be used on artificial stones. Always soak a new stone in oil until it is saturated. Keep it in a box. If a stone becomes clogged with metal particles, scrub it with a stiff brush dipped in paraffin or petrol;

Care of oilstones

Lid

Medium stone

Fine stone

Hardwood
end-grain stop

Cleat

Make a box to hold oilstones to keep out dust. With a forstner bit, drill out two recesses in a solid block. Fit hardwood end-grain stops at each end, level with the top of the stones. Screw a cleat to the bottom to hold the box in the vice. Then make a well-fitting lid from five-ply and 19 mm/¾ in battens.

When an oilstone wears hollow grind it flat again on a paving stone or marble slab, using silver sand and water for natural stones and carborundum powder and water for artificial stones. Work the stone in a circular movement. A hollow stone cannot produce a straight edge.

Slipstones are for sharpening shaped blades such as gouges and moulding plane blades. They can be of natural or artificial stone and are sold in sets of assorted shapes and sizes. If a shape is not suitable, buy a larger size and rub it down on a paving stone (see method above).

When emery and wet-grinding wheels become glazed with accumulated dust and particles, scrape off this layer and expose a new layer of abrasive with a dressing stick. Use a metal star wheel dresser for emery wheels and a carborundum or silicon carbide stick for wet-grinding stones.

An emery wheel can be an attachment for a portable power drill held in a horizontal stand, or it can be an integral power tool.

On wet-grinding wheels the revolving, horizontally mounted abrasive cylinder is constantly washed with a flow of water during operation.

soak a badly clogged stone overnight, then scrub it. Soak the stone in oil again.

Many woodworkers use an electrically powered emery wheel for grinding. This has many disadvantages. It is used dry and revolves at around 3,000 rpm so there is danger of drawing the temper from the blade unless the tool is constantly dipped in water to cool it. It is difficult to produce an even edge on a narrower edge than the plane blade or chisel surface, and it is dangerous as it can chip or shatter. If it is used, always wear goggles and work with great care. Wet-grinding machines with horizontal wheels are much more suitable for both grinding and honing cabinetmakers' tools. The artificial stone is either a coarse 50 grit, a medium 180 grit or a fine 280 grit abrasive. The stone revolves at only 150 rpm and is constantly saturated with water or oil, so it is not dangerous and the tool is kept cool. Honing is completed on a fine stone.

To hone a tool at the correct angle, hold the tool in both hands, place the grinding bevel flat, then raise the hands slightly. Hone on an oilstone with a forward and backward motion. Push forwards, keeping pressure constant; return using no pressure. Keep the wrists rigid — rocking will cause the bevel to round over. After a few strokes, check that the bevel is forming evenly. Adjust the pressure if it is not. Keep the stone lubricated and keep honing until a wire edge, or burr, appears. Wipe the oil from the tip and test with the thumb to feel if the wire edge has formed along the whole width of the tool. To remove the wire edge, lay the blade absolutely flat and gently rub once on the stone. Wipe off the oil, and check. Finish the edge by stropping the blade across the palm or on leather.

Sharpening follows the same basic procedure for all edge tools. When sharpening narrow blades, it is vital that grooves are not worn in the oilstone or blades will not be sharpened flat. Move blades about in a figure of eight to utilize the whole stone. Be careful not to dig the corners of blades into the stone. Sharpen very narrow blades on the edge of the oilstone.

Using a honing guide

Width adjustment screw

Bed

25°
30°

Honing guide.

Honing and grinding bevels.

Using a honing guide
Honing guides hold chisel and plane blades at the correct angle. The guide consists of a frame mounted on wheels or rollers. The frame is adjustable to take blades of varying widths and has a bevel scale so it can be set at the angle required. To hone, push the guide backwards and forwards along the oilstone. Woodworkers eventually dispense with these guides but they are useful as an aid for beginners.

Sharpening plane blades

1. Hold the blade at an angle.

2. Remove the wire edge.

Sharpening plane blades
Hold a wide blade at an angle so its whole edge is in contact with the stone (1). Remove the wire edge when it appears on the reverse side (2). Hone jack plane and smoothing plane blades with a very slight curvature for fast cutting. Make a few figures of eight to produce the slight curve. Hone jointer plane blades dead square; round the corners slightly to prevent the edges digging in. Hone rebate, block and combination plane blades dead square.

Replacing plane blades

1. Position the cap iron.

2. Turn the cap iron.

3. Lay them on the frog.

Replacing plane blades
Hold the cap iron at right angles to the blade (1). Insert the lever cap screw. Slide the cap iron back along the slot in the blade and turn it in line with the blade (2). Move it forwards until it is the required distance from the cutting edge. Hold the two together and tighten the screw. Lay them on the frog (3). On a wooden plane replace the wedge; on a metal plane, replace the lever cap. Then adjust the blade projection as explained on page 78.

Grinding and honing 2

Sharpening chisels

1. Hone the chisel.

2. Remove the wire edge.   3. Strop the chisel.

Sharpening in-cannel gouges

1. Hone an in-cannel gouge with a slipstone.

2. Remove the wire edge on the oilstone.

Sharpening out-cannel gouges

1. Hone an out-cannel gouge on the oilstone.

2. Remove the wire edge with a slipstone.

Sharpening drawknives

1. Hold the tool bevel up.

2. Remove the wire edge with the oilstone.

Sharpening chisels

To hone a chisel, hold it bevel down at the correct 30° angle on the oilstone. Hold the end of the handle, with the fingers of the other hand applying pressure towards the cutting edge (1). Chisel blades must be absolutely square across. An off-square blade cannot make a true cut and is dangerous as it tends to slip sideways. Turn the chisel over to remove the wire edge on the fine oilstone (2). Keep the blade absolutely flat. If not, a secondary bevel will be formed on the flat back of the blade and when paring vertically the cut, instead of going straight down, will follow the line of the bevel. To finish the edge, strop the chisel on the palm of the hand (3).

Sharpening in-cannel gouges

To sharpen an in-cannel gouge, first hone the bevel on the inside of the blade with a slipstone (1). Use a slipstone that matches the curve of the blade or has a slightly sharper curve. When the wire edge appears, remove it on the fine oilstone, working from side to side with a rocking motion (2). Strop the gouge on the palm or on a piece of leather glued to a wooden board.

Sharpening out-cannel gouges

To sharpen an out-cannel gouge, hone the bevel first on the oilstone until the wire edge forms (1). Move the gouge in a figure of eight motion and roll it throughout its width during the movement. This should produce a smooth curve on the bevel. Remove the wire edge by rubbing a slipstone of the appropriate section back and forth within the curve (2).

Sharpening drawknives

The drawknife has such a large blade that it is more convenient to bring the oilstone to the blade. Brace one handle against a bench-stop, holding the tool bevel up (1). Take a firm grip on the oilstone and rub it the full length of the blade, holding the stone flat against the bevel. Remove the wire edge on the reverse side by turning the drawknife over, putting the oilstone against the flat of the blade and rubbing back and forth (2).

Sharpening spokeshaves

1. Hold the blade by the tangs. 2. Rub the blade lengthways. Hone on the oilstone.

Sharpening cabinet scrapers

1. File the edges square.

2. Drawfile to remove the file marks.

3. Hold the scraper upright across the oilstone.

4. Remove the wire edge.

5. Consolidate the metal.

6. Form the hook.

Sharpening spokeshaves

Remove the blade from a wooden spokeshave by tapping the two tangs with a hammer. Grip the oilstone on its edge in the bench vice. Put the blade bevel down, and hold it by the tangs (1). Hone it like a chisel or plane blade. Remove the wire edge by rubbing the blade lengthways (2). Metal spokeshave blades are similar to plane blades, but being shorter are difficult to hold. Make a wooden holder with a kerf at one end to take the blade. Sharpen it in the same way as a plane blade.

Sharpening cabinet scrapers

File the edges square with a smooth metal file (1). Hold the file at an angle so its teeth are at right angles to the scraper edge. Move the file diagonally both across and along. Drawfile to remove the first file marks (2). Hold the file lightly and at right angles to the blade. Then hone the edge square on the oilstone, holding the cabinet scraper upright at an angle across the oilstone to avoid forming a groove (3). Rub back and forth using strong pressure. To counteract any tendency to lean more to one side than the other, turn the blade round and repeat. Now lay the blade flat on the oilstone and remove the wire edge by rubbing first one side of the blade, then the other, applying pressure with the fingers along its length (4). Form the hook with a burnisher. This is simply a piece of silver steel rod harder than the cabinet scraper. It can be a special tool with a handle, or the back of a gouge can be used. First consolidate the metal (5). Lay the scraper flat on the bench and, with very strong pressure, rub the burnisher up and down. This presses the molecules together, so, when the razor edge hook is formed, it will be maintained longer. Then form the hook. Put a drop of oil on the blade; then hold it vertically on the bench, gripping the top in a soft cloth. Form the hook in two strokes. On the first stroke, hold the burnisher 5° away from the right angle, and on the second stroke, a further 5° away (6). Use firm pressure with each stroke. Treat the other three edges in the same way. The hook can be burnished down and re-formed a number of times before it is necessary to repeat the complete process using the file and oilstone.

Abrasives

After shaping, wood will require further cutting with an abrasive before it is ready for the final finish.

Abrasives, which are backed with paper, cloth or metal, are graded according to the coarseness of the grit used: 800 grit is the finest and 12 is the coarsest. Gradings used to be from Flour, 180 grit, through to Strong, about 50 grit. Grits spaced close together are called close-coat abrasives, while those spread more thinly are known as open-coat abrasives. The latter cut much faster because they clog up with dust less quickly.

Work an abrasive along the grain. Progress from a coarse abrasive, through medium, to a fine one.

Power sanders save considerable work when smoothing a piece of wood. Always switch them on before lowering them on to the wood. A belt sander is a heavy machine that will smooth rough stock fast. An orbital sander is much lighter and can produce a very fine finish. A drum sander can be used for smoothing hollows and contoured wood.

Type of abrasive	Glasspaper	Garnet paper	Aluminium oxide	Silicon carbide
Type of grit	powdered glass	crushed garnet	bauxite	coal and quartz
Abrasive quality	fairly soft	medium	hard	extremely hard
Suitable materials	hard- and soft-woods	hard- and soft-woods	hard-woods	hardwoods, particle boards
Uses	paintwork; bare wood finishing	by hand and with machine sander	general smoothing; bare wood finishing	wet on paintwork; dry on bare wood
General comment	cuts slowly	obtainable in very fine grit size	its hard grains take fast machine smoothing	also known as carborundum paper and wet-and-dry paper

When smoothing with an abrasive use a block to produce an even surface. A cork block is firm and resilient.

Hand sanding block

A metal-backed tungsten carbide abrasive lasts much longer than a conventional abrasive but is harsher.

For economy and a good fit around the block, tear a standard-sized sheet in six against the workbench.

Clear the dust on open-coat papers with a file card; rinse wet-and-dry papers under running water.

Smooth with the shoulder and block in line, with the chamfers on top. The paper should be tight around the block.

To maintain the sharpness on an edge hold the paper tightly around the block. On a wider surface hold it diagonally.

To smooth a corner work the abrasive between points A and B. Then work between C and B, avoiding surface AB.

To work an abrasive against a concave curve use the chamfered rather than the sharp edges on the block.

To smooth a moulding use a specially shaped sanding block with an abrasive paper held tightly around it.

Belt sander

To fit the belt release the tension lever between the rollers. Slip on the belt with its arrows pointing clockwise.

To stop the belt wandering along the rollers, adjust the angle of the front roller with the tracking adjustment knob.

Always switch on a belt sander before lowering it on to the wood. Allow the sander to pull itself along the surface.

Switch lock

On/off switch

Dust bag

Sanding belt

Front roller

Tracking adjustment knob

Orbital sander

Always fit a proprietary abrasive paper to an orbital sander, following the manufacturer's instructions.

When using an orbital sander do not press hard. Smooth in any direction. Finish by hand, smoothing with the grain.

Switch lock

On/off switch

Rubber pad

Abrasive paper

Drum sander

A drum sander has a foam rubber drum that follows the contours of the work being smoothed.

Drills and braces 1

An auger bit is the basic wood-boring tool and is used in a brace. At its tip is the threaded feed-screw that centres the bit and pulls it into the wood. Two spurs scribe the diameter of the cut and give precise centring so the bit remains accurate in grain of any direction. After the spurs, the cutters bite into the wood, lifting the wood chips and feeding them up the throat to the twist, which conveys them up and out of the hole.

A woodworkers' twist drill has a throat specially designed to clear away the wood chips on both hard- and softwood when boring at high speed. An engineer's twist drill is, however, the drill in common use even though its twist is specifically designed to clear the swarf produced when drilling metal. It is unable to clear wood chips efficiently at high speeds; nor is it suitable for unseasoned softwoods.

Because they are the same diameter all the way up the shank, auger bits and twist drills are more accurate than bits that are relieved behind the cutters.

A forstner bit, like many others, has a central point to lead the bit into the wood. The actual cutting is done by its circular rim and two cutters; the bit is therefore unaffected by knots and grain direction.

One expansive bit can stand in for a range of centre bits. To check its size, after adjusting the cutter, measure from the tip of the feed-screw to the outside edge of the spur. At the top of the feed-screw is a cutter that severs the wood ahead of the extended cutter.

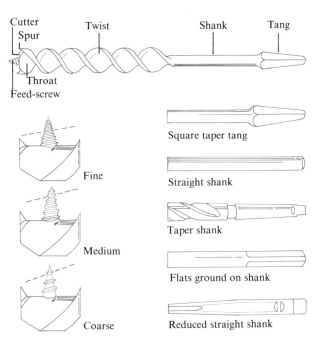

Cutter | Spur | Twist | Shank | Tang | Throat | Feed-screw

Fine

Medium

Coarse

Square taper tang

Straight shank

Taper shank

Flats ground on shank

Reduced straight shank

The pitch of the feed-screw thread determines the cut made by an auger bit. Use coarse and medium threads for general work; fine for a smooth finish.

A straight, taper or flattened shank fits a three-jaw self-centring chuck on a hand or power drill. A square-taper tang fits only a brace jaw.

Bradawl
Tip width 2–3 mm/$\frac{3}{32}$–$\frac{1}{8}$ in. For boring small holes and starting bits, drills, nails and screws.
Automatic push drill
Length 240 mm/9$\frac{1}{2}$ in. For rapid boring of small holes.
Archimedes drill
Length 290 mm/11$\frac{1}{2}$ in. For tiny holes. Bits are stored in the hollow handle.

Bradawl

Automatic push drill

Archimedes drill

Power drill

Power drill
Chuck capacity 6–16 mm/ $\frac{1}{4}$–$\frac{5}{8}$ in. For general-purpose boring. Graded by chuck capacity, which indicates the maximum size hole the drill can make in steel; this figure can be more than doubled when drilling wood. Various speed models are available.

Brace

Twist drill (A)
Diameter 0.38–38 mm/
$\frac{1}{64}$–1$\frac{1}{2}$ in for general drilling of
woods, metals and plastics in
hand and power drills.

Woodworkers' twist drill (B)
Diameter 6–25 mm/$\frac{1}{4}$–1 in. For
general drilling of hard- and
soft-woods in a brace.

Solid-centre auger bit (C)
Diameter 5–38 mm/$\frac{3}{16}$–1$\frac{1}{2}$ in. A
strong, fast-cutting general-
purpose bit.

Jennings-pattern auger bit (D)
Diameter 5–38 mm/$\frac{3}{16}$–1$\frac{1}{2}$ in.
More accurate than the solid-
centre auger bit and better for
fine work because of the
smooth finish it leaves.

Scotch auger bit (E)
Diameter 5–38 mm/$\frac{3}{16}$–1$\frac{1}{2}$ in.
For boring hardwoods; also
end grain.

Centre bit (F)
Diameter 5–56 mm/$\frac{3}{16}$–2$\frac{1}{4}$ in.
Fast-cutting bit for shallow,
large-diameter holes.

Forstner bit (G)
Diameter 6–50 mm/$\frac{1}{4}$–2 in. For
accurate flat-bottomed holes
and, where the auger cannot be
used, for end grain, thin wood
and three-ply.

Flat bit (H)
Diameter 19–38 mm/$\frac{3}{4}$–1$\frac{1}{2}$ in.
For general large-hole boring.
The lead point enables angled
holes to be started easily.

Expansive bit (I)
Diameter 13–150 mm/$\frac{1}{2}$–6 in.
For fast cutting shallow, large-
diameter holes only in
softwood. Has adaptable
interchangeable cutters.

Countersink bit (J)
Diameter 6–25 mm/$\frac{1}{4}$–1 in. For
widening the mouth of a
countersunk screw-hole,
allowing the screw-head to be
set flush or below the surface.

Combination drill bit (K)
Sized to suit common sizes of
screw. For drilling, countersinking and counterboring to
the required depth all in one.

Drill and countersink bit (L)
Sized to suit common sizes of
screw. Bores a screw-hole and
countersinks.

Screwdriver bit (M)
Blade width 6–16 mm/$\frac{1}{4}$–$\frac{5}{8}$ in.
Use in a brace for inserting or
extracting screws.

Hole saw (N)
Diameter 16–100 mm/$\frac{5}{8}$–4 in.
For large-diameter holes. A
central pilot bit is surrounded
by interchangeable saw blades.

Plug cutter (O)
Diameter 10–16 mm/$\frac{3}{8}$–$\frac{5}{8}$ in.
For cutting wood on dowel
plugs and pellets to conceal
screw-holes and nail-heads.

Fluted bit (P)
Diameter 2–16 mm/$\frac{3}{32}$–$\frac{5}{8}$ in.
For boring tiny holes. Fits only
the automatic push drill.

Hand drill

Brace
Sweep 150–350 mm/6–14 in.
Sized by the radius described
by the handle. For large, deep-
hole boring. Can be worked in
confined spaces.

Hand drill
Chuck capacity up to
6 mm/$\frac{1}{4}$ in. Accurate and
convenient for general boring.

Drills and braces 2

Brace

Use a try square to check if a drill is leaning forwards or backwards. The drill leaning to one side is more noticeable and easier to correct.

To bore a series of holes at an angle, make a simple jig. Place a block of wood against the rod (*see* page 37); mark in the angle of the slope. Bore a

vertical hole right through the wood. Then saw down the slope and plane it smooth. Hold the jig securely on the work with a cramp.

Bit shank

Jaws

Sleeve

A through hole bored with an auger bit will splinter. As soon as the feed-screw tip emerges, turn the work around and bore from the other side.

Another way to prevent splintering is to clamp a piece of waste wood to the back of the work to support the fibres as the bit emerges.

To fit a bit lock the ratchet. Holding the sleeve, swing the frame clockwise until the shank enters the jaws. Then tighten anti-clockwise.

The corners of the bit shank must fit into the V-grooves in the jaws. Brace jaws can be replaced if they slacken after considerable use.

Power drill

A drill stand makes it easy to drill a series of holes to a fixed depth. Screw the base to a board with a cleat and grip the cleat in the vice.

To use the drill position the bit on the wood and start it while applying light pressure. Remove from the wood before switching it off.

To fit a drill open the jaws, turning the chuck key anti-clockwise. Turn it clockwise to secure the drill, tightening all three holes in rotation.

Hand drill

When drilling vertically push down on the handle; apply extra force if necessary by leaning the head against the uppermost hand.

When drilling horizontally extra pressure can be brought to bear by pushing the body weight against the hand that is holding the drill.

To fit a drill hold the sleeve and turn the handle anti-clockwise. Insert the bit and turn the handle clockwise to tighten the chuck.

Special bits

Countersink

Counterbore

D   E

Clearance hole   Pilot hole

Depth stops

A   B   C

Use a forstner bit (A) to cut clean flat-bottomed holes. This bit is best used in a drill stand with a depth stop, and it is ideal for removing the bulk of waste from a recess. A plug cutter (**B**) bores to a fixed depth. After boring, break the pellet at the root, using a small screwdriver. Glue and insert

the pellet into the hole in line with the grain; then plane it flush. Plug cutters are sized to match standard bit sizes. To bore with a hole saw (**C**), first secure the required size of blade to the pilot bit. Unlike other large diameter drills, the hole saw removes the waste as a complete disk.

Screws require a pilot hole to take the threaded portion, a clearance hole for the threadless portion, and a countersink if the head is to be flush with the surface. The drill and countersink bit (**D**) does all this in one. A combination drill bit (**E**) is shaped to form a counterbore as well.

To drill to a fixed depth without a drill stand, a depth stop is fitted to the bit itself. This can be a metal clamp (**A**), which locates in the flutes of an auger bit, or a screw-on sleeve (**B**) for a twist drill. Simplest of all is a short length of dowel, with a hole bored through the centre (**C**).

Sharpening bits

Spur

Cutter

Sharpen spurs on an auger bit from the inside not lower than the cutters, using a smooth file. Sharpen cutters on the edge facing the shank.

Place the cutting edge of a twist drill against the wheel; rotate the cutting edge, lifting at the same time. Repeat for the other edge.

A jig will hold a twist drill at the correct angle for sharpening. Push the jig over a sheet of 180 grit abrasive paper to sharpen the drill.

Twist drill sharpeners powered by the drill itself are made to fit some drills. On some the chuck is removed (as above); others fit into the chuck.

Hammers, mallets and screwdrivers 1

The first hammer was a stone held in the hand; the first mallet, a cudgel. The Romans used a hammer with a claw pein for pulling nails, while medieval pictures show a hammer with a square head that is similar to current European hammers.

Hammers are sized by the weight of their head. A hammer should be well balanced with a forged head; a cast head tends to shatter. The claw should be carefully ground, tapering to a fine V so it can pull nails of all sizes. A hammer handle is traditionally made from ash or hickory—both tough, long-grained woods. The end of the wooden shaft is impregnated with oil to prevent moisture loss and splitting. Hammers with metal or fibreglass shafts are a modern development. The head is securely wedged on to a wooden handle or is forged and locked on to a metal handle. A wooden-handled claw hammer usually has an extended eye, like the eye of an adze, to prevent excessive strain on the shaft when pulling large nails.

Every workshop needs at least four screwdrivers to fit all sizes of screw likely to be used. A traditional screwdriver has a beech or boxwood handle strengthened with a metal ferrule. A modern plastic handle is moulded directly on to the blade. The bulbous end to most handles enables more torque to be applied, although some workers prefer fluted plastic handles.

Hammer parts

Eye · Bell · Pein · Face · Cheek · Neck

Square-headed claw hammer

Adze-eye claw hammer

Steel-shafted claw hammer

Pin hammer

Cross-pein hammer

Pin push

Joiners' mallet

Nail-punch

Nail-set

Nail-punch and nail-set
Length 100 mm/4 in. For driving nails below the surface and where a hammer would damage the surface when driving nails flush. The tip must fit the nail.

Joiners' mallet
Head size 100–175 mm/4–7 in. For joint assembly.

Pin push
Length 100–150 mm/4–6 in. For driving small nails in awkward places. The magnetic tip holds the pin.

Pin hammer
Weight up to 110 gm/4 oz. Lightweight cross-pein hammer for small pins and nails.

Cross-pein hammer
Weight 170–450 gm/6–16 oz. A general-purpose joiners' hammer. Use the cross-pein for starting nails.

Steel shafted claw hammer
Weight 450–570 gm/16–20 oz. For heavier jobs than a cross-pein hammer. Can remove nails that have projecting heads.

Pincers
Length 150–250 mm/6–10 in.
For removing nails where a
claw hammer cannot reach.
The claw at the end of the
handle is for lifting tacks.

**Cross-head
screwdriver**

**Self-grip
screwdriver**

**Ratchet
screwdriver**

**Cabinet
screwdriver**

**Cabinet
screwdriver**

**Heavy-duty
screwdriver**

**Offset
screwdriver**

Stubby screwdriver

**Spiral ratchet
screwdriver**

Self-grip screwdriver
Blade 75–175 mm/3–7 in. The
spring-loaded sleeve around
the blade holds the screw.
Cross-head screwdriver
Various types and sizes. Use
only with screws slotted in the
same pattern as the tip.
Ratchet screwdriver
Blade 50–300 mm/2–12 in. For
driving screws without having
to shift the grip on the tool.
Ratchet can be adjusted for
clockwise or anti-clockwise
drive, and can be locked.
Spiral ratchet screwdriver
Blade 240–710 mm/9½–28 in
fully extended. Downward
pressure on spiral grooves
causes tip to turn.
Cabinet screwdriver
Blade 75–250 mm/3–10 in.
Modern style with round
straight blade.
Cabinet screwdriver
Blade 75–250 mm/3–10 in.
Traditional screwdriver with
flat blade.
Heavy-duty screwdriver
Blade 100–200 mm/4–8 in.
Forged from solid steel; riveted
wooden inserts form the
handle.
Offset screwdriver
Length 75–150 mm/3–6 in. For
awkward spaces or where extra
torque is required. Can be
tapped with a hammer to shift
stubborn screws.
Stubby screwdriver
Blade 25–38 mm/1–1½ in. For
confined spaces. Its thickened
handle provides torque. Use
tommy bar for increased
torque.

Screwdriver blades

Flared tip

Ground-back flared tip

Parallel tip

Cross-head

Traditional screwdrivers have a
flared tip. Modern tools tend
to have parallel or ground-
back flared tips. These can turn
at the bottom of holes in which
a flared tip might bind. Various
styles of cross-head screwdriver
tip are available.

Hammers, mallets and screwdrivers 2

The process of hammering nails and pins and driving screws is not that simple. Skill is required to hammer in a nail perfectly every time, and careful preparation and choice of screwdriver are necessary for flawless work. Keep the hammer-head free from grease and rub off rust spots with a fine abrasive. When nailing near end grain, the danger of splitting is reduced if the nail tip is blunted by cutting off the tip or banging it on metal. Use clench nailing only where strength is more important than appearance.

A screwdriver blade becomes rounded through use, so restore the flat sides and tip occasionally by honing on an oilstone. Grind any sharp corners off the screwdriver blade tip to avoid damaging the wood on the last few turns, when driving countersunk screws.

Hammers and nailing

Hold a hammer by the end of the handle, not in the middle. Swing the arm, pivoting from the elbow and keeping the wrist straight but flexible. Keep an eye on the nail, hitting with a firm, clean stroke so that the hammer-head meets the nail-head at right angles at the moment of impact.

To start a nail in the wood tap it gently with the cross-pein. When it is able to stand unsupported, drive it in with the hammer face.

Short nails and pins that cannot be held in the fingers can be gripped with a small pair of pliers while they are tapped into position in the wood.

Short nails and pins can also be held by being pushed through a strip of card. Then hammer the nail through the card into the wood; when the nail grips, tear away the card. This method is particularly useful if the nail is to be inserted in an awkward place such as a corner or into the ceiling.

If only one hand can be used start a heavy nail by gripping its head against the side of the hammer and drive both in together until the nail holds.

For clench nailing tap a long nail through both parts of the wood. Hammer the tip over and then flush, with the work resting on a firm surface.

Dovetail nailing in end grain grips better than straight nailing. Insert the nails at opposing angles like the slopes of a dovetail.

Remove a nail if it starts to bend. Pincers and claw hammers work by leverage so pressure on the handle is magnified at the nail end.

The force on the pivoting section can damage the work, so place a cabinet scraper or waste wood beneath the tool to spread pressure.

Bent nails should be discarded, but if one must be re-used place it on a piece of scrap metal and straighten it with a few taps from a hammer.

Fitting a new hammer handle

1. Plane the handle.

2. Saw a kerf in the handle.

3. Tap the handle firmly.

4. Finish with a mallet.

5. Hammer the wedge flush.

Fitting a new hammer handle
If a wooden hammer handle breaks or splinters, it can be replaced with a new one secured by a metal wedge. Saw off the old handle close to the head. Drive out the remainder with a chisel or punch, working from the underside towards the top, because the eye is tapered in that direction. Plane the head of the new handle to fit the hammer eye (1). Tap it gently partway into the eye. Remove and plane any shiny parts, which indicate where the wood is binding. In the top of the handle, saw a kerf in line with the hammerhead to the depth of a metal wedge (2). Place the head on the handle and tap firmly on the bench until the head is driven on to the shaft by its own weight (3). Turn the hammer over and use a mallet for the final blows (4). If the kerf closes, open it with a chisel or screwdriver. Insert the wedge and hammer it flush (5).

Punches

To use a nail-punch hold it vertically just above the nail-head. Hit the top so the spring tip punches the nail below the surface. Fill the punched hole with stopping and smooth the surface flush for an invisible finish. The smaller the hole made by the tapered punch tip, the neater the finish will be.

Hold a nail-set just above the nail against the fleshy part of the middle finger. After impact the nail-set will automatically spring up again.

To use a pin push drop the nail into the sleeve — the magnetic tip will hold it even upside down. Press down on the handle to operate.

Screwdrivers

When using a ratchet screwdriver in awkward places, it can be difficult to get sufficient pressure on the blade. For right-handed workers, in such cases, it may be easier to push on the screwdriver handle with the left hand and support the blade with the right; do this vice versa if left-handed.

When using a spiral ratchet screwdriver apply downward pressure on the spiral grooves to turn the tip. Small models have a mild spring that is potentially less dangerous than the strong spring in large models. If these latter slip, they can damage the woodworker and the work.

Table saw

The basic function of a table saw is ripping and cross-cutting wood, both fast and accurately. The saw is sized by the diameter of its blades, which are similar to but larger than those used on the portable circular saw. A 200–250 mm/8–10 in saw is suitable for the home workshop. The blade is fitted on a revolving arbor and can be projected the required amount above the flat, iron table. The work is fed into the revolving blade, with the aid of fences and jigs, by the operator. An adjustable metal rip fence is positioned parallel to the blade, acting as a guide when ripping. A mitre fence slides in one of two grooves in the table, on either side of the blade, to act as a guide when cross-cutting and mitre-cutting. The fences aid accurate and safe work-ing and should always be used. For making bevelled cuts, a tilting arbor saw is much safer than one where the table tilts.

A table saw should always have a blade guard directly over the blade and a riving knife. This is a metal tongue directly behind the blade, which keeps the kerf open and prevents the wood binding on the blade and being kicked back towards the operator. The riving knife must be used for all ripping. If the blade guard must be removed, always use other safety devices such as a push stick, a holding jig or a guide. Turn off the mains isolator switch before making any major adjustment to the table saw. When operating the saw, allow it to reach full speed before beginning a cut.

Removable table plate — Blade — Riving knife — Blade guard — Mitre fence lock — Mitre fence groove — Sliding extension table

Mitre fence groove — Rip fence — Rip fence slide (and table extension rod)

Table

Mitre fence

Sliding extension table — Rip fence lock — Rip fence adjustment knob — On switch — Mushroom-headed off switch

Blade height control — Angle of tilt scale — Blade tilt control

Drop-down tool tray

Mains isolator switch

Sawdust outlet

Push stick
For feeding the work into the saw. Made from hardwood; has a notch at one end. Hang within reach near the saw.

A springboard, kerfed on the bandsaw, is clamped against the work, providing pressure and flexibility. Always hold the work against the fence.

When ripping hold the work against the fence with one hand; feed it in with the other, which should stay near the table edge.

Ripping is much safer if a push stick and a springboard are used. Stand slightly to one side in case the board should suddenly kick back.

When bevel ripping set the saw with the blade tilt control. The tilt scale gives the angle of cut; for accuracy, check the saw angle with a sliding bevel.

When cross-cutting and mitre-cutting use the mitre fence. Bolt or screw on a higher wooden auxiliary fence so it is easier to hold the work.

When cross-cutting use both hands to hold the work tightly against the fence. If only one hand is used, the work could slide during the cut.

To cross-cut several boards to the same length, clamp a stop-block to the mitre fence. A G-cramp is ideal for this. Glue abrasive cloth to the face of the wooden auxiliary fence to prevent the wood creeping along the fence during the cut. This makes accurate cross-cutting much easier.

When making mitre cuts at any angle feed the work slowly into the saw to minimize movement, which would result in inaccurate mitres.

To make bevelled mitre cuts use a mitre fence and tilted blade. Before starting the saw, check that the fence will not touch the blade.

To cut wedges and tapers use a jig. Make a kerf in the baseboard parallel to one long side. Draw in the shape of the wedge from this datum cut. Pin the two stop-blocks in place. Put the work in the angle between the blocks. Rest the baseboard against the rip fence and feed the jig into the blade.

To cut a groove make a kerf. Then re-set the fence, a fraction away from the blade, and make another kerf to widen the original one.

If the blade guard must be removed a length of wood clamped to the fence holds the work down and also prevents the hands going near the blade.

To cut a groove in an edge hold the board against the fence. Use a sliding jig to hold work that is more than twice the fence height.

Cut rebates in two passes, tongues in four. For the second cut, hold the work so that the waste is against the fence, covering the blade.

Tapered wobble washers are used in pairs and are fitted on either side of the blade to angle it so that a wider kerf can be made in one pass.

To cut rebates, grooves and tongues use wobble washers. Run the saw at a slow speed to ensure the blade does not bow inwards, forming curved sides.

Safety points for fixed power tools

○ Disconnect the tool when making adjustments to blades.
○ Always use the guards and fences provided. If they must be removed, improvise with push sticks and jigs.
○ Never sweep waste off the table with the hand. Switch off the tool and use a stick or brush.
○ Never reach over blades; always walk around the tool.
○ Check when buying that the tool has an emergency mushroom-headed stop button or foot-press stop button.
○ When working long boards, enlist the aid of an assistant or use a roller on a stand to support the work as it comes off the tool.
○ Where possible, check the movement fully by hand before switching on.
○ Never hurry. Always be on guard against any potential danger.
○ Never leave the tool running unattended.
○ Avoid any clothing that may become caught in the tool.

Bandsaw

The bandsaw blade is a flexible steel strip, running continuously around two, or sometimes three, wheels. The blade is toothed on one edge like a handsaw blade. The bandsaw's primary function is to cut curves, although it also makes straight ripping cuts, cross-cuts and mitre cuts. It is also the best tool for resawing and for cutting shapes with compound curves. The saw is usually sized by the wheel diameter; one with less than 350 mm/14 in is suitable for a home workshop. Sometimes, however, it is sized by throat depth, that is, the distance between the blade and the frame of the machine. This affects the size of wood that can be swung across the table on curved cuts. Before use, the blade must be tensioned correctly so that it is still possible to flex it slightly. This is done by raising or lowering the top wheel. The blade must also be adjusted so that it tracks correctly between the blade guides. This is done by angling the top wheel. The guides keep the blade from deflecting to either side when cutting curves. The back-thrust wheel rotates with the blade and supports it against the feed pressure of the work. If the blade guides are not correctly set, the blade will be unable to make a true cut. The guide assembly is adjustable for height to allow for the thickness of the work. When in use, always follow the basic safety points listed on page 107.

Blade tensioning knob

Blade

Blade guard

Blade guide assembly

Guide fence

Blade

Table

Groove for fence

Table tilt control

Fence lock

On/off switches

Stand facing the blade, slightly to one side (*left*). Feed the wood gently through, pushing it with one hand and guiding it with the other. When ripping, hold the work firmly against the fence. To resaw, hold the wood against the fence; clamp guide on the other side (*above*).

Blade width	Cutting radius
6 mm/$\frac{1}{4}$ in	19 mm/$\frac{3}{4}$ in
10 mm/$\frac{3}{8}$ in	38 mm/$1\frac{1}{2}$ in
13 mm/$\frac{1}{2}$ in	56 mm/$2\frac{1}{4}$ in
19 mm/$\frac{3}{4}$ in	100 mm/4 in

Cutting curves is the bandsaw's primary function. The narrower the blade, the tighter the curve it will cut.

Radius   Kerf   Bolt

Cleat

Screw

Baseboard   Pivoting table

Make an adjustable jig for cutting circles. Butt the base cleat against the table. Kerf the base and pivoting table.

Direction of feed

Work

Fix the work to the screw on the pivoting table. Swing the pivoting table to the radius. Turn the work into the blade.

To cut compound curves draw the profile of the shape on all four sides. Tape the waste in place after each cut.

The table on most bandsaws tilts up to 45° on one side for making bevelled cuts. It tilts only slightly on the other side.

Radial arm saw

The radial arm saw is extremely versatile. It has an arm that can be swung through 360° to the right or to the left of an upright column. To adjust the depth of cut, the arm is raised or lowered on the column by turning the elevating handle. Each complete circle moves the arm up or down 3 mm/⅛ in. The yoke is suspended from the arm and holds the motor and blade. The yoke can be moved along the arm when cross-cutting and mitre-cutting, or can be locked at any point on it. The yoke can also be swivelled around to turn the blade parallel to the fence. The motor and blade can be swung within the yoke to make bevelled or even horizontal cuts. The saw is sized by the diameter of its blades. These are similar to the blades fitted to a circular table saw. A diameter of around 250 mm/10 in is suitable for a home workshop. Although the radial arm saw can perform many tasks, it is safest and most efficient when cross-cutting. This is because the blade rotates down and away from the operator, pushing the work in against the fence. When ripping, the blade rotates up and towards the operator, and so the anti-kickback fingers must always be used to prevent the wood from being shot out of the saw back towards the operator. The saw can also be fitted with accessories, including shaping cutters and sanding disks. Always observe the safety points listed on page 107.

Elevating handle
Mitre scale
Yoke clamp
Arm lock
Radial arm
Mitre lock
Ripping scale
Column
On/off switches
Sawdust spout
Yoke
Blade guard
Handle
Bevel lock
Table
Bevel angle scale
Fence
Blade
Anti-kickback fingers

When cross-cutting hold the work against the fence and pull the saw to the end of the arm. Return the saw to the fence.

When ripping set the yoke the required distance from the fence, using the ripping scale. Feed the work through.

When ripping wide materials cut with the yoke turned around and the blade locked at the outer end of the arm.

When mitre-cutting swing the arm to right or left of the column and lock it. Make the cut like a cross-cut.

For bevelled cuts tilt the motor and blade to the required angle. Rip, mitre- and cross-cuts can be made.

The motor can be swung so that the blade is horizontal within the yoke. Use this position for rebating and grooving.

To make grooves by kerfing adjust the depth of cut with the elevating handle and make a series of cross-cuts.

x

Spindle moulder

The spindle moulder cuts and shapes the edges of straight and curved pieces of wood. It can make mouldings, rebates, tenons and grooves. It consists of a flat table with a hole in the centre near the back edge. A rotating spindle projects through the hole, and a cutter is fitted on or through the spindle. The spindle can be raised and lowered to adjust the height of the cutter. The table has a groove, to take a sliding mitre fence, and threaded holes, to take two wooden fences on either side of the spindle. The fences move independently backwards and forwards, to adjust the amount by which the cutter projects, and from side to side, to provide clearance on each side of the spindle. The work rests against the fences and is fed into the cutter against the direction of rotation. The spindle revolves at up to 10,000 rpm. Cutters are available in a wide range of profiles. Some cutters are sold in matching positive and negative pairs. Blank cutters are available for filing to any profile. Split collar cutters consist of a pair of cutters that are fixed into parallel slots in grooved collars. French cutters consist of a single cutter passing through the spindle shaft. Disk cutters make cuts to a greater depth in the wood. They can be used singly or in pairs separated by adjustable spacing collars (see page 128). Before making any cut, turn the spindle by hand to check that it clears all guides and fences. Always make a test cut on waste wood first. To shape the edge of curved work, fit the ring fence. The uncut portion on the edge of the work rides against the ring fence. When the complete edge of curved work is to be shaped, pin a wooden template to the work; the ring fence will ride against the template. When the spindle moulder is in use, always follow the basic safety points listed on page 107.

Cutter — Hold-down assembly — In-feed fence — Mitre fence — Mitre hold-down — Sliding table — Split collar cutter — Disk cutters — French cutter

Spindle — Fence adjustment knob — Fence slide knob

Out-feed fence — Mitre fence groove — Vertical hold-down — Horizontal hold-down — Slide bars

Cutter profiles

Cutters can remove a complete edge, or only part of it. For safety, always try to arrange work so the cutter shapes the lower edge.

Use hold-downs when making straight cuts. When shaping a curved edge, always fit the ring guard on the ring fence to protect the fingers.

Sight along the fences and adjust them so the cutter protrudes to produce roughly the profile required. Make test cuts on waste wood before making the final adjustments. The fences should just clear the cutter on either side.

The work must be supported by both the in-feed and the out-feed fences along its whole length during the course of the cut. If only part of the edge is being cut away, then both fences should be set in line with each other.

When the whole of an edge is to be cut away, set the out-feed fence forwards so the newly shaped edge is supported as it clears the cutter. If the cut is deep, first make a thin cut; readjust the fences and complete the cut.

Use the hold-downs wherever possible. An overhead arm clamped behind the cutter supports a wooden shoe to hold the work down, while allowing it still to move, and a spring steel plate holds the work against the fence.

To shape the edge of a straight board let the cutter reach full speed. Press the wood against the in-feed fence and push it forwards. Allow the wood to

bridge the cutter gap. Then transfer one hand to press it against the out-feed fence. Keep movement smooth and continuous.

To shape end grain the wood must have the extra support supplied by the sliding table and the mitre fence. Clamp the work to the mitre fence. Place

some waste wood beneath the work to support the cutter, and place another piece of waste wood behind the work to prevent the grain from splintering.

To shape end grain at an angle hold the work at the required angle against the mitre fence and push it past the cutter using the sliding table.

When shaping a wide board use the vertical hold-down. Raise the horizontal hold-down in front of the cutter and press the work against the fence.

To make moulding strips shape both edges of a board. Then rip off the strips on a table saw. Repeat, until sufficient moulding is made.

Combine cutters to make a deep moulding. Position the second cutter for continuity with the first and readjust the fences as necessary.

To shape curved edges remove the wooden fences and hold-downs. Press the work against the ring fence and allow the cutter to protrude beneath it.

Mark the minimum (A) and maximum (B) cutter projection on the ring fence. Introduce the work at A and pivot it round to B.

Make the cut along the length of the work at point B. Always fit the ring guard. (For clarity it has been omitted in the illustrations *left* and *far left*.)

To smooth shaped work fit a drum sander. Fit a sleeve of abrasive paper over the rubber cylinder. Screw down the cap so the rubber expands.

Combined planer & thicknesser

The planer and thicknesser perform related tasks and are often combined. The planer smooths and trues up faces and edges on a piece of wood. The thicknesser smooths the other face of the wood to a uniform thickness, provided one face is already flat and true so the wood can register against the flat bed of the thicknesser. Cutting in both planer and thicknesser is done by a rotating cylindrical metal cutter block.

On the planer, the work is fed over the cutter block between two metal tables. These are raised and lowered independently. The out-feed table must be the same height as the cutters at their highest point so the newly planed surface rides smoothly on to it. The in-feed table is set lower — by the amount of wood to be removed. The maximum depth of cut should be no more than 3 mm/$\frac{1}{8}$ in. Make deeper cuts by a series of passes. To plane a cupped board, place the concave side downwards and take several thin cuts. If a board is "in winding", remove wood from the high corners.

Wood is fed into the thicknesser on a flat bed, which is raised or lowered to adjust the depth of cut. Corrugated in-feed rollers grip the work and draw it beneath the rotating cutter block. The feed rollers hold the wood flat while it is being smoothed.

When using these tools, always observe the safety points listed on page 107.

Stand to one side when feeding the work into the thicknesser in case of kickback. Rollers at each end of the bed support the work.

On simple combination tools one cutter block serves for both parts. Feed rollers in the thicknesser pull the wood in.

Table rise and fall control — Fence

Cutter block

Out-feed table

In-feed table

Blade guard

Table rise and fall control

Support roller

Planer on/off switch

Bed

Support roller

Speed control

Bed rise and fall control

Mushroom-headed stop button

Thicknesser on/off switch

Thicknesser gauge

To plane a rebate remove the blade guard and adjust the fence to the rebate width. Cut the full depth of the rebate in steps in a number of passes.

To plane bevels and chamfers tilt the fence in- or outwards (*above*), using the mitre scale behind the fence. Check the setting with a sliding bevel.

Use a push block for short or thin wood. Wood less than 300 mm/12 in long is too short to be safely planed with power tools and must be hand planed.

Start planing with both hands holding the wood on the in-feed table (1). Gradually move the hands over the blade guard to the out-feed table (2, 3).

Drill press

The drill press can bore and drill a large number of holes quickly and accurately to a pre-determined depth. It is available in both bench and floor-standing models, the only difference being in the length of column. The size of the drill press is determined by measuring the distance from the chuck centre to the column and then doubling that measurement: this is the maximum diameter that can be accommodated on the table. The table can be moved up and down the column and can be locked to hold work of varying thicknesses. It may also be tilted to bore angled holes or to support wood for boring into end grain. Set the table by aligning the bit with a sliding bevel.

Place the work beneath the bit and lower the bit directly, and with even pressure, into the work, using the feed lever. Drill press speeds range from around 300 rpm to 6,000 rpm. Follow the manufacturer's instructions for the correct speed for different materials; the fastest speeds are for using accessories such as router cutters and a drum sander.

Open and close the three-jaw chuck with a key. The chuck capacity is usually up to 13 mm/½ in. The drill press takes the same range of bits and drills as the portable power drill (*see* pages 98–9).

When using the drill press, it is extremely important to observe the safety points listed on page 107.

On/off switches

Speed control

Feed lever

Spindle

Depth stop

Chuck

Mains isolator switch

Table

Table slide

Column

Stop button

To bore holes to a uniform fixed depth mark the required depth of the hole on the edge of the wood (*above*). To set the depth stop (*left*) lower the bit, using the feed lever, until the tip lines up with the mark on the wood. Secure the locking nuts on the depth stop.

For accurate boring mark the hole clearly and provide a locating point for the bit tip with an awl. Then switch on the drill press.

Lower the feed lever until it is just above the work. Move the work so the bit will be centred accurately. Hold the work down firmly.

Bore deep holes halfway from each side. Position the work for the second hole by fitting the first hole over a locating dowel inserted in a jig base.

To bore holes in end grain and in board edges tilt the table until it is at right angles to the bit. Clamp the wood to the table. Then bore.

Methods

A comprehensive demonstration of all the
essential techniques in woodworking

Joints

A joint must be strong enough to resist the stresses that will be imposed on it. (For uses of joints *see* pages 150–65 and pages 8–29; for terms peculiar to each joint *see* under the appropriate joint.) The design of most joints has evolved over the centuries to solve the particular problems posed by solid wood construction. Few of these joints work successfully with manufactured boards except for multi-ply (*see* page 149). All joints, except those that are dismantled or pivoted, must be glued. The greater the area on the side and edge available to be glued, the more a joint's strength is increased. End grain does not hold glue well.

Consider the grain direction carefully before starting to make a joint. There should be no knots in the joint area. Decide how the pieces are to be arranged (*see* page 151). Choose the best surfaces of the wood to be the face side and face edge. Cut and plane the wood to size and square it up, marking the faces (*see* pages 56–7). Then cut the joint. The surfaces of the joint left by the saw will be quite rough; this is an advantage as it helps the glue to grip. Remove ragged edges; smooth the faces that will be inaccessible when the joint is assembled, but leave pencilled reference marks on until the whole project has been glued and assembled. Before gluing, a joint can be tested for fit — known as a dry assembly. A well-made joint will be friction tight. Glue all the inside surfaces of the joint on both pieces. Then knock the joint pieces home with a hammer. The hammer has the same weight as a mallet but the impact area is smaller and is consequently easier to control. Use waste wood as a buffer. Wipe off excess glue before it dries using a damp cloth. When dry, level all surfaces with a smoothing plane and smooth with glasspaper.

Halving joints

A

B

C

D

E

F

Halving joints

Halving joints provide a simple way of joining two pieces that cross or meet in an L or T formation. They are used for small simple frames and for intermediate frames and divisions within a carcass. They do not have the strength and rigidity of joints such as mortise and tenons, dovetails or housings. The cross halving joint (**A**) can be cut in manufactured boards crossing in their width, making it suitable for internal dividers in boxes and small carcasses. The lap halving joint (**B**) needs to be reinforced by screwing underneath, or by dowels or bolts. Variations on the halving joint include the housed and halved joint (**C**) and the mitred, rebated and halved joint (**D**) — a useful joint for picture and mirror frames. Secure the mitre by dowelling or screwing from the back. The straight shoulders on the oblique halving joint (**E**) give it strength and resistance to twisting. In the dovetail halving joint (**F**), the strength of a dovetail joint is added to that of a T-halving joint. Use it for jointing carcasses and frames.

Mortise and tenon joints

A

B

C

D

E

F

G

H

J

Comb joint

Mortise and tenon joints

These are the strongest end to side edge joints and they are used in cabinetmaking for frame jointing. The through mortise and tenon joint (**A**) is the basic form of this joint. The mortise is cut right through the wood showing the end grain of the tenon. Shoulders on the tenon provide stops for the tenon and a resistance to twisting. Wedges can be inserted into either tenon or mortise to give additional strength. In the stub or blind mortise and tenon joint (**B**), the tenon is shortened to avoid showing end grain on the outer surface. The barefaced mortise and tenon joint (**C**) is used when a thin slat must be tenoned into a thicker upright to finish flush on one side. The tenon has only one shoulder. This allows the mortise to be displaced safely away from the front edge. The bridle joint (**D**) is often used for leg and rail joints where a thick leg must be connected to a thinner rail. On the haunched mortise and tenon joint (**E**) the width of the tenon is reduced to prevent the joint being withdrawn upwards. Instead of a complete strip of the tenon being removed, a small portion near the shoulder is left — called a haunch. The haunch helps resist any tendency to twist. The haunch can be tapered by placing it against a matching slope in the mortise piece. The long and short shoulder mortise and tenon joint (**F**) is necessary when using rebated members. The mortise and tenon joint with a mitred front (**G**) gives a neat appearance and is useful when working mouldings on the inside edge. The projected and wedged mortise and tenon joint (**H**) forms the leg and rail connection on a table that might need to be dismantled. The tenon passes right through the leg, or truss, and is wedged on the outside. The pinned joint (**J**) is extremely strong. There is a very large gluing area and the joint can resist downward and twisting pressure.

Comb joint

This joint is used for boxes and drawers, particularly when many drawers are needed. The tongues make a tight fit in the kerfs, and the joint has a large gluing area. A comb joint is formed quickly and accurately with a table saw.

Dovetail joints

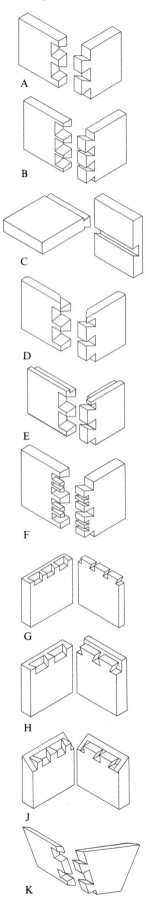

A

B

C

D

E

F

G

H

J

K

Dovetail joints

Dovetail joints are the strongest way of connecting pieces of wood together in their width. They are used to join carcasses rigidly and to make boxes and drawers. They have a comparatively large gluing area and are therefore particularly strong. Generally, the longer the tails, the better the grip. Properly made tails only fit once, so a joint should only be half entered on a dry assembly. The carpenter's through dovetail joint (**A**) is the basic form of the joint. End grain shows on both pieces. When hand-made the tails are wider than the pins. The fineness of the pin is judged as a sign of quality workmanship, and in the cabinetmaker's dovetail joint (**B**) the pin often comes to a point. In the dovetail housing joint (**C**), the tail is cut across the width of the wood. The joint is usually tapered on assembly to avoid excessive friction across such a wide area. This is a particularly strong joint to use for securing shelves. The through dovetail joint with mitre (**D**) has the top edge mitred and usually rounded over for a neat appearance on trays and boxes. The through dovetail joint with rebate (**E**) is used with a rebated frame. The decorative through dovetail joint (**F**) makes a feature of the fact that end grain shows on both pieces. The small tails add to the strength of the joint by increasing the gluing area on the very large tails. The lapped dovetail joint (**G**) is used when the end grain is required to be hidden on one of the pieces. The through tails are modified by shortening the tails and letting the socket piece lap over the end. The joint is often used for drawers where the end grain is not required to show on the front. The double lapped dovetail joint (**H**) is used where tails are not required to show on either piece. One piece presents a flush surface while the other shows only a thin line of end grain. No end grain shows at all on the secret mitre dovetail joint (**J**), which from the outside looks like a simple butted mitre joint. The bevelled dovetail joint (**K**) is used to join the sides of boxes where all four sides slope outwards; it is one of the most difficult of all joints to make. Through and lapped dovetails can be cut by machine, using a power router and jig. This is useful if many joints are to be cut.

Housing joints

A

B

Dowel joints

A

B

C

Edge joints

A

B

C

D

Pivoting joints

A

B

Housing joints

The through housing joint (**A**) is used for fixing shelves in carcasses and for holding intermediate rails in carcass frames. The housing can be stopped, so there is an unbroken vertical line on the carcass. In the barefaced housing joint (**B**), used for jointing a top to a side, the horizontal piece is reduced in thickness by having a tongue cut in it and only this is housed. This makes the joint better able to resist twisting.

Dowel joints

Dowels can be used to join wood edge to edge (**A**) or at right angles edge to end (**B**). They can also be used for mitre joints (**C**) and to secure solid-wood or manufactured-board shelves. In traditional work they were rarely used as the dowels had to be cut by hand. Dowel joints are now often substituted for mortise and tenon joints, as they are easier to make and almost as strong. They are especially suitable when awkwardly shaped or angled pieces of wood meet as in canted or round table legs joining a rail.

Edge joints

To build up a wide surface in solid wood two or more boards can be joined edge to edge. The most basic way is to use the rubbed glue joint. It is a perfectly strong joint if the mating edges are planed and glued together correctly. The tongued and grooved joint (**A**) has a large gluing area. The tongue can be cut in one operation using a tonguing cutter or be formed by cutting a rebate on both edges. Both pieces can be grooved and a loose tongue glued in. The slot-screwed joint (**B**) may be used as an alternative. A mitre joint can be strengthened with a loose tongue glued in grooves (**C**) or by keys inserted after assembly (**D**).

Pivoting joints

The knuckle joint (**A**) is cut when a pivoting joint is required. It is traditionally formed on the brackets supporting the flaps on Pembroke tables. The rule joint (**B**) is traditionally used for fall flaps such as on a gateleg table. It looks neat when the flap is both up and down and adds strength as pressure on the flap is transmitted to the main top when the flap is up. It must be used with a special rule joint hinge (*see* page 258).

117

Halving

A cross halving joint

Edge   Side

The finished joint.

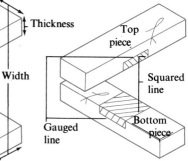

Length   Thickness

Depth   Width

Thickness

Length

The joint pulled apart.

Top piece

Squared line

Gauged line

Bottom piece

The wood marked up.

Making a cross halving joint

1. Mark the width of the top.

2. Square down both edges.

3. Gauge half the thickness.

4. Saw to the gauged line.

5. Check the marked lines.

6. Chisel out the waste.

7. Saw the wood fibres.

8. Check with a straight edge.

9. Check the joint for fit.

Variations on the cross halving joint

Lap halving joint.

View of the underside.

Mitred, rebated and halved joint.

Housed and halved joint.

Making a cross halving joint
Both pieces must be of equal thickness. Place the top piece on the bottom piece, face sides uppermost, and mark the width of the top piece on the bottom piece (**1**). Square the marks across the bottom piece and halfway down both edges (**2**). Place the pieces in their original position and mark the width of the bottom piece on to the underside of the top piece. Set the marking gauge to half the thickness of the wood and gauge between the marks on the edges of both pieces from the face sides (**3**). Hold one piece in the bench-hook and saw across the grain just inside the squared line, down to the gauged line (**4**). Put the two pieces together and check that they will make a tight fit when the second cut is made to the marked line (**5**). Move the saw in relation to the squared line if necessary. Make one or two kerfs in the centre of the waste to enable it to be removed more easily. Secure the piece in the vice. With a bevel-edged chisel and mallet, chisel out the waste from the housing in stages (**6**). Work halfway in from each edge. With a saw, remove the fibres that do not come away cleanly (**7**). Check the flatness of the housing with a straight edge (**8**). Level out any remaining unevenness, chiselling with hand pressure only. Cut the second housing. Check the joint by putting the end of one piece into the housing on the other and vice versa (**9**). The joint should be tight enough to enable one piece to be lifted up by the other.

Variations on the cross halving joint
The lap halving joint is one of the easiest joints to make for frames. It needs reinforcing either with a through dowel or by gluing and screwing from the underside. The housed and halved joint is another variation on the cross halving joint and is similar to the bridle joint. Although more wood is removed than in the cross halving joint, the variation is stronger because of the two housings, which eliminate lateral movement. The mitred, rebated and halved joint is suitable for picture and mirror frames and it is stronger than the plain mitre joint. The lap allows a screw to be inserted from the underside. Drill the screw-hole near the mitre shoulder for additional strength.

An oblique halving joint

Side

Edge

The finished joint.

Length

Depth

Width

Length

The joint pulled apart.

Thickness

Top piece

Squared line

Bottom piece

Gauged line

The wood marked up.

Making an oblique halving joint

1. Place the sliding bevel on the rod.

2. Mark the length of the housing.

3. Mark in the housing.

4. Make the saw-cuts.

5. Chisel away the waste.

A dovetail halving joint

Side　　　End

The finished joint.

Edge

Length

Tail piece

Width

Thickness

Depth

Housing piece

Length

Thickness

The joint pulled apart.

Squared line

Gauged line

Gauged line

The wood marked up.

Making a dovetail halving joint

1. Gauge the wood.　2. Saw across the grain.　3. Mark in the tail slope.

4. Remove the waste.　5. Mark the housing.　6. Cut the housing.

Making an oblique halving joint
Both pieces must be of equal thickness. Take the oblique angle from the rod of the whole project. Hold the top piece in position on the rod, face side up. Place a sliding bevel against the edge, aligning the stock with the marks for the bottom piece (1). Set the bevel blade to this angle. Mark the width and position of the oblique housing on the edges of the top piece (2). Check the marks against the sliding bevel and use it to draw the oblique housing on the underside of the top piece (3). Square the marks halfway down the edges. Then mark the housing on the face side of the bottom piece in the same way. Gauge the depth of the housing on both pieces from the face sides. Remove the waste at the centre of each housing, where it is squared across, using a saw and bevel-edged chisel. To make the oblique saw-cuts, use a bench-hook and clamp the wood where necessary so that the cut can be made at the easiest angle. Make two straight saw-cuts. (4). Then chisel away the waste in the oblique corner pieces (5).

Making a dovetail halving joint
Mark the housing piece width on the tail piece. Square the marks across the underside and down both edges. Set the marking gauge to half the thickness of the wood and gauge along both edges and around the end (1). Remove half the thickness of the dovetail piece from the underside; saw a 3 mm/⅛ in kerf with the wood upright in the vice. Then clamp the wood at an angle and saw down the line gauged along one edge. Turn the wood around and repeat. Then put the wood upright in the vice again and complete the cut to the squared line. Put the wood on the bench-hook and saw across the grain (2). Square the line of the cut edges across the face of the tail piece. With a pencil, mark the angle of the tail slope by eye, or with a rule measuring 1 in 6 or 1 in 8 units (3). Repeat the slope on the other side. Saw the tail shoulders across the grain to the pencil marks. Remove the waste with a chisel, working along the grain towards the saw-cut (4). Mark the housing from the tail (5). Saw and chisel out the waste (see method above) (6).

119

Mortise & tenon 1

A through mortise and tenon joint

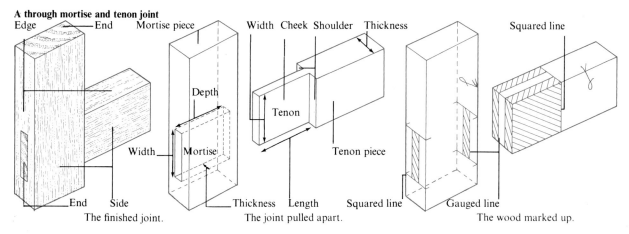

The finished joint. The joint pulled apart. The wood marked up.

Marking up a through mortise and tenon

1. Mark the length of the tenon.

2. Square all around the lines for the tenon.

3. Mark the mortise width from the tenon.

4. Square around the lines for the mortise.

5. Set the spurs of the gauge.

6. Set the gauge stock.

7. Check from the other side.

8. Gauge from the face side.

9. Gauge around the tenon end.

Marking up a through mortise and tenon

A tenon should generally be one-third the thickness of the tenon piece. The grain of the mortise piece should run along the width of the mortise so that the mortise can be chopped out against the grain. This will ensure a clean cut that is the exact width of the chisel being used. Mark the length of the tenon from the mortise piece, using a marking knife (1). Square the line around the tenon piece (2). Mark the width of the mortise from the width of the tenon piece (3). Square the line around to both edges (4). To mark the mortise thickness set the spurs of the mortise gauge to the width of the chisel to be used for chopping out the mortise (5). Set the gauge by eye so the marks are in the centre of the mortise piece (6). Check by placing the stock against the other side to see if the spur marks coincide (7). If they do not coincide, readjust the stock. When the mortise gauge is correctly set, gauge the mortise on both edges from the face side (8). To set out the tenon leave the gauge at the same setting but adjust the stock if joining woods of different thicknesses. Grip the tenon piece in the vice and gauge around one edge and the end from the face side (9). Then turn the wood around and gauge the other edge from the face side.

Chopping out a mortise

1. Chop from the middle of the mortise.

2. Stop 3 mm/⅛ in from the other end.

3. Lever out the waste from each end.

4. Chisel vertically, bevel inwards.

Sawing a tenon

1. Make a level cut.

2. Saw into tilted wood.

3. Saw to the line.

4. Saw off each shoulder.

5. Check the corners for fit.

Wedging a through mortise and tenon

A. Outside wedges.

B. Inside wedges.

Chopping out a mortise

Place the mortise piece on a piece of protective waste wood and clamp to the workbench. To prevent the wood splitting, the mortise must be chopped halfway through from each side. Begin chopping out by making an upright cut in the middle, then move the chisel backwards about 3 mm/⅛ in at a time with the bevel towards the middle (1). Stop 3 mm/⅛ in from the squared line (2). This allows for compression when levering out the waste. Reverse the chisel and continue from the middle to within 3 mm/⅛ in of the other end. Turn the chisel round and lever out the waste from each end to the centre (3). Finish by chiselling vertically on the end lines, bevel facing inwards (4). Unclamp the mortise piece and shake out any loose wood chips. Sweep the chips off the bench. Placing the uncut edge uppermost, reclamp the mortise piece to the bench. Repeat the chiselling and waste removal process to meet the previous cut from the other side of the mortise piece.

Sawing a tenon

Grip the tenon piece upright in the vice. At each stage of sawing work on both gauged lines on each side of the tenon. Position the saw against the waste side of the gauged line. Tilting it so it bites into the edge of the wood, saw down about 3 mm/⅛ in. Level out the saw and cut about 3 mm/⅛ in down (1). Regrip the tenon piece at a 45° angle. Saw to the squared line (2). Turn the tenon piece around and saw the other edge, again at 45°. Grip the tenon piece upright in the vice and saw straight down to the gauged line (3). Then, with the tenon piece flat, saw off the waste wood at each shoulder (4). To check the fit, try each corner of the tenon in the mortise (5).

Wedging a through mortise and tenon

Wedges give the joint extra strength. They can either be inserted on the outside of the tenon (A) or into saw-cuts in the tenon (B). Extend the mortise on the outside edge by chiselling at an angle 3 mm/⅛ in from the squared line to about half the mortise depth. If the tenon is very tight, grip the mortise piece in the vice so it does not split. Glue and insert the tenon and tap in the wedges alternately. Saw off the excess and plane flush.

121

Mortise & tenon 2

A stub mortise and tenon joint

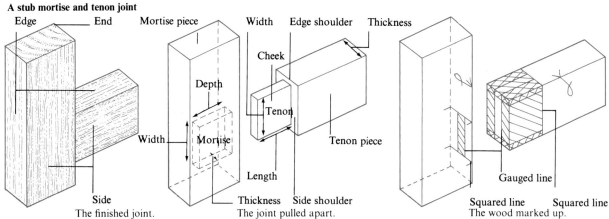

The finished joint.

The joint pulled apart.

The wood marked up.

Making a stub mortise and tenon

1. Establish the tenon length.

2. Saw the tenon.

3. Saw the edge shoulders.

4. Mark the mortise width.

5. Set the mortise depth.

6. Chop out the mortise.

Fox wedging

1. Insert the wedged tenon.

2. Clamp the joint.

Barefaced and offset mortise and tenon joints

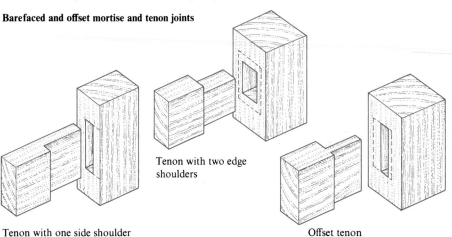

Tenon with one side shoulder

Tenon with two edge shoulders

Offset tenon

Making a stub mortise and tenon

Establish the required length of the tenon by holding it against the mortise piece (1). Mark up and saw the tenon (*see* pages 120 and 121) (2). With a marking gauge, mark the edge shoulders, which should be minimal so as not to weaken the tenon. (The edge shoulders will ensure that a gap does not appear when the wood shrinks.) Saw down to the squared lines and cut off the waste (3). Mark the mortise width from the completed tenon (4). Holding the chisel against the tenon, wrap masking tape around the blade to mark the depth of the mortise to be cut (5). Chop out the mortise to a little more than the required depth (6).

Fox wedging

Cut two wedges the thickness of the tenon. In the tenon make kerfs slightly longer than the wedges. Undercut the mortise base by 3 mm/⅛ in each end. Glue and insert the wedges into the kerfs. Glue and insert the tenon into the glued mortise (1). Tighten with a sash cramp (2). This exerts greater and safer pressure than hammering.

Barefaced and offset mortise and tenon joints

When joining a thin rail to a thick leg a "standard" tenon, with its equal side shoulders, will not give a strong joint at the front of the leg if the rail and leg are to finish flush. Therefore a barefaced mortise and tenon with only one side shoulder on the tenon is used. Make the mortise and the tenon (*see* pages 120-1). If the rail is to finish in the middle of the leg the tenon can have two edge shoulders. If the rail is to be inset from the front of the leg a slightly offset "standard" tenon can be used.

A bridle joint

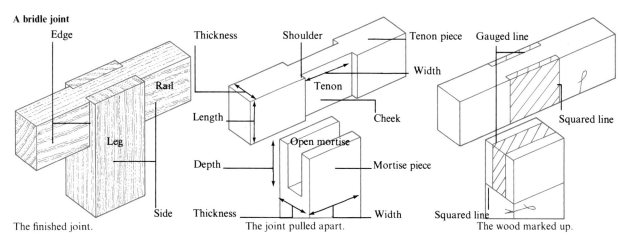

Edge
Rail
Leg
Side

Thickness
Shoulder
Tenon piece
Width
Tenon
Length
Cheek
Open mortise

Depth
Mortise piece
Thickness
Width

Gauged line
Squared line
Squared line

The finished joint.

The joint pulled apart.

The wood marked up.

Making a bridle joint

1. Mark the width of the mortise.   2. Mark the length of the tenon.   3. Saw down to gauged line.

4. Chisel the waste from the tenon.

5. Sever the fibres cleanly.

6. Check for flatness.   7. Level out.

8. Set the mortise gauge for the mortise.

9. Bore out the base.   10. Saw to the hole.   11. Remove waste.   12. Square up.

Making a bridle joint

A bridle joint is a reversed mortise and tenon and is used where the leg is thicker than the rail. Mark in pencil the width of the mortise on to the tenon (1). Then, to ensure a tight fit, square all around with a marking knife slightly inside the pencil lines. Mark the length of the tenon on to the top end of the mortise (2). Square all around the mortise piece. To form the tenon, mark a 5 mm/$\frac{3}{16}$ in recess either side of the tenon piece. Hold the tenon piece on the bench-hook and saw to the gauged line on the waste side of the line (3). Make one or two saw-cuts in the centre of the waste wood, which can then be removed more easily. Secure the tenon piece in the vice. With a bevel-edged firmer chisel and a mallet begin removing the waste wood. Rest the elbow on the bench and hold the chisel bevel upwards with the hand near the cutting edge. Hold the mallet just below its head. Chisel away a bit at a time halfway across; chiselling directly at the gauged lines may cause the wood to break away along the grain to a greater depth than required (4). If the fibres do not come away cleanly, saw slightly deeper into the waste wood to sever them (5). Check the tenon for flatness (6). Level out any remaining unevenness, chiselling with hand pressure` only — not a mallet (7). Set the mortise gauge to the thickness of the tenon (8). Adjust the stock on the top of the mortise piece and gauge around for the open mortise. Start cutting the mortise by boring a hole at the base, drilling into the middle from both sides (9). Saw along each gauged line down to the hole (10). Remove the waste wood (11). Square up the bottom of the mortise with a mortise chisel (12).

Mortise & tenon 3

A haunched mortise and tenon joint

Edge   End

Side   Edge

The finished joint.

Haunch   Haunch   Haunch
thickness   depth   width

Tenon
piece

Tenon

Thickness   Width   Cheek   Length   Depth

The joint pulled apart.

Mortise piece
Thickness
Width

Mortise

Gauged line

Gauged line
Horn
Haunch width

Squared line

The wood marked up.

Making a haunched mortise and tenon

1. Mark out the mortise.

6 mm/¼ in

2. Chop out the through mortise.

3. Saw either side of the crosshatched area.

4. Chisel out the waste.

5. Mark the haunch depth.

6. Mark the tenon width.

7. Cut wedges from the waste.

8. Check the joint for fit.

9. Saw off the horn.

Making a haunched mortise and tenon

Chiselling a mortise near the end of a piece of wood is likely to split the wood. To prevent this, mark up the mortise 19 mm/¾ in from the end. This waste, or horn, is cut off when the joint is complete. Mark the tenon piece width on the mortise piece, allowing for the horn and square across one edge. From the top mark come in the haunch width, which should be no greater than one-third the width of the tenon piece, and again square across the edge. Transfer this haunch mark and the lowest mortise mark to the outer edge, to give the limits of the through mortise (**1**). Set the mortise gauge and mark the thickness of the mortise, continuing 6 mm/¼ in around the end of the horn to allow for the depth of the haunch. Crosshatch the waste to distinguish it from the through mortise. Chop out the through mortise (*see* page 121) (**2**). Extend the mortise on the outside edge to take the wedges (*see* page 121). To make the entry for the haunch saw down to the 6 mm/¼ in gauge mark (**3**). Then chisel out the waste (**4**). Mark up and saw the tenon (*see* pages 120 and 121). Mark the depth of the haunch (**5**). Then mark the width of the tenon against the through mortise on the mortise piece (**6**). Cut two wedges from the waste on the tenon (**7**). Then cut off the remaining waste to form the haunch. Check the corners of the tenon for fit (**8**). If there is a gap at the shoulders check that the haunch is not too deep. If it is, deepen the haunch recess on the mortise piece rather than shortening the haunch. Glue and tap the mortise and tenon together. Glue and tap in the wedges alternately from the outside edge of the mortise piece. Then saw them off flush. Saw off the horn (**9**).

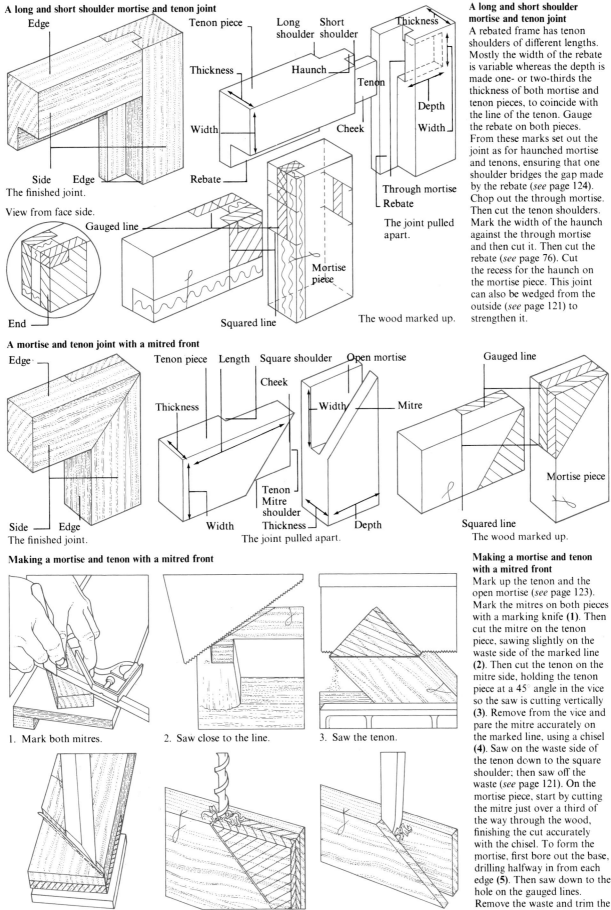

A long and short shoulder mortise and tenon joint

Edge

Side **Edge**
The finished joint.

View from face side.

Gauged line

End

Tenon piece **Long shoulder** **Short shoulder** **Thickness**

Haunch

Thickness

Width

Rebate

Tenon

Cheek

Thickness

Tenon

Depth

Width

Through mortise

Rebate

The joint pulled apart.

Mortise piece

Squared line

The wood marked up.

A long and short shoulder mortise and tenon joint

A rebated frame has tenon shoulders of different lengths. Mostly the width of the rebate is variable whereas the depth is made one- or two-thirds the thickness of both mortise and tenon pieces, to coincide with the line of the tenon. Gauge the rebate on both pieces. From these marks set out the joint as for haunched mortise and tenons, ensuring that one shoulder bridges the gap made by the rebate (*see* page 124). Chop out the through mortise. Then cut the tenon shoulders. Mark the width of the haunch against the through mortise and then cut it. Then cut the rebate (*see* page 76). Cut the recess for the haunch on the mortise piece. This joint can also be wedged from the outside (*see* page 121) to strengthen it.

A mortise and tenon joint with a mitred front

Edge

Side **Edge**
The finished joint.

Tenon piece **Length** **Square shoulder** **Open mortise**

Cheek

Thickness

Width

Mitre

Tenon Mitre shoulder

Width **Thickness** **Depth**

The joint pulled apart.

Gauged line

Mortise piece

Squared line

The wood marked up.

Making a mortise and tenon with a mitred front

1. Mark both mitres.

2. Saw close to the line.

3. Saw the tenon.

4. Chisel the tenon mitre.

5. Bore out the mortise base.

6. Trim the mortise base.

Making a mortise and tenon with a mitred front

Mark up the tenon and the open mortise (*see* page 123). Mark the mitres on both pieces with a marking knife (**1**). Then cut the mitre on the tenon piece, sawing slightly on the waste side of the marked line (**2**). Then cut the tenon on the mitre side, holding the tenon piece at a 45° angle in the vice so the saw is cutting vertically (**3**). Remove from the vice and pare the mitre accurately on the marked line, using a chisel (**4**). Saw on the waste side of the tenon down to the square shoulder; then saw off the waste (*see* page 121). On the mortise piece, start by cutting the mitre just over a third of the way through the wood, finishing the cut accurately with the chisel. To form the mortise, first bore out the base, drilling halfway in from each edge (**5**). Then saw down to the hole on the gauged lines. Remove the waste and trim the base with the chisel (**6**).

Mortise & tenon 4

A projected and wedged mortise and tenon joint

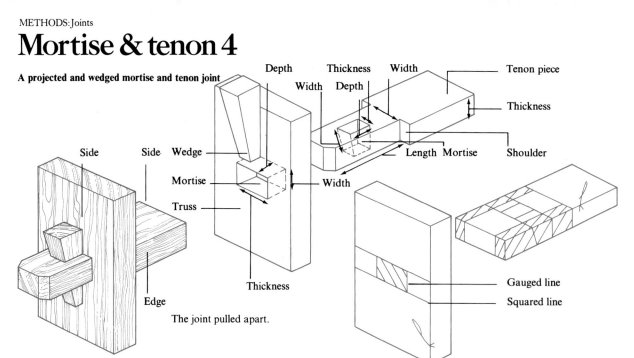

The finished joint.

The joint pulled apart.

The wood marked up.

Making a projected and wedged mortise and tenon

1. Place the tenon edge on the truss edge.

2. Mark the tenon position.

3. Gauge the mortise on the other side.

4. Bore out the waste.

5. Finish with a chisel.

6. Mark the truss thickness.

7. Mark the wedge angle.

8. The mortise shape.

9. Gauge the mortise thickness.

10. Cut the slanting side.

11. Saw the tenon shoulders.

Making a projected and wedged mortise and tenon

Mark the position of the mortise on the truss. The mortise width must be equal to the thickness of the tenon piece. Square these lines on both sides. Mark the tenon shoulders. The width of the tenon should be one-third the width of the truss. Position the edge of the tenon against the edge of the truss (1). Measure the remaining width and divide by two. This gives the distance of the tenon from each edge (2). Gauge the mortise marks on the other side of the truss (3). Bore out the waste from the mortise with a brace and bit (4). Complete the mortise using a chisel (5). Mark the thickness of the truss on the tenon (6). Then mark the tenon mortise slightly in from this first mark. Mark the depth of the tenon mortise, so, at its deepest, it is about half the protruding tenon length. Cut a wedge for the mortise. The wedge length should be about four times the thickness of the tenon. Mark the profile of the mortise by holding the wedge with its straight side tight against the first mortise mark. Then mark along the tapered side (7). The mortise and wedge shapes (8). Gauge lines for the thickness of the mortise on both sides of the tenon (9). Remove the waste with a brace and bit and finish with a chisel. Cut the straight side first, then the slanting side (10). Saw the tenon shoulders (11). Lightly chamfer the edges of the tenon and the wedge. Use this joint for collapsable structures, so do not apply glue unless a permanent joint is required.

A pinned joint

Back edge

Front edge

Top

The finished joint.

Tenon piece

Gauged line

Housing depth gauge line

Mortise depth gauge line

Mortise

Mortise depth

Tenon (or pin)

Tenon length

Width

Housing depth

Thickness

Front shoulder

Stopped housing

The joint pulled apart.

Gauged line

Mortise piece

The wood marked up.

Making a pinned joint

1. Saw away the tenon waste.

2. Mark the first shoulder.

3. Mark the housing depth.

4. Set the bit to the housing depth.

5. Clear the housing.

6. Saw the housing.

7. Chisel out the waste.

8. Level the housing.

9. Mark the mortises.

10. Bore out the mortise waste.

11. Check the tenon width.

Making a pinned joint

Mark the thickness of the tenon piece on the mortise piece in pencil. Then mark just inside the line with a marking knife to ensure a tight fit. Set the cutting gauge to the mortise depth and gauge around the tenon piece, except on the back edge. Gauge around 3 mm/⅛ in inside the first line except on the front edge. This gives the housing depth. The front edge of the mortise piece takes the form of a stopped housing. Gauge the front shoulder line on the top, end and bottom of the tenon piece 10 mm/⅜ in from the edge, as far as the housing gauge mark. Mark the front of the first tenon a further 10 mm/⅜ in in from the front edge to guard against splitting. Gauge this line on the top, end and bottom to the mortise depth gauged line. Divide the remaining width of the tenon piece into equal spaces for the tenons (*see* page 56). Gauge the width for each tenon on the top, end and bottom of the tenon piece, between the mortise gauge marks. Saw off the front shoulder. Then saw down the sides of the tenons on the waste side of the lines. Remove most of the waste with a coping saw (**1**). Finish with a chisel. Place the tenon piece on the mortise piece and mark the position of the front shoulder (**2**). Then mark the depth of the housing on the edge of the mortise piece (**3**). Set a forstner bit to drill to this depth (**4**). Bore a series of overlapping holes at the end of the housing to form clearance for the saw when cutting the sides of the housing. Remove the waste at the stopped end of the housing with a chisel (**5**). Saw down the sides of the housing (**6**). Then chisel out the waste (**7**). Level out the housing to a depth of 3 mm/⅛ in with a router (**8**). From the tenons, mark the positions of the mortises in the housing, making sure the face edges are coincident (**9**). Set the forstner bit against the front edge of the mortise piece to drill to the depth of the tenons. Bore out most of the waste for the mortises with the forstner bit (**10**). Before chopping out the mortises, check the width of the individual tenons against the mortises (**11**). Chisel out the waste, and try the joint. If it is too tight, plane the bottom of the tenons; do not attempt to widen the housing. This joint has a large area for gluing, making it particularly strong.

Mortise & tenon 5

Power tools are particularly useful if a number of joints of the same size are to be cut. To speed up the marking-out process, clamp the pieces together and square the marks across. Once the tools have been set up, the joints can be cut quickly and accurately. The hollow square mortise chisel and bit, shown here in a power drill fitted in a special mortising stand, can be used in many different power tools, from factory production mortisers to drill presses and portable drills. Not all drill manufacturers make mortising stands.

Mortising stand for power drill

Feed handle

Power drill

Drill support

Column

Hollow chisel lock

Hollow square mortise chisel and bit

Hollow chisel

Depth stop

Vertical hold-down

Vertical hold-down height adjustment knob

Horizontal hold-down

Base

Using a hollow square mortise chisel and bit

The bit, which is similar to an auger, fits inside the hollow chisel. It bores just ahead of the chisel, which squares up the hollow as it is lowered into the work; it does not revolve. The chisel and bit cut mortises ranging from $6\,mm/\frac{1}{4}$ in to $13\,mm/\frac{1}{2}$ in. The mortise is cut as a series of overlapping square holes from one end to the other. First adjust the mortiser for depth of cut. A through mortise should be cut halfway through from each side. Position the work with the chisel lined up to make the first cut at one end of the mortise (1). Set the hold-downs so it is possible to slide the work under them. Start the drill. Lower the chisel and bit. Cut the mortise (2).

1. Position the work.

2. Cut the mortise.

Using a power router

Mortises can be cut quickly using a power router and square cutter. The wood thickness must be no more than twice the maximum depth of the cutter for a through mortise. The depth of a stub mortise is restricted by the cutter depth. Set up guides to restrict the side to side travel of the router. Then switch on and cut the mortise.

Using a power router.

Cutting tenons

The bandsaw is the ideal machine for cutting tenons. To cut a series of tenons quickly and accurately, set the guide fence and make all the cross-grain shoulder cuts first. Readjust the fence and then make all the cuts along the grain for the tenon cheeks at the same time.

Spacing collar

A disk cutter on a spindle moulder makes deep cuts. Form a series of tenons using two disk cutters separated by spacing collars adjusted to the tenon thickness.

Sliding fence

Waste wood

Work-piece

Set the disk cutters and make a sample tenon; check for fit in the mortise. When the cutters are correctly set, back each tenon piece with waste wood to prevent the wood from splintering. Cut each tenon, supporting the wood on the end-grain extension table.

Comb

A comb joint

The finished joint.

Thickness of work-piece

Length of tongue

Width of kerf

The joint pulled apart.

Making a comb joint

Because this joint is cut on the table saw, the pieces are all exactly the same shape. The large gluing area gives the joint its strength. The comb jointing fence must be used. This has a kerf to clear the blade and a metal stop that is finely adjusted by a knob at one side (**1**). It is attached to the mitre fence, which is set at 90°. The tongues should be square so their length is equal to the thickness of the work-piece. Set the blade height to this thickness (**2**). Fix wobble washers to the blade to enable it to make a wide kerf. The tongues are the same width as the spaces between them. This distance must be no more than the maximum width of the kerf (**3**). Use two pieces of waste wood (A and B) that are the same thickness as the work-pieces (X and Y) to determine the width of the tongues. Adjust the stop on the comb fence, and make a kerf on piece A so that the tongue left on the edge is narrower than the kerf (**4**). Adjust the stop, and make a kerf on piece B so that the tongue is wider than the kerf (**5**). Then gradually diminish the tongue on piece B until it makes a sliding fit into the kerf on piece A (**6**). Do this by bringing the stop in closer to the blade and taking fine cuts from the tongue. Lock the comb fence in position when the fit is right. Then take work-piece X. Hold it face side towards the blade and, with its edge tight against the stop, make a kerf (**7**). Lift the piece over the stop and, with the edge of the kerf tight against the stop, make a second kerf (**8**). Repeat this process across the edge of piece X. Reverse piece X so its face side rests against the fence. Place the last kerf against the stop. Set work-piece Y face side towards the fence, and hold it tight against piece X. Make the first kerf in piece Y (**9**). Remove piece X. Continue making kerfs across the edge of piece Y to complete the joint (**10**).

Making a comb joint

Stop

1. Use the comb jointing fence.

2. Adjust the blade height.

Saw table

Wobble washer

Maximum width of kerf

3. Assess the tongue width.

4. Cut a kerf in piece A.

5. Make the tongue wider than the kerf.

6. Fit the tongue into the kerf.

7. Hold work-piece X against the stop and kerf.

8. Make a second kerf.

9. Make a kerf in piece Y.

10. Continue to make kerfs in piece Y.

Dovetail 1

A carpenters' through dovetail joint

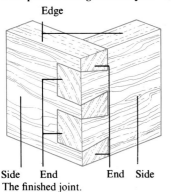

Edge

Side End End Side
The finished joint.

Socket piece

Tail piece

Socket Pin Tail Shoulder
The joint pulled apart.

Half thickness of socket piece

6 mm/¼ in

Gauged line Squared line Gauged line
The wood marked up.

Dovetail proportions

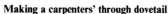

6

1

8

1

Softwoods Hardwoods

Using a dovetail template.

Dovetail proportions

The optimum slope for a dovetail is 1 in 6 for softwoods and 1 in 8 for hardwoods. Softwood cells compress more easily and so require a steeper slope. Too steep a slope produces a sharp dovetail, leaving weak short grain at the corners. Too shallow a slope would be ineffective as the joint could be pulled apart. For repeated marking, make a dovetail template from hardwood or aluminium.

Making a carpenters' through dovetail

1. Set the gauge to the wood thickness.

2. Set out the tails.

3. Mark the tail slopes.

4. Saw the tails.

5. Cut the shoulders carefully.

6. Remove most of the waste.

Making a carpenters' through dovetail

Set the cutting gauge to the wood thickness (1). Gauge the thickness of the socket piece all around the tail piece and the thickness of the tail piece on both sides of the socket piece. On each end of the tail piece mark in from the edge a distance equal to half the thickness of the socket piece. Measure the distance between the lines marked on the end as there should be a 6 mm/¼ in gap to accommodate a pin between each tail. Subtract 6 mm/¼ in for each pin. Divide the remainder by the required number of tails to give the width of the tails (2). Mark the tail slopes using a dovetail template or sliding bevel (3). Secure the wood in the vice at a slant so the proposed saw-cuts are vertical. Saw on the waste side of the lines. Then change the angle of the tail piece and make the cuts on the other side of the tails (4). If the saw wanders from the marked line, continue in a straight line. (The sockets will be cut to fit the tails.) Saw off the shoulders on the waste side of the line, keeping a finger against the waste to prevent it from suddenly falling away and causing the saw to slip (5). Remove most of the waste between the tails quickly and neatly with a coping saw (6). Chisel out the remainder of the

7. Chop out the remaining tail waste.

8. Chalk the end of the socket piece.

9. Line up the plane with the socket piece.

10. Mark around the tails.

11. Square the lines down.

12. Saw the pins.

13. Chop out the sockets.

14. Remove the sharp corners.

15. Tap the joint home.

waste. Using as wide a chisel as possible, chop halfway through the tail piece, first from one side then from the other. Chop near the line first, chisel upright, bevel outwards. Then chop precisely on the line. When only a few tails are being made, a quick and simple method is to hold the wood by sitting on it (7). Mark the sockets directly from the tails. Use the following method whenever possible as it is simple, quick and accurate. Rub chalk all over the end of the socket piece so that any scribed marks will show up clearly (8). Lay a plane on its side close to the vice and secure the socket piece in the vice with the end level with the top of the plane (9). Tighten the vice and push the plane away. Rest the tail piece on the plane and the end of the socket piece, keeping the edges flush and the shoulders in line with the inside surface of the socket piece. Mark round the tails with a scriber (10). Square the marked lines down to the cutting gauge mark (11). Place the socket piece back in the vice, projecting it only slightly to minimize vibration. Make vertical saw-cuts just inside the scribed lines (12). Remove most of the waste with a coping saw. Finish by chopping out the sockets with a chisel held at an angle, following the slope of the tail (13). Chisel halfway from each side. Remove the inside sharp corners of the tails with the chisel to give the sockets a lead-in (14). Dovetail joints fit correctly only once, so try the joint by tapping only partly into position. Remove, smooth the inside surfaces and glue both pieces. Then, using a piece of waste wood to spread the pressure, hammer the joint home (15).

Dovetail 2

A cabinetmakers' dovetail joint

The finished joint.

Edge

Side   End   End   Side

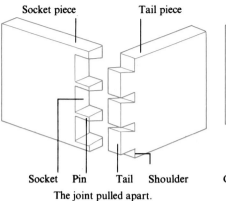

Socket piece   Tail piece

The joint pulled apart.

Socket   Pin   Tail   Shoulder

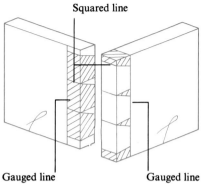

The wood marked up.

Squared line

Gauged line   Gauged line

Making a cabinetmakers' dovetail

1. Square the tail marks.

2. Make the vertical saw-cuts.

4. Saw the socket piece.

3. Draw the saw through the kerfs

5. Clean out the waste with the saw tip.

Experienced cabinetmakers' method

1. Hold the saw at an angle.

2. Saw off the shoulders.

3. Chop out the tails.

Making a cabinetmakers' dovetail

Set the cutting gauge to the thickness of the tail piece and gauge round the socket piece. Then set it to the thickness of the socket piece and gauge round the tail piece. Chalk all over the tail piece end grain; then mark and square across 6 mm/$\frac{1}{4}$ in from each end. Divide the distance between by the number of tails required. Square across and mark in the tail slopes (**1**). Cut the tails (**2**). Chalk the end of the socket piece and set it upright in the vice. Rest the tail piece on the plane and the edge of the socket piece. Draw a dovetail saw through each of the kerfs (**3**). Square the marks down the face side. As a guide to which side of the marked line to saw out the sockets, align the tail piece with the socket piece, then saw (**4**). Remove the waste with a coping saw and finish cutting the sockets with a chisel. Use a 3 mm/$\frac{1}{8}$ in bevel-edged chisel to chop out the tails. Clean out the waste using the chisel and the tip of the dovetail saw (**5**).

Experienced cabinetmakers' method

Mark up the tails on all the relevant pieces. Put all the tail pieces together upright in the vice. Make all the saw-cuts for one side of the tails first, holding the saw at the angle of the tail slope (**1**). Then make all the cuts for the other side of the tails. Chalk and mark the socket pieces, pairing them with individual tail pieces. Clamp the tail pieces back in the vice and saw off the shoulders (**2**). Stagger the tail pieces one on top of the other, and clamp. Chop the tails halfway through on each piece. Turn the wood over. Stagger and clamp the pieces and complete the tails (**3**). Stagger and clamp the socket pieces similarly and chop out the pins and sockets.

A through dovetail housing joint

Side
Top
Edge

The finished joint.

Tail piece   Tail

The joint pulled apart.

Gauged line

The wood marked up.

A stopped dovetail housing joint

Housing piece

Through housing

The finished joint.

Tail

Gauged line   Shoulder

The joint pulled apart.

Stopped housing

Making a through dovetail housing

1. Mark the housing edge.

2. Gauge around the tail end.

3. Gauge along the housing.

4. Mark the tail slope.

5. Chisel the tail.

6. Saw the sides.

7. Chisel the housing.

Making a stopped dovetail housing

1. Mark the stopped housing.

2. Saw down the housing sides.

3. Chisel out the housing.

4. Mark the tail length.

5. Saw off the waste.

Making a through dovetail housing

Mark the thickness of the tail piece on to the edge of the housing piece (1). Square round. Set the cutting gauge to half the thickness of the housing piece. Gauge round the end of the tail piece (2). Then gauge along the edges of the housing piece (3). On the edge, mark 3 mm/⅛ in in from both sides of the tail piece (4). Repeat on the other edge. Connect each gauge point to its adjacent corner. Saw the tail shoulders. Chisel out the waste along the grain (5). Mark the tail outline on the housing piece, holding the tail piece tight to the half thickness gauged line. Repeat on the other edge of the housing piece and square the marks across the side. Then saw down the housing sides (6). Chisel out the waste (7).

Making a stopped dovetail housing

Mark and cut the tail (*see* method above). Mark the housing; then mark where it is to be stopped (1). Saw as far as possible down the sides of the housing from the stop mark to the half thickness gauged line (2). Make a saw-cut in the centre of the waste. Chisel away the waste horizontally, going no deeper than the saw-cuts. (Alternatively bore a series of overlapping holes along the housing, using a forstner bit set to the half thickness gauged line.) To clear the waste from the housing, start chiselling vertically in the middle; work towards the sides (3). Mark the housing length on to the tail (4). Saw off the waste at the tail shoulder (5). Saw across the grain first.

Dovetail 3

A through dovetail joint with mitre

The finished joint.

The joint pulled apart.

The wood marked up.

Edge

Mitre shoulder

Tail piece

Socket piece

Tail

Shoulder

Socket

End   Pin

Side

Side

Side

Gauged line

6 mm/¼ in

Squared line

Gauged line

6 mm/¼ in

Making a through dovetail with mitre

1. Saw the mitre edge.   2. Saw the shoulder.

3. Mark sockets from the tail piece.

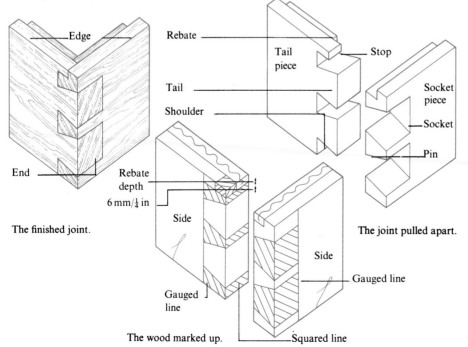

4. Finish the mitre with a chisel.

Making a through dovetail with mitre

Both pieces must be the same thickness. Set the gauge to this thickness and mark the sides and bottom edge of the tail piece. Gauge both sides of the socket piece. Mark the mitre on the face edge of both pieces with a marking knife. Mark 6 mm/¼ in in from the face edge of the tail piece for the mitre shoulder and then another 6 mm/¼ in. Mark 6 mm/¼ in in from the bottom edge. Set out the tails between these marks. Saw the mitre edge on the tail piece near the mitre (1). Finish with a chisel. Then saw down to the mitre shoulder (2). Finish with a chisel. Saw and remove the waste between the tails. Mark the sockets from the tail piece (3). Saw the mitre. Finish with a chisel (4). Round the mitre edge with a plane and a fine abrasive.

A through dovetail joint with rebate

The finished joint.

The joint pulled apart.

The wood marked up.

Edge

End

Rebate depth

6 mm/¼ in

Side

Gauged line

Rebate

Tail piece

Tail

Shoulder

Stop

Socket piece

Socket

Pin

Side

Gauged line

Gauged line

Squared line

A through dovetail joint with rebate

Leave a projection on the shoulder of the tail piece to act as a stop for the rebate on the socket piece. Cut the rebates first. Mark in the depth of the rebate on the edge of the tail piece. Mark 6 mm/¼ in in from the rebate for the first tail. Mark 6 mm/¼ in in from the bottom edge for the last tail. Set out the tails between these marks and make saw-cuts between the tails. Remove the waste between the tails. Chalk the end grain of the socket piece. Mark and chop out the sockets (see pages 130–1). Cut the rebate shoulder and the shoulder on the bottom edge of the tail piece.

A decorative through dovetail joint

Edge End Edge

Pin Tail Shoulder

Socket piece   Tail piece

Socket

The finished joint.

The joint pulled apart.

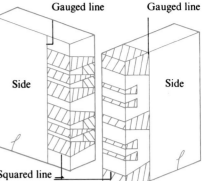

Gauged line   Gauged line

Side   Side

Squared line

The wood marked up.

Making a decorative through dovetail

1. Saw the dovetail slope.

2. Chop out the waste.

3. Clean out the corners.

4. Gauge the end of the socket piece.

5. Mark the pins.

6. Saw between the pins.

7. Remove the waste.

8. Form the small pins.

9. Chisel to the cut fibres.

10. Work down to gauged line.

11. Chop two pins at once.

Making a decorative through dovetail

Set the cutting gauge to the thickness of the wood and mark around the tail piece and along both sides of the socket piece. (If both pieces are not of the same thickness, set out the thickness of the tail piece on the socket piece and vice versa.) Mark 6 mm/¼ in in from each edge for the shoulders. Set the gauge to half the thickness of the wood and gauge across the sides of the tail piece to give the length of the small tails. Set out the tails. The small tails need not be spaced equally within the large tails; they should be finely proportioned — more like cabinetmakers' dovetails than carpenters' dovetails. With the wood upright in the vice, saw down the slopes of the tails, making all the cuts on one side first (1). Saw off the shoulders. Remove the waste between the large tails with a coping saw. Chisel out any remaining waste between the tails (2). Clean out the corners (3). Chalk the end of the socket piece. Gauge half the thickness of the wood on the end of the socket piece to mark the depth of the small pins (4). Mark the pins from the tails, using a saw (5). Hatch and crosshatch the waste areas carefully. Make vertical saw-cuts between the pins (6). Remove the waste with a coping saw (7). Form the small pins by chopping across the grain (8). Then chisel as far as the severed fibres (9). Gradually work down to the half thickness gauged line (10). Using a wide chisel, chop out two pins at once for a cleaner line (11).

Dovetail 4

A lapped dovetail joint

Edge   End   Edge

The finished joint.

Socket   Pin

Lap

Socket piece

The joint pulled apart.

Tail

Shoulder

Tail piece

6 mm/¼ in

Tail length

Gauged line

Squared line

Inside surface   Inside surface

The wood marked up.

Making a lapped dovetail

1. Mark the sockets.

2. Saw the sockets.

3. Saw away the corners.

4. Cut across the grain.

5. Cut along the grain.

6. Clean out the corners.

A double lapped dovetail joint

Edge   End   Edge   Lap   Pin

Socket

Socket piece

The finished joint.

Lap width

Gauged line

Squared line

Inside surface

Tail

Lap
Rebate
Shoulder

Tail piece

The joint pulled apart.

Inside surface

6 mm/¼ in

Gauged line

The wood marked up.

Making a lapped dovetail

The tails are hidden by being cut shorter than usual and by being overlapped by the socket piece. First decide on the length of the tails. Long tails have a stronger hold but, if they are too long, only a thin lap will be possible on the socket piece. As a general rule, leave about 6 mm/¼ in for the lap. Set the gauge to the tail length and gauge the end of the socket piece from the inside surface. Gauge all around the tail piece. Mark and cut the tails (see pages 130–1). Chalk the end grain of the socket piece up to the gauged line. Mark the sockets from the tails **(1)**. With the wood upright in the vice, saw the sockets tight against the line **(2)**. Stop when the saw touches the gauged lines on the inside surface and the lap. To enable it to come away more easily, saw away the corners of the waste **(3)**. Place the socket piece flat on the bench and remove the waste, chopping across the grain **(4)**. Then chop along the grain as far as the severed fibres **(5)**. Avoid the corners when chopping along the grain, otherwise the wood may split. Clean the corners out carefully, using a 6 mm/¼ in bevel-edged chisel **(6)**.

Making a double lapped dovetail

The tail piece can overlap the socket piece, as shown, or vice versa. (If the socket piece overlaps, the tails must be marked from the sockets.) Decide on the width of the lap (see method above). Gauge this width on the end of both pieces from the face sides. From the tail piece end, gauge the rebate, with the same setting as the lap width, around the inside surface and both edges. Set the gauge to the thickness of the socket piece and gauge the inside surface of the tail piece. To form the rebate, saw across the grain **(1)**. Then chisel down the grain. Clean up the rebate with a shoulder plane, working from both edges to the centre **(2)**. Mark 6 mm/¼ in in from

Making a double lapped dovetail

1. Saw the rebate for the lap.

2. Clean up the lap.

3. Set out the tails.

A secret mitre dovetail joint

Edge

The finished joint.

Mitre

Mitre shoulder

Socket

Socket piece

Tail

Mitre shoulder

Mitre

Pin

The joint pulled apart.

End

Inside surface

Squared line

Gauged line

6 mm/¼ in

End

Gauged line

Inside surface

The wood marked up.

Making a secret mitre dovetail

Gauged line

1. Mark the mitre on the edges.

2. Mark the pins with the template.

3. Saw the mitre edge.

4. Form the mitre lap.

5. Mark the tails from the pins.

6. Saw the mitre.

7. Chop out the waste.

each edge of the tail piece and set out the tails between these marks (**3**). Remove the waste at the shoulders and between the tails in the same way as chopping out the sockets in the lapped dovetail joint.
Chalk the end grain of the socket piece and mark the sockets from the tails. Saw and chisel away the waste, cutting the corners away first to ease the chiselling process.

Making a secret mitre dovetail

Both pieces must be the same thickness. Set the cutting gauge to the thickness of the wood and gauge the inside surfaces of both pieces from the end. To mark the rebates, set the gauge to 6 mm/¼ in and, on both pieces, gauge the end from the face side and the inside surface from the end. Mark the mitre on the edges of both pieces, using a knife or chisel (**1**). Square the rebate line down to the mitre line on both edges. Cut both rebates (*see* method above). For this joint it is necessary to form the pins and sockets before the tails. Chalk the end of the socket piece. Mark lines 6 mm/¼ in from the edge of the rebate on the socket piece, parallel to the edge. Then mark in a further 6 mm/¼ in. Mark the pins using a cardboard template the width of the widest part of the tails and with the required slope on each side (**2**). For marking in a rebate, a cardboard template is more convenient than a wooden one, which would be awkward and the sliding bevel could not be adjusted close enough. Square the marks down the inside surface. Saw the mitre edges on each side (**3**). Then saw down to the mitre shoulders. Chop out the sockets in the same way as in the lapped dovetail joint. Place a backing piece, cut and planed to 45°, behind the socket piece and align it with the top of the mitre shoulder. Secure it in position so it supports the plane. Form the mitre lap with a shoulder plane (**4**). (The backing piece is needed as the mitre area is so small.) Mark the tails from the pins on the inside surface of the tail piece (**5**). Square the lines into the rebate. Saw the mitre (**6**). Then chop out the waste between the tails and the waste between the mitre shoulders and the tails (**7**). Plane the mitre lap.

Dovetail 5

A bevelled dovetail joint

Edge

Side

End

The finished joint.

End-grain bevel

Tail

Socket piece

Tail piece

Socket

Pin

Shoulder

The joint pulled apart.

Thickness line

Bevel

Centre of tail

Bevel end marks

The prepared wood marked up.

Elevation

Y

Y₁

X

Plan view

Y₃   Y₂   Y

A₁

A

End-grain bevel angle

X₂ X

Side angle

B₁

B

Z

Rod, or full-size drawing.

Making a bevelled dovetail
Before this joint can be made, the true shape of the end must be obtained from a rod, or full-size drawing, because the sides as seen in elevation and in plan are sloping and are therefore foreshortened. Draw the elevation showing the slope and the thickness of the wood. Directly underneath, draw the plan view. If the side elevation is pivoted to lie flat, the true shape is seen when looking straight down on it. On paper in the elevation, pivot Y around X to Y_1. Project Y_1 vertically to Y_2, that is, until the line is level with Y in the plan view. Join X in the plan to Y_2. The angle between XY_2 and XZ is the angle of the sides. To work out the end-grain bevel angle, draw the outside edge of the side on the plan (Y_3X_2). From any point on line XY_2, draw a line AB at right angles. Draw a line A_1B_1 parallel to AB, the thickness of the wood away, reaching to line Y_3X_2. Join A to A_1. The angle between AB and AA_1 represents the end-grain bevel angle.

Preparing the pieces for jointing

1. Set the side angle.

2. Transfer the angle.

3. Set the end-grain bevel.

4. Mark this on the edges.

5. Plane the end grain.

Preparing the pieces for jointing
Both pieces of wood must be the same thickness. Set the side angle using a sliding bevel against the rod (**1**). Transfer the angle to both pieces of wood (**2**). Saw and plane the ends. Check the angles with the sliding bevel. Set the sliding bevel to the end-grain bevel angle against the rod (**3**). Mark this angle on the top and bottom edges of each piece (**4**). Connect up the lines along the inner and outer sides of each piece. Plane the end grain to these lines (**5**). Check with the sliding bevel.

Cutting the tails and sockets

1. Mark out the thickness of the wood.

2. Saw the tail slopes.

3. Chop out the waste.

4. Mark the socket lines parallel with the edges.

A machine dovetail joint

Side

Groove

Front

A

B

Parts of a drawer or box.

Back

C

D — Side

Stop screws

Stop screws

B   B

A   C

1   2

D   D

C   A

3   4

Order of cutting the joints.

Making a machine dovetail

1. Insert the guide collar.

Cramping bar

A

B

Stop screws   Cramping bar

2. Clamp the pieces in the jig.

3. Clamp the template on top.

4. Cut the joint.

5. Let the bit cut each tail.

6. The completed cut.

Cutting the tails and sockets

Mark the thickness of the wood on both sides of each piece (1). Set out the centres of the tails parallel to the top edge. Then set out each tail relative to its centre line. Place the wood in the vice so one set of tail slopes is vertical. Cut these (2). Change the angle and complete the cuts. Connect up the two thickness lines across the edges. With the thickness lines vertical, saw off the shoulders. Saw out the waste between the tails. Chop out the remaining waste, working to the centre from each side (3). Chalk and mark the socket piece from the tails (*see* page 131). Mark the socket lines on the side parallel with the edges (4). With socket lines vertical, saw away most of the waste. Chop out the sockets. Plane a bevel on the top and bottom edges so they are horizontal when the joint is put together. The angle is the same as the end-grain bevel.

Making a machine dovetail

Through or lapped dovetail joints can be cut with the power router fitted with a dovetail bit guided by a jig and template. Both sides of the joint are cut at the same time. The sides are offset against stops in such a way that, as the router follows the template fingers, it cuts the recess between tails in the vertical piece at the same time as it cuts a socket in the horizontal piece. For a four-sided box or drawer, mark the pieces and make the cuts in the order shown. Always cut a joint in waste pieces first to determine the depth of cut. If the drawer sides are grooved to take the bottom, cut the groove first. Insert the template guide collar into the router sole plate (1). This will ride against the template. Cut and plane the pieces to size. Clamp them with face sides against the jig and the ends flush and abutting against the stop screws on the jig; this will automatically give the required amount of offset (2). Use the stop screws on the left or the right according to which of the four corners are being jointed. Clamp the template on top (3). To cut the joint, run the router fully round the contour of the template fingers (4). The guide collar runs against the template, while below it the bit makes the tail cut (5). The completed cut (6). Then unclamp the pieces and cut the next joint.

Housing

A through housing joint

Side

End

Edge   Housing depth

The finished joint.

Squared line

Edge

Gauged line

The housing piece marked up.

A stopped housing joint

End

Side

The finished joint.

Housing
piece

Through
housing

Shelf

Shelf
piece

The joint pulled apart.

Stopped
housing

Shelf

Shoulder

The joint pulled apart.

Making a through or stopped housing

1. Mark the shelf thickness.

2. Gauge the housing depth.

3. Chisel on the lines.

4. Chisel horizontally.

5. Level with a router.

Chisel the stopped end square.

A barefaced housing joint

Housing width   Thickness

The finished joint.

Rebate   The joint
pulled apart

Housing depth The wood
marked up

Making a through or stopped housing

Mark the thickness of the shelf piece on the side of the housing piece with a marking knife or a chisel (1). Square the lines across the face side and down both edges. Set the marking gauge to one-third the thickness of the housing piece and gauge the housing depth between the squared lines on both edges (2). With a bevel-edged chisel and mallet cut across the grain inside the squared lines. Then chisel on the lines (3). To provide shoulders for the router to run against, chisel horizontally to a depth of approximately 3 mm/⅛ in (4). Work into the centre from both edges. Level the housing with a router (5). Test the joint for fit; if it is too tight, plane a shaving off the bottom of the shelf piece. (For alternative methods *see* pages 76, 127, 133.)

In a stopped housing joint a shoulder must be cut in the face edge of the shelf piece. Mark the thickness of the shelf on the housing piece in pencil. Square the lines down the rear edges, and gauge the housing depth between these marks. With the gauge at this setting, gauge around the face side, underside and face edge of the shelf. Decide how far in from the edge the housing will be stopped and cut a shoulder at this point on the shelf piece. Re-mark the thickness of the shelf on the housing with a marking knife or chisel. Mark the stopped end of the housing. Clear the stopped end by drilling a few overlapping holes with a forstner bit. Chisel shoulders for the saw to run against. Chisel the stopped end square. Cut the housing in the same way as the through housing joint.

A barefaced housing joint

Pencil the thickness of the top on the housing piece. Square the marks down the edges. Mark the housing width to one-third this measurement. Square the lines down the edges. Gauge the housing depth from the inside surface. Cut the housing. Gauge the housing width on the end of the top and gauge the depth on the edges. Saw across the grain down to the gauged marks. Then gradually chisel down to the sawn line. Finish the rebate with a shoulder plane.

Dowel

A dowel joint

Side —

End — Edge —

The finished joint.

Width

Length —

Thickness

The joint pulled apart.

Squared line

Gauged line

The wood marked up.

Making a dowel joint

1. Drive through the plate.

2. Cut equal lengths.

3. Chamfer the dowel ends.

4. Saw a kerf in the dowel.

5. Mark the joint with pins.

OR with dowel centres.

Fence lock Fence

Drill bush

Adjustable head

Steel rod

Reference head

Carrier lock

A dowelling jig. Cramp head Carriers

Bushes guiding the drill bit.

Variations on the dowel joint

Edge to end dowel joints are often used as a substitute for mortise and tenons. Dowels can also strengthen mitres and join pieces meeting at an awkward angle. Stagger dowels when joining thick pieces of wood. When dowelling into end grain, drill the end grain holes first. When joining at an angle, insert the dowels at right angles to the joint surface for a strong joint. Clamp the wood at an angle so that the holes are drilled vertically wherever possible.

Variations on the dowel joint

Edge to end joint.

Dowelled mitre joint.

Making a dowel joint

Dowels can be made with a metal dowel plate, which has holes of varying sizes. (Proprietary dowel rods and standard-size dowels are the alternatives.) Roughly chisel a cylindrical shape from square-sectioned beech wood cut to the diameter of the appropriate hole. Cut a lead-in at one end and drive the wood through the hole with a hammer (1). To cut all dowels to the same length first make a jig. Butt the dowel rod against a nail the required distance from a kerf in the back batten. Saw through the kerf (2). Chamfer both ends of the dowel for easy entry into the hole; use a dowel rounder in a brace or power drill (3). Saw a kerf along the dowel to allow air and surplus glue to escape from the hole (4). Dowel holes must be accurately aligned in both pieces. Mark up one piece, squaring the hole positions across and gauging them centrally along the wood. Tap in panel pins and cut off their heads. Align the second piece and tap it down. Remove it, revealing the central impressions (5). Remove the pins. (Alternatively, drill the holes in the first piece, and insert a dowel centre into each hole. Align the second piece and tap it down.) All holes in both pieces must be the same depth — the combined depth being slightly greater than the length of the dowel — so use a depth stop. Countersink all dowel holes for easy entry. A dowelling jig makes accurate dowelling easier. The type shown has two steel rods on which two carriers slide. Select the right sized bushes and insert them in the carriers to guide the drill bit. Position and tighten the carriers and fences, with the reference head against one end of the work. Lock the adjustable head against the other end. Drill the holes in one piece. Invert the jig and drill the second piece.

Edge and tongue & groove

A rubbed glue joint

A tongued and grooved joint

A slot-screwed joint

Groove

Tongue

Slot piece

Screw piece

Making a rubbed glue joint

1. Plane the first edge.

2. Check the mating edge.

3. Check the alignment.

4. Glue both edges.

5. Rub the edges together.

6. Check the joint.

Making a tongued and grooved joint

1. Make a cut at one end.

2. Mark the blade position.

3. Centre the tonguing blade.

Making a slot-screwed joint

Screw position lines

Slot end lines

1. Square slot lines across.

2. Gauge along the edges.

3. Insert the screws.

Making a rubbed glue joint
Hold one piece in the vice and plane the edge with the longest bench plane available (1). Try to plane a hollow in the centre of the piece. The length of the plane will make this impossible, but the attempt will help to prevent the ends being rounded over. Finish planing by taking one continuous shaving. Check for perfect squareness. Plane the mating edge similarly, checking it continually by moving it against the first edge to feel for points of friction at the ends (2). Check the alignment of the sides with the plane edge (3). Hold the edges of both pieces in contact, and glue them (4). Rub the edges together to remove any air from the joint (5). Clamp up the joint. Apply light pressure at first, then tighten, checking the evenness of the joint as the pieces are tapped down flush with a hammer (6).

Making a tongued and grooved joint
Cut the whole joint with a plough plane. To centre the groove, make a cut at one end with the rebating blade (1). Then reverse the plane and make a second cut. When the cuts coincide, cut the groove. Lay the rebating blade centrally on the edge of the tongue piece and mark its position (2). Guided by the marks, centre the tonguing blade and cut the tongue (3).

Making a slot-screwed joint
Select the face sides and mark accordingly. Mark the positions for the screws 44 mm/1¾ in from each end and at intervals of 150 mm/6 in. Place the pieces in the vice with the screw piece offset by 13 mm/½ in. Square screw position lines across both pieces. Square slot lines across the slot piece 13 mm/½ in to the left of the screw position marks (1). Gauge half the wood thickness along the marked

4. Bore holes at the slot ends.

5. Chisel the slots.

6. Tap the ends flush.

edges (2). Insert the screws, leaving the heads projecting by 13 mm/$\frac{1}{2}$ in (3). Bore holes to take the screw-heads in the slot piece on the screw position marks, 13 mm/$\frac{1}{2}$ in deep. Drill holes to take the shanks at the end of the slot lines, 13 mm/$\frac{1}{2}$ in deep (4). With a narrow chisel, cut slots 13 mm/$\frac{1}{2}$ in deep (5). Fit the larger holes in the slot piece over the screw-heads and tap the ends flush (6).

A mitre joint with loose tongue

A keyed mitre joint

The finished joint.

The joint pulled apart.

The finished joint.

The joint pulled apart.

Making a mitre joint with loose tongue

1. Mark the tongue width.

2. Measure across the mitre.

3. Gauge around the mitre.

4. Chisel the groove.

5. Mark the waste on the tongue.

Making a mitre joint with loose tongue
Cut the mitre in a mitre box. Cut a strip of wood for the tongue about one-third the thickness of the mitred pieces and about 16 mm/$\frac{5}{8}$ in wide. Put the mitre pieces together. Lay the tonguing strip centrally on top and mark its width (1). Square the marked line parallel to the mitre and down both edges. Place the tongue on edge on a mitre end, flush with one side. Measure across what remains of the mitre (2). Divide by two. Set the marking gauge to this measurement and gauge around the mitre to the squared lines (3). Saw down the mitre to the squared lines. Chisel the groove in the mitre end (4). Fit the joint together with the tonguing strip in place and mark the waste on the tongue (5). Remove the tongue; saw it to size. Glue the joint and tongue together.

Making a keyed mitre joint

1. Saw two kerfs.

2. Tap the key into the kerfs.

3. Saw the keys off flush.

Making a keyed mitre joint
Cut and glue the mitre pieces; clamp and leave to dry. Position the mitre in the vice so the saw cuts level with the work surface. Cut two kerfs, angling each slightly inwards (1). Cut the key strips from 2 mm/$\frac{3}{32}$ in three-ply or from veneer, depending on the size of the kerf. Glue the key strips and the kerfs and tap the keys into the kerfs (2). Allow to dry. Saw the keys off and plane them flush with the joint (3).

143

Pivoting

A knuckle joint

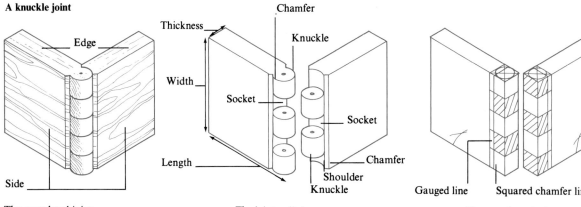

Edge

Side

The completed joint.

Thickness

Width

Socket

Length

Chamfer

Knuckle

Socket

Chamfer

Shoulder

Knuckle

The joint pulled apart.

Gauged line   Squared chamfer line

The wood marked up.

Making a knuckle joint

1. Draw diagonals.

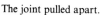
2. Draw a circle on each edge.

3. Square around both pieces.

4. Saw the chamfer.

5. Plane the chamfer.

6. Round the knuckle.

7. Smooth the rounded end.

8. Divide the width equally.

9. Gauge around the knuckles.

10. Saw between the knuckles.

11. Remove the waste.

12. Shape the curve.

Making a knuckle joint

The pieces must be of equal thickness. Set the cutting gauge to the thickness of the wood; gauge round the sides and edges of both pieces. Draw diagonals on the edges (1). Set a compass to half the wood thickness and draw a circle on each edge (2). Position a try square where the diagonals bisect the circumference of the circle near the gauged line and square around the sides and edges of both pieces to mark the chamfer lines (3). With a dovetail saw, cut along each chamfer line down to the circle (4). Before forming the chamfers, make a 45° backing piece; clamp it behind the chamfer line. With a shoulder plane, form the chamfer flush with the backing piece (5). Partially round the knuckles from the chamfers using the shoulder plane (6). Round the end of the wood to the circle mark using first a smoothing plane and then the shoulder plane. With a gouge make a concave-shaped sanding block to fit the curve. Using the block and a coarse and then a fine abrasive paper, smooth the rounded end of the work-piece (7). Divide the width of the work-piece equally by the total number of pins in the knuckle (in this case, five) (8). Set the gauge for each mark and gauge around the knuckles from the face edge on each piece (9). Hatch in the waste areas. Saw down between the knuckles on the waste side of each gauged line allowing for a filed finish (10). Saw off the shoulders. Remove the waste between the knuckles with a coping saw (11). Clean out the sockets with a chisel. Shape the curve on the shoulders using a chisel with a rocking motion and an in-cannel gouge (12). Finish by paring vertically with an in-cannel gouge up to the knuckle (13). For a smooth movement,

13. Pare the shoulders.   14. File the knuckles.   15. Drill a hole through the joint.

file the knuckle surfaces lightly and test the joint for a friction fit (14). Complete the rounding of the sockets with a narrow chisel. Clamp the joint. Bore a hole through the centre of the joint, working from both sides (15). To ensure that the drill remains vertical, position a try square alongside the bit or use a drill stand. Insert a steel pivoting rod through the hole and cut it flush.

A rule joint

The joint with flap up.   The joint with flap down.   Section through the joint.   The wood marked up.

Making a rule joint

1. Plane to the quadrant mark.   2. Shape with a scratch stock.   3. Smooth the quadrant.

4. Mark the cove.   5. Form the cove.   6. Shape with the scratch stock.

7. Mark around the hinge.   8. Chisel the knuckle recess.

Making a rule joint
Glue waste wood to the edges to prevent splintering. Finger gauge a line 3 mm/⅛ in down from the face side of the top along the end and both edges. Repeat on the underside. The distance between these two lines is the radius of the quadrant. Set a plough plane to this distance and cut rebates on the face of the top and the underside of the flap. Square the shoulder line down one edge of the top; where it intersects the bottom shoulder line is the circle centre. Draw the quadrant with a compass. Clamp a square backing piece flush with the shoulder and plane to the quadrant mark (1). Shape the quadrant finally with a scratch stock made to fit (2). Smooth using a shaped sanding block (3). Mark the cove from the quadrant (4). Chamfer the cove edge of the flap against a 45° backing piece. Roughly form the cove profile with an out-cannel gouge (5). Check the profiles of the edges together, then finish with the cove cutter in the scratch stock (6). Smooth. Chisel and plane off the waste wood. Square the rebate line around to the underside of the top. Align the hinges, knuckles up and centred on the line. Mark around each hinge (7). Chop out flap recesses with a scooping action. Mark and chisel the knuckle recess (8).

Working manufactured boards 1

The most popular manufactured boards are plywoods (three-ply, multi-ply, battenboard, blockboard and laminboard), chipboard and hardboard. They make maximum use of wood material that might otherwise be wasted, and so they are usually more economical than solid wood. The natural figure in plywoods is generally plain due to the rotary slicing process; chipboard and hardboard have no figure.

The chief advantage of working with manufactured boards is that they do not distort as a result of shrinkage or natural warping. Carcass construction is therefore made considerably simpler because allowance does not have to be made for dimensional change. Distortion in battenboard, blockboard and laminboard is minimal as the plies sandwiching the solid wood strips restrain the tendency of the growth rings to straighten themselves. Any distortion that might occur in three-ply or multi-ply, where each veneer is laid at right angles to the next, is balanced out by its construction. Both chipboard and hardboard have no natural grain direction across which to shrink.

Manufactured boards, however, will warp if they are incorrectly stored. Damp boards usually warp and may even disintegrate. They should be stacked vertically against a dry wall resting fully on their edges with the top corners supported and protected from damage. Apart from chipboard, manufactured boards can only be used outside when specially treated. Tempered hardboard is impregnated with oil, and marine multiply is resin bonded, making it water resistant.

In addition to their stability, manufactured boards are useful because they are supplied in large sheets.

Cutting

A. Support a large sheet.

Cutting

A power saw is the most effective tool to cut manufactured boards, but, unless laminated, they may also be cut with a panel or a tenon saw in the same way as solid wood. A tenon saw with its fine teeth held almost horizontally is preferable for thin boards. Never use a rip saw. The resin adhesive in marine three-ply and chipboard quickly blunts saw teeth, so for these boards tungsten-carbide-tipped teeth are best. Make sure the saw blade always cuts into the face so any ragged edge that may result will be on the underside. To minimize this ragged edge, stick adhesive tape on the underside along the cutting line. When sawing, support both sides of the board close to the cutting line. To cut a large board, climb on to the workbench and kneel close to the cutting line. Have an assistant support a large overlap to prevent it from snapping off unevenly towards the end (A). Three-ply that is up to 3 mm/$\frac{1}{8}$ in thick can be scored with a cutting gauge and snapped cleanly in two by holding it along the work-top edge against a stop and pressing on the overlapping piece (B). A laminated board can be sawn with a panel or tenon saw, but the leading edges on the teeth should be raked back more than usual. Always saw into the laminate and keep the teeth well clear of the laminate on the backward stroke to prevent it from chipping. To hold a laminated board firmly while sawing, clamp two battens close to the cutting line. Place blocks of the same thickness as the laminated board between the two battens at both ends. Then saw halfway across the board from both sides (C). This will leave a clean edge.

B. Hold the piece against the work-top edge.

C. Saw halfway across a laminated board.

This makes them particularly suitable for wide, flat components. Hardboard and sheets of three-ply or five-ply are commonly used for panelling; multi-ply is for carcass tops, shelving and doors. For shelving, the solid core strips must run from end to end for greatest support. For doors, the strips should run vertically as screws do not hold in the end grain. Chipboard is most suitable for carcass construction and doors.

The edges of manufactured boards are both unsightly and easily damaged if they are not lipped, either with veneer or solid wood. Nails, screws and pins should be set between 100 mm/4 in and 150 mm/6 in from one another, and should never be fixed closer to the edges than 13 mm/$\frac{1}{2}$ in as the edges are liable to break. Use a twist drill for boring small holes in manufactured boards and a flat bit for large holes.

Before drilling plastic laminated surfaces, stick two layers of adhesive tape over the spot to be bored. Then make a pilot hole with a small twist drill.

It is not always necessary to apply a surface finish to manufactured boards because most are ready primed and sealed; many are also laminated or veneered. If not treated, three-ply, multi-ply and blockboard may be finished in any way suitable for solid wood. Both these and chipboard are porous and should be well sealed and may be gently keyed for veneer.

While three-ply and hardboard are conducive to bending, chipboard and blockboard are rigid. To achieve the maximum curve, three-ply should be steamed and bent across the short grain of the outer veneers. Hardboard is even more flexible when bent with the rough textured side on the outside.

Smoothing

A. Plane the edges from the ends inwards.

B. Plane laminated board edges at an angle.

Smoothing
The wide surfaces of a manufactured board should not be planed, as they are pre-finished. Plane the edges from the ends inwards (A). If the plane runs off the end, chipping will occur. Cut resin-bonded boards to exact size to avoid planing as resin blunts the blades. Smooth chipboard edges with a Surform or rasp. Remove the woolly burr left on planed hardboard edges by glasspapering with a sanding block. Smooth the edges of laminated boards away from the laminate and at an angle with a Surform (B).

Lipping

A. Veneer lipping laid second.

B. Veneer lipping laid first.

C. Solid wood lipping.

D. Feathered lipping.

E. Grooved multi-ply.

F. Grooved chipboard.

G. Grooved laminboard.

H. Loose tongue lipping.

J. Tongued multi-ply.

Lipping
Where edges have split, re-glue them and clamp until dry before lipping. Hardboard is lipped only in combination with solid wood. If veneer lipping is laid after face veneer, the thin lipping edge will show on the face. If the lipping is done first, the face veneer will cover the lipping edge, but there is a risk of the face veneer lifting. To avoid both problems smooth the top edge of the face veneer to a 45° angle (A, B). All solid wood lipping that shows on the face side should be mitred. Lipping should be left proud of wide surfaces until the glue has dried. It can then be smoothed to any shape. Apply self-adhesive strip veneer lipping with a warm iron. Edges can also be lipped with solid wood (C). Feathered lipping does not show on the top surface (D). Lipping that is tongued and grooved provides the strongest join. Multi-ply, blockboard and chipboard may be grooved (E, F, G). Loose tongues can be used (H). It is always best to cut the tongue from solid wood if lipping blockboard or chipboard, though a tongue in multi-ply is quite strong (J).

Working manufactured boards 2

Fixing

Three-ply and multi-ply can be fixed with screws or nails against a solid wood frame or another sheet of three-ply or multi-ply. Choose nail and screw sizes to ensure a firm grip in the underneath piece. Nails can be used to secure glue joints. Their heads must be left projecting above the surface so they can easily be withdrawn when the glue is dry (**A**). As well as fixing with nails, veneer pins, panel pins and oval brads can also be used (**B**). When using screws, drill a clearance hole, which can be countersunk (**C**). The most durable method of fixing three-ply and multi-ply is with a combination of glue and nails (**D**) or glue and screws (**E**). Nails and screws must not be fixed into three-ply and multi-ply edges as they will split the plies.

Knock-down fittings

If three-ply or hardboard is used to panel hollow doors, secure a fitting, such as a handle, to the face with a hollow door fitting (**H**). Push the anchor partially through a drilled hole in the face with a hammer; then screw it tight. Once the anchor is in position, its arms will have opened and will be pulled flat against the other side of the face. A chipboard screw (**J**) has a thread profile designed specifically to grip in chipboard without the need for a bush. The countersunk screw-head will lie flush with the surface. It can be concealed with a cover cap, which is pressed or screwed into a special recess in the head. Use a block joint (**K**) to join chipboard panels at right angles. Screw one part into the chipboard side and screw the other into the side of a perpendicular piece of chipboard. The two dowels in one part fit into the recesses in the other. The parts are then screwed together tightly. Use a modesty block (**L**), which is less obtrusive, for corner joints in light constructions or for strengthening. The knock-down dowel fitting (**M**) is strong and neat. Fit the plastic dowel into a drilled hole in the side of chipboard and fit the bush into a perpendicular board in the same way. Then tighten a machine screw into the bush. A strong joint can be made with a cross dowel and guide dowels (**N**). The metal cross dowel has a threaded hole across its axis to accommodate a machine screw.

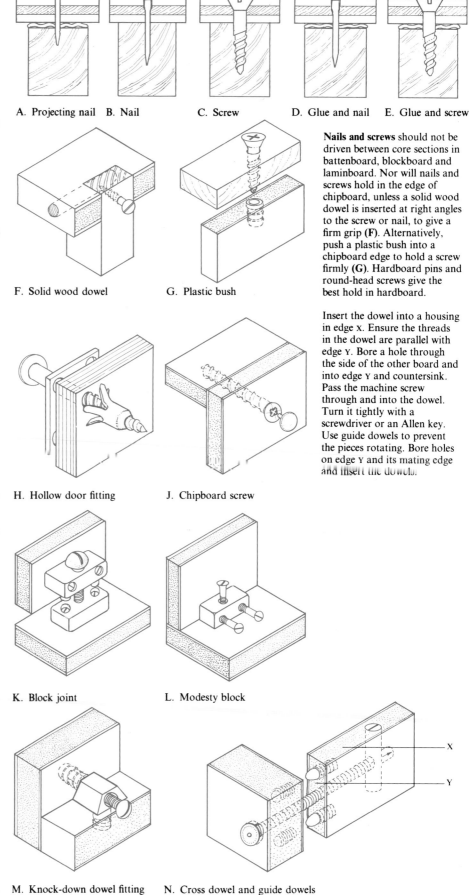

A. Projecting nail B. Nail   C. Screw   D. Glue and nail E. Glue and screw

F. Solid wood dowel   G. Plastic bush

Nails and screws should not be driven between core sections in battenboard, blockboard and laminboard. Nor will nails and screws hold in the edge of chipboard, unless a solid wood dowel is inserted at right angles to the screw or nail, to give a firm grip (**F**). Alternatively, push a plastic bush into a chipboard edge to hold a screw firmly (**G**). Hardboard pins and round-head screws give the best hold in hardboard.

Insert the dowel into a housing in edge x. Ensure the threads in the dowel are parallel with edge Y. Bore a hole through the side of the other board and into edge Y and countersink. Pass the machine screw through and into the dowel. Turn it tightly with a screwdriver or an Allen key. Use guide dowels to prevent the pieces rotating. Bore holes on edge Y and its mating edge and insert the dowels.

H. Hollow door fitting   J. Chipboard screw

K. Block joint   L. Modesty block

M. Knock-down dowel fitting   N. Cross dowel and guide dowels

Jointing multi-ply

A number of solid wood joints can also be cut in multi-ply. These include the barefaced housing joint (**A**) and all other housing joints; the pinned joint (**B**) and the dowel joint (**C**). The cross halving joint (**D**) can be cut in the width of the multi-ply. The barefaced tenon joint (**E**) and bridle joint (**F**) can be cut if the mortise piece is thick enough. The tongued and grooved joint (**G**) makes a strong edge joint. Joints such as the through dovetail (**H**), decorative through dovetail (**J**) and double lapped dovetail (**L**) can be cut, provided the tails and pins are coarse. The comb joint (**K**) can be cut only on a table saw. With the projected and wedged mortise and tenon joint (**M**), the wedge must be cut from solid wood and should be about four times the thickness of the tenon.

Jointing boards other than multi-ply

N. Dowel

P. Tongued and grooved

Q. Barefaced tongued

R. Housed dowel

S. Tongued and grooved

T. Reinforced with glue blocks

V. Dowel

W. Rebated solid wood

Jointing boards other than multi-ply

In many respects battenboard, blockboard and laminboard can be jointed in the same way as solid wood. Amongst the most suitable joints are dowel joints (**N**) and housed dowel joints (**R**). A tongued and grooved joint can be cut across solid core strips — never along their length (**P**). Battenboard, blockboard and laminboard can be cut under similar conditions for a tongue but not a groove; a loose tongue can also be used. A barefaced tongued joint cut into solid wood (**Q**) is quite strong. Few of the traditional joints can be cut in chipboard as the fibres tend to crumble. Joints are usually made in conjunction with solid wood, the chipboard being rebated into the solid wood and reinforced with glue blocks (**T**). A tongued and grooved joint can be used, providing only the groove and never the tongue is cut from the chipboard (**S**). The tongue must always be cut from plywoods or solid wood. Grooves in chipboard are best cut with a portable circular saw used with wobble washers. A dovetail joint is not strong in chipboard but dowels give adequate strength (**V**). Since hardboard is generally used for panelling in conjunction with a solid wood frame, hardboard rarely needs jointing. However, a strip of solid wood double rebated to take a sheet of hardboard on either side and secured with panel pins can make a strong joint for panelling (**W**).

149

Carcasses and frames

Every piece of furniture can be classified into one or more of three types of unit — storage, supporting or seating. Each type of unit consists of components assembled into one of three basic constructions — frame, box or stool. From these basic constructions any kind of furniture unit can be made.

Common to all are the allowances for movement of the wood. When a solid board is fixed to another splitting along their length may occur because wood shrinks across the grain. The development of frame and panel construction allowed for this movement in the wood as the panels were able to move independently of the frame. The direction of movement must be considered when boards have to be joined side edge to side edge, or end to end at right angles as for a corner joint. Wood moves across the grain and the growth rings tend to straighten as the wood dries, causing cupping. Join narrow boards side edge to side edge so that the movement of one board is counteracted by the next. Ideally, join boards with their growth rings at right angles to the wide surface.

Before assembling a carcass, make a preliminary unglued knock-up to ascertain the order of assembly and to check fit. Wherever possible, break the carcass down into sub-carcasses each comprising several components, and assemble each unit separately. Assemble and roughly adjust all cramps; prepare any cross-bearers and cramping blocks. Collect the relevant tools: a hammer, a mallet and a striking block of waste wood, a soft pencil, measuring and testing tools, a damp rag for wiping off surplus glue and a quirk stick for cleaning glue out of corners. Mark joints and components with the soft pencil on the face side and number them with the order of assembly. Smooth all inside surfaces and inside all joints with a smoothing plane and abrasive paper. Glue and assemble the components into their parts. Any dowels or loose tongues can be glued into one side only; then check for length. Wipe off all surplus glue before it sets. Check for squareness and leave until the glue has set before assembling the units into a complete carcass. Remove heavy cramps as soon as possible.

Types of structure

Piece of furniture	Constructional form		
	Frame	Stool	Box
Blanket chest	*	*	
Bureau		*	*
Dresser	*	*	*
Table		*	
Chair		*	
Bed		*	

Frame

Stool

Box

Frame, box and stool are the three basic solid wood constructions from which all units of furniture can be made. They give strength and also allow for the free movement of the wood.

The dresser is a complex form of storage unit consisting of a stool frame supporting two kinds of storage unit — a shelf unit, or large solid-sided box, and a cupboard closed by frame and panel doors.

Why frame and panel construction developed

Early planked oak chests, made from solid boards nailed together, split at the front and back because the vertical grain of the boards at the sides resisted the movement in the wood at the front and back.

In frame and panel construction a solid frame, mortised and tenoned together, is filled in with panels that are free to move in grooves formed along the inside edges of the rigidly fixed frame.

How wood moves

A

B

C

D

To counteract shrinkage and the tendency of growth rings to straighten (**A**), try to use boards with their growth rings as near as possible at right angles to the wide surface (**B**) of the completed work.

A joint made with the heart side inwards as at C will tend to loosen as the outside edges curl away. For a tight, well-fitting joint, arrange the boards with the heart side outwards and the grain as shown at D.

For a solid wood box construction arrange the boards so that the grain in the top, bottom and cheeks runs around the carcass, allowing all the boards to move in a uniform manner.

Measuring and testing carcasses

E

F

G

H

To check if a carcass is square measure the diagonals with a squaring rod placed inside one corner. If the diagonals differ, then the carcass is out of square by half that distance; readjust with cramps.

Check the openings of all carcasses, frames and boxes for squareness. Check all four corners. Put small flat frames on a known level surface and check them for winding.

If a frame is out of square (E) correct it by slanting the cramps to pull the frame square. If the frame is "in winding" (**F**), apply cramps to pull the higher corners down and the lower corners up.

When clamping across the width of a carcass use crossbearers from front to back (**G**). Any surfaces that bow inwards can sometimes be corrected by clamping in the opposite direction (**H**).

Basic carcass construction 1

Carcass types

Back rail

Side rail

A₂

Front rail

A₁

M

X Y

Side rails

A. Solid wood carcass

Pilaster

Side rail

B₁

B₂

B. Chipboard carcass

C. Knock-down carcass

D   E   F   G   H

Carcass backs

J
Side

Top

J. Rebated back

Side   Back

K

Side

Front

Side

Side

Bottom

M

Side

K. Muntin back

L

Side

Shelf

Side

L. Grooved-in back   M. Frame and panel back

Carcass types

In solid wood carcasses, rails are lap dovetailed to the corner posts, which are mortised to receive the tenons on the side rails (**A₁**). Posts and side rails are grooved to accept fielded panels. A triangular fillet, dowelled to the front or back rail and dovetailed to the side rail, is often added for strength (**A₂**). Note that the short grain at x is weak and may split, so replace the acute angle at y with a right angle. M can be a tongue in a groove (as shown), or a mortise and tenon. Front pilasters, added for rigidity, may be tongued and grooved or attached with small glue blocks on the inside. Carcass construction in manufactured boards can be simpler than solid wood construction as movement is negligible; tenons and dovetails are structurally weak so corner joints can be barefaced tongued and grooved (**B₁**), rebated (**B₂**) or mitred and glue blocked. For other joints *see* pages 148–9. A lap joint can be reinforced by screwing and pelleting. Most knock-down fittings, such as the block joint (**C**), have been designed for use with chipboard (*see* pages 256–7). If a carcass is not rigid, distortion can lead to doors and drawers jamming, and failure of joints. Methods of ensuring rigidity include fixed shelves and partitions, and the addition of pilasters secured to the carcass front or back at the sides (**D**), at the centre (**E**), attached to a bottom rail (**F**), in T (**G**) or in H (**H**) form.

Carcass backs

A back does more than cover a gap: the carcass depends on it for rigidity and stability. The simplest form of back is a five-ply panel screwed into rebates worked in the sides and top (**J**). The carcass bottom is flush with or overlapped by the back. Hardboard may be screwed or pinned. Five-ply and hardboard can also be fitted in grooves worked in the sides. The carcass bottom and any shelves must be flush with the groove to allow the back panel to be slid in after assembly (**L**). A frame and panel back, suitable for a large carcass, can be screwed into a rebate, or may be tongued and grooved (**M**). A muntin back (**K**) consists of one or two grooved uprights, or muntins, tenoned or rebated and screwed into the top and bottom with fill-in panels, usually of three-ply.

Plinths

Dovetailed bracket
Mitred plinth

A₂

Lapped dovetail

A₁

A. Loose mitred plinth

B. Projecting plinth with mitred moulding

Front

Back

C. Bracket feet   D. Recessed plinth

E. Tongued-in rail

Cheek or plinth

Front rail

Back rail

Carcass top or bottom

F. Screwing through slots

G. Pocket screwing

Plinths

Complex secret dovetail joints may be used on plinths, but it is more common to make a plain mitre joint at the front, reinforced by a glue block or dovetailed bracket (**A₁**). The back may be housed into the sides, tongued and grooved or lap dovetailed (**A₂**). A large plinth will require a cross-bearer, which should be housed or slot dovetailed to front and back. A projecting plinth with moulding is constructed with mitred corners. The moulded board supports the carcass and is mitred at the front and glue-blocked in the corners beneath and along the sides (**B**). Bracket feet are used on antique and reproduction furniture. The front feet are mitred together and glue-blocked while the back feet are lap dovetailed (**C**). Recessed plinths, which do not require precise fitting, allow room for standing up against the furniture. A lapped dovetail at the front is typical (**D**). A variation often used with cupboards and wardrobes is to bring the cheeks down to floor level and rest the bottom on an inset plinth rail tongued into the cheeks (**E**). Plinths and tops can be secured in the same way. Solid wood ones should be fixed by gluing and screwing to the front rails and screwing through slots at the back (**F**). Wooden buttons (*see* page 163) or metal shrinkage plates (*see* page 257) can also be used. Plinths and tops of manufactured board can be glued and pocket screwed (**G**).

Carcass tops

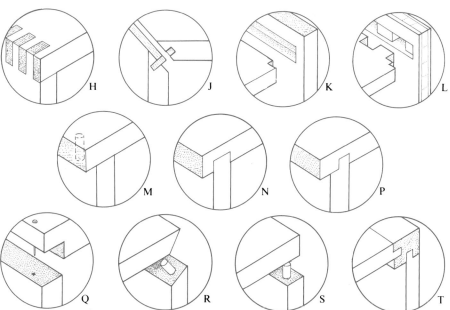

H

J

K

L

M

N

P

Q

R

S

T

Carcass tops

Where the top forms an integral part of the carcass and is not screwed on, dovetail or lapped dovetail are the most common joints. Double lapped and secret mitre dovetails are used for a hidden joint. The machine-made comb joint can also be worked (**H**). A mitre joint should be reinforced with a loose tongue (**J**). Tops that are set below the top ends of the carcass cheeks can be secured in a stopped housing (**K**). However, a pinned joint, because of its greater gluing area, is stronger (**L**). With manufactured boards oversailing tops can be fixed to the cheek ends by dowels (**M**), housings (**N**) or tongues (**P**). Flush tops can be housed in a grooved corner block of solid wood (**T**), rebated, then pinned and the holes filled (**Q**), mitred and dowelled (**R**) or butted and dowelled (**S**).

Basic carcass construction 2

A carcass without a back
Strong, well-fitting corner joints are necessary to ensure strength and rigidity. In solid wood, secret dovetails with a single lapped joint at the bottom (A_3) and a double lapped joint at the top (A_1) are usual. Shelves increase strength and prevent the cheeks bowing. All forms of housing joint are suitable, in any materials, although a through housing looks unsightly on the front edge. A stopped housing is neater and preserves the vertical line at the sides of the

carcass. The addition of stub tenons, making a pinned joint, increases the strength. A barefaced dovetail housing (A_2) can be cut only in solid wood; this joint is strong as it resists any outward pull. The housing is tapered in its length and the shelf is inserted from the rear. Fixed shelves in manufactured boards may be dowelled (B_1) or tongued (B_2) to the cheeks. Other methods include screwing through the cheeks into the ends of shelves or using knock-down fittings (*see* page 256).

Pinned joint

A_1

A_2

Through housing

Stopped housing

A_3

A. Solid wood carcass with fixed shelves

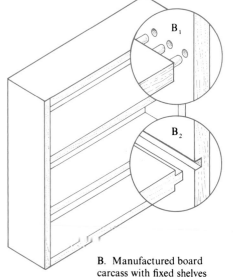

B_1

B_2

B. Manufactured board carcass with fixed shelves

C_1

C_2

C_3

C. Adjustable shelves

Adjustable shelves
These are best made from manufactured boards as they are less likely to warp. They may be supported by plastic studs tapped into holes in the cheeks (C_1); ideally the holes should be fitted with a metal or plastic bush. Metal bookcase fittings (C_2) should be let flush into the cheeks. Magic wires (C_3) provide a concealed fitting (*see* page 264). When adjustable shelves are included it is advisable to have a back panel to ensure rigidity. Increase the strength by fixing one of the shelves permanently in position by the addition of a rail to the front or back, or by screwing through the back panel into the back edge of one or more shelves.

Carcass rails
In the construction of a carcass without a back, such as a bookshelf, that is likely to be subjected to heavy loading and have a tendency to ricking, the addition of full-width rails will increase rigidity considerably. Most large knock-down cupboard or shelving units made of chipboard need rails to hold the side panels vertical. They may be pediment rails, front rails, back rails or plinth rails inset under the base. The rails may be lap dovetailed to the cheeks, dowelled (D_2), stub tenoned (D_1), tongued or secured with a knock-down fitting such as a block joint or a bolt and cross dowel (*see* pages 256–7). Rails can be used for fixing the carcass to a wall; this will increase the rigidity in the same way as the addition of a back. Rails may also be used for hanging the carcass.

Pediment rail

Back rail

Front rail

D_1

D_2

Plinth rail

Hanging a carcass without a back

A bevelled rail tongued to the carcass or screwed to the carcass back can hook over a corresponding rail attached to the wall. Flushmount fittings and keyhole plates can also be used, as can cabinet hangers (*see* page 257).

A carcass with a back and drawers

The inclusion of a drawer needs careful planning from the start as the position of drawer rails, runners, kickers and guides, and how to fix them, has to be considered as does the construction of a central division. A basic chest of drawers made with multi-ply or blockboard sides and bottom should have solid wood carcass rails and a drawer rail, which is stub tenoned to the sides (A_3). Drawer runners of solid wood are glued and screwed to the sides. A similar unit in chipboard should have solid wood runners screwed to the sides of the carcass and have dowelled rails (**B**).

Drawer runner

Drawer rail

B. Basic frame for a chest of drawers in chipboard

Carcass rail

Fix rails with a lapped dovetail. Use double tails for solid wood if the rail is wide enough (A_1). Make the single tail in blockboard extra wide so it will hold in the varying grains of the core (A_2).

A. Basic frame for a chest of drawers with solid ends

Rails, runners, kickers and guides

Hanger

Centre kicker

Kicker

Side

C_1

Side runner

Drawer rail

C. Carcass with solid ends

Drawer guide

C_2

Centre runner

Centre upright

Drawer guide

Side runner

Post

D

Drawer rail

D. Frame and panel carcass

In a traditional frame and panel carcass (D), the drawer rails are tenoned into the front posts and are cut around them at the back so that the rail ends touch the side panels. Their back edges are grooved to take the front ends of the side runners, which are stub tenoned. The side runners are set into grooves cut in the back posts and screwed into position. Guides on the side runners fill the space between the posts and the panels.

Rails, runners, kickers and guides

In a solid carcass, a drawer rail is grooved along its back edge, enabling a dustboard to be fixed and providing a means of securing the drawer runners, which are stub tenoned at the front (C_1). If no dustboard is required, a groove is cut locally to provide a mortise for the stub tenon. Side runners are grooved and fitted into stopped housings in the sides. No glue is used. At the back the wood is cut away at an angle and secured with a screw. If a centre upright is fitted at the back, it is often possible to cut a groove across it to accommodate the back end of the centre runner. If this is not possible, a hanger must be dovetailed to the top back rail and into the centre runner. Centre runners are stub tenoned to the front rail (C_2). Both edges of the centre runner may be grooved for a dustboard. The drawer guide is screwed to the top of the drawer runner. A solid top dovetailed to the sides acts as a kicker to prevent the drawer from tipping forwards when opened. In a carcass with solid ends, short kickers can be tongued into grooves in the rails or fillets. Secure them with two screws into the carcass sides, fixing the back screw in a slot to allow for movement in the wood. A centre kicker is stub tenoned into the front and back carcass rails.

Drawers

The corners of drawers are always dovetailed into solid wood in quality work. The sides are lap dovetailed to the front and through dovetailed to the back. This is the strongest form of construction as the dovetails resist the tendency of the front and back to pull away from the sides while the drawer is being pulled and pushed. A feature of the best hand-made drawers is that the corners of the lapped dovetails almost meet, giving a neat appearance because of the narrow pins. For large drawers, the front should be approximately 22 mm/$\frac{7}{8}$ in thick. Medium-size drawers have fronts about 19 mm/$\frac{3}{4}$ in thick, and small drawers about 16 mm/$\frac{5}{8}$ in thick. The sides and back should be kept as thin as possible, from 6 mm/$\frac{1}{4}$ in to 10 mm/$\frac{3}{8}$ in thick.

A. Dovetailed drawer

Drawer grooves and slips
Groove the inside front to take the drawer bottom, so the lowest front pin must be positioned low enough for the groove to be contained in the socket (**A**), otherwise the grooves will show on the pin. If the sides are thick enough, they too are grooved level with the lowest dovetail. In the best quality work the sides are too thin, so special grooved slips are glued in place to take the bottom (**B**). The simplest slip, commonly used with a three-ply bottom, has a quadrant moulding worked on its top edge. The drawer back must be arranged so that its bottom edge and lowest pin rest on the drawer bottom.

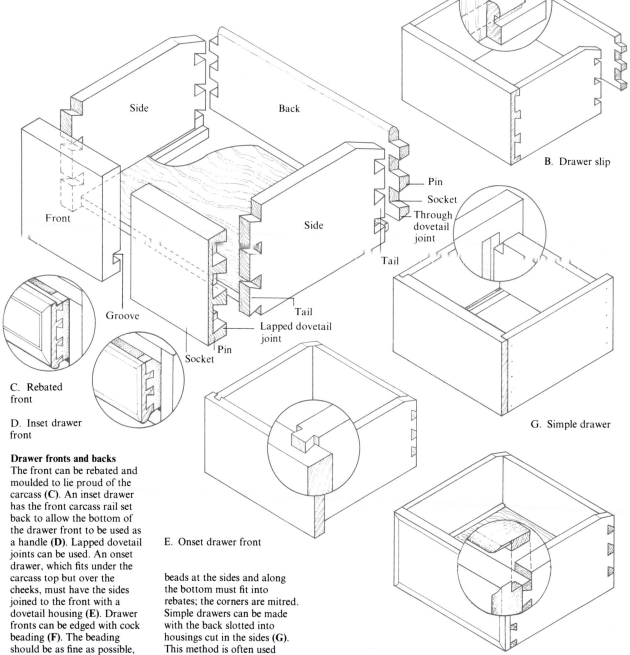

Side

Back

Front

Pin

Socket

Through dovetail joint

Side

Tail

B. Drawer slip

Tail

Groove

Lapped dovetail joint

Pin

Socket

C. Rebated front

D. Inset drawer front

G. Simple drawer

E. Onset drawer front

F. Cock beading

Drawer fronts and backs
The front can be rebated and moulded to lie proud of the carcass (**C**). An inset drawer has the front carcass rail set back to allow the bottom of the drawer front to be used as a handle (**D**). Lapped dovetail joints can be used. An onset drawer, which fits under the carcass top but over the cheeks, must have the sides joined to the front with a dovetail housing (**E**). Drawer fronts can be edged with cock beading (**F**). The beading should be as fine as possible, about 3 mm/$\frac{1}{8}$ in thick. The top length of beading covers the top edge of the drawer, but the beads at the sides and along the bottom must fit into rebates; the corners are mitred. Simple drawers can be made with the back slotted into housings cut in the sides (**G**). This method is often used combined with a plain lapped dovetail joint between the sides and front.

Drawer bottoms

A. Muntin bottom

B. Rebated bottom

C. Grooved sides

D. Fitting front and sides

Drawer bottoms

Three-ply is generally used, but make small drawer bottoms from hardboard. If solid wood is used, the grain must run from side to side, otherwise the bottom may be pulled out of the side grooves. Cut the bottom over-wide to project at the back and secure it with screws in slots; then if it shrinks it can be unscrewed, tapped forward and screwed in place again. Fit a muntin down the centre of drawers over 600 mm/24 in wide (A). Dovetail it into the drawer front or stub tenon it. Notch and screw it to the drawer back. For a shallower drawer, the bottom can be rebated in and secured by gluing and pinning (B).

Side-hung drawers

Modern drawers are often side hung, so the drawer sides must be grooved to take the runners (C). These are attached to the carcass side. (No guides or kickers are needed.) The runners can be wooden fillets screwed to the sides, or special plastic strips that are secured by pressing projecting studs into holes bored in the sides of the carcass.

Drawer stops

Stops keep the drawer in the correct position and prevent it from hitting the carcass back (F). Gauge the drawer front thickness on the rail. Glue two stops and place them slightly forward of the gauged line. Carefully slide the drawer into place. Remove it and the stops will be correctly positioned. Fix them with pins.

F. Drawer stops

Making a drawer

Make each drawer to fit its own opening in the carcass. Cut the front and plane the edges to fit, in the correct order (D). Follow the same procedure for the back, which should have its top edge set down by 6 mm/¼ in and its bottom edge resting on the drawer bottom. Fit the sides into the carcass and plane the ends square. Mark each side "Left" and "Right", and check they are equal in length. Gauge in any grooves for the drawer bottom in the front and sides before marking out the dovetails. Mark mating ends A:A, B:B, C:C and D:D. Mark and cut the dovetails (*see* pages 130–9). Form the grooves; clean up the inside faces. To assemble the drawer, fix the front vertically in the vice, sockets outwards. Glue one side into the front. Remove from the vice. Glue the pins and sockets on the drawer back. Place the back in the vice and partially tap it into the glued side and front. Release from the vice. Place the U frame, front upwards, on the bench and tap the joints fully home. Glue the tails on the second side. Turn the frame upside down and tap the side home. Wipe off surplus glue and check for squareness.

When dry, fit the bottom in place but do not secure it yet. Fit the drawer into the carcass, locating tight spots carefully. These are revealed by a shiny surface on the wood when the drawer is pushed in and pulled out of the carcass. Remove them by taking fine shavings with a plane. Clean up the drawer, supporting it with the vice and a board secured with the bench holdfast (E). If the drawer is racked about, the joints could fail. Then secure the bottom, using a few drops of glue in the front groove and screws or pins to secure the back.

E. Supporting the drawer for finishing

Drawer front
Drawer bottom
Drawer rail
Hardwood stop

Doors 1

A solid wood framework gives a frame and panel door its strength; it is made using mortise and tenon joints. Horns are left on the stile ends to prevent the wood from splitting during working. The exact construction of the frame depends on the method used to fit the panels. These are simply fill-in pieces and may be of solid wood or five-ply, fitted into grooves or rebates. Grooved-in panels are usually made of five-ply, while fielded and raised panels are normally made of solid wood. Flush panels may be of either material. All types

of panels may be beaded into a rebated frame. To allow for movement, solid wood panels must never be glued, and care must be taken during assembly so that no glue is squeezed out of the joints. As it does not move as much as solid wood, five-ply may be glued to stiffen the whole structure. The panel area may be divided into smaller sections by vertical dividers called muntins. These are often used purely for visual effect, but they do help to stiffen the panel area. Muntins are stub tenoned and glued in place.

Panels and frame construction
A grooved-in panel made from a manufactured board, which is to have a brushed or sprayed surface finish, should be assembled in its frame before the finish is applied. If the finish is to be applied in any other way, or if the panel is made from solid wood, the surface should be coated before being assembled. Framed carcass backs do not need a surface finish. A haunched mortise and tenon is used for the frame (**B**). With a rebated frame, the panel can be fitted after assembly and application of a surface finish. A long and short shoulder joint is used (**E**). The panel is beaded in from the back. Moulding may be applied to the front edges of a plain frame to form the rebate. The panel is beaded in (**D**). In the best moulded and rebated frames the moulding is worked in the solid. It is cut away locally at the mortise and is mitred (**C**).

A. Door parts
1. Horn
2. Meeting stile
3. Hinging stile
4. Top rail
5. Middle rail
6. Bottom rail
7. Muntin
8. Top panels
9. Bottom panel

B. Haunched mortise and tenon

Grooved-in panel

Flush panel

Fielded panel

Raised panel

Rebated frame

C. Moulded door frame

D. Applied moulding

E. Long and short shoulder joint

Making a frame and panel door

1. Mark one stile.

2. Mark the rails.

Stile   Rail

Stile

3. Clamp the pieces together.

Rear shoulder marks

Front shoulder marks

Door height

Rail width

Horn   Mortise   Stile

Making a frame and panel door
Mark out directly from the door opening in the constructed carcass. If the frame is rebated, gauge in the rebate. Place one stile against the carcass. Mark the height in pencil, very slightly oversize to allow for trimming (**1**). Place the stiles in the carcass and mark the rails, adding a trimming allowance (**2**). This must also allow for the length

of the tenons and long front shoulders. Clamp the stiles and rails together to mark out the joints (**3**). Cut the joints, then the rebates. Glue and clamp the frame together. Plane the edges of the frame in the correct order until it fits the door opening (**4**). Plane the bottom edge so that, combined with the hinging edge, the door fits the bottom right corner. To fit the top edge, rest the door on a piece of glasspaper placed on the carcass bottom, to give clearance for the surface finish. Plane the meeting edge, leaving it slightly oversize. Hinge to the carcass and complete the fitting on the meeting edge, giving the door a clearance fit. Bevel the meeting edge slightly inwards (**5**).

Hinge edge   Top

Meeting edge

Bottom

4. Plane the edges in order.

5. Bevel the meeting stile.

Increasing use is being made of manufactured boards for flush doors. Multi-ply, laminboard and chipboard must have their edges covered to ease shaping and application of a surface finish and to conceal the core material. Wide edgings of solid wood are necessary to provide a secure grip for hinge and lock screws because manufactured boards do not give a secure grip on screws inserted into their end grain (*see* pages 148–9). The edging can be butted and glued on, or tongued and glued into a groove for extra strength (*right*).

Flush doors

A traditional flush door (**A**) is made with a core of straight-grained, well-seasoned wood formed of strips 50 mm/2 in wide glued together. Smooth both sides, then face them with constructional veneer laid at right angles to the grain of the core. Veneers of the same thickness must be used on both sides. Over the constructional veneers, lay decorative veneers with their grain parallel to the strips. Multi-ply (**B**) and laminboard doors should have their grain at right angles to that of the face veneer. A framed and covered door (**C**) has a solid wood frame covered with three-ply. The covering is supported by cross rails, which should be drilled to allow the internal air pressure to equalize with that of the surrounding atmosphere, otherwise sinking or bulging may occur in the three-ply. Bore holes in the bottom rail, not in the top rail.

A. Traditional flush door

Tongued edging

B. Multi-ply door

Internal supports for framed and covered doors can vary. Lighter methods of supporting panels on covered doors are particularly useful for large doors. These include slats of insulation board (**D₁**) arranged as shown and cardboard honeycombing (**D₂**).

C. Framed and covered door

D. Internal supports

Fitting hinges

E. Inset door

F. Lay-on door

G. Inset door

2. Set the gauge.

1. Square hinge position across.   3. Saw the waste.   4. Chisel the recess.

Fitting hinges

The butt hinge is the most common in cabinetmaking. The hinge flaps can be recessed equally into the carcass and the door (**E**) or the whole knuckle can be let into the door with one flap taper recessed. The other flap is recessed from the extreme edge of the carcass and tapered to the flap thickness in both lay-on (**F**) and inset doors (**G**). As a general rule, position a hinge its own length from the end of the stile. On a framed door the top end of the hinge is usually lined up with the inner edge of the rail. To position a hinge, square pencilled position marks across the door frame and carcass (**1**). Set a marking gauge to the hinge (**2**). Gauge its width and thickness from the knuckle to the edge on the door frame. Make vertical saw-cuts in the waste and on the waste side of the gauged lines (**3**). Chisel across the ends (**4**). Then pare the recess flat. Form the recesses in the carcass and screw the door in position, centre screws first.

Doors 2

Sliding doors

These are usually made of chipboard or laminboard edged all around with hardwood. Lightweight doors have a softwood frame, faced with three-ply. The simplest way to make doors slide is to cut grooves in the carcass top and bottom (A) or to attach grooved hardwood, fibre or stainless steel guides to the carcass. Doors may be tongued to slide in the grooves (B). Grooves must be slightly wider than the thickness of the door or tongue, for easy running. Allow sufficient extra depth in the top grooves for the doors to be inserted by pushing them up and then dropping them into the bottom groove. Fibre track cuts down friction. Glue it into grooves worked in the carcass top and bottom. Let mating plastic gliders into a groove in the bottom of the door, which should fit close to the carcass bottom (D). At the bottom, fit the fibre track in two lengths. Glue the first

piece in place, slide in the doors, then glue in the remaining length. Large doors are usually top hung with two wheels per door, running in channels (C_1). Buffer stops prevent heavy doors pinching fingers (C_2). The door bottoms slide in nylon guides (C_3).

A. Grooved carcass

D. Carcass with fibre track

B. Tongued door

C. Heavy doors

Tambours

Feed-in groove

False interior

Locking rail

Finger grip

Fixed end-stop

Baseboard

Edging strip

Cramping block

Edging strip

E. Assembling the slats

Tambour slats

10 mm/⅜ in

6 mm/¼ in

Tambours

A tambour is a sliding door made of wooden slats glued to a canvas backing. Tambours can be pulled down to close, pushed up or into the sides. Surface finish the slats before assembling them face down on a board between edging strips and a fixed strip at one end, all slightly thinner than the slats. With a cramping block at the other end lightly clamp up the slats (E). Ensure absolute squareness. Then nail or screw the cramping block to the board and remove the cramps. Glue fine canvas over the slats, stretching it well. Leave sufficient canvas at one end for it to be attached to the locking rail. The tambour runs in grooves in the carcass sides. Widen the grooves around the curves so that the slats can negotiate the curves. Run out the side grooves at the carcass back, which must be detachable, so the tambour can be slid in after the carcass has been assembled and finished. Then fill in the feed-in grooves. The locking rail, which is thicker than the slats and is rebated at the ends, is then sprung into the grooves from the front after the tambour is in place. The canvas is then beaded into a rebate cut in the back of the rail (see inset). To prevent the contents of the carcass from interfering with the travel of the tambour, and for appearance, fit a false top, sides and back.

Fall flaps

Fall flaps

These can be made from manufactured boards, ideally laminboard, or they can be framed and panelled. To provide an uninterrupted surface for writing on when the flap is down, back flap hinges are traditionally used where the flap covers the carcass edges, with an extra concealing rail fitted under the front edge of the carcass bottom. This rail is hollowed out so that it can accommodate the swing of the fall flap. However, modern hinges have been developed that do away with the need for the hollowed-out rails and allow the flap to sit within the carcass (see pages 258–9). Pivot hinges can be recessed into the side edges of the flap and the inside of the carcass. Stopped pivot hinges hold small flaps in the open position without additional support. All but the smallest flaps need more support than can be provided by the hinges alone. Lopers can be built into the carcass beneath the flap (see pages 14–15), or a stay must be fitted to support it.

Flap open   Supporting rail   Flap closed

Barred doors

The tracery in barred doors comprises a face moulding with a separate stiffening rib grooved into the back to form rebates for the glass, which is beaded or puttied in (**B**). Lay out the ribs first on a three-ply panel that has been cut to fit the exact size of the door frame rebates. Set out the pattern, working to the centre of the moulding. Cut the ribs and hold them in place with wooden blocks pinned to the three-ply panel (**C**). Join the ribs together with cross halving joints or simple butt joints reinforced with glued canvas (**D₁**). Two curved ribs meeting an upright can be spliced together and slotted into the end of the upright (**D₂**).

A_2

A_1

A_3

A_4

A_1

A_2

A_3

A_4

A. Barred door patterns

Frame

Face moulding

Stub tenon

Rib

Beading

B. Tracery construction

Wooden block

Rib

Three-ply panel

C. Assembling the ribs

D_1

D_2

D. Rib joints

Stub tenon the rib assembly into the frame. Place the frame over the assembly to mark the tenon lengths and the mortises in the rebates. Cut the joints. Glue the tenons and spring the whole assembly into the frame. The face mouldings are mitred where they meet each other and where they meet the frame (**A₁**), so they must be the same section as the frame moulding. The mitre always bisects the angle between adjacent parts. Cut the face mouldings and glue them on to the ribs. Cut the glass panes with a slight clearance all round; then bead or putty them into the ribs.

Tables

Leg and rail joints

The mortise and tenon is the most common joint. Wide underframe rails should have haunched tenons as the haunch supports the upper third of the rail without it pulling free (C). Mitre tenons where they meet within the leg (D). Leave a small gap between the mitred faces to allow for the contraction of the leg and so the shoulders can be pulled tight. To avoid the haunch showing on the top of the leg, use a tapered haunch resting in a correspondingly tapered mortise (E). A dowel joint between rail and leg is simpler but not so strong (F). Stagger the dowels. Reinforce leg and rail joints with blocks glued to the inside (A, B). To join rails to round legs, either scribe the shoulder of the rail so that it fits the leg, in which case a dowel joint (H) is easiest, or plane a flat section on the leg (G) and work a mortise and tenon joint in the usual way.

Cabriole legs

Tables with cabriole legs are constructed differently from other styles. Make the leg and rail frame with mortise and tenon joints. Glue the joints and allow them to dry. Then fit the ear pieces to each leg. These should be dowelled for the strongest fixing (N). They can also be glued, have screws driven into counterbored holes and then be pelleted (P).

Canted legs

When a table has canted legs, cut the tenon shoulder to slant at the same angle (J) or plane an area flat at the top of the leg to take a standard tenon (K). For a strong frame, first join the four rails together with through dovetails. Then saw and plane off the corners of the frame. Hold a leg in the vice. Place the frame corner on top and scribe its outline on the end of the leg (L). Saw and chisel out a recess in the leg to the frame depth. Slide the frame into the recess (M). Reinforce the joint with glue blocks and with a screw that is long enough to run through the leg and the joint and bite into the leg on the other side.

Knock-down fittings

These can be particularly useful on tables. Make firm secure fittings with a bolt and cross dowel (A). Insert the steel cross dowel in the rail at right angles to the threaded bolt, which passes through the leg and is screwed into threads in the dowel by an Allen key. The table plate is a straightforward fitting (B). Screw each side to a rail. Screw a threaded bolt into the corner of the leg and secure the table plate with a wing nut. Use two short locating dowels with knock-down fittings to prevent the components twisting. Do not glue the dowels if the table is to be dismantled.

Curved rails

Dovetail curved rails on a round or D-shaped table into housings on the legs. If a leg is in the middle of the curved rail and is flush with it, join it to the rail with a combined bridle and tenon (E). If the rail is inset, use a bridle joint (C). When the lower edge of a rail is curved where it meets the leg, a weak feather edge will be formed if the rail is simply planed to a curve. To prevent this, cut a small housing in the edge of the leg around the tenon, and shape the rail (D).

Stretcher rails

These add strength and rigidity to the whole frame. They are usually thinner and narrower than the underframe rails and are joined to the leg in the same way, but without a haunch. If the rail is very thin, it can be fitted completely into the mortise; the tenon, however, should have a top shoulder to give it a definite length and to enable the top edge of the rail to be moulded (F). If stretchers run diagonally, work a flat section on each leg (G). Where diagonal stretchers join a central stretcher to form a Y configuration, tenon them into the central stretcher (H), or mortise them to receive the tenon on the central stretcher (J). Flat stretchers are sometimes required. Make up the stretcher frame with mortise and tenon joints or tongued mitres. Secure turned feet with dowels passing through holes bored in the stretcher frame and into the bottom of the legs (K).

Solid wood tops

Fix solid wood tops in such a way that the wood is allowed to shrink or expand. Wooden buttons screwed to the table top and sliding in grooves on the inside of the rails are the traditional method (L). Metal shrinkage brackets are a more modern method of holding the top down (M). These have slots on one face for the screws to slide along.

Chairs

The chair is the most used and abused piece of furniture in the average household. It has to withstand being rocked backwards and sideways as well as having to stand up to the torsional stresses imposed by the continual readjustment of the sitter's position. All chair joints must fit well and be strong. Make up front and back frames first and then join them to the side rails. Always make a full-size drawing of the projected chair to enable angles to be measured correctly. Any design more elaborate than a simple dining chair should be made up in softwood as a full-size working model to test the design and construction.

The modern dining chair can be quite simple to construct. Use mortise and double stub tenon joints to fix the front and back rails to their legs. Attach the side rails with dowels. Increase the strength and rigidity of the frame by gluing and screwing stout corner blocks in place. Screw a fillet to the back rail to support the three-ply base of the seat. Tenon any stretcher rails if they are used. Position them so as not to catch the back of the sitter's legs and so they cannot conveniently be used as footrests. Make the chair back from a dowelled frame; pad and screw it to the back posts from the inside. Take the cover over to hide the frame.

Crest rails

These may be tenoned into the back post (C) or be mortised to receive the tenon on the back post (D). Alternatively, use a dovetail bridle joint (E). Where these joints would be difficult because of shaping or the awkward joint line, use dowels to fit the rail (F).

Seat frames

Mortise and tenon joints are traditionally used, but modern chairs rely more on dowel joints or on a combination of dowel and mortise and tenon joints. Set down the front rail flush with the rebates in the side rails. A drop-in seat requires rebates to be cut around the inside edges of the rails (A). Use a haunched tenon to accommodate the rebate. Angle the side rails and connect them to the front and back frames with dowel joints, a canted tenon (B) or a canted mortise. If the leg is to be flush with the rail, plane off the outer part of the leg after the frame has been assembled.

Armrests

Stub tenons, dovetail bridle joints or dowels can be used to join armrests to front arm posts. At the back, notch an armrest and stub dowel it into the back leg (G), or tenon it. The armrests can be housed in, screwed from the back and pelleted (J). A down-swept arm must be tenoned and housed (K). House the front arm post into the seat rail, and glue and screw it (H).

Turned chairs

A turned spindle or leg should ideally fit into a tapered hole, bored with a tapered bit. If the hole has parallel sides, however, a spindle fitted into it requires a shoulder on it to limit the depth of entry (**B**). A small flat area must also be formed on the leg. When fitted to a flat arm, a turned leg must have a spigot formed on the end (**A**). The spigot is taken through and wedged.

Front to back folding chairs

Folding chair frames may be dowelled or mortised and tenoned. Hinge the back frame to the top rail of the front frame (**C**). Pivot the back of the seat on steel pins running in stopped grooves in the back leg. Rest the seat frame on dowels or steel pins with the ends riveted over washers (**D**).

Beds

H. Halved bed frame

J. Divan bed

Side to side folding chairs

Mortise and tenon the side frames. Tenon the folding X frames into the seat rail on one side (**F**) and bore them to accept spigots turned on the other seat rail. Use steel pins to connect the folding frames to the side frames (**G**) at the bottom. Fix the straps at the top with screws (**E**).

Beds

The divan type of bed (**J**) has a box framework on stump legs. Its slatted base is simple to make. The side and end rails are of softwood about 150 mm/6 in wide and 22 mm/$\frac{7}{8}$ in thick. The slats are 100 mm × 22 mm/4 in × $\frac{7}{8}$ in. These may be let in flush with the side rail, where they are glued and screwed, or screwed into slots. Make a flush headboard or use frame and panel construction. Screw the wooden uprights directly to the back of the bed, slotting them for height adjustment (**L**). Make a bed frame with the top and bottom rails halved to the side rails (**H**). Bolt the side rails to the head- and footboards. Lengthen the uprights to act as legs for the bed. Side frames can also be tenoned into head- and footboards (**K**). Dowels bored through the tenons lock the joints; they can be knocked out to dismantle the bed.

K. Tenoned bed frame

L. Divan headboard

Solid wood bending

Solid wood can be bent for structural purposes. The degree of effective curvature depends on the species of wood. Gradual curves can be made by bending dry wood around a framework, such as a former, and clamping it, but the wood has a tendency to spring back at least partially to its original shape when released. Cutting curves from solid wood results in short-grain weakness around the curve or at the ends. By making saw-cuts across the grain on a piece of wood its effective thickness will be reduced, allowing the wood to be bent; it will retain its bent shape when the kerfs are glued.

The most satisfactory method for bending solid wood, however, is to steam it first to make it supple. Using this method solid wood can be bent without kerfing and its shape will be retained when the wood has dried. As the wood is subjected to the steam the wood cells will soften and consequently become more amenable to compression. The cells are not, however, equally amenable to expansion and are liable to fracture. The outer surface of the curve must therefore be supported.

The wood to be bent should be straight grained and free from defects. It should be longer than will ultimately be necessary and must be planed smooth. Steaming is done in a rectangular or cylindrical chest, made from wood, metal or plastic, that is large enough to hold the wood to be bent. The chest should be set at a slight incline, so that the condensed water will run to one end. Holes at the bottom of the chest will allow condensation moisture to escape. Place wooden slats inside to support the timber to be bent and to allow the steam to circulate around it. Bore one end of the chest to allow for the insertion of the tube supplying the steam. Loosely block the other end with a cloth to prevent steam loss. Exterior lagging will help reduce condensation and heat loss.

An adequate supply of steam is essential. A 23 litre/5 gal. drum, filled two-thirds with water and heated by a gas burner, will give a sufficient quantity of steam. Bore a hole in the top of the drum to take the width of the rubber tubing, and connect the tubing to the chest. An average temperature of 100°C/212°F at normal atmospheric pressure should be maintained

Cross-kerfing

1. Select a piece of waste wood.

2. Mark the radius.

3. Mark the position of line B.

4. Mark the surface again.

5. Cut a series of kerfs.

6. Bend the glued wood.

Cross-kerfing

Before dry wood can be cut and bent to the required radius, the distance between kerfs must be calculated. To do this take a thin piece of waste wood of the same width as the thickness of the wood to be bent (1). Mark the required radius measurement along its length, 50 mm/2 in from one end (2). Square the first line (A) across the waste wood. Gauge two-thirds the width of the waste wood. On line A make a single kerf down to the gauged line. Clamp the end to a flat surface. On this surface mark the position of line B (3). Push that end until the kerf at A closes at the top. Holding that position, mark the surface again at line B (4). The distance (x) between the two marks on the surface is the distance that should be left between each kerf in order to make a curve of the required radius. From the face side of the actual wood to be bent, gauge a line on the edges two-thirds the thickness of the wood. With the same saw, cut a series of kerfs down to the gauged lines, allowing the calculated distance between each (5). Insert glue into every kerf. Then bend the wood (6). Hold the curve with a loop of cord, thus closing all the kerfs at the top. Clamp the wood in position when all the kerfs are closed. When the glue has dried release the cramps and cord. Smooth the bent wood; then veneer its edges to conceal the kerf marks.

within the chest for approximately 3 hours for every 25 mm/1 in of wood thickness.

Steamed wood is bent around a former, which may be constructed from solid wood and/or manufactured boards and should, where necessary, allow for cramps. The radius of the former should be slightly smaller than that ultimately required on the wood to be bent as the wood will straighten a little when unclamped. Each former is usually a one-off construction as its curves are difficult to adapt to a different shape. Smooth the former frame so that the wood to be bent can lie directly against it and protect it with a surface coating. A metal strap is used to support the wood on the outside of the bend. Usually the strap is made of steel, but where the wood is particularly acid it must be of aluminium. The strap must be flexible, wider than the wood to be bent and longer so that some form of handle can be fixed to each end. Each handle comprises the backplate, the metal strap end and an end-stop, bolted together. Backplates are essential; they extend along the outside of the strap and prevent the wood from twisting out of plane. End-stops prevent the

wood from stretching longitudinally during the bending process. Wedges may be inserted between the end-stops and the bent wood to tighten the fit. A sash cramp should be used to hold the bent wood ends tightly to the former. Concentrated pressure on any one part of the metal strap will dent the wood to be bent, so place a block of waste wood between the cramp and the strap to prevent any damage. The wood may take at least 5 hours to dry in the former in a room at 15°C/60°F.

Some good timbers for steam bending	
Acer pseudoplatanus — Sycamore	*Quercus rubra* — Red oak
Carya spp. — Hickory	*Quercus mongolica* — Japanese oak
Fagus sylvatica — European beech	*Robinia pseudoacacia* — Robinia
Fraxinus excelsior — Ash	*Ulmus americana* — White elm
Juglans regia — European walnut	*Ulmus glabra* — Wych elm
Prunus avium — European cherry	*Ulmus hollandica* — Dutch elm
	Ulmus procera — English elm
	Ulmus thomasii — Rock elm

Steam bending

Lagging Chest Rubber tubing Cap Water Drum Wood to be bent Heat source Wooden slat

1. Steam the wood in the chest.

Waste wood block — Backplate — Wood to be bent — Metal strap — End-stop

2. Clamp the centre.

3. Draw the handles inwards.

4. Leave to dry.

Steam bending
Steam the wood to be bent in the chest until supple (1). Then remove from the chest. Immediately set the middle of the steamed wood against the centre of the curved former. Place the metal strap and some waste wood centrally on the other side of the wood. Then clamp the assembly (2). Draw both handles of the metal strap towards the sides of the former, sandwiching the wood (3). Using an assistant, secure the backplates with a sash cramp so that the ends of the wood are against the sides of the former. Hold the top of the backplates with G-cramps. Leave the wood to dry (4). Then release it from the former and allow to settle.

Laminated wood bending

A strong, durable, curved component may be constructed from a number of glued veneers bent around a former. Some complex shapes can be formed by this process, which is known as laminating, but it does have aesthetic limitations as the edge of any laminated component will be parallel layers of veneer and glue.

All veneers must be of the same thickness, which should be no more than $2\,mm/\frac{3}{32}$ in each. Their width should be at least half as wide again as the finished component, to allow for trimming and smoothing of the edges when the glue has dried. Allow an extra $50\,mm/2$ in length for each veneer. The number of veneers glued together can range from two to 18, depending on the strength and pliability.

The veneers are glued together with their grain running lengthwise in the same direction. Urea formaldehyde is the most suitable type of glue for laminating. It will take up to 8 hours to dry in a temperature of $15°C/60°F$, provided the atmosphere is dry and the room is well ventilated. Once the glue has dried, the veneers are unlikely to move. It is then that the component can be cut to its final length before its edges are smoothed.

The veneers are bent to shape in formers, which are purpose-built for each project from solid wood or manufactured boards. The former must accommodate the excess length and width of the veneers. The area around which the veneers are bent should be smoothed and surface coated before use. Protect the former surface from the glue with a plastic sheet or newspaper. Where small radii are to be bent, veneers can be made more pliable by dampening them and leaving them clamped and unglued between formers to dry out.

Depending on the size and shape of the component required, there are various types of former and different ways of holding the veneers in position while the

Laminating with a pair of male and female formers

1. Cut the formers to shape.

2. Glue the veneers.

3. Place the male former on top.

4. Leave the glued veneers to dry.

Laminating with a pair of male and female formers
Cut the formers and shape them to the required component shape (1). Smooth and coat them. Stack the veneer leaves, with any decorative veneers at the top and bottom. Then apply glue to one side of each leaf with a brush, restacking them in reverse order (2). Place a plastic sheet over the female former. Then lay the glued veneers on the sheeting. Put another plastic sheet on top of the veneers. Place the male former on top (3). Clamp the formers together, using three or more pairs of cramps placed opposite each other. Apply pressure first at the centre and work outwards in order to squeeze the glue to the side edges and ends. Then tighten all the cramps and leave the glued veneers to dry (4).

Laminating with a segmented female former

Laminating with a segmented female former
Cut the formers to the required shape. Smooth and seal each former section. Glue one side of each veneer leaf, using a brush. Then stack them in the required order. Place a plastic sheet around the male former. Set the centre of the veneers against the centre of the male former. Put a plastic sheet on top of the veneers. Place the appropriate segment of the female former against the veneers at this point and clamp the whole together. Bend the veneers around the male former progressively from the centre to the ends, clamping the female segments in position. Each segment must fit the curve perfectly. Re-tighten the cramps from the centre outwards. Leave the glued veneers to dry.

glue dries. If the shape is comparatively flat or has a reverse curve a pair of formers would be most suitable.

Where a more complex shape is required one former is less likely to slide easily into place over another. The female former can then be made in a number of segments of different shapes and sizes designed to fit closely around the unbroken edges of the male former. Provision must be made within the male former for the insertion of cramps wherever segments of the female former need securing.

Shallow, wide shapes can be made from a male former alone by creating a vacuum around the former and veneers placed in an airtight bag, usually made from thick rubber or plastic. A vacuum cleaner can be used to remove the air from the bag. The pressure is sufficient to make the veneers wrap around the former. This method can only be used for lightweight components. To test their shape use a paper template cut to the required curve. Wrap the template around the male former; when it fits, cut the veneers accordingly.

If a curve is required only in the end of a piece of solid wood, glued veneers can be inset into kerfs cut into the end to be bent.

Some good timbers for laminating	
Acer pseudoplatanus — Sycamore	*Mansonia altissima* — Mansonia
Cassipourea malosana — Pillarwood	*Quercus cerris* — Turkish oak
Fagus sylvatica — European beech	*Quercus rubra* — Red oak
Fraxinus excelsior — Ash	*Sterculia rhinopetala* — Brown sterculia
Gossweilerodendron balsamiferum — Agba	*Ulmus americana* — White elm
Juglans regia — European walnut	*Ulmus glabra* — Wych elm
	Ulmus hollandica — Dutch elm
	Ulmus thomasii — Rock elm

Vacuum bending

Plastic sheet — Veneers — Adhesive tape — Airtight bag — Batten — Baseboard — Wooden blocks — Male former — Air pump nozzle

Vacuum bending

Cut a male former to the required shape. Smooth and coat it. Where necessary make a template and cut the veneers accordingly. Place a baseboard in an airtight bag. Rest at least four wooden blocks on the baseboard; then set the male former and a plastic sheet on the wooden blocks. (The blocks and baseboard will ensure efficient air extraction.) Glue and stack the veneers on the former. Place a plastic sheet on top of the veneers. Check the assembly carefully. Secure in position over the former with adhesive tape. Insert the nozzle of a vacuum pump well into the bag. Seal the ends with battens and cramps. Tie string around the bag where the nozzle is inserted. Turn the pump on. Leave the veneers in the vacuum while the glue dries.

Veneer insets

1. Cut stepped kerfs.

2. Insert each veneer.

3. Clamp between formers.

4. The final product.

Veneer insets

Cut stepped kerfs into the end of the wood, so each tongue of wood and each kerf is approximately the same thickness (1). The longest kerf must be that closest to the side that will become the outside curve and should be cut so that it reaches right round the curve; the shortest kerf must be on the inside of the curve. Cut leaves of constructional veneer slightly wider than the component and slightly longer than the kerfs. Shape one end to fit the circular saw curve. Glue them and insert well into the kerfs (2). Place plastic sheets either side of the component. Clamp the component between formers until the glue has dried (3). Then saw off the excess veneer and smooth the end. The final product (4).

The lathe

Turning wood on a lathe is a particularly absorbing skill for the woodworker, who will work more closely with the lathe than with most other power tools. As the work revolves, the cutting tools will make symmetrical cuts in the wood.

When selecting a lathe it is best to limit the choice to manufacturers that are well known in the field, as they will have overcome any design problems and will be able to supply additional equipment and spares if necessary. First decide on the type of work to be turned; the size of the work should dictate the size of the lathe. For major woodturning operations, such as table legs and large diameter bowls, the lathe illustrated is best. When purchasing a lathe with its own stand remember to check that it is at a comfortable working height. An approximate guide is for the elbow to be level with the centre of the tailstock, so no bending or stooping is necessary. Ensure that a bench-mounted lathe is supported on a solid base.

Whatever its size, a good quality lathe should have the following features. The motor, usually a $\frac{3}{4}$- or 1-horsepower induction motor, should be totally enclosed. Motors that are cooled by air passing through vents in the casing are to be avoided as they will draw in wood dust and chippings. The headstock should be sturdy and free from vibration and nipples should be provided for easy lubrication of the bearings. A plain phosphor bronze bearing running on a taper is an ideal arrangement. The lathe bed must be strong and should be of heavy casting. In service, a few drops of oil on both parts of the bed will allow easy movement of the tailstock. The more expensive tailstocks eject the centres when wound fully back — a useful luxury.

Most lathes have the capacity for three or four speed changes. The changes of speed are made using a system of stepped pulleys in the headstock. Easy access to the pulley system is therefore important. In general, cleaner cuts can be made with the lathe turning at its highest speed. Any speed adjustment is dependent on both the size of the stock and the type of wood being turned. Thus heavy stock, such as uncut wood for a bowl, requires a slow initial speed. As the wood is removed the speed can be increased.

The type of wood to be used should be one of the first considerations when planning a woodturning session. Coarse textured timbers such as oak as well as the majority of the softwoods will not hold sharp corners or minutely detailed profiles; if attempted the fibres will crumble. These timbers are best suited to designs incorporating rounds, slow curves and straight sections. For intricate profiles, choose fine textured timbers such as mahogany or beech.

As a general rule, wood should be well seasoned and free from knots and shakes. Knots can cause tools to jump, possibly resulting in injuries to the operator or damage to the stock. It is possible to rough turn the stock first and then leave it for a while in a room of similar humidity and temperature to the place for which it is ultimately intended. Especially when rough turning bowls, fresh surfaces are exposed, which may not be thoroughly seasoned and so, later on, the finished article may distort under changes of temperature and humidity.

Headstock
The headstock contains the pulleys, which provide the driving mechanism from the motor. The lathe speed is altered by slipping the driving belt from one pulley to another after first releasing the tension. The pulleys are mounted on a spindle that projects beyond the headstock on both sides and is threaded so that a faceplate can be screwed on to it. The spindle facing the lathe bed is also fitted with a morse tapered hole for holding attachments that are not threaded.

Micro switch

Inboard headstock spindle

Bed

Outboard headstock spindle

T-rest

On/off controls

Motor

Safety
○ Before switching on check that all levers are tight.
○ Before switching on turn the stock by hand for one full revolution to check that there are no obstructions.
○ Always turn the lathe off before making any adjustments.
○ Never leave the lathe running unattended.
○ Wear goggles to protect the eyes from flying wood chips.
○ Avoid any clothing that may become caught in the stock.
○ When glasspapering wear a facemask to protect the lungs.
○ When polishing never wrap the rag around the hand.

T-rest

A T-rest provides support for the lathe tools when turning. Its height is fully adjustable and can be fixed in position by a clamping lever; its head can also be moved round and clamped at any angle. Always stop the lathe while adjusting a T-rest. The top edge of a T-rest is rounded to give the tools greater ease of movement and support. T-rests are available in different lengths and are interchangeable between the headstock side and the lathe bed. They can be slid along the lathe bed.

Tailstock

The tailstock is used when turning between centres. It is fitted with a spindle, which has a morse tapered hole to accommodate a tailstock centre. The spindle feed hand wheel is for moving the spindle and centre against the piece of wood to be turned until the wood is held firmly. The hand wheel can be locked in position, usually with a screw at the side of the tailstock. The whole tailstock can be slid along the lathe bed and held in position by the cam operated lever at the side.

Locking screw — Hand wheel
Tailstock spindle —
Clamping lever

Accessories

A A faceplate is a metal disk with screw holes and a central threaded hub that is fastened on to the headstock spindle. Each faceplate is threaded to tighten when the lathe is switched on. Each faceplate is threaded to fit either the outboard or the inboard spindle; faceplates are therefore not interchangeable. A faceplate is used when bowl turning to hold the stock on to the inside or outside of the lathe. A leather or fibre washer can be fitted between the faceplate and the spindle to prevent the faceplate jamming.

B A screw flange chuck is a small faceplate with a central wood screw and a tapered shank or threaded hub. When a stock is screwed to this chuck all surfaces, both inside and out, can be shaped.

C An adjustable screw flange chuck is similar to the screw flange chuck except that the length of its screw can be altered to suit various thicknesses of wood.

D A drive centre is attached to the inboard side of the headstock spindle when turning between centres. At one end it usually has a morse tapered shank, which slots into the spindle, and at the other it has a central point and two spurs, which are fitted into the stock. A four-spurred drive centre is also available and is particularly suitable for small-diameter and light work as it gives a very positive drive.

E A tailstock centre supports the other end of the stock when turning between centres. It has a tapered shank, which fits into the tailstock, and a point at the other end, which is often called a dead centre as it does not turn with the stock. The centre is usually removed by tapping a dowel rod against the shank base.

F Alternatively the other end of a tailstock centre may rotate on bearings with the stock. It is then called a revolving centre. Its advantage is that heat and friction are avoided.

G A drill chuck holds drill bits for boring operations and usually has a maximum shank size of 13 mm/$\frac{1}{2}$ in.

H A universal chuck embodies the four traditional chucks — screw, ring, internal screw and faceplate — as well as the recently developed split ring chuck and expanding collet chuck. It has a wide range of uses and is a good investment for any woodturner.

Woodturning tools

The hand tools for woodturning are divided into those that cut and those that scrape. Gouges, chisels and parting tools cut into the wood and give a clean finish. Scraping tools are easier to use but as the name implies they scrape and this tends to give a rougher finish, so considerable glasspapering is necessary. Sparing use of scrapers is a useful adjunct to the craft of woodturning, but the turner should resist the temptation to follow the initially easier scraping method most of the time. Once the art of using cutting tools has been mastered, the turner will produce much better results.

Gouges have channelled or fluted blades with curved or flat cutting edges. They are used for roughing down and reducing stock to a cylindrical shape as well as for cutting coves, beads and sweeping curves. Gouges are bevelled on the convex side at an angle of 30° to 45°, depending on use. A large angle is often required when turning bowls and a smaller angle when turning work between centres.

Chisels have flat blades and straight cutting edges either at right angles or skewed at an angle of 70° to 80° to the edge of the blade. Skew chisels are used to make V cuts, beads and tapers, to cut down cylindrical stock and to smooth shoulders. They are bevelled on both sides and are sharpened to form a combined bevelled edge of 20° to 30°.

Gouges and chisels are held with the bevel of the tool rubbing the stock behind the cutting edge. This also gives the tool support when cutting.

Parting tools are used to cut through the stock and to make narrow recesses or grooves to a desired depth, forming a cut with parallel sides and a square bottom. The tool is bevelled on both sides to give a combined angle of 20° to 30°.

Scrapers are flat bladed with bluntly angled bevels and variously shaped cutting edges. They are correctly used for light finishing cuts when turning on the faceplate or between centres and for end-grain work. The cutting edge is ground at an angle of 70° to 80°. Never use old files as scrapers as they are brittle and therefore dangerous.

The tools illustrated form a good basic kit for woodturning and they will enable the turner to tackle a variety of interesting work from chair legs to large-diameter bowls. Always buy good-quality turning tools from a reputable manufacturer. Cheap tools will only prove a continual disappointment and they will also make it difficult to acquire the basic woodturning skills.

Tools must be sharp when woodturning so they will give a clean crisp cut that will require the minimum of effort by the turner. During a lengthy turning session the tools will need sharpening periodically because the cutting edges will have removed a considerable amount of wood very rapidly and will thus have become dull. It is not necessary to regrind the tools completely every time but, as flat bevels are so essential in woodturning, they must not be allowed to become too round. Careful use of the oilstone will be sufficient to renew the cutting edges many times between grinding sessions. While grinding, the blade must be kept cool. Dip it frequently in cold water when using an emery wheel; where possible a sandstone running in water is preferable.

Deep fluted bowl gouge
10 mm/⅜ in for general shaping inside and out when working on the faceplate.
Spindle gouge
6 mm/¼ in and 13 mm/½ in for coving, shaping, hollowing and rounding over.
Roughing gouge
25 mm/1 in for roughing down to cylinders, waste removal and long curve shaping.

Deep fluted bowl gouge

Spindle gouge   Roughing gouge

Angles for sharpening

Gouge (see pages 92–5)

Skew chisel

Parting tool

Round-nosed scraper

Skew chisel
19 mm/¾ in and 25 mm/1 in for
V grooves, beading and
smoothing.
Round-nosed scraper
19 mm/¾ in for final end-grain
shaping and smoothing
concave surfaces in faceplate
work.

Square-nosed scraper
25 mm/1 in for smoothing
convex and flat surfaces.
Parting tool
6 mm/¼ in for cutting work to
length and quickly forming
narrow grooves.
Sizing tool
Used with the parting tool for
cutting grooves or for setting
out diameters.

Sizing tool

Parting tool

Skew chisel   **Round-nosed scraper**   **Square-nosed scraper**

Methods of sharpening

A parting tool needs frequent
sharpening. Using a tool-rest,
which can be adjusted to the
bevel required, grind the blade
to a 20° to 30° angle between
bevels. Move the blade across
the face of the wheel while
exerting light pressure. Hone
with the bevels laid flat against
the oilstone and work it back
and forth. When a wire edge
appears, hone each side
alternately until the edge
disappears.

Sharpen a skew chisel on a
grinding wheel to an angle of
20° to 30° between bevels.
Make the angle of the skew
between 70° and 80°. Place the
centre of the bevel against the
rotating wheel. Press until the
complete bevel is ground to the
shape of the wheel. Grind the
other bevel in the same way.
Then hone each bevel
alternately on an oilstone,
working it back and forth to
remove the wire edge.

A round-nosed scraper may be
sharpened to any convex
tailor-made shape. Hold its
single bevel on the tool-rest at
a 70° to 80° angle to the
grinding wheel. Swing the tool
from left to right to keep the
shape even until a wire edge is
produced. At the grinding
angle hone the bevel on the
oilstone, with a rocking
motion. Then lay the blade flat
and move it back and forth to
remove the wire edge.

Sharpen a square-nosed scraper
on its single bevel at a 70° to
80° angle. Using an even
rhythm move the tool from
side to side across the grinding
wheel until a wire edge is
produced. Dip the blade in
cold water at frequent intervals
to stop the steel overheating.
Then hone the bevel, back and
forth, at an angle of 70° to 80°
to the oilstone. Finally rub the
blade flat on the stone to
remove the wire edge.

Turning between centres 1

When turning between centres, the wood to be turned is supported at one end by the tailstock centre and at the other by the headstock driving centre. The grain of the wood always runs parallel with the lathe bed, which means that the turning tools will always be cutting across the grain of the wood. It is from this technique that long slender items and cylindrical work with shaped profiles can be produced.

Until some confidence and skill have been acquired, it is advisable to plane the stock to an octagon before turning it on the lathe, because turning from a square can present problems. When roughing down to a cylinder or glasspapering, the stock must be revolved at a low speed. Continually adjust the T-rest so that the gap between the stock and the T-rest is 3 mm/$\frac{1}{8}$ in.

When turning between centres, try to develop the habit of keeping an eye on the general shape of the stock, especially the rear profile. Initially the temptation will be to look at the cutting edge of the tool, but this should be resisted as it will be difficult to assess whether the stock is cylindrical.

Both a scraping and a cutting method can be used in turning between centres. Although the scraping method may appeal to the beginner as being a more cautious approach, the finished surface will always be rougher than a surface that has been cut, and practice using the cutting method will in the long run be rewarded with more professional results. All cutting tools can scrape but not all scraping tools can cut, and so glasspapering will be required after scraping.

Preparing the stock and mounting it on a lathe

1. Draw diagonals.

2. Punch a hole in one end.

3. Make a cut in the other end.

4. Plane to an octagon.

5. Mount the stock on the lathe.

6. Adjust the T-rest.

Preparing the stock and mounting it on a lathe

To locate the centre of the stock draw diagonals from corner to corner at both ends (1). Then, with dividers, mark out circles on both ends of the stock. Make a location hole at the centre of one end, using a nail-set or bradawl (2). At the other end make a saw cut about 3 mm/$\frac{1}{8}$ in deep across one of the diagonals (3). This should stop the wood splitting. To relieve some of the initial stress of cutting a cylinder from a square, it is advisable to plane the stock to an octagonal section before mounting it on the lathe (4). Fasten a revolving or dead centre on to the tailstock spindle. If using a dead centre on the tailstock apply a spot of grease to the central hole in the stock to avoid friction when the work is turning. (This is unnecessary when a revolving centre is used.) Then fit a drive centre into the headstock spindle and press the centre of the kerfed end of the stock into the spurs on the drive centre. Push the tailstock up to the centre of the stock and clamp into position with the lever. Then turn the spindle feed hand wheel to drive the tailstock centre fully into the stock centre (5). Retract the centre a fraction to ease friction, then fix in position with the tightening screw. Adjust the T-rest parallel and central to the stock, 3 mm/$\frac{1}{8}$ in from the edge (6). Before turning, spin the stock by hand to check that there are no obstructions.

Cutting down to a cylinder

1. Lay the bevel on the stock.

2. Rough down the stock.

3. Check the diameter.

4. Finish with a skew chisel.

Cutting down to a cylinder

Place a 25 mm/1 in roughing gouge on the T-rest and move the bevel lightly against the stock so that the middle of the blade tip will cut away the waste (1). For quick roughing, place a hand over the gouge (2). For more control, place the hand under the gouge. Begin to cut at one end; gradually move the gouge along to the other end of the stock before bringing it back. The cylinder is then cut down to rough size using a smooth, even rhythm. Continually stop the lathe to adjust the T-rest and check the diameter of the stock, using calipers (3). Finally raise the T-rest 3 mm/⅛ in above centre and smooth off the stock with a skew chisel (4). It is important for the cut to come from the centre of the blade and not from the blade corners as this would result in the wood tearing or the chisel digging into the stock. To avoid the chisel digging into the shoulder start the cut a little way in from the tailstock and work towards the headstock. Then reverse the chisel and work towards the tailstock. If the skew chisel is used correctly the stock will not require glasspapering.

Scraping down to a cylinder

1. Rough down with a round-nosed scraper.

2. Finish with a square-nosed scraper.

Scraping down to a cylinder

Adjust the T-rest to just below the stock centre. Tilt the handle of a round-nosed scraper slightly above horizontal (1). Work the tool from one end of the stock to the other. When the stock has been reduced to the required diameter use a square-nosed scraper to remove any unevenness, using a similar motion to that of the round-nosed scraper (2). Glasspaper the stock smooth.

Using a sizing tool

1. Set to the required diameter.   2. Place over the stock.   3. Lift the handle gently.

Using the sizing tool

The sizing tool is a parting tool fitted with an arched attachment and is frequently used for repetition work. Set the sizing tool to the required diameter and screw it in position (1). With the T-rest positioned parallel and central to the stock, make a cut with the handle held slightly below the horizontal (2). Hold the position of the blade while gently lifting the handle until the required diameter is cut in the stock (3).

Turning between centres 2

Making a groove

1. Scribe lines on the stock.

2. Make cuts with a skew chisel

OR with a parting tool.

Making a groove
Grooves are commonly cut to shape profiles on cylindrical work. Clamp the T-rest centrally. With a wing compass, score the required widths along the stock (1). Set the toe of a skew chisel against the scribed lines and make vertical cuts 3 mm/⅛ in deep. Hold the handle well down (2). For wider grooves use a parting tool, starting with the tool held straight on to the stock and gently lifting the handle from below horizontal until the point is cutting 3 mm/⅛ in into the stock.

Cutting a cove

1. Make angled grooves.

2. Start at one shoulder.

3. Cut down to the cove centre.

4. Cut from the other shoulder.

Cutting a cove
Mark the required cove width with a wing compass. With the T-rest central to the stock make grooves at alternate angles, using a skew chisel (1). Then take out the waste from the centre of the cove with a spindle gouge, inclining the handle of the gouge downwards. Twisting the wrist, cut from left down to the centre and then from right down to the centre, using a rhythmic movement (2, 3, 4). Only cut on the down stroke. On the up stroke the gouge should not touch the wood but the action helps to create an even rolling motion. If a cut is made from the bottom to the top of the cove it will tear the wood. Gradually cut closer to the grooves each time, twisting the wrist from the one cove shoulder to the other. This shaping process is carried out bit by bit on each side of the cove until the required depth is achieved and the cove width stretches from angled groove to angled groove.

Scraping a cove

1. Scrape the cove centre.

2. Work from each shoulder.

3. Glasspaper to finish.

Scraping a cove
Scribe the stock and cut out grooves that are angled alternately. Adjust the T-rest to just below the centre. Using a round-nosed scraper that is slightly narrower than the intended width of the cove, feed the tool straight into the centre of the stock until the desired depth is reached (1). Then work the tool from either shoulder down to the centre of the cove (2). Remove the T-rest. Switch on the lathe at a low speed. Smooth the coves, without removing any corners, using glasspaper wrapped tightly around a purpose-shaped sanding block (3).

Cutting a bead

1. Draw lines on the stock.

2. Cut from the pencilled line.

3. Roll the chisel into the groove.

4. Cut the other side.

Cutting a bead

Clamp the T-rest centrally. Scribe the stock, using a wing compass. Then make a vertical groove 3 mm/⅛ in deep on each scribed line. Mark the centres of the beads by holding a pencil against the revolving stock (1). Hold the skew chisel against the stock at 25° to 30° with the handle dropped to just below the T-rest. Lay the cutting edge of the chisel heel close to one of the pencilled lines. Push the tool forwards so that the cutting edge of the heel is in contact with the surface of the stock, close to the bead centre (2). The bevel should be flat against the stock without the heel digging into it. Raise the handle slightly as the chisel is rolled slowly up and over in the direction of the groove. Push the chisel forwards in one continuous motion so that the tool finishes in an almost vertical position (3). Cut the other half of the bead in the same way with the angles reversed (4).

Scraping a bead

1. Scrape from the pencil line.

2. Move the toe into the groove.

3. Glasspaper to finish.

Scraping a bead

Prepare the stock as if cutting a bead. Then hold a skew chisel flat against the T-rest with the handle slightly below horizontal. Place the cutting edge of the toe close to the central bead line. Work it round towards the groove and back (1). As the bead shape forms the tool should rock, causing the toe of the tool to point into the groove (2). Never allow the toe tip to plough into the stock. Work each side separately before building up a completely balanced and rounded bead, again from each side. Glasspaper to finish (3).

Making duplicate turnings

1. Draw the important points.

2. Transfer the points.

3. Set a sizing tool.

4. Check the finished work.

Making duplicate turnings

First sketch the design on card either side of a centre line. Draw up the design accurately on one side, cut along the outline, fold the card flat on the centre line and draw along the outline to give the exact symmetrical shape. Draw all the important points, at right angles to the centre line, down to the bottom edge (1). With this edge against the stock, transfer the points (2). Set a sizing tool to the diameters on the symmetrical drawing for exact depth of cut (3). Use the "negative" piece of card from the cut outline to check the finished work (4).

Turning on the faceplate 1

Bowls, trays and many other circular objects can be turned on a faceplate, which is fixed either inside the headstock or outside when working on large-diameter stock. Successful turning requires much skill, practice and a certain amount of luck because of the inherent structure of wood. As with turning between centres, the stock must be well seasoned and generally free of knots, although knots can sometimes enhance the work if they are in the base. The stock must be cut with the grain running across its diameter; otherwise the edges of the stock will split and crack. There will however be two distinct end-grain patches on the stock where the chisel or gouge is cutting into the grain and it is these areas that will cause trouble as they tend to tear out under the action of the chisel or gouge. Cutting must be done between the centre and the right-hand edge. If the tool is held elsewhere it will be lifted away. As always tool sharpness is most important.

There should be minimum delay between turning the outside and inside of the stock because the wood will shrink slightly across the grain, causing the rim of the stock to become unevenly thick. Ideally, the outside should be turned and finished one day and the inside either that same day or the next.

Preparing the stock and mounting it on a faceplate

1. Plane the stock.

2. Circumscribe one face.

3. Cut away the waste wood.

4. Drill the screw-holes.

5. Secure the screws tightly.

6. Mount the faceplate.

7. Position the T-rest.

Preparing the stock and mounting it on a faceplate
With a jack plane, flatten one face of the stock against a bench-stop so that there are no gaps when it is placed on a faceplate (1). This will avoid vibration during cutting. Locate the centre by drawing diagonals across the stock, using a pencil and rule. With a wing compass, mark out a circle that is slightly larger than the intended diameter of the bowl (2). Then cut away the waste wood, using either a bowsaw or a bandsaw (3). Ensure the stock is as near round as possible to minimize the forces during roughing down. It is highly dangerous to turn a stock on the faceplate with the corners left on. Select a faceplate that is of smaller diameter than the stock. When the tools are unlikely to come into contact with the faceplate while turning, a faceplate that is larger than the stock can be used. (Alternatively take some waste wood of larger diameter than the stock, plane both sides flat and screw it to the stock.) Place the planed side of the stock on the faceplate and visually centre it. Select at least four screws that will penetrate through the 6 mm/$\frac{1}{4}$ in thick faceplate so that it cannot judder or vibrate during the cutting process. Drill the screw-holes with a hand drill, ensuring the holes are not aligned along the grain (4). Lubricate the screws with tallow or soft soap before securing them as tightly as possible in the holes (5). Check that there is a leather washer on the hub of the outer faceplate spindle, giving a resilient cushion to prevent jamming. Secure the faceplate firmly to the lathe by turning the faceplate on to the spindle with one hand and pulling the pulley cone gently in the opposite direction with the other (6). Finally position the T-rest so that it is central and parallel with the stock 3 mm/$\frac{1}{8}$ in away (7).

Turning the underside

1. Keep the handle well down.

2. Rough shape the stock.

3. Work from inside to outside.

4. Adjust the T-rest continually.

5. Neaten the sides.

6. Cut a plinth in the base.

7. Smooth with a scraper.

8. Mould the lip with a scraper.

9. Glasspaper the outside.

10. Remove from the faceplate.

Turning the underside

Spin the stock to ensure there are no hindrances. Then switch on the lathe. Initial roughing down speed should be low. Mark the required diameter of the base with a pencil and steel rule while the stock is spinning. The work of trueing up the edge of the stock and rough shaping now begins, using a 25 mm/1 in roughing gouge. With forearm resting lightly on the leg, keep the handle well down and the bevel touching the stock (1). The other hand should steady the tool as it lies on the T-rest. Rough shape the stock by cutting a chamfer at the edge of the stock (2). Gradually increase it towards both the rim of the stock and the diameter of the base (3). Continually adjust the T-rest so it stays parallel with the edge of the stock 3 mm/⅛ in away (4). Once the basic shape has been cut, speed up the lathe. A 13 mm/½ in deep fluted bowl gouge is then used to cut a more accurate shape (5). In order to form the plinth at the base, cut the stock with the gouge turned round (6). Adjust the T-rest to just below the centre and use a very sharp square-nosed scraper to smooth the outside of the stock. Point the scraper slightly downwards, steadying it on the T-rest (7). Work outwards and inwards rhythmically. Then use a round-nosed scraper to clean the lip, pivoting it round on the T-rest to make the lip more pronounced (8). Remove the T-rest. Then glasspaper (9). Never use coarse glasspaper as it will cause radial scratches. Set a slow speed and allow the paper to trail in the direction of the stock's rotation. Mould across the shape of the stock, paying special attention to corners and edges. Stop the lathe. The stock is ready for its surface finish. Olive oil, for example, is ideal for a salad bowl and wax suits a fruit bowl. Many other finishes, however, can be applied to the stock. Once the oil or wax finish has dried it should be lightly buffed into the grain. Switch the lathe to the slowest speed and with a clean cloth work out from the centre, supporting the wrist with the other hand. Apply a couple of coats within 2 to 3 hours. Leave the stock overnight to dry. Then glasspaper the surface carefully. Remove the stock from the lathe and take out the four screws holding it to the faceplate (10).

Turning on the faceplate 2

Mounting the stock base

1. Screw on the faceplate.

2. Mount on the lathe.

3. Draw a circle.

4. Scrape out a recess.

5. Leave the glued base to dry.

Mounting the stock base

Before turning the inside of the stock take a 19 mm/$\frac{3}{4}$ in thick piece of waste soft wood that is larger than the diameter of the stock base. Plane the waste wood flat so that the faceplate will fit flush against it and remove its corners, which could be dangerous when turning at speed. Screw the waste wood to the faceplate **(1)**. Mount the faceplate on the spindle and position the T-rest parallel to the waste wood just below its centre **(2)**. Turn the waste wood by hand to ensure there are no hindrances. With a steel rule and pencil mark out a circle that is the same diameter as the stock base **(3)**. Remove the waste within the circle to a depth of 3 mm/$\frac{1}{8}$ in, using a square-nosed scraper **(4)**. Stop the lathe frequently to check that the base of the stock fits closely into the recess. Remove the faceplate from the lathe. (For wide work, measure and make a note of the stock depth. Use the measurement at a later stage of turning as a check against the inside depth.) Cut out a piece of thick brown paper to fit the recess exactly. Using a sparing amount of PVA or animal glue stick the paper into the recess; then glue the stock base on to the paper so that the grain of the stock is at right angles to that of the waste wood base. Place a weight on top of the stock and leave to dry **(5)**.

Turning the inside

1. Clamp the T-rest.

2. Make a cut into the middle.

3. Twist the gouge round.

4. Twist the gouge into the stock.

5. Measure the inside depth.

6. Sight the depth cut.

7. Finish off with a scraper.

8. Buff with a clean cloth.

9. Release the stock.

10. The final product.

Turning the inside

Mount the faceplate, together with the waste wood and stock, on the lathe. Clamp the T-rest slightly lower than the stock centre and spin the stock manually to check clearance (1). Hold the handle of a deep fluted bowl gouge slightly below horizontal and start cutting into the middle, placing the gouge at right angles to the stock (2). Keep the bevel touching the stock. When cutting for depth, the handle should be lifted up slightly so that the edge of the blade cuts into the stock. As the cut develops, twist the handle round to about a 45° angle to the stock (3). As the hollow becomes wider and deeper the twisting movement becomes more pronounced. Continually adjust the T-rest so that it remains close to the work. Once the hollowing procedure is well under way a roughing gouge may be used to cut away further waste quickly. Using body pressure twist the gouge into the stock (4). Stop the lathe periodically to dust down the stock and to check its depth. To do this, place a steel rule across the rim and rest another at right angles to it (5). With the second rule held at the inside depth place the rule against the outside and sight the depth cut (6). At the required depth raise the T-rest to the centre of the stock and use a round-nosed scraper to finish off the inside and to smooth the rim. Hold its handle up and the blade down, thus lifting the bevel off the stock (7). Then switch the lathe to its lowest speed and glasspaper the stock, working from the centre outwards. Stop the lathe and apply the chosen surface finish. Where necessary buff it into the grain with the lathe on its slowest speed (8). After the surface finish has been applied, remove the stock from the lathe and unscrew the faceplate. Position the waste wood upright on the edge of the bench, with its grain running vertically. With an assistant holding the stock, place a chisel on the edge of the waste wood, with its blade aligned along the grain. Split the grain by giving the chisel a sharp tap with a mallet (9). Work the chisel along from each edge until the stock is released. Remove any surplus glue and paper from the base of the stock and lightly glasspaper it. Touch up the surface finish. The final product (10).

Woodcarving tools and basic techniques 1

Woodcarving provides the opportunity of combining woodworking skill with creative ability, whether used purely to embellish a piece of wood or to produce a complete work in itself. When choosing wood for carving ensure that it is free from knots, shakes and splits and is preferably fine textured for clean cutting. Lime is thus particularly suited to carving, and the attractive grains of yew and various species of pine are ideal for abstract shapes.

Woodcarvers have several different names for each implement. Those illustrated below make up the basic carvers' tool kit; a selection for the more advanced woodcarver is shown opposite. All carving tools are bevelled on both sides to permit easy entry into and through the wood. Their blades are made of tempered steel to give maximum strength and are bought with unsharpened edges and without inner bevels. Therefore, before a session, the woodworker must always sharpen his carving tools. Bevels should be made to an approximate length of 13 mm/½ in. The harder the wood the shorter the bevel required. The inner bevel on a gouge must be honed on a slipstone (*see* page 94).

With tools that have sharp edges accidents can all too easily occur unless certain safety precautions are taken: always check the stability of the work surface and the wood itself before commencing work. One good light source is essential. The tools should be laid out on the bench with their handles towards the carver.

Skew chisel
6 mm/¼ in. Useful for undercutting. The skew blade is bevelled on both sides.

Parting tool
60° 6 mm/¼ in and 45° 13 mm/½ in. For incised lettering, pattern detail and outlining. It has two straight edges to form a V shape of varying angles.

Basic cutting tools

Skew chisel

Parting tool

Straight gouge

Fluter

Straight gouge
3 mm/⅛ in, 6 mm/¼ in, 10 mm/⅜ in, 13 mm/½ in and 16 mm/⅝ in. For general carving. It must be sharpened to a bevel on the inside as well as the outside. Its depth ranges from almost straight to semicircular.

Fluter
10 mm/⅜ in and 13 mm/½ in. A gouge with a sweep greater than a semicircle.

Sharpening a parting tool
Grind each side to a 70° to 80° angle holding the tool to the side of the wheel and twisting it slightly to avoid grinding a concave outside bevel (**1**). Hone the sides on an oilstone (**2**). Rock the bottom of the V to avoid it acting as a rudder in the wood. Hone the tool up and down on a triangular slipstone (**3**). Slide one side up and down the slipstone then repeat for the other side. Strop to perfect the cutting edge.

1. Grind on the wheel.

2. Hone on the oilstone.

3. Hone on a slipstone.

Salmon-sweep gouge

Spoon-bit gouge

Back-bent gouge

Spade

Fishtail

Macaroni

Flutaroni

Veiner

Sweeps and angles
Gouges have widths ranging
from 0.75 mm/$\frac{1}{32}$ in to
25 mm/1 in and depths ranging
from near flat to semicircular.
Parting tools have varying
widths and angles of 30°, 45°,
60° and 90°.

Macaroni
6 mm/$\frac{1}{4}$ in. For cutting straight
sides with a flat bottom.
Flutaroni
6 mm/$\frac{1}{4}$ in. For cutting straight
sides with a flat bottom and
curved corners where the
parallel sides meet the bottom.
Veiner
1.5 mm/$\frac{1}{16}$ in. For very fine
narrow gouge-type cutting.

Salmon-sweep gouge
6 mm/$\frac{1}{4}$ in and 10 mm/$\frac{3}{8}$ in. For
cutting curves and recesses.
Spoon-bit gouge
Deep 10 mm/$\frac{3}{8}$ in and shallower
10 mm/$\frac{3}{8}$ in. For cutting acute
curves and recesses.
Back-bent gouge
6 mm/$\frac{1}{4}$ in. For reaching into
awkward places.
Spade
10 mm/$\frac{3}{8}$ in and 16 mm/$\frac{5}{8}$ in. Its
splayed-out blade enables the
carver to see the wood
skimming away.
Fishtail
25 mm/1 in. For heavy work
and, when it is inverted, for
rounding over.

183

Woodcarving tools and basic techniques 2

Carving methods

A running cut.

A reverse running cut.

A setting in cut.

Carving stance.

Driving a tool with a fist.

Carving methods
For greatest control when carving always stand up. Ensure the workbench is at a level that is comfortable so it is not necessary to stoop over the work, which should be held securely. To keep control of the tool always rest an arm on the work or workbench. Never allow the body to block the path of any cut. Move the work round as each part is carved so the wood being worked is always close to hand.

For a running cut rest the thumb and the middle finger on the tool while the index finger exerts a backwards pressure to prevent the tool running through the wood too quickly. Push the tool forwards with the other hand and point the index finger down the shank. Gauge the depth of an incision by how much blade is showing out of the wood.

Where it is not always possible to cut away from the carver, move the body away from the direct path of the tool and let the thumb provide the backwards pressure.

For a setting in cut stab the tool vertically into the wood. Clench the fist and place the fingers of the other hand close to the wood to ensure accurate positioning.

Where a mallet would prove too forceful and an ordinary running cut not forceful enough, hit the tool handle instead with the fleshiest part of the palm.

For hard wood and large work wrap the fingers around the tool to provide a backwards pressure and rest the wrist against the work. Hit the tool handle with a mallet.

Always cut in the direction of the wood grain where possible. When cutting a circle make four separate cuts in the directions indicated in the diagram.

Carving a circle.

Driving a tool with a mallet.

Mallets

A round wooden mallet is traditionally used for driving cutting tools. Mallets with malleable iron heads are a modern improvement. They require less exertion from a carver and do not bounce on the wooden handles of the cutting tools so much as a wooden mallet.

Punches and tooled textures

Punch and punch tips.

Tap the punch head gently.

Punches and tooled textures

Wooden surfaces, especially backgrounds, may be punched or tooled. To make a small impression hit the punch head with a hammer. The frosting punch impressions overlap; the impressions of a ring punch just touch. A wide variety of patterned punch impressions are available.

A tooled surface is often preferred to a smooth or punched surface. The surface of the wood is carved so as to give it a particular texture. The texture may be chosen at random for, say, a background or it may have been chosen specifically for the purpose of enhancing or emphasizing the character of the carving.

Frosting punch.

Star punch.

Ring punch.

Textures that can be tooled.

Woodcarving tools and basic techniques 3

Rasps and rifflers

Rifflers.

Rasps and rifflers

A rasp will quickly remove wood so use it cautiously and only for large pieces of wood. A riffler is used for smoothing smaller and more delicate carvings. It is in fact two tools in one as it has a different shape and smoothing surface each end. Like a rasp and file, it may be flat, round, half-round, square, oval or triangular in cross-section. It may also have a fine or coarse, file or rasp cut.

Using a riffler.

Using a rasp.

Using a carvers' bench-screw

Carvers' bench-screw.

Securing from above the bench.

Securing from below the bench.

To secure the wood while carving
use a carvers' bench-screw, wooden strips nailed around the base of the work or G-cramps. The carvers' bench-screw can hold the work from above or below the workbench. Each wing nut has a square hole that, when locked on the screw-head, acts as a spanner.

Using a carvers' bench-screw
To secure a frame on a flat surface drill a small hole in the workbench. Drill another hole, slightly wider than the bench-screw, through a batten that is slightly longer than the frame length. Twist the tip of the screw securely into the bench and put the frame around it. Fit the batten over the screw-head, and place its ends over the frame edges. Screw down the wing nut on to the batten until the structure is steady. If the batten bends it is either too thin or too much pressure has been exerted.

To secure the work from below the bench, drill a small hole in the underside of the wood to be carved. Twist the screw tip securely into the hole. Then drill a clearance hole in the workbench. Put the screw-head through the bench hole. From beneath the bench screw up the wing nut until the wood is held tightly and securely against the bench.

Marking up with carbon paper

1. Secure the design firmly.

2. Trace on the design.

3. The design transferred.

Marking up with a stencil

1. Secure the stencil to the wood.

2. Dab on the paint.

3. Touch up the design.

Marking up with tools

1. Transfer the measurements.

2. Fill in the design.

Checking work in progress

1. Measure the model.

2. Measure the carving.

Using a height gauge.

Marking up with carbon paper
Draw the required design on a piece of paper. Lay some carbon paper face down on the selected piece of wood and, on top, place the design paper (1). Check that no part of the design overreaches either the edges of the wood or the carbon paper. Secure both papers with tape. Using a wooden stick with a very thin point, trace around the design (2). When complete lift away both papers. Where necessary touch up the design. The design transferred (3).

Marking up with a stencil
Draw a design on some stiff paper. Then cut away the major features, using a sharp, pointed knife, to create a stencil. Secure the stencil to the wood to be carved (1). With a brush dab some paint wash through the holes (2). Carefully remove the stencil. When the paint is dry draw in the complete design using the paint marks as a guide (3).

Marking up with tools
Set dividers against salient points on the design. Move them on to the wood to be carved and transfer the measurement, using a pencil (1). Using these datum marks, complete the rest of the design freehand (2).

Checking work in progress
Once a carving is under way, use dividers to check the work against the design and calipers to take measurements when high-relief carving or carving in the round (1). The curved legs of the calipers allow them to reach around any projection on the original model. Then check the measurement against the work (2). Make a height gauge to measure relief depths. The arm should slide vertically and horizontally and should swing through almost 180° so that depths can be checked against any model. Like the calipers and dividers, the height gauge is secured with a nut.

Chip and incised carving

Chip carving

Chip carving is the simplest method of carving. The technique is based mainly on cutting inverted pyramids. To mark up an inverted pyramid first draw a triangle. Then bisect each of the angles to give the centre (1). Any design will consist of a number of pyramids. Transfer the design on to the wood, then secure the wood firmly (2). With a parting tool make a pilot cut from each corner of the triangle to its centre (3). Set in along these cuts with a cabinetmakers' chisel, increasing the depth towards the centre (4). Pare back towards the lines of the triangle, gradually removing the waste (5). Sharpen up all sides ensuring that they slope evenly. Cut out each inverted pyramid in the design similarly. The final chip carving (6).

Chip carving

1. Bisect each angle.

2. Secure the wood firmly.

3. Cut from each corner.

4. Set in from each corner.

5. Cut along the outside lines.

6. The final chip carving.

Incised lettering

1. Intersect the angle.

2. Cut down the centre.

3. Make an angled inside cut.

4. Make an angled outside cut.

5. Cut cleanly around the edges.

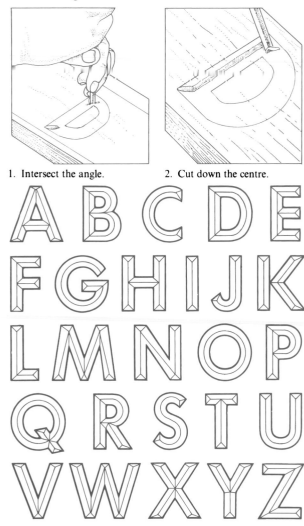

Incised lettering

Transfer a design on to the wood. Secure the wood to the bench. Where a right angle occurs in a letter use a parting tool to intersect the angle from the edge to the centre of the letter (1). Cut down the centre of the letter between the design lines with the parting tool (2). Using a shallow gouge or chisel, cut along the inner design line into the centre of the letter at an angle of approximately 55° (3). If the tool is held at a steeper angle it is likely to jam in the wood. Cut cautiously to achieve a uniform depth. If too shallow the cut can always be made deeper. Cut the other side, using a chisel or a gauge from the outer edges of the lettering (4). Take out the waste as the cuts progress so that the design can be seen clearly. Cut cleanly round the edges with a wide gouge so that they are sharp and perfectly shaped (5). Finally any open right-angled corner should be cut away as an inverted pyramid, as for chip carving. Cut at an angle of 55° to the edge and at a similar depth to the incisions already cut at the centre.

Repeat carving

Repeat carving

1. Make a tapered downward cut.

4. Set in the curved line.

6. Round over the egg.

8. Cut the dart.

9. The finished dart.

2. Cut down from the semicircle.

5. Cut the semicircle.

7. Carve the waste wood from either side of the dart.

10. Punch in the decoration.

3. Set in around the egg.

Repeat carving

Having mastered the techniques of chip carving and incised lettering, repeat carving should seem a natural progression. It most often occurs on mouldings. Make each cut throughout the length of the moulding before moving on to the next. This is to reduce the time spent picking up and putting down tools. With the parting tool make a tapered downward cut either side of the egg (1). Using the same tool cut a curved downward line from the semicircle towards the bottom centre of the egg (2). Remove the waste wood. With a wide gouge that fits the contour of the moulding set in around the egg (3). Set in the curved line as well (4). With a suitably shaped gouge held vertically cut the semicircle between the eggs (5). Round over the egg with an inverted gouge (6). Carve out the waste wood from either side of the dart leaving a straight vertical line down the centre (7). Set in the point of the dart with a spade (8). Then finish the point of the dart. Clean out the waste wood, using a spade (9). Decorate the centre of the semicircle with a punch or nail to complete the design (10).

Egg and dart moulding parts

Egg   Semicircle   Dart   Punch decoration

Relief carving

Unlike incised carving where the design is sunk into the wood, relief carving has the design raised above a cut-away surface. Low relief carving can be very simple. The outline is cut to a uniform depth and the waste wood is removed from the background to the depth of the relief line. The design is then ready for setting in and modelling.

What is termed "high relief" is in fact deep relief and the deeper the relief the greater the number of planes on which the design must be carved. The techniques in high relief work are similar to those required for carving in the round and demand considerable skill and confidence. The main technique of undercutting gives a more three-dimensional effect. Undercutting is done by carving inwards beyond the vertical to give each feature a greater shape and to cast shadows, thus enhancing the three-dimensional effect. Bent gouges and chisels are used to form the corners and crevices.

As with carving mouldings each stage of relief carving must be completed throughout the design before moving on to the next. The background can be either punched or given a tooled texture. Check the finished work for areas that may appear too deep or shallow under fixed viewing light. The Tudor rose design used to illustrate the technique is carved on a number of different planes.

Relief carving

1. Draw a relief line.

2. Cut the outer circle.

3. Remove the groundwork.

4. Level the groundwork.

5. Mark between each petal.

6. Set in the petals.

7. Curve around each petal.

8. Make two vertical cuts.

Relief carving
Before commencing relief carving transfer a design on to the wood. Then draw a line round the edges of the block to indicate the depth of the groundwork (1). The position of this line depends on what depth of relief is intended. Secure the block on four sides with wooden strips and then begin by cutting the outer, middle and inner circles around the rose with a fluter (2). Cut closely with the grain where possible. With a larger gouge remove the groundwork to within 3 mm/⅛ in of the relief line, pressing backwards with the other hand to prevent the tool running into the design (3). With a shallow tool flatten away the groundwork and smooth down to the relief line (4). Using a parting tool, mark the division between each petal with a vertical cut (5). Set in with a wide gouge (6). Curve around each petal to make individual shapes (7). Keep referring to the original design to check that no part, such as where an outer petal or leaf is to be carved, is being cut away. It is easy to make a mistake when the design is being carved on many different levels, so always work with great care. Remove the waste wood continually throughout the process. To carve the leaves emerging from under the outer petals, make two vertical cuts down to the levelled groundwork (8). Remove the

waste (9). Cut the turnover shape on the inner and outer petals with a fluter (10). Carve gently down into the centre on both inner and outer circle of petals, using a shallow gouge (11). With a pencil draw in the outer petal stems. Then using a small fluter take away the wood on either side of each of the stems (12). Set in with a shallow gouge or spade (13). With an inverted gouge round over the petal edges and the central button of the flower (14). Soften the inner and outer turnovers (15). Undercut the outer petals and the little pointed leaves (16). For a final effect use a punch and hammer to texture the groundwork (17). The Tudor rose carved in relief (18).

9. Remove the waste wood.

10. Cut the turnover shape.

11. Carve into the petal centre.

12. Remove the waste wood.

13. Set in each stem.

14. Round over the petal edges.

15. Soften the turnovers.

16. Undercut the outer leaves.

17. Texture the groundwork.

18. The final carving.

Veneering

Veneering is an invaluable part of woodworking. Many woods are very expensive or have grains that are unsuitable to work in solid form; thin slices of wood, known as veneers, offer the opportunity of using some of these rare woods and their figures. Beautiful decorative patterns can be achieved with veneers, especially by incorporating stringing and borders of contrasting colour to the central veneer panel. Leaves of veneer stacked as they were cut from the log are particularly suitable for matching veneers.

There are two methods of laying veneers: by using cauls and by hand. Cauls are used for laying thick or difficult pieces and for built-up patterns such as in marquetry and parquetry. The veneers are all taped together before being laid with either animal or resin glue. Hand veneering requires fast and organized working because each veneer is laid separately with hot animal glue, which must remain hot until the veneer is correctly positioned. Impact adhesives do not give good results as positioning the veneer on the ground is difficult, bumps in the surface are almost unavoidable and blisters are difficult to deal with.

Veneers should always cover the base or ground on to which they are to be glued, with a little extra width and length. Avoid veneering over surface joints or end grain wherever possible, especially on face veneer, as sinkage usually results. When veneering both sides of the ground always lay the underneath veneer before the face veneer.

To cut veneers use a knife and a metal straight-edge, except on oak or sycamore when a hardwood straight-edge should be substituted. A veneer knife must have a stiff pointed blade that has a long, thin, straight cutting edge. A trimming knife and scalpel are ideal.

Any splits in veneer must be taped with gummed paper tape once the veneer is laid on the ground. Always tape veneer joints with gummed paper tape. This holds the joints together so the veneers will shrink from the sides. Any other adhesive tape is very sticky and can easily tear the veneer on removal.

Veneer grounds
The ground is the base for veneers and can be of any thickness. It can be of solid wood provided the growth rings run at right angles to the surface and it is flat, true, unsplit and free from knots and any other defect. Manufactured boards are also suitable as grounds. On all manufactured boards and all solid wood of less than 13 mm/½ in thickness lay a plain inexpensive counter veneer on the reverse side of the ground to prevent the ground curling as the glue dries and the veneer contracts.

Preparing the veneers
Unpack the batch of veneers carefully. Keeping the leaves in order, number them consecutively with a soft pencil (1). The adjoining leaves will then match almost perfectly. Gently rub the veneers on both sides with a warm damp cloth to flatten them (2). Lay no more than ten leaves at a time between flat boards, and clamp for at least three hours or overnight until they are almost, but not quite, dry (3). On a flat board cut the sheets singly to the required size, allow 6 mm/¼ in extra all round. To facilitate a close join lean the knife blade slightly away from the straight-edge (4). Cut the veneer with several light strokes. Too much pressure, especially across the grain, will split the veneer. It might be helpful to cut the last bit away from the uncut end.

Veneer grounds

Manufactured boards

Thick solid wood

Preparing the veneers

1. Number the veneer leaves.

2. Damp the leaves.

3. Place in a cramp.

4. Cut to the required size.

Matching veneers

A

B

C

D

Veneers may be cut from the crown, burr, butt or main trunk of a tree. When matching veneer bear in mind where the piece will be placed in relation to the light as this can considerably alter the colour of the veneer.

A Plain quartering is excellent for short stock.

B Butt end quartering is the most commonly used quarter matching pattern.

C Quartering diamond can be used when the veneer is straight grained and has a plain figure.

D Book matching has every other sheet turned over.

Using cauls

Pressing veneers using cauls

When using cauls, veneers and ground are glued together, placed between bearers and clamped. The caul itself is a stout piece of laminboard or blockboard, at least 19 mm/¾ in thick, which is clean, flat and free from defects. Its length and width should exceed that of the ground. Use of a jointed board is inadvisable. The caul is placed against the veneered side of the ground with newspaper inserted between the veneer and the caul to absorb the excess glue. When the ground is counter veneered, newspaper and a caul are placed against each veneer. Bearers in pairs are clamped over and under the caul and veneered ground, no further than 250 mm/10 in away from each other. Bearers are made from sound solid wood, cut on the bandsaw. For a single caul the bottom bearers are flat while the top bearers have a slight curve. For a double caul one edge of each bearer is curved. The width of the bearer should be twice its thickness and its length should extend 100 mm/4 in beyond the caul's width.

Jointing veneers

1. Plane the veneers flush.

2. Make right-angled cuts.

Jointing veneers

When using cauls, veneers must be jointed, pinned and taped together before being glued and laid as one piece. To joint two veneers place them between two straight-edged battens with the veneer grain running parallel with the battens. Allow a little of the veneers to appear above the battens. Grip one end of the assembly in a bench vice and hold the other in a G-cramp. Plane the veneers flush (1). Remove from the vice and lay the veneers on a flat surface. With a knife and try square cut the ends of the veneers at right angles to the planed sides, using several light strokes (2). Cut the unplaned side of the veneers with a sharp knife and straight-edge.

Using cauls with resin glue

1. Tape the veneer joints.

2. Evenly spread the glue.

3. Lay the veneer.

4. Press down the veneer.

5. Leave to dry.

Using cauls with resin glue

Pin and tape the jointed veneers closely together in the required pattern with short pieces of tape (1). Remedy any defects on the ground to be veneered (see page 223). Roughen the ground diagonally with a toothing plane. Dust off. Assemble the press. Pour the glue on to the ground. Spread it evenly over the surface with a spatula (2). Lay the veneer on the ground, leaving an extra 6 mm/¼ in of veneer around the sides (3). Smooth it down by hand. With a roller, press the glue from the centre to the edges (4). If counter veneering, lay the veneer on the other side of the ground in the same way. Cover the veneered ground with newspaper and place in the press. Using an assistant, clamp the pairs of bearers together, gradually exerting pressure from the centre outwards. Leave to dry (5). Then remedy any blisters.

Using cauls with animal glue

Pressure from cramp

Bearer

Caul

Heated plate

Newspaper

Veneer

Ground

Using cauls with animal glue

Prepare the ground as for hand veneering (see page 194). Pin and tape the jointed veneers together. Brush the glue on to the ground. Lay on the veneer, leaving 6 mm/¼ in extra veneer around the edges. If counter veneering, lay veneer on the other side in the same way. Cover the veneered ground with newspaper and a preheated zinc or alloy plate and place in a press. Clamp the pairs of bearers together from the centre outwards. When dry, remove from the cramp and check that the veneer has stuck to every part of the ground. Remedy any blisters that may have occurred.

193

Hand veneering

Preparing the ground

1. Key the ground.   2. Size the ground.   3. Mark up the ground.

Laying veneer by hand

150 mm/6 in

Hardwood

Brass strip

88 mm/3½ in   1. Make a veneer hammer.

2. Assemble the equipment.

3. Press down the veneer.   4. Use two hands.

Preparing the ground

Cut out any defects and patch (see page 223). Using a toothing plane key the ground to be veneered diagonally across the grain in both directions (1). Dust off. Size all the ground to seal the pores (2). Size the end grain repeatedly until the pores are filled. Leave each coat for at least three hours to dry. Smooth the sized ground diagonally with a medium abrasive paper around a sanding block. Wipe the surface clean. Mark both sides and edges of the ground with a pencil and rule to indicate where all veneer pieces, including borders, will lie. Mark a 6 mm/¼ in overlap on each side on any joins (3).

Laying veneer by hand

To lay veneer by hand a veneering hammer must be made (1). The handle and flat or tapered head of the hammer are of hardwood and are screwed or dowelled together. The grain of the head should run at right angles to the brass or aluminium strip inserted at the bottom end. Always hand veneer in a room that is at least 21 C/70 F and have all the required tools and materials to hand so the hot glue does not chill and thus lose its adhesive properties. Collect together the following: freshly prepared hot animal glue, a straight-edge, a rule, a knife, a pencil, a brush, an electric iron (a domestic one will do), clean hot water, a clean damp cloth, gummed paper tape, a cross pein hammer and a veneer hammer (2). Dip the veneer hammer in the hot water to heat its metal edge. Warm the ground gently over a flame or against a radiator. Brush a thin even coat of hot glue on to the ground. Position the veneer against the ground marks, allowing a 6 mm/¼ in overlap for any edge and join. Brush the top side of the veneer lightly with glue. Then press the veneer against the ground with the veneer hammer, working from the centre outwards with a zigzag motion and pushing the warm glue and any air bubbles to the edges (3). Avoid bringing too much pressure across the grain as this will stretch the veneer and will cause more shrinkage when the veneer is drying. For greater pressure, use two hands on the hammer (4). If the glue needs reheating lay a damp cloth on the veneer and lightly run a warm iron over the

5. Press with a warm iron.

6. Lift the V-cut veneer.

7. Position the second veneer.

8. Apply glue to the top side.

9. Cut through the two veneers.

10. Remove the underneath strip. 11. Reglue the veneer join.

12. Press the join.

13. Tape the join.

surface (5). Then press the veneer against the ground again. When the veneer has been evenly pressed in position, clean away any excess glue. It is important to keep the veneer clean but take care to avoid unnecessary cleaning as too much water in the glue will cause it to lose its adhesion. Test for blisters or foreign bodies under the veneer by brushing the surface with the palm of the hand and tapping suspect areas with a finger nail. Remedy any blisters (see page 222). To take out a foreign body make a V-cut, running as closely with the grain and figure as possible. Lift the veneer, remove the defect and insert a little more glue (6). Then press the veneer down. To lay the second veneer, glue the ground. Then lay the veneer on the glued ground, overlapping it against the first veneer where marked (7). Brush the top side with glue (8). Press the veneer to the ground. Place the straight-edge against the marked centre and cut through the two veneers (9). Peel away the top strip. Lift the veneer slightly to remove the second veneer strip and any dirt particles from underneath (10). Reglue the veneer edges (11). Press the centre join (12). Clean the area and tape the join so the veneer shrinks from the edges as it dries (13). Repeat this process on any further pieces of veneer.

Banding and finishing

Banding

Inlay banding

Plain banding

Crossbanding

Herringbone

Banding

Banding is the overall term for any veneer decoration, of whatever width or pattern, surrounding a veneer panel. The inner decoration is known as stringing and is usually a very fine line of black or cream veneer. The outer decoration is known as a border. Plain borders are cut along the grain as one continuous strip. Crossbanding is cut at right angles to the grain as one or more strips. Herringbone banding is made from two strips cut at 45° to the grain and laid together with one strip turned over.

Laying banding by hand

1. Lift the waste veneer.

2. Check the width.

3. Position the stringing.

4. Cut corners with a chisel.

Laying banding by hand

Both stringing and borders are laid in the same way. The process of cutting and laying stringing is illustrated. Set a straight-edge or cutting gauge on the ground against the border marks and cut away the waste veneer from the central panels while the glue is still at the jelly stage. Lift the waste with a chisel (1). Clean the area well. Measure the stringing, allowing 6 mm/$\frac{1}{4}$ in overlaps. Check the evenness of width with a rule set against a straight-edge(2). Cut the stringing and apply glue to both sides. Place it on the ground, tight to the central veneer panels. Press the stringing to the ground with a veneer hammer or the cross pein of a hammer. Glue both sides of a second piece of stringing and lay it at right angles to the first, overlapping at the corner (3). Mitre the corners with a wide chisel cutting vertically through both veneer layers (4). (For borders use a knife and straight-edge, making a short cut from the outer corner before cutting from the inside corner outwards.) Remove the top waste veneer and lift the mitred corner to extract the underneath waste (5). Reglue the corner. Rub it down and wipe clean. Lay all stringing and then the borders similarly. Tape the mitred corners (6). Then tape the join between the banding and the central panels.

5. Remove the waste veneer.

6. Tape each corner.

Laying banding prior to using cauls

1. Tape the banding in position.

2. Cut the corner.

Laying banding prior to using cauls

Measure and cut each strip of banding so it overlaps 6 mm/$\frac{1}{4}$ in at the ground corners and over the edge. Tape each strip tight against the central veneer panel, leaving the corners free (1). Either mitre each corner with a wide chisel, cutting vertically through both layers of veneer, or use a knife and straight-edge to make a short cut from the outer corner before cutting from the inside corner outwards (2). Remove the waste. Tape the corner. Repeat for all corners. Then lay the veneers as a single leaf (*see* page 193).

Trimming excess veneer

1. Chisel away excess veneer. OR Trim with a knife.

2. Plane the sides straight.

Trimming excess veneer

When the glue has dried, place the veneered ground in a bench vice, protecting the veneer with cork. Chisel the veneer sides flush with the ground sides, working inwards towards the ground (1). Pay careful attention to the direction of the grain. Alternatively tilt the ground slightly on a piece of waste wood. Cut the bottom excess veneer away with a knife. Repeat all round the ground. Using a jack plane smooth the sides straight and square (2).

Edges

Whether the veneer has been laid by hand or using cauls, ground edges must be sized with animal glue. When dry, smooth with abrasive paper. Cut veneer strips of the same colour as the borders, allowing 6 mm/$\frac{1}{4}$ in extra width and length. Glue both sides of a strip with hot animal glue and press it against the ground edge (1). Trim both ends with either a chisel or a knife. Lay and trim the other strips in the same way. Tape all the corners. When the glue has dried trim the edges flush with the sides of the veneered ground. (2).

1. Hammer the veneer down.

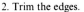

2. Trim the edges.

Cleaning up

Remove any tape and dried excess glue by gently rubbing both sides and all edges of the veneer with a warm damp cloth (1). Lightly scrape off any tape and glue that remains, using a cabinet scraper (2). (The surface must be absolutely clear as no surface finish will adhere to any sticky patches.) Smooth the sides and edges of the veneer with an 80 grit abrasive paper. Then use a finer abrasive paper (3). Apply sand sealer unless a french polish or oil finish is required.

1. Rub with a warm damp cloth.

2. Scrape off tape and glue.

3. Smooth with abrasive paper.

Parquetry

Parquetry is the laying of veneers to form a geometrical design. It is a companion craft to marquetry but, whereas in the latter almost all the cutting is done freehand, for parquetry a straight-edge guides the knife through the veneer. Most parquetry designs are made from polygon-shaped pieces of veneer — usually diamonds, squares and triangles. Plain figured and straight grained woods are most suitable.

For accurate cutting use a simple jig with a straight-edge of steel or wood fixed to it. Cover the jig with vinyl or linoleum to protect the knife blade and, from a single point on the straight-edge, mark out 30°, 45°, 60° and 90° angles. A movable fence, used as a guide for the veneer, can be set to the required angle. A fence made of veneer rather than of metal or solid wood is preferable as it can be cut into without damaging the knife blade. Use a veneer knife with a comfortable handle and with a pointed blade. When cutting veneer, spacers are required to measure and maintain an equal width throughout a strip of veneer. They are made from wooden or metal squares or rectangles. Used in pairs of the same width they should be positioned against the straight-edge at the ends beyond the veneer. Always set out veneer strips in the order they are cut to prevent any inconsistencies in the design and join the veneer pieces with short strips of gummed paper tape.

When the design is complete, check that it has right-angled corners. Then add any banding (*see* page 197). Mount the design on a ground, using cauls and resin glue (*see* page 193). Counter veneer if necessary. Lay veneer strips on the edges and then clean up all the surfaces and edges (*see* page 197).

Cutting veneer strips

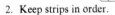

1. Cut along the grain.

2. Keep strips in order.

Patterns based on squares and rectangles

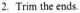

1. Tape strips together.

2. Trim the ends.

3. Cut the strips across.

Pattern variations based on squares and rectangles

4. Reverse alternate strips.

5. Tape strips closely.

Cutting veneer strips

Trim one side of a veneer leaf parallel with the grain. Place it against the fixed straight-edge together with spacers of the desired strip width. Set the spacers either side of the veneer leaf. Place a rule against the spacers and with the knife blade at a low angle cut the veneer along the grain (**1**). Twist the blade into the rule slightly. Remove the strip. Continue to cut in this way laying the strips in order as they are cut (**2**). To make a basketweave pattern, half the veneer strips must be cut across the grain and laid alternately.

Patterns based on squares and rectangles

Cut four dark and four light strips of veneer of identical width. Use short pieces of gummed paper tape to stick alternate dark and light strips closely together (**1**). Place the veneer fence along the 90° line on the jig. Turn over the taped strips and lie one side flush with the veneer fence. Trim one end of the assembled strips (**2**). Place the trimmed strip ends and the spacers that were used to cut the strips against the jig straight-edge. Hold the rule against the spacers and cut the veneers through with several long strokes. Cut the rest of the veneers in the same way, keeping each strip in the order it is cut (**3**). Discard any waste veneer. To make a chessboard pattern turn around every alternate strip (**4**). Tape each end of the strips closely into position (**5**). Then turn over the assembled strips and tape along them. Remove the positioning tape from the underside. Endless variations can be obtained using this technique. To make triangles halve squares diagonally. Cut rectangles by using different spacer widths.

Patterns based on diamonds

1. Lie the strips together.

2. Cut the strips through.

3. Tape the pattern.

4. Cut a zigzag line.

5. Tape to the opposite side.

A zigzag pattern.

A chevron pattern.

A pattern of triangles.

Cubes

1. Place diamonds in position.

2. Cut around the outline.

3. Let in the design.

Stars

Splitting diamonds.

Star motifs.

Patterns based on diamonds

Cut strips of equal width as for any pattern based on squares. Tape the veneer fence along the 60° line on the jig. Lie alternate light and dark strips tight to the veneer fence so that the corner of each strip touches the straight-edge (1). Tape the strips closely together. Trim the corners using the rule and spacers, so that they can be positioned tightly against the straight-edge. Using spacers of the same width as were used originally to cut the strips, lie the rule against the spacers and cut the veneers through with several long strokes (2). To make a chequered pattern move each succeeding strip along by one diamond. Tape the strips closely together (3). To make the overall pattern square, cut a zigzag line down the sides of a row of diamonds (4). Place the straight side against the opposite straight side (5). Tape together. To make a zigzag pattern cut through the centres of all the diamonds of one colour and move each alternate strip along half a diamond. To make a chevron pattern, repeat the same procedure described for the zigzag on both sets of diamonds. To make a pattern of triangles turn over every alternate strip.

Cubes

A cube is made from three 60° angled diamonds of different shades. Cut the diamonds and assemble the design on paper. Pin self-adhesive plastic, sticky side up, on grid paper and lift the diamonds on to it with the point of a knife (1). When the design is complete cut around the outline and through the plastic (2). Hold the design firmly in position on the background veneer and cut around the outline. Let the design into the veneer (3).

Stars

Star motifs are built up with diamonds. Construct and lay them into veneer in the same way as cubes. To calculate the appropriate angle for a star, divide 360° by the required number of points. A six-pointed star, for example, is made from six 60° angled diamonds. Some star motifs are made from split diamonds cut with a plane blade held vertically across the diamond and tapped with a hammer.

Marquetry

Marquetry is the laying of veneers, cut freehand, to form a design. Using this technique, the endless figure variations found in wood can be exploited.

Originally a fretsaw was used to cut awkward veneer shapes, but this is no longer necessary now that veneers as thin as $0.7\,\text{mm}/\frac{1}{32}$ in are available. These can be cut with a craft knife, provided the blade has a fine point. The "window" method is the most satisfactory technique for modern marquetry as the worker can see the exact grain effect of any veneer piece before it is cut.

With the "window" method the design is traced on the veneer selected as the background. A design feature is then cut out from the background veneer and a new piece of veneer of different colour or figure is placed under the opening or "window" in the background veneer. The new veneer is cut to shape, using the window edges as a template, and is then glued in to the window.

Depending on the subject, plain or figured veneer can be used for the background. Where the background veneer represents the sky, any darker part should be at the top of the sky. In general, cut the background features first and gradually work through to the foreground, cutting out one feature at a time.

Cut veneers on a piece of hardboard or plywood covered with linoleum or vinyl tiles to prevent the knife blade from dulling. Curved shapes should be cut with the knife almost upright in small stabs made with the knife point. Begin at the nearest end and start each stroke slightly farther away each time. Cut straighter shapes with the knife held at a low angle and with the blade at a 90° angle to the surface. If possible simplify the shape and strengthen the edges of the pieces by overcutting into the borders and into background veneer that is later to be cut away. The completed picture must be absolutely square so that when the banding is laid the corners can be mitred accurately.

When practising marquetry, use PVA glue, but where this is insufficient to hold a feature in place, stick a little gummed paper tape over the join on the face.

Shading

1. Heat up the sand.
2. Spoon on to the veneer.·
3. Remove the hot sand.

Shading

Veneer can be shaded darker by scorching it with hot sand. Place a metal container filled with silver sand over a moderately high flame or hot plate (**1**). Test the sand temperature with a piece of waste veneer. When hot enough, either dip the veneer into the sand or spoon the hot sand on to the area to be tinted (**2**). Remove after a few seconds (**3**). The sand will remove moisture, leaving the veneer brittle, so dampen it a little with a moist cloth.

Cutting the design

1. Transfer the background details and registration mark.

2. Pencil in any gaps.

3. Overcut the line if possible.

Cutting the design

Draw the design on tracing paper; make a registration mark at the bottom. Choose a suitable veneer for the background, ensuring that it extends over the design borders on every side. Reinforce the end grain on the piece of veneer with some gummed paper tape to prevent splitting. Select which side of the veneer to position at the top. Tape the top of the tracing paper to the top of the background veneer, using gummed paper. Place a sheet of black carbon paper between the veneer and the tracing paper. (Use white carbon for dark veneers.) Trace the background design features, the registration mark and the borders on to the background veneer, using a worn-out ballpoint pen or stylus (**1**). Fold back the tracing paper and remove the carbon paper. Join up any gaps in the traced lines where details will later be positioned (**2**). Cut around one of the traced features on the background. Overcut into borders or areas that are later to be replaced (**3**).

4. Remove the piece.

5. Select a new veneer.

6. Score the selected veneer.

7. Glue in the selected veneer.

8. The background set in.

9. Set in small features.

10. Flatten the sliver.

11. Work the sliver into the slot.

Tidying up

1. Check the diagonals.

2. Cut along the border lines.

Remove the piece (**4**). Select a suitably figured veneer and move it around in the opening or "window" left in the background veneer (**5**). When the best grain effect shows through the window, hold the selected veneer in place with paper clips or gummed paper tape and score it around the window edges in small stabs, always cutting back into the previous score mark (**6**). Remove the piece of selected veneer from under the window. Then cut along the scored line. With a pointed piece of waste veneer apply PVA glue to the window edges. Fit the selected veneer piece into the window and rub the edges into place with the knife handle (**7**). Replace the tracing paper and carbon paper on the background veneer, aligning the registration marks, and retrace any lines that have been cut away. Cut and set in each feature of the background design, following the process described above (**8**). Then trace on the remaining features of the design. Cut and set in the selected veneer pieces for these last features. Sometimes it is better to set in small features before adjacent large features; the overcutting will strengthen them (**9**). To cut out very thin lines on the design, first cut on one side of the line and then on the other. Remove the tiny sliver from the background veneer to make a slot. With a rule and knife cut a thin long sliver from a straight grained veneer and stroke it with the knife handle to flatten it (**10**). Insert one end of the selected sliver into the slot. Put a dab of glue on it to hold it in place. Work in the rest of the sliver and then rub a little glue into the join with the back of the knife handle (**11**).

Tidying up
When all the veneer pieces have been fitted correctly re-mark the lines of the border. The picture must be absolutely square before the banding is laid, so check that the sides of the design are at right angles to each other by ensuring the diagonals are the same length and that the sides are the same length (**1**). Cut along the border lines, using the knife and straight-edge (**2**). Add any banding (*see* page 197). Mount the design on a ground, using cauls and resin glue (*see* page 193). Counter veneer if necessary. Veneer the edges and then clean up the surfaces and edges (*see* page 197).

201

Surface finishes 1

The purpose of applying a surface finish to wood is to protect it from oil, grease, liquids and other general pollution by sealing the pores. The surface finish will also enhance the natural beauty of the wood, if a transparent rather than an opaque finish is applied. To prevent the wood from shrinking and thus the finished surface breaking down, any centrally heated room should contain a humidifier or an abundance of plants to maintain adequate levels of moisture in the air.

Choosing the best materials to apply to a particular piece of work can cause confusion especially as the materials must be compatible. The eventual use of the piece is the prime consideration. Will it be subject to hard wear and tear or have liquids spilled on it? Does it need to be heat resistant? (The qualities possessed by the important surface coatings are described on pages 208–11.) Will the piece look more attractive if it is coloured? If so, will a stain be satisfactory or would an opaque finish be more suitable? Is an open-grained surface preferable—or a close-grained woodfilled one?

Before applying any surface finish, it is essential that the wood is thoroughly prepared and its surface is absolutely clean. Any residual grease and dirt will repel the materials and thus give an uneven finish. Plane all protruding joints; punch nails and panel pins below the surface and remove any pencil marks, oil and grease stains, paint and bruises. Fill in any holes later.

Once the wood has been prepared, consult the chart (*right*) for the order in which the appropriate surface finishes should be applied.

Preparing the wood

1. Press with a warm iron.

2. Thoroughly clean the wood.

Preparing the wood
Surface finishes tend to accentuate rather than conceal bruises and they are repelled by dirt so special care should be taken with the preparation of the piece of work. Any bruises in the wood must be removed before any finish is applied. Dampen the damaged area with a wet cloth. Heat an old iron file or an electric soldering iron so that the warmth from the iron can be felt 150 mm/6 in from the face. Place a wet cloth over the bruise and press with the iron, moving it about gently (**1**). The resultant steam causes the wood fibres to expand and rise, thus removing the bruise. Smooth the area with glasspaper. To clean the wood, rub the surface vigorously with a cloth and clean water (**2**). The water will raise the grain. When the wood has dried completely, smooth it with a grade 6/0 or 7/0 garnet paper and dust off. The wood is then ready for its first surface finish.

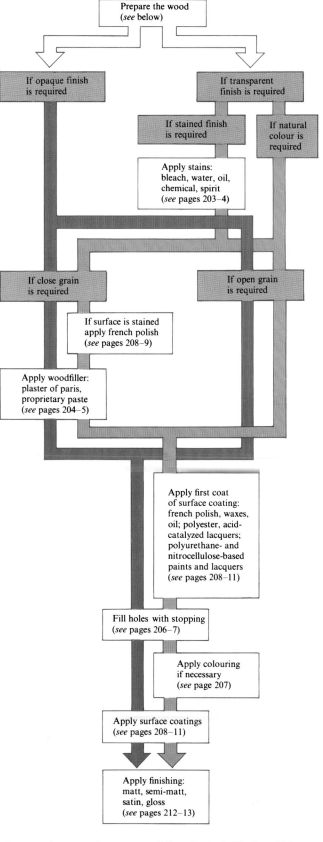

Prepare the wood
(*see* below)

If opaque finish is required

If transparent finish is required

If stained finish is required

If natural colour is required

Apply stains: bleach, water, oil, chemical, spirit (*see* pages 203–4)

If close grain is required

If open grain is required

If surface is stained apply french polish (*see* pages 208–9)

Apply woodfiller: plaster of paris, proprietary paste (*see* pages 204–5)

Apply first coat of surface coating: french polish, waxes, oil; polyester, acid-catalyzed lacquers; polyurethane- and nitrocellulose-based paints and lacquers (*see* pages 208–11)

Fill holes with stopping (*see* pages 206–7)

Apply colouring if necessary (*see* page 207)

Apply surface coatings (*see* pages 208–11)

Apply finishing: matt, semi-matt, satin, gloss (*see* pages 212–13)

To ensure the appropriate materials are applied in their correct order once the wood has been prepared, follow the arrows in the chart. Starting from the top of the page, follow the shaded boxes, which indicate the type of finish selected, and complete the actions mentioned in the unshaded boxes, in the order in which they appear.

On a transparent surface coating, a stain will often emphasize the natural figure of the wood as well as colour it. A stain is unnecessary where an opaque surface coating is to be applied.

There are four different groups of stains: water, chemical, oil and spirit. Only stains in the same group are intermixable. Each group of stains may be diluted by its base solvent.

The art of staining is based on one simple principle: use plenty of the stain at the outset. It is advisable to allow a couple of hours for the wood to dry after staining. Any polishing carried out on wet wood will, at a later stage, cause a reaction that will spoil the final finish. The grain may whiten, pimples may form, a cloudy film may appear or the polish may flake off.

Water stains

These are known as direct dyes. They are made by mixing dry pigment powders with water. The pigment powders are intermixable and so a wide range of shades can be achieved. The depth of the colour is determined by the amount of powder used: the more powder, the darker the stain. Pigment powders are comparatively cheap to buy and large quantities of stain can be made up from fairly small amounts of the powder. Some powders may take a while to dissolve, so leave the mixed stain for an hour before using so the final colour is certain.

Chemical stains

Some chemicals such as blue copperas and ammonia can be mixed with water and applied to wood as a stain. They react with the tannic acid that is present in varying amounts in the wood and thus change the wood colour. The problem is that the woodworker cannot see what colour these stains will make until they are applied to the wood. Some chemicals such as bichromate of potash and copper sulphate have a little colour content of their own while others, such as ammonia and caustic soda, are colourless.

Oil stains

These are available in a variety of colours, which can be mixed. They are simple to use but are relatively expensive. Oil stains do not penetrate the wood fibres and thus will not raise the grain. Their strength therefore tends to be greater than other stains.

Spirit stains

Spirit stains are made by dissolving dry pigment powder in methylated spirit and then adding french polish in a ratio of four parts methylated spirit to one part french polish. The french polish will act as a binder; if it is not used the methylated spirit will evaporate, leaving behind the dry powder. The rapid evaporation rate of the solvent in spirit stains does tend to make them difficult to use on large surfaces. They also have a tendency to fade.

Bleaches

There are three main bleaches that can be used on wood: sodium hypochlorite, oxalic acid and super bleach.

Sodium hypochlorite is one of the constituents of household bleach and it can be used for removing dark marks, but it will not substantially alter the colour of wood. Oxalic acid, which is a poisonous white crystalline powder saturated in water or methylated spirit, has similar uses. It should be neutralized with acetic acid and washed with water.

Super bleach is extremely powerful. Always wear gloves and avoid splashing it. It is available as a two-pack bleach. The first solution is an alkaline, which is applied liberally and allowed to soak into the wood. This may temporarily darken the wood. The second solution is concentrated hydrogen peroxide. When it is applied to the wood after the first solution, the bleaching action takes place. If the overall reduction in colour is not sufficient, repeat the whole process.

Whichever bleach is used, wash the wood with clean water afterwards and allow it to dry completely.

The effect of stains on various woods

	Mahogany	Vandyke	Black	Blue copperas	Bichromate of potash	Ammonia	Sodium hypochlorite	Oxalic acid	Super bleach
Beech	reddish	brown	grey	greyish	light tan	brown	slightly lightens	slightly lightens	almost white
Mahogany	red	brown	subdues red; produces greyish tone	eliminates red; produces browny-grey	deep rich brown	deep brown with greyish tone	removes dark marks	slightly lightens	lightens considerably
Oak	red	deep brown	grey	grey-blue	greenish-brown	slightly greenish deep brown	removes dark marks	slightly lightens	almost white
Pine	reddish	brown	grey	greyish	pale yellow	greenish-brown	removes dark marks	slightly lightens	almost white
Teak	reddish	brown	grey	greyish	yellowish-brown	greenish-brown	removes dark marks	slightly lightens	lightens considerably
Walnut	reddish	brown	grey	greyish	pale yellow	greenish-brown	slightly lightens	slightly lightens	lightens considerably
Manufactured boards	reddish	brown	grey	greyish	deep brown	greenish-brown	removes dark marks	removes dark marks	almost white

Surface finishes 2

Staining with a water stain

1. Test the colour of the stain.

2. Tip in the powder.

3. Test the solution.

4. Apply with an absorbent cloth.

5. Brush uneven surfaces.

Staining with a water stain
To test the colour of a stain rub some water and a little powdered stain into the palm of the hand (1). Tip some powder from a creased piece of abrasive paper into hot water (2). Make a strong solution. Stir and bring to the boil. Test the shade on the back of the hand (3). Dilute if necessary. Saturate end grain in clean water. Soak a soft absorbent cloth in the stain solution and work the stain into the pores with a circular motion (4). Use a brush on uneven surfaces, ensuring it does not splash (5). Apply the solution to the surface quickly so the whole area is still moist when the operation is complete. While still wet wipe the surface dry in a circular motion with a clean dry cloth. Then wipe dry along the grain. Dry all corners and recesses carefully. Adhesion problems will occur later if all excess stain is not removed. Leave to dry for a couple of hours. When completely dry, seal with french polish.

Woodfillers

Woodfillers are used to fill up the pores of wood to obtain a full-grained finish and also for a high-gloss finish; they are rarely used on carved wood. They are based on a variety of chalks to which colouring, oils and solvents are added. Woodfillers are cheaper, quicker and more effective than french polish or any other surface coating that could be used as a filler.

Both plaster of paris and proprietary oil-based fillers are available. Plaster of paris is only used when the work is to be french polished. Combined stain and woodfillers are available, but they are generally unsatisfactory. Some surface coatings require specific woodfillers, so check with the suppliers. Always use a filler that is slightly darker than the wood surface.

Woodfillers can be applied to stained and unstained surfaces. Stained surfaces must be sealed by spreading a thin coat of french polish on the wood before it is covered with woodfiller. If left unsealed, the stain might possibly be lifted later on.

The art of successful woodfilling is to apply the filler quickly and evenly and to cover the entire surface before the filler has begun to dry. Clean all corners and recesses with a quirk stick and allow the woodfiller to dry for at least 4 hours before glasspapering, dusting off and applying the surface coating.

The effect of oil-based woodfillers on various woods							
	Light oak	Medium oak	Dark oak	Light mahogany	Medium mahogany	Dark mahogany	Black
Beech	yellowish with light grain	light tan with slightly dark grain	dark brown with dark grain	pale pink with light grain	pinkish with slightly dark grain	pale red-brown with dark grain	dirty grey with dark grain
Mahogany	yellowish with white grain	yellowish tinge with slightly white grain	darkish brown with slightly dark grain	pinkish with slightly light grain	darkish with slightly dark grain	red-brown with dark grain	greyish-brown with very dark grain
Oak	yellowish with slightly white grain	light brown with slightly dark grain	darkish with dark grain	pinkish with slightly light grain	reddish with slightly dark grain	red-brown with dark grain	grey with very dark grain
Pine	yellowish with light grain	slight tan with slightly dark grain	brownish with dark grain	pale pink with light grain	pinkish with slightly dark grain	brownish with dark grain	greyish with very dark grain
Teak	yellowish with light grain	brown with slightly dark grain	brown with dark grain	pale pink with light grain	pinkish with slightly dark grain	reddish brown with dark grain	greyish with very dark grain
Walnut	yellowish with light grain	darkish with slightly light grain	darkish brown with slightly dark grain	pinkish with light grain	pinkish with slightly dark grain	brownish with dark grain	greyish with very dark grain
Manufactured boards	yellowish with light grain	brownish with slightly dark grain	brown with dark grain	pinkish with light grain	light red-brown with slightly dark grain	red-brown with dark grain	grey-brown with very dark grain

Making a quirk stick

1. Split off a sliver of wood.

2. Shape the wood.

3. The finished product.

Woodfilling with a proprietary paste

1. Fill the pad with paste.

2. Rub into the surface.

3. Clean out any mouldings.

Woodfilling with plaster of paris

1. Mix the powders and plaster.

2. Test the colour.

3. Press into the mixture.

4. Rub into the grain.

Making a quirk stick
Split off a piece of hardwood with a chisel and mallet (**1**). Work the quirk stick to shape with a chisel (**2**). The stick may be pointed or rounded, large or small, depending on the shape of the recesses it is intended to clean (**3**).

Woodfilling with a proprietary paste
Scrape the paste out of its container with a loose pad of hessian (**1**). If too thick, dilute the paste with turps. Rub the paste into the surface of the wood, using a circular motion (**2**). Work the paste well into any corners and mouldings. Then, keeping the pad loose, rub the paste across the grain. While the filler is still wet, wipe away the excess with hessian and then a soft, absorbent cloth. With an appropriately shaped quirk stick clean corners, edges and recesses where any woodfiller remains (**3**). Leave to dry.

Woodfilling with plaster of paris
Tip out some superfine white plaster on to a piece of newspaper and add the required pigment powders. Mix together the powders and plaster by tipping them about in the newspaper (**1**). To test the colour, put some water on the back of the hand, dip a finger into the plaster mixture and rub it on the wet hand (**2**). The colour will appear much chalkier than desired, but this whiteness will be removed later. Then soak a piece of hessian in cold water. Squeeze it out gently and press it into the plaster mixture (**3**). Rub the filler into the grain, using a circular motion (**4**). When the entire surface has been filled, wipe it clean across the grain with clean hessian held loosely. Clean corners, edges and recesses with a quirk stick. Leave to dry for about 4 hours. The water from the plaster will evaporate and leave a white residue. Remove this with linseed oil on a soft cloth, applied to the surface with a circular motion. Smooth the still wet wood with 320 grit glasspaper, rubbing lightly along the grain. Wipe across the grain with clean dry hessian, pushing the excess filler into the grain pores. Rub up with a dry cloth.

205

Surface finishes 3

The process of filling holes and cracks is known as stopping. For an opaque finish, stopping is done after any woodfiller has been applied (if a full-grained finish is desired) but before any surface coating is applied. For any transparent finish, stopping and colouring are done after the woodfiller process and after one layer of surface coating has been applied. If woodfiller is not used the surface for a transparent finish must still be coated once before stopping and colouring.

There are several materials that are suitable for filling holes. Some, such as beaumontage and shellac, are known as "hard stopping" and are melted in use while others, such as beeswax and japan wax, are applied cold and are better suited to filling small holes. Shellac is immensely sticky and it is much cleaner to use beaumontage. Any of these stopping materials can be coloured by melting them down and mixing in dry pigment powders.

Colouring entails touching up a surface to one overall colour. It is best to make up spirit stains in strength and then mix them together. Dilute in a new solution of four parts methylated spirit and one part french polish. Bismarck brown and spirit black are the main spirit stains that, combined in varying quantities, will give warmer or colder shades respectively. To lighten dark spots in wood combine lemon chrome, orange chrome and titanium white. The colour should blend into the background and not show up as an obvious blob of colour.

Two thin coats of spirit stain are better than one thick one so bear this in mind when mixing up a colour. If more than three applications are required, seal the stain in with a layer of the selected surface coating before continuing with the colouring. Failure to do this could cause the stain already on to drag off later.

Fads and rubbers
The professional way to apply french polish is with a rubber or a fad (*see* page 209). Rubbers are also used to apply a pull-over solution (*see* page 211). A rubber is a piece of absorbent wadding covered in soft absorbent material. The wadding is carefully folded so it is pear shaped with a point at one end. Pound wadding is best as it remains soft and springy for a long time whereas medicated cotton wool and upholsterers' wadding tend to harden very quickly.

After much use, the wadding in the rubber will become slightly hardened. When this occurs, the cloth covering the wadding is removed. The hardened wadding is then known as a fad and is used by itself to apply polish. Fads and rubbers should be stored in an airtight container such as a lidded jar.

Filling large holes

1. Undercut the sides.

2. Heat the tang of a file.

3. Melt the beaumontage stick.

4. Chisel away the excess.

5. Smooth with a sanding block.   6. Smooth by hand.

Filling large holes
Proprietary wax sticks, made in a variety of colours, can be used; alternatively make a beaumontage stick by melting beeswax and carnauba wax in 10:1 proportions in a double pot. Add pigment powder. Cool down the mixture and bind with a little french polish. Allow to solidify. Enlarge the hole to be filled by undercutting the sides so the stopping remains lodged in place (1). Heat the tang of a file so that when held 150 mm/6 in away from the face the warmth can be felt (2). Wipe off the soot. Hold the beaumontage stick over the hole and melt it into the hole with the hot tang (3). Press it in well. With a chisel, held bevel downwards, gently scrape away the excess beaumontage (4). Smooth the surface by glasspapering lightly with a sanding block (5). Then glasspaper further by hand (6).

Filling small holes

1. Remove shavings of coloured wax.

2. Press the shavings into the hole.

Colouring

1. Dilute the spirit stain.

2. Touch up with the brush tip.

Making a rubber

1. Fold into three equal parts.

2. Fold into three again.

3. Form a point.

4. Fold the sides inwards.

5. Squeeze the wadding.

6. Place the cloth over.

7. Fold one side of the cloth.

8. Secure with the thumb.

9. Twist the cloth firmly.

Filling small holes

Dip beeswax into the required pigment powders. Remove shavings of the coloured wax, using a knife (1). Press the shavings well into the hole with a chisel (2). Remove the excess wax with the chisel held vertically. Smooth the surface, first with the back and then with the front of a piece of glasspaper.

Colouring

Make a small "boat" with old glasspaper. Make up spirit stains in strength. In the boat mix the stains to the required colour. Dilute with four parts methylated spirit and one part french polish (1). Dip the tip of a fine brush into the new solution and test the colour on the back of the hand. Adjust colour as necessary. Then touch up any unevenly coloured areas with the brush tip (2). Leave to dry. Repeat if necessary.

Making a rubber

Rubbers can be made in various sizes. Small ones are most suitable for awkward corners and carvings whilst larger ones are convenient for big flat surfaces. The soft absorbent cloth should always be a little larger than the wadding. To make an average-sized rubber use a piece of pound wadding about 225 mm/9 in square and fold it into three equal parts (1). Turn the wadding around 90° and fold the wadding again into three equal parts (2). Fold the top corners into the centre middle to form a point (3). Then fold the sides into the centre bottom and overlap them (4). Squeeze the wadding into a pear shape with a point at one end (5). Place the square piece of soft absorbent cloth over the wadding (6). Holding the wadding tightly, tuck one side of the cloth under the point of the wadding (7). Secure with the thumb. Then pull the other side of the cloth tightly under the point of the wadding. Again secure with the thumb (8). Wrap the cloth around the rest of the wadding. Twist up the rest of the cloth at the back firmly and hold in the palm of the hand to prevent it trailing across the work (9).

Surface finishes 4

Surface coatings can be used both to protect a surface and to enhance the beauty of the grain. Most protect against dirt and make cleaning easier. All to some extent protect against moisture. Some are heat resistant; others protect against insect or fungal attack. They all have good adhesive qualities provided the surface to which they are applied is absolutely clean. All work should be done in a well-lit room but not in direct sunlight. The room should be clean, and have a constant temperature of about 17°C/65°F.

The important surface coatings are french polish, wax and semi-wax, oil, nitrocellulose, polyurethane, acid-catalyzed lacquers and polyesters.

French polish

French polish, though a weak surface coating in that it has little heat and moisture resistance, still remains popular amongst craftsmen. It is a sticky resinous mixture and so difficult to apply, but when applied correctly it gives one of the best gloss or matt finishes. The aim is to produce a high gloss by applying numerous thin coats of polish; this can then be matted down if required.

The basic ingredients of french polish are shellac, which is a substance exuded by the lac insect, and methylated spirit, which is used as a solvent. The main colours of polish are pale, button and garnet. French polish is also available tinted with dyes of black and red; black-dyed french polish is used to ebonize a surface over black stain. Sycamore, mahogany and birch are some of the best woods for ebonizing.

French polish should be worked in slowly and deliberately with a fad or rubber, gradually building up a film of polish, which is left to dry before the next coat is applied. Always lift the fad or rubber promptly from the surface sides and ends to prevent polish from dripping over the edges. Fadding and bodying up and down the grain is done to prevent the polish from streaking. The slower the polishing process, the more time the previous coat will have had to release its solvents and become dry. It is easier to work on a number of surfaces in rotation so each surface has an opportunity to dry off before the next application of polish. Each coat will partially dissolve the coat beneath so the layers will amalgamate. The quantity of polish worked into a surface determines the degree of gloss; for a full even gloss, apply many thin coats.

French polish

Beech
Use a pale polish on light or natural beech. Button polish may be used after staining.

Mahogany
Use button or garnet polish.

Oak
Use a pale polish on light oaks; button polish on stained oak.

Pine
Pale polish is normally used. Button polish is used on a stained piece.

Teak
Pale or button polish, depending on colour required.

Walnut
Pale polish is normally used. Button polish may be used for a cast.

Manufactured boards
Pale, button or garnet polish depending on colour required.

Wax and semi-wax polish

Wax gives an attractive shine and is easy to maintain, but it has only slight moisture resistance, little or no heat resistance and is easily marked. It also holds dust, which, unless the grain is sealed, will become deeply embedded in the wood. Most proprietary waxes are based on soft paraffin wax and are unsuitable for application to unsealed wood. If using wax as a surface coating, heat 0.45 kg/1 lb of shredded beeswax with 280 ml/½ pt turpentine and some carnauba wax. It is possible to colour beeswax with oil-soluble colours or dry pigment powders. Bleached beeswax is also obtainable. Allow the mixture to cool. Apply the wax paste to the surface with a soft brush or cloth along the grain. Leave it to dry. Then burnish it with a soft dry cloth. On uneven surfaces, apply the wax with a short-bristled brush made of bear hair or mixed hair and burnish with a dry soft-haired brush. Once the surface has been sealed with the beeswax mixture further coats of proprietary wax may be used to produce a finish with depth and warmth.

To apply a semi-wax polish, first seal the wood with a couple of coats of french polish, using a cloth, brush or fad. When dry, smooth with a 7/0 garnet paper, wipe clean and then apply a further coat of french polish. When dry add wax polish to 000 or 0000 steel wool and rub down the surface. Burnish with a soft dry cloth.

Oil

The advantages of oil polish are that it does not crack or blister, or show heat or water marks. Its application, however, takes a great deal of time as oil is not only slow drying but requires numerous coats. Layer upon layer painstakingly applied will give effective protection to wood exposed to the open air and to liquids. It is therefore most suited to garden furniture, table tops, bar tops, counters and spirit cabinets.

The traditional oil to use as a polish is linseed oil; this will produce a high gloss that will be moderately heat and water resistant if applied sparingly over a period of months. Each application must be hardened by oxidization and at least 12 coats are necessary. The addition of small amounts of turpentine and terebene makes it easier for working and will speed up the drying process. Using either raw or boiled linseed, add 5 per cent turpentine and 5 per cent terebene and simmer the mixture in a double pan for 15 minutes. Vigorously rub the mixture into the wood with a clean cloth. Allow at least one day for the oil to dry; then smooth it with fine glasspaper and dust clean. Numerous coats should be applied in this way, leaving at least one week between sessions. Remove any dust that has settled on the surface between sessions and use a clean cloth for every session.

Several proprietary oils containing oxidizing agents are available, but, compared with linseed oil, these give an inferior quality finish.

Teak oil, olive oil and Danish oil are also suitable as polishes for wood, especially teak, oak, mahogany, walnut and cedar, as they enhance the natural grain and colouring. Teak oil is extremely combustible so always soak an oil-filled cloth in water overnight. Then wash it out thoroughly before disposing of it.

French polishing

1. Charge the fad with polish.

2. Rub the fad along the grain.

3. Smooth the surface.

4. Fill the rubber with polish.

5. Work along the grain.

6. Work in figures of eight.

7. Work in circles.

8. Work along the grain.

Using the rubber's nose in corners.

Using the rubber's nose in crevices.

Methods of holding work

Waste wood nailed to a small door.

Heavy door laid on wedges.

Frame held with bench-sticks.

Carcass propped up.

French polishing

Charge the fad or rubber well with polish. To charge the rubber remove the cloth. Saturate the wadding with polish (1). Replace the cloth and squeeze until the polish oozes through. Work the fad or rubber along the grain with a minimum of downward pressure, overlapping each stroke (2). Too much downward pressure will force out the polish too rapidly, resulting in a sticky surface. Leave to dry for 10 minutes. Rub 180 grit abrasive paper together to make it finer and smooth the surface (3). Dust with a soft cloth. Fill any holes and adjust the colour. Then body the surface with a rubber. Charge with polish (4). Work the rubber in strict sequence: first along the grain, overlapping each stroke until the entire surface is covered (5); then in a figure-of-eight movement (6); then in a circular movement (7); and finally work the rubber along the grain again (8). Leave the surface to dry off. Apply more coats, repeating this process until a high gloss has been achieved. Towards the end of the bodying process, lubricate the hardening rubber with a spot of linseed oil. Remove any excess oil with the dried out rubber, using considerable pressure along the grain. Test the surface by breathing on it: if a mist forms, continue to rub until the oil has gone. With experience, methylated spirit can be used on the dried out rubber, to give a perfectly smooth surface. Leave the surface to harden. Then smooth with very fine abrasive paper.

Methods of holding work

Hold a small door by nailing a piece of waste wood at right angles to the unpolished bottom edge of the door. Lay a large or heavy door on four wooden wedges. The door weight will keep it in position. Lay a table upside down to polish the legs and rails. Then stand it upright to polish the top. Polish a chair from the legs upwards. With a frame, first polish the inner and outer edges, then place the frame flat in home-made bench-sticks, nailed to the workbench, and polish the top. Prop up a carcass with a block of waste wood at one end and place folded abrasive paper at the other so the grit is in contact with the carcass and the floor to prevent slipping. Hold a drawer from the inside.

Surface finishes 5

Manufacturers use the words "lacquer" and "varnish" synonymously, so for clarity the term lacquer is used throughout this book. There are four basic types: nitrocellulose, polyurethane, acid-catalyzed lacquers and polyester. Lacquers and paints give a harder and more resistant finish than french polish, wax or oil. Generally they are applied with a brush or a spray gun. The hard finish is produced when the solvents have evaporated on the surface. Always read and follow the manufacturer's instructions and check that the method of lacquer or paint application does not contravene any legal stipulations.

Some lacquers are toxic and inflammable so ensure that the workshop is well ventilated, without being dusty. The humidity should not exceed 70 per cent as dampness will cause blooming and chilling. Evaporation time varies according to the lacquer and method of application, but if a lacquer is too slow drying or too thick the surface will remain soft. Lacquers can be cleaned off brushes and spray guns with lacquer thinners. However, brushes may be destroyed by lacquer to such a degree that cleaning proves a waste of time; therefore always use a cheap mixed hair brush. When using a spray gun pay particular attention to cleaning the air cap, horn holes, fluid tip, fluid needle and the inside of the gun body. Use cocktail sticks and pipe cleaners to reach into inaccessible parts. Whether for cleaning or thinning buy a thinner of the same brand as the lacquer.

The best paints are nitrocellulose based; polyurethane paint, however, can also be used. All but non-drip thixotropic paints should be stirred to suspend the pigments. To give a surface the smoothest finish it is best to apply paint with a spray gun. A primer coat should be applied before going on to give a further two undercoats and a top coat. It is advisable to use the same manufacturer's top and base coat throughout the work. Clean oil-based paints off brushes and spray guns with white spirit; use warm water and detergent on water-based paints. Paints can be bought with a matt, semi-matt, satin or gloss finish.

Before painting or lacquering, wood that has not already been stained should be treated with water to raise the grain; it should then be dried and smoothed with an abrasive. Whatever the surface it must be dry, dust free and greaseless before application. The work should be left for at least an hour between coats.

Nitrocellulose

Nitrocellulose may be applied with a brush but is more generally applied with a spray gun. Lacquers made for brushing have slow evaporating solvents to allow for the longer application time. Nitrocellulose is cheap, quick drying and produces a hard heat- and moisture-proof surface. It has an unlimited pot life. Up to 10 per cent polyurethane solution may be added to give a still harder finish. Layers are applied "wet on wet" so that they amalgamate well. Nitrocellulose lacquering is followed by an application of a pull-over solution; this is a diluted nitrocellulose solution, which is applied with a rubber 24 hours after lacquering and before finishing, to give an even surface. Always use a pull-over solution of the same brand as the lacquer.

Polyurethane

Polyurethane may be applied with a brush or spray gun. It is expensive but produces an excellent hard surface with good heat-, moisture- and wear-resistant properties, though it is rarely burn resistant. It can be bought in different forms, usually in a twin pack consisting of liquid plastic and a catalyst containing the solvent, which promotes the drying process. The solution may have a pot life of as little as 8 hours. Oil stained wood should be tested for discoloration. Polyurethane is available both as a transparent and opaque lacquer and its colour can be adjusted by mixing the lacquer with spirit stains.

Acid-catalyzed lacquer

Acid-catalyzed lacquers give a very durable heat- and moisture-proof surface. They should be applied with a spray gun. The layers set by polymerization. Most acid-catalyzed lacquers come in a one- or two-pack form and once the solution is made up it has only a 1-day pot life. A surface covered with this lacquer is not easy to repair.

Polyester

Polyester is the hardest and most durable of all the lacquers and has good heat- and moisture-resistant properties. Because it dries fast it can only be applied with a spray gun; one coat is sufficient. Polyester can be burnished to give a high-gloss finish. As with acid-catalyzed lacquers, it is difficult to repair the surface, which usually will have to be stripped and relacquered.

Brush application

1. Make a pool.

2. Brush along the grain.

3. Suspend the brush.

Brush application

If lacquer comes in a two-pack form pour both solutions into a container in the recommended proportions. Mix with a wooden stick. Leave for half an hour. Fill the brush with solution. Make a pool on the near side of the work, halfway between the ends (1). Do not allow the solution to drip. Exercising maximum pressure on the brush at the centre, brush back and forth along the grain. Reduce the pressure as the brush moves from the centre and lift the brush tip promptly at the ends (2). Each stroke must overlap. When the area is covered, brush over the entire surface lightly to straighten the strokes and remove any surplus lacquer. Leave the surface to dry (about 1 hour). Keep the brush supple by suspending it over the solution (3). (After applying polyester or nitrocellulose wash the surface with soapy water.) Smooth with 320 grit wet-and-dry paper. Dust the surface. Fill holes and adjust the colour if necessary. Apply a second coat. Leave to dry; do not smooth. Apply a third coat. Smooth with 320 grit paper; dust. Smooth with 400 grit paper. Dust the surface.

Spray gun application

Lacquer container

Horn hole

Fluid needle

Air cap

Trigger

Gravity spray gun.

Air from compressor

Suction feed spray gun.

A converted swivel chair.

1. Spray past the surface.

2. Spray from the front.

3. Place on nail points.

Applying pull-over solution

1. Rub with a soapy cloth.

2. Smooth with abrasive paper.

3. Work with a rubber.

Spray gun application
Spray guns distribute lacquer with a viscous flow that can be carefully controlled to a fine spray. To ensure good working order always clean the gun thoroughly. A gravity spray gun has a lacquer container positioned above the gun; the lacquer drains down into the fluid tip. A suction feed spray gun has a lacquer container positioned below the gun; the lacquer is sucked up into the fluid tip. A trigger action controls the air and lacquer flow. The air is forced through two horn holes in the air cap, usually activated by compressed air. Guns and air compressors must be compatible. The horn holes can be set horizontally for side to side spraying or vertically for up and down spraying. It is best to put the work on a turntable such as a converted swivel chair. Fill the lacquer container with solution. Test the viscosity by spraying some waste wood. Spray at 45 , 150 mm/6 in to 200 mm/8 in away from the surface. Add thinner if necessary. Adjust the horn holes to the appropriate position for the work. Spray the edges of the work first. Always spray in a straight line along the grain, overlapping the previous stroke by 50 per cent. Start spraying before the surface and continue past it (**1**). Then spray the top, working from front to middle (**2**). Turn the work round and spray the other half. Place the lacquered surface on nail points (**3**). Then spray the underside. Rack the work carefully. Leaving an hour between coats, apply two or three coats.

Applying pull-over solution
Rub the dry surface in a circular motion with a soapy cloth (**1**). Smooth with 320 grit wet-and-dry abrasive paper (**2**). Rub the edges with wet abrasive paper held flat. Dust the surface. Smooth with 400 grit paper and dust again. Dip a rubber into some pull-over solution. Squeeze until just moist. Work the rubber along the grain. Wipe any excess from the edges. Then work the rubber in a circular motion and finally, with a slightly moister rubber, along the grain again to give a brilliant surface (**3**).

Surface finishes 6

All surface coatings can be treated to give a matt, semi-matt, satin or gloss finish. For a matt, semi-matt or satin finish a dulling process is used, which diminishes the original shine. For a gloss finish a greater build-up of surface coating than for any other finish is required to produce a surface with a deeper sheen and brightest possible shine. The process used to create a gloss finish is known as burnishing and it may be done by hand or by machine. Dulling brushes have long bristles that are made from bear hair or mixed hair. Whether dulling or burnishing, the more the surface coating is rubbed the greater the effect, so work cautiously. Both processes can be repeated, but to reverse dulling a reviver has to be used on the surface.

After their final layer has been applied, surface coatings should be left for at least 24 hours before they are ready for any finishing treatment. If treated earlier than this, streaks may appear on the surface. Between applying a surface coating and finishing, considerable sinkage may occur, especially where the grain has not been filled with woodfiller. If this takes place, smooth the whole surface lightly with a fine abrasive paper, lubricated if necessary. Then wipe clean before starting the final finish.

Matt finish

1. Rub the wool along the grain.   2. Rub with a circular motion.   Brush uneven surfaces.

Matt finish
Rub the surface along the grain with flattened grade 000 or 0000 steel wool (1). Dust off. Hold the work to the light to check that all the shine has been removed. Wipe wax on to a soft absorbent cloth. Rub it on to the surface with a circular motion (2). Leave overnight. Then burnish the surface with a clean soft cloth. Use a brush impregnated with wax on uneven surfaces.

Semi-matt finish

1. Put some powder on a brush.   2. Rub along the grain.

Semi-matt finish
Sprinkle some pumice powder on to a dulling brush (1). Work the brush up and down the grain with considerable pressure (2). Wipe off frequently. When the polish has been sufficiently matted down wipe the surface clean with a soft cloth.

Satin finish

1. Load steel wool with wax.   2. Rub along the grain.   3. Buff up with a soft cloth.

Satin finish
A greater build-up of surface coating is required for a satin finish than for a matt or semi-matt finish. Fold some 000 or 0000 steel wool into a pad and load with beeswax (1). Rub along the grain with moderate pressure (2). Too much pressure will dull the satin finish. Turn the pad over and remove the residual wax with the clean side. Then buff up the surface with a clean soft cloth to the required sheen (3).

Gloss finish

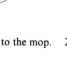

1. Rub the block on to the mop.   2. Hold the surface to the mop.   3. Hold the edge to the mop.

Gloss finish
Rub a block of wax and abrasive powder back and forth against the rotating linen mop of a burnishing machine (1). Hold the work lightly but firmly against the rotating mop in the position shown (2). Move the work slowly from side to side. Place one hand under the work when burnishing the edges (3). Regularly replenish the mop with wax and abrasive powder. Polish with the sheepskin mop.

Linen mop

Sheepskin mop

Sheepskin bonnet

A small burnishing machine.

Burnishing and polishing machines
A small burnishing machine can be used to make a gloss finish. The linen mop at one end of the machine is for the initial burnishing and the sheepskin mop at the other is for polishing. Alternatively the surface can be burnished by hand and polished with an electric drill attachment, consisting of a polyurethane disk over which a sheepskin bonnet is fitted. To burnish by hand use a mild rubbing compound such as those available from motor supply shops and a soft cloth made from natural fibres. Put the compound on to the cloth and rub the surface along the grain. When the compound dries the burnishing action begins. Continue to rub until the finish is bright. Wipe with a clean cloth and polish with the drill attachment. Remove any smears with a reviver.

Stripping

A surface coating may be recognizable by the solvent that will soften it. Application of a reviver, made from equal parts linseed oil, household vinegar and methylated spirit, will also aid recognition as it will conceal scratches on a french polished surface whereas on a lacquered surface the scratches will remain white.

To assess accurately whether the work needs to be stripped, first remove the surface dirt, grease and wax with a reviver. Shake the reviver before applying it to the surface with a soft absorbent cloth; then rub the surface with a clean cloth.

A thorough cleaning of the surface may be all that is required to restore the original patina. If the surface needs a further application of surface coating, clean it with white spirit or a weak solution of soda crystals before rubbing it down with fine steel wool. Then apply the relevant surface coating. If, however, the surface is badly cracked or patchy it will need to be stripped. Should the piece be a valuable antique that has only minimal surface damage it is usually better to leave it as it is. A surface should not be partially stripped as its colouring will be uneven when it is resurfaced.

Almost all surface coatings can be removed with a proprietary stripper. Protect the floor and workbench with newspaper when using the stripper and wear goggles as well as an overall and gloves. Stripper is toxic and inflammable so read all instructions with care and neutralize any splashes immediately with water.

Before beginning to strip, assemble the stripper, a scraper, a 38 mm/1½ in flat brush, 000 steel wool, some hessian or canvas, a small stiff bristle brush, a tin to hold the stripper, some upholstery wadding and some methylated spirit. A cabinet scraper may also prove useful. Steel wool is sometimes substituted for a scraper where the coating is soft, for example french polish. Hessian will also remove the coatings and is useful for wiping the scraper. The brush will take off the coatings from awkward places.

Any part of the surface may be stripped first, but attempt only a small area at a time. Scrape when the surface finish is soft. Test frequently and strip rapidly as soon as easy removal is possible. Scrape towards or away from the worker. If a surface dries too fast another layer must be applied. The number of stripper layers will vary according to the type and thickness of the surface coating. When the surface has dried, all stripper must be neutralized with methylated spirit or cold water to stop the stripper continuing to react. Leave the work to dry before resurfacing.

Stripping

1. Scrape the broken coating.

2. Strip recesses thoroughly.

3. Rub with steel wool.

Stripping
Brush stripper liberally on to an area. Leave until nearly dry. Scrape the broken coating along the grain (1). Then rub steel wool along the grain. Repeat this process as necessary. Strip recesses thoroughly (2). Neutralize the whole surface with methylated-spirit-soaked upholstery wadding and rub well into the grain with a circular motion. Remove the film with steel wool (3). Then smooth.

Restoring

When embarking on a job of restoration first of all examine the piece of furniture carefully. Look for evidence of insect damage, chipped mouldings and beading, worn bearing surfaces and warping. Rock frame structures to see if any joints are loose and check veneers for splits and blisters. Then make a list of all the defects and decide on the order in which they should be tackled. The scope of the work that can be undertaken will depend on the skill and confidence of the worker. Wherever possible surface finishes should be retained, and as a general rule repair is preferable to renewal as it is frequently impossible to imitate the patterns and craftsmanship of the past. The age and value of the piece must also be taken into account. It may be that the piece of furniture has fallen into such a state of disrepair that the extent of work required to restore it would not prove worth while.

To prevent pieces falling into bad condition always attend to a repair immediately, otherwise the one defect may cause strain on another area and lead to a series of further problems. Where it is necessary to replace old wood, match the new wood closely by paying careful attention to species, grain, figure and even, sometimes, the rays so that the repair will be unobtrusive. If at all possible do a repair without dismantling, but where it does prove necessary to dismantle remember to protect the surface finishes with wedge-shaped blocks or battens to prevent bruising. When the joints are knocked apart remove all old glue with a chisel or shoulder plane.

Removing nails

1. Prise up any capping pieces.

2. Remove pins and loose nails.

3. Punch in embedded nails.

4. Drill out large nails.

Removing nails
Before dismantling a piece of furniture it is important to remove all nails and screws. These may be well concealed, especially in tenons. Remove any capping pieces by prising them up with a chisel (1). Then remove any panel pins by gently twisting and levering them out, using side cutters (2). Lift out any loose nails. Nail-heads that are flush or below the surface of the frame should be hammered through using a nail-punch, because levering them out could cause damage to the piece of furniture (3). Where hammering through is not practical, use a brace and plug cutter to penetrate the wood around the nail (4). Then remove the nail with a pair of side cutters.

Dealing with pellets and screws

1. Chisel out any pellets.

2. Heat stubborn screw-heads.

3. Glue loose joints.

Dealing with pellets and screws
Place the piece of furniture on a workbench or floor and protect the points of contact with some cork or a cloth. With a mallet and chisel, gently prise out any pellets (1). Then remove the countersunk screws. Loosen stubborn screws by heating their heads with a soldering iron to make them expand (2). Expansion breaks any seal of rust so that when the screws cool and contract they can be loosened. Prise open loose joints once the screws have been removed. Force glue in, using a hypodermic syringe (3). Replace the screws.

Dismantling

Separating frames.

Dismantling carcasses.

Dismantling

Letter each piece of wood at each end so that matching joints can be identified. Before separating anything, decide on the order of dismantling and check that nothing else is holding the parts together. Always work parallel joints together to prevent straining. Using a hammer or rubber mallet, start to knock frame joints apart using the side of a wedge-shaped block. Place one end of the wedge between the opening formed and gently knock the joints apart. Dismantle carcasses with a hammer and batten, hitting the centre of the batten so that the impact is distributed evenly.

Removing dowels

1. Chisel any broken dowels.

2. Drill out the dowel end.

Removing dowels

Chisel any broken dowels until they are flush with the surrounding surface **(1)**. Using the same size drill bit as the dowel diameter, drill into the bottom of the dowel. Once the drill bit has firmly embedded in the dowel, pull it out from the surrounding wood **(2)**.

Clamping

Sash cramp.

G-cramp.

Cam and tourniquet cramps.

Clamping

Awkwardly shaped pieces of furniture were originally clamped with the aid of projections that were later sawn off. Clamping while restoring is far more complicated. The even distribution of pressure in the required places can become a skilled juggling trick and specially shaped clamping blocks may be needed. Always ensure that components are clamped true and at the angle at which they were originally designed. All surfaces must be protected with wooden blocks or cork. Sash cramps are often used with wooden bearers or specially cut saddles to spread the load evenly. G-cramps are generally for holding parts together away from edges. Cam cramps are especially useful to a restorer as an extra edge cramp can be added for three-sided clamping pressure. Tourniquet cramps are for rounded corners or extremely awkward shapes.

Natural defects

Wood beetle infestation

1. Clamp the wood firmly.

2. Cut into the infected area.

3. Remove the infected wood.

4. Check for flatness.

5. Measure the new wood.

6. Clamp the glued patch.

7. Plane the patch flush.

8. Treat with an insecticide.

9. Fill the holes with wax.

Wood beetle infestation

In temperate zones, the pin-hole borer, the furniture beetle, the longhorn and the death-watch beetle are among the insects that burrow into timber, particularly sapwood. Their tell-tale marks are the flight holes appearing on the surface of the wood. Where the attack is severe the infected area will need to be replaced with good wood, retaining the original front surface if possible. Clamp the piece of furniture firmly to the bench (1). Ensure the infected area is accessible. Using a dovetail saw make a sloping cut at the edge of the heavily infected area (2). Do not mark the front surface. Make a similar cut at the far end of the infected area. With a chisel carefully remove the infected wood between the two saw kerfs (3). Whether working on a curved or straight piece of wood always chisel the surface flat. Check the cut-away area for flatness with a try square or straight-edge both along and across (4). Take a piece of wood of similar grain direction and figure to the main piece and measure it against the cut-away area (5). Making it slightly wider and higher than the cut-away area, cut the patch to shape. Plane its sides. Apply PVA glue to the patch and tap it into the cut-away area. Clamp all round for 30 minutes to dry (6). Take off the cramps and plane both sides so the patch lies flush with the main piece (7). Then smooth with an abrasive paper. Colour the patch so it blends in with the adjacent wood. If the infestation has only just begun to appear, or when the above treatment for severe infection has been completed, the entire piece of furniture should be treated with an insecticide. Use a proprietary liquid in a bottle with a nozzle and squirt the liquid into every visible flight hole (8). Sometimes liquid appears from another flight hole some distance from the hole that is being treated. This is evidence of a multitude of galleries running just below the surface. Block the flight holes after treatment by working some coloured wax into the holes, wearing gloves (9). When the wax has dried buff the area with a soft cloth. Whatever time of year the initial treatment was done, respray the flight holes the following spring, when the surviving insect eggs may be hatching.

Joint defects 1

Loose joints

1. Grip the wood firmly.

2. Bore a hole.

3. Insert animal glue.

4. Select a piece of wood.

5. Mark a curve at the front.

6. Screw in position.

Loose joints

Loose joints can frequently be remedied by reinforcement gluing and the addition of a corner block. Protecting the surface finish with some cork, grip the piece of furniture in the bench vice (1). With a hand drill bore an inconspicuous hole in the loose joint cavity (2). Insert animal glue into the hole, using a hypodermic syringe (3). Do not substitute a resin glue as it would dry too fast. Clamp the reglued joint so that the pressure is distributed evenly and leave for 8 hours. For the corner block, select a piece of wood with its grain running between adjacent sides of the frame (4). The edges may need to be bevelled to fit the frame closely. Mark a curved front on the corner block to facilitate the entry of screws (5). Cut out the block, using a bowsaw, and drill clearance holes for the screws. Glue and screw the block into position, countersinking the screws (6).

Over-wide mortises

1. Clean out the mortise.

2. Measure a wooden plug.

3. Chisel it to fit.

4. Hammer in the glued plug.

5. Lever the plug to one end.

Over-wide mortises

Where a dismantled joint reveals a loose tenon in an over-wide mortise, clamp the component to the bench and clean out the mortise with a chisel (1). Then choose a piece of wood with matching grain direction to the main piece and mark out the length, width and depth of a wooden plug that will fit into the mortise and hold the tenon closely (2). Saw out the plug and chisel it to fit (3). Glue the plug and hammer it into the mortise (4). Lever the plug tightly against one end of the mortise, using a tool such as a screwdriver (5). When the glue has dried, plane the plug flush with the surface. Smooth with an abrasive paper. Stain and polish where necessary.

Joint defects 2

The general principle of how to splice on new wood applies both to repairing broken legs and rails and to cutting a new mortise or new tenon. The restorer must maintain as much as possible of an original piece of furniture and every effort should be made to preserve rather than replace components. Splicing is a means of putting this principle into practice. Broken components and joints should be attended to as soon as possible when the breaks are fresh, leaving no time for grease and dirt to accumulate, for pieces to be mislaid or for surfaces to break further. New wood should be tapered to 15° to 20° to provide as large a gluing area as possible and to make the joint strong and inconspicuous. It should also have the same grain pattern as the main piece.

Having dismantled the failed piece check to see if it has been set square or at an angle in the wood. Cut the new piece in such a way as to leave it a little proud of the surface when glued in position. When dry, plane the piece flush with the adjoining surface, taking care to remove as little of this surface as possible. Always smooth with an abrasive paper to ensure the surface is absolutely flat before staining and polishing the new piece to match the original wood.

Where dismantling proves difficult or causes undue strain on other parts of the structure, false tenons can be used to repair broken mortise and tenon joints. This is particularly common with chair back rails and stretchers. Before cutting new ones it is important to check whether the original tenons were set square or at an angle and whether the mortise is over-wide. There are several kinds of false tenon, such as stepped ones, and these reflect the variety of mortise and tenon joints, so always check which type is required.

New mortises

1. Check the wood carefully.

2. Chisel away old tenon.

New mortises

Where a mortise has been severely damaged the entire area may need to be replaced (1). Grip the component in the bench vice with cork for protection. Saw away any tenon protruding from the mortise. Remove the rest of the tenon from the mortise with a chisel and mallet, looking out for nails (2). Clean away the old glue with a chisel. Consider carefully how best to cut into the good wood to allow for maximum strength when the new piece is fitted. Saw away the damaged area, making a shallow slope on to which the new piece will be spliced (3). With a shoulder plane, smooth the slope (4). Check it for flatness with a try square or straight-edge. Select some new wood of matching grain pattern to the old wood. Cut the wood to fit the cut-away area, leaving it proud. Plane the sloping side smooth. Mark the position of the mortise (5). Saw and chisel out the marked area (6). Glue the sloping side and fit it in position against the component and clamp firmly (7). When the glue has dried take off the cramps. Using a smoothing plane, level to just above the surface of the adjacent wood (8). Smooth the new piece flush, using an abrasive paper. Colour the repair carefully to match the original wood.

3. Saw away damaged mortise. 4. Plane the slope.

5. Mark the mortise.

6. Chisel out the mortise. 7. Fit the glued new piece.

8. Plane the new piece.

New tenons

1. Plane the damaged wood.

2. Clamp the new glued piece.

3. Plane the new piece.

4. Gauge the new tenon.

5. Saw the new tenon.

False tenons

1. Glue in the false tenon.

2. Slot the rail over glued false tenons.

Clamped joints

1. Plane the edges.

2. Clamp the glued edges.

New tenons
Saw or plane away the damaged area around the broken tenon, making a shallow slope on to which a new piece of wood can be spliced (1). Choose a piece of wood with a grain that matches the old piece and cut it almost to size. Grip it in the vice and plane one edge to fit the sloping side of the component. Glue the component and new piece together and clamp (2). When the glue has dried, remove the cramp. Plane the new piece flush; take care to remove as little of the finish on the adjoining surface as possible (3). Smooth with an abrasive paper. Set a mortise gauge to the dimensions of the mortise and then use it to gauge the size of the new tenon (4). Grip the component, protected with cork, firmly in the bench vice and saw the marked tenon (5).

False tenons
Clean out the old mortise with a chisel and mallet. To make a false tenon cut a rectangular piece of wood to twice the depth and the exact width and thickness of the mortise. Glue the wood into the mortise (1). Mark the measurements of the protruding false tenon on to the rail end and underside. Saw from the bottom at an angle along the marked lines; then chisel out the waste. Vertically chisel away the rest of the waste, making the slot square. Repeat the process at the other end. Glue the false tenons and slot the rail over them (2).

Clamped joints
Remove the relevant parts and place them in the bench vice. Plane the edges straight and square (1). Take out of the vice. Glue the edges and lay them flat on a board covered with newspaper to prevent them sticking to the board. Place some paper and a batten over the joint and clamp it down. (With wide boards clamp a second batten on the opposite side.) Clamp the two edges together with one or more sash cramps (2). Leave the joint to dry. Remove the cramps and smooth away any excess glue.

Surface defects 1

Worn surfaces

Rub candlewax along the runner.

1. Clamp the drawer.　　2. Secure in the vice.

3. Clamp the glued new piece.

4. Plane to shape and size.

Split surfaces

1. Saw in the split wood.

2. Plane a thin strip of wood.

3. Hammer in the glued strip.

Worn surfaces

Where a drawer is sticking it may be sufficient to rub a little candlewax along the runner or drawer side to enable the drawer to move smoothly. Where the bottom edge of a drawer side has been worn away it will need to be built up with a new piece of wood. Clamp the drawer upside down, leaving the worn surface free to be worked on (1). Plane the worn surface flat with a shallow sloping side. For the new piece choose wood similar to that of the drawer side and of the same grain direction. Secure it in the vice and saw off a tapered piece that will closely fit the sloping edge of the drawer side (2). As the inside edge will become inaccessible after gluing, plane this edge at this stage. Apply PVA glue to the planed worn surface. Place the new piece with its inside edge in position and clamp it to the drawer (3). When the glue is absolutely dry remove the cramps and plane the new piece to the required shape and size (4).

Split surfaces

Splits running along the grain often occur in the bottoms of drawers. Remove the drawer bottom and grip it in the bench vice. Using a rip saw, cut down to the base of the split (1). Select a thin strip of wood of similar type and grain direction to the drawer bottom and plane it against a bench-stop until it fits into the saw kerf (2). Glue the strip and insert it into the saw kerf. It may be necessary to hammer it into position (3). When the glue is absolutely dry, plane the strip flush on all sides and stain if necessary.

Bowed surfaces

1. Nail stops to the fence.

2. Lower the wood.

3. Cut even, parallel grooves.

4. Clamp open the grooves.

5. Square off the groove ends.

6. Hammer in the glued strips.

Bowed stiles and rails

1. Chisel out the marked area.

2. Cut the patch to fit.

3. Clamp the glued patch.

Warped doors

Using G-cramps.

Using a puncheon.

Bowed surfaces

Set the blade of a table saw to three-quarters the thickness of the bowed wood. Position the guide fence so that the saw blade will cut 19 mm/¾ in in from the side and nail wooden stops to prevent the wood being cut nearer than 13 mm/½ in from both ends (1). Switch on the saw. Lower the wood on to the blade, holding it against the fence and nearest wooden stop (2). As the saw cuts push the wood gently towards the far wooden stop. Having reached the end switch off the saw. When the blade stops rotating lift off the wood. Make similar parallel grooves 19 mm/¾ in apart. Stop 19 mm/¾ in from the far side (3). For a convex bow clamp the wood over gently curved bearers in the opposite direction to the bow (4). (For a concave bow clamp the grooved surface flat.) Cut strips of wood to the thickness of the clamped grooves. Chisel the groove ends square to take the strips (5). Glue the strips and tap into the grooves (6). When the glue has dried remove the cramps. Plane the strips flush. Smooth with an abrasive paper.

Bowed stiles and rails

With the concave side uppermost clamp the bowed wood flat. Where the bow is greatest mark out a tapered area with undercut sides. It should be no longer than 75 mm/3 in and no deeper than half the thickness of the main piece. Cut away and level the marked area (1). Select a piece of wood similar to the rail or stile and of the same grain pattern. Bevel it to fit tightly into the cut-away area (2). Glue the patch and push it well in. Grip it in the vice (3). When dry, remove; plane the patch flush and colour to match.

Warped doors

Lay the door flat with wooden blocks beneath the straight or downward-bent corners. Clamp upward-bent corners with G-cramps. Lay large doors on the floor. Put wooden blocks under the straight and downward-bent corners. Place puncheons between the upward-bent corners and wooden planks laid against the ceiling. From opposite sides knock the thin ends of two triangular wedges between the puncheon and the door. Force glued wedges into the open joints. Release the pressure and plane the wedges flush.

Surface defects 2

Damaged mouldings

1. Make two bevelled kerfs.

2. Chisel the damaged area.

3. Check the flatness.

4. Check the patch for fit.

5. Clamp the glued patch.

6. Plane the patch.

Damaged mouldings

Where an area of moulding is missing or damaged it can usually be replaced by a new piece. Make a bevelled kerf on either side of the damaged area so that the top opening in the moulding is wider than the bottom and so that the front is narrower than the back (1). Chisel out the area between the two kerfs, working across the grain (2). Test for flatness with a try square or straight-edge (3). Select a piece of wood with a grain that matches the moulding. Making it slightly larger than the cut-away area, plane it to shape to make a perfect fit in the cut-away area (4). Glue the patch, insert it firmly into the cut-away area and clamp (5). When the glue has dried, remove the cramp and plane the patch to shape with a shoulder plane for convex curves and a moulding plane for concave ones (6). Smooth with an abrasive. Then colour the patch to blend in with the surrounding moulding.

Veneer blisters

1. Slit open any blisters.

2. Insert glue in both sides.

3. Clamp until dry.

Veneer blisters

Brush over the surface with the palm of the hand and tap suspected air pockets and blisters with a finger. Make a slit along the grain through the middle of the blister (1). Gently lift the veneer with the knife point and insert animal glue under each side (2). Push the veneer down so the excess glue is squeezed out. Clamp until dry, protecting the veneer with cork (3).

Making new pellets

1. Mark the required shape.

2. Chisel the pellet to fit.

3. Chisel the pellet flush.

Making new pellets

Where pellets have been damaged new ones must be made from suitable wood with a matching grain to the main piece. Where possible use the old pellet as a template to mark the new one (1). Pare the wood, slightly tapering it. Keep it attached to the main piece for as long as possible (2). Put some glue in the hole and gently tap in the tapered pellet until it fits tightly. When dry, chisel the pellet flush with the adjacent surface (3). Smooth with an abrasive paper. Stain and polish as required.

Patching holes

2. Plane the patch.

3. Chisel the hole to shape.

4. Remove the under edges.

5. Plane the patch.

6. Colour in the patch.

Patching holes

Where removed fittings have left holes, the surface must be patched. The wood should be carefully matched: even the ray direction is important (1). Cut out an irregular diamond-shaped patch. An asymmetric shape will blend in well with the adjacent surface and so make the patch less conspicuous. Slightly taper the edges of the patch with a block plane (2). Lay the patch over the hole on the surface. Align the grain and rays as perfectly as possible; then draw around the patch with a very sharp pencil. With a mallet and chisel cut inside the marked lines; gradually move outwards until the chisel is working on the marked lines (3). Take special care when cutting into the acute angles. Chisel the edges with a slight taper. On the patch remove the sharp under edges with a chisel (4). Glue the patch with PVA. Spreading the pressure with a wooden block, hammer the patch into the hole. Plane the patch almost flush with the adjacent surface (5). Smooth the patch flush with the surface using an abrasive paper. Colour and polish as necessary (6).

Treatment of surfaces

Reviving surfaces
To shift grease and dirt apply a thin coat of proprietary soft furniture wax. Rub off with a soft cloth to leave a thin film. An alternative method is to clean the surface with a soft cloth dampened with soap and warm water. Allow it to dry. If the surface remains dull after this treatment, apply a mixture of equal parts linseed oil, household vinegar and methylated spirit. Rub the surface gently. Where deep scratches occur omit the oil. Gently wipe off the mixture, using a clean cloth. Then apply a coat of good-quality wax polish and rub up well.

Stains caused by water
When wood is dry, rub area well with genuine turpentine. Restain where necessary.

Stains caused by alcohol
Where a surface is polished treat as for water. Where varnished, smooth lightly with an abrasive and rebuild surface finish with varnish.

Stains caused by grease and oil
Sprinkle talcum powder over stains. Cover with tissue paper or blotting paper and warm with an iron to draw grease and oil from wood. Repeat until marks disappear. On non-veneered surfaces apply trichlorethylene to the stain. Never use this chemical on veneered and manufactured boards as it attacks glue.

Ink stains
Bleach with oxalic acid. Afterwards neutralize acid with a weak soda crystals solution.

Heat marks
Rub camphorated oil into marks with soft cloth. Wipe the surface clean.

Cigarette burns
Smooth away or scrape to below the burned surface. Stain as necessary and rebuild the surface finish. Paint out deeply ingrained burn marks with spirit stains.

Light scratches
Smooth with very fine glasspaper dipped in linseed oil.

Deep scratches
Fill with shavings of suitably coloured beeswax. Press the shavings into the scratch with a knife. When dry remove excess wax and smooth with fine abrasive paper.

Dents
Cut through finish with fine knife, making several parallel cuts along the grain. Fill depression with water and allow to soak in. Apply cloth and hot iron to swell the wood. Allow to dry and refinish with the appropriate surface coatings.

Materials

An extensive study of the most sympathetic of all materials

Growth and structure

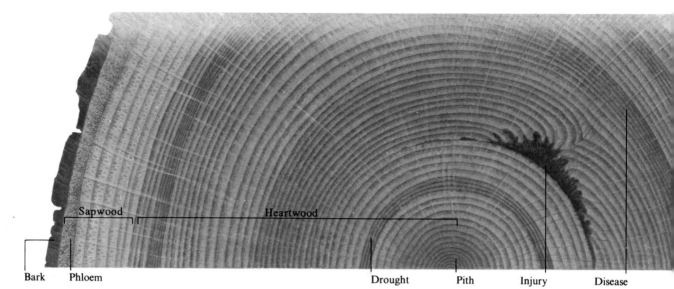

Sapwood | Heartwood

Bark   Phloem   Drought   Pith   Injury   Disease

The **bark** is the outermost layer of the tree. Its function is to protect the vital inner tissue from extremes of temperature and some diseases. It covers the inner bark or **phloem** which conducts synthesized food (the product of photosynthesis) from the leaves to the rest of the tree. It also allows vital gaseous exchanges.

The **cambium** is the growing layer of the tree. It is a thin delicate layer of tissue responsible for the production of new wood both outwards to the phloem and inwards to the sapwood, adding girth to the trunk and branches throughout the growing season; in temperate areas this is spring and summer.

The **sapwood's** main function is to conduct soluble mineral salts from the roots to the leaves. It is usually distinguishable from the heartwood — the main part of the tree — by its paler colour. It can measure up to 50 mm/2 in wide, although in tropical species it can be even wider — up to 200 mm/8 in.

The **heartwood** lies within the sapwood. It is composed of dead cells that give rigid support and store food. The majority of timber comes from this part of the tree. At the centre of the heartwood lies the **pith** or medulla, which is usually invisible but can sometimes be seen with difficulty in certain species.

The tree is unique in the plant kingdom for two reasons, its size and longevity. There are some 44,000 known species of tree varying in height from 1 m/3¼ ft — the dwarf pine of Alaska — to over 120 m/394 ft — the Californian redwood. The record girth measurement is 53 m/174 ft and belongs to a Mexican cypress known as the Giant Tree of Tule, which is thought to be three trees that have grown together. Some species such as the lowland oak can produce a root system almost twice as extensive as their branch system or crown. The variation in life span is even more dramatic. The English silver birch is considered over mature at 80 years of age, whereas a bristlecone pine felled in 1964 in Nevada lived for 4,900 years. Other relatively long-lived species such as the oak and Californian redwood can live for 1,000 years or more.

Like all other plants, trees are dependent on the process of photosynthesis, which is necessary for the production of new cells and, subsequently, growth. In a tree the growing points are called primary meristems and these are responsible for increasing the height. They are situated at the tip of the trunk and each branch and twig. To increase the girth of the tree the secondary meristems, or cambium, produce new phloem and sapwood during the growing season. The new wood is laid down in sheath-like formations called growth rings. Under ideal conditions a tree growing in fertile soil will produce wider growth rings than a tree growing in infertile soil. The study of a tree's growth-ring formation, known as dendrochronology, can provide an accurate record of these environmental conditions as well as the biological and traumatic incidents that occur throughout a tree's life.

At the centre of the tree is the heartwood. This acts as a rigid support structure and also contains many substances such as oils, resins, gums, dyes and latex. Many of these are extracted from the stumpwood after the tree is felled, but some, such as latex, are tapped from the living tree. In spite of the introduction of synthetic materials many industries such as paint and pharmaceutical manufacture are still reliant on these natural substances.

Some substances in the wood, such as gums and resins, affect the wood colour. The numerous dark-coloured veins in African walnut, for example, actually enhance the wood and give it a characteristic figure. Less beneficial, from the woodworker's point of view, are mineral deposits, which may cause hard and soft patches in the wood, making it difficult to work.

Although all trees grow and produce wood in a similar way, some trees belong to a more primitive plant type than others. Trees are therefore divided into two main classifications. The first and more primitive are the gymnosperms or conifers; these are cone-bearing needle-leafed trees known as softwoods. The second are angiosperms; these are subdivided into two classes, the monocotyledons, which include the palms and grasses and are, therefore, of little interest to the woodworker, and the dicotyledons. It is the dicotyledons, or broad-leafed deciduous trees, which include the most varied species of trees known as hardwoods. The terms hardwood and softwood are botanical terms and do not reflect the physical properties of the tree. The softwoods pitch pine and yew, for example, are much harder than the hardwoods balsam, willow, lime, obeche and gaboon.

Cambium

The **growth rings** are the annual increments of wood laid down by the cambium. Faults in the pattern are caused by **disease** and **drought**, which inhibit the growth of a tree, resulting in the production of narrow growth rings, and traumatic injury such as fire, which can leave a scar buried in the tree.

The three main reference planes by which wood can be recognized are illustrated. A transverse section is on the end grain, a radial section is on a quarter-sawn surface and the tangential section is on a plain-sawn surface.

The wide range of wood textures reflects the many varied patterns of growth among trees. As a general guide, when the wood is even textured there is little contrast between the wood produced at the beginning of the growing season (earlywood) and that produced later on (latewood). A high contrast results in a wood of uneven texture. Wood is also described as fine or coarse textured, the difference here being defined by the size of the cells (be they vessels in hardwood or tracheids in softwoods) and the ray widths. Wood with large cells and wide rays is coarse textured and that with small cells and narrow rays, fine textured. The transverse sections show a fine, even-textured wood (*right*) and a coarse uneven-textured wood (*far right*).

Transverse

Radial   Tangential

Latewood
Earlywood
Resin canal

Thick-walled axial tracheids

Thin-walled axial tracheids with pits

Ray cells

The cellular structure of softwoods is relatively simple. There is one main type of cell known as the axial tracheid, which is long, thin and hollow. The larger tracheids have pitted thin walls and occur in the earlywood. The smaller ones have thicker walls and are found in the latewood, and they give the timber its strength. The rays appear as long thin horizontal lines radiating outwards from the pith to the phloem of the tree. In most softwoods they are very fine and barely visible. Food storage occurs mainly in the parenchyma cells, which can also produce resin. Some species, such as true pine and larch, have special resin canals that run horizontally and vertically throughout the structure and are lined with parenchyma cells.

Latewood
Earlywood
Fibres
Ray

Ray cells

Axial vessels with wall pits

The cellular structure of hardwoods is more complex than that of softwoods, the main difference being the presence of axial vessels, which aid conduction of water and soluble substances throughout the tree. The vessels are usually of relatively even size and distribution in the growth ring; this is known as diffuse porous wood (*above*). On rare occasions vessels formed in the earlywood are larger than those of the latewood; the wood is then termed ring porous. The support cells, which give hardwood its strength, are known as fibres and can be thin or thick walled. As in softwoods the rays run from the pith to the phloem and help distribute the soluble food materials in the tree. Food storage occurs in the parenchyma cells.

Forestry and distribution

Wood is generally superior in its fabricating and aesthetic qualities to many of its competitors. The two main types of wood of interest to the woodworker are softwoods and hardwoods. The hardwoods are the more popular and versatile as well as being the more plentiful of the two woods, making up 60 per cent of the world's forests.

There are over 44,000 known species of timber, of which 12,000 are in use as commercial timber. Many extractive materials, such as resins, gums and latex, also provide the raw material for many separate but equally important industries that, for example, manufacture chemicals and medicines. As new areas of tropical and subtropical forests become accessible, many more species will become available.

At one time two-thirds of the world's surface was covered by natural forest. Man's intervention has reduced this to only one-third of the surface area. This shrinkage of natural forest, coupled with the growing needs of industry, has resulted in an increase in the cultivation of man-made forests. Success in this venture depends on the forester's knowledge of topography, to ensure the correct climatic conditions, and his skill at silviculture, to ensure that the right species are planted in the most beneficial soils.

To ensure as high a yield as possible, the forester must plant the trees using a system of rotation and in planned cropping areas, known as settings, to allow for natural and artificial re-seeding. Seeds may be planted by hand, machine or by air from a helicopter.

Forests cover one-third of the world's land surface. They can be divided into three main zones (*right*). Softwoods tend to be used as building materials and for packaging and paper pulp, while the hardwoods are preferred for specialized uses such as cabinetmaking. The total amount of wood supplied to the world market in 1979 was nearly 2,000 million cubic metres/6,562 million cubic feet, and demand is increasing, despite the introduction of many wood substitutes such as plastic laminates. Through the cultivation of man-made forests, man is trying to meet both present and future demands for timber, within the limits of the natural cycle of the timber crop.

| Coniferous forests (softwoods) | Temperate hardwoods | Tropical hardwoods |

To ensure a sustained yield of trees, a forest is divided into settings (*left*). A selected setting is cleared and then replanted with seeds or young trees. Once the cleared setting re-establishes itself, an adjacent setting may be cut and replanted. One of the major hazards of the forest is fire, both natural and man-made. One method of combating fires is from a small plane or helicopter, which "bombs" the blaze with retardant chemicals (*below left*).

The harvesting of larger trees from the higher slopes of mountains has, in the past, proved impossible because the areas have been inaccessible to transport. With the advent of bulldozers, however, it has been possible to build roads so trucks could bring in machinery such as the tower yarders (*right*). These are self-powered, telescopic steel towers, which may extend to 33.5 m/110 ft. They are equipped with enough cable to haul in logs from ranges of up to 800 m/880 yd.

The harvesting of trees requires different techniques, depending on the location and species of the tree. Selecting trees to harvest from man-made conifer forests that contain only a few species is relatively easy, but in the natural tropical forests of Africa, south-eastern Asia and South America, where hardwood species tend to occur only in isolated groups, the process of selecting and marking is much more difficult and expensive, requiring more manpower and considerably more time.

Part of modern forestry management involves protecting trees from insects, diseases, fungi and fire. Nine out of ten forest fires are caused by man and should therefore be preventable. Even though watchtowers are manned continually throughout the summer, extensive damage is caused annually in the huge forest tracts of northern America, Africa and Australia. Although fire can devastate forests completely, together insects and disease destroy more timber than fire. Diseased trees can be detected by infra-red photography from a satellite and can be counteracted by spraying the trees with protective chemicals.

The achievements of modern forestry management have only partially dispelled fears that the world's rapidly increasing population would necessitate large forest depletion for both food production and firewood. Also, there is still debate as to whether the world's forestry resources will be sufficiently large to support all the world's forseeable requirements and still provide for its ecological needs.

Felled trunks (*above*) are trimmed and then cross-cut (bucked) into logs, using chain saws. Also available are machines, such as the multi-processor, that can fell, de-limb and buck the trunks in one operation — and infinitely faster than a team of woodsmen.

Enormous 20-wheeled trucks (*above*), weighing up to 40 tonnes, can be loaded with a dozen or more logs that together may add a further 80 tonnes or more to the load.

The cost of transporting logs, including the building and maintaining of the access roads, is one of the greatest expenses incurred by timber companies.

In many parts of south-eastern Asia and west Africa water remains the cheapest form of transporting the logs (*above*). In order to cross still lakes and wide estuaries, the logs are fastened together and held by large poles (booms) to form a raft. They are then towed by a small tug to their destinations, which may well be the conversion mills.

Acacia melanoxylon

Acer pseudoplatanus

Afzelia spp.

Aucoumea klaineana

Blackwood
Indigenous to mountain areas of eastern and south-eastern Australia

Sycamore
Indigenous to Europe

Doussié
Indigenous to Cameroon, east Africa, Mozambique, Nigeria

Gaboon
Indigenous to equatorial Africa

Buxus sempervirens

Cardwellia sublimis

Carya spp.

Castanea sativa

European boxwood
Indigenous to south and north-western Europe

Silky oak
Indigenous to brush forests of north-eastern Australia

Hickory
Indigenous to eastern and southern North America, southern Canada

European chestnut
Indigenous to Europe, Middle East, north Africa

Castanospermum australe

Ceratopetalum apetalum

Chlorophora excelsa

Dalbergia latifolia

Black bean
Indigenous to north-eastern Australia

Coachwood
Indigenous to brush areas of the Australian east coastal districts

Iroko
Indigenous to west Africa

Indian rosewood
Indigenous to southern India

Diospyros spp.

Dryobalanops spp.

Endiandra palmerstonii

Entandrophragma cylindricum

Ebony
Indigenous to the Andaman Islands, India, Sri Lanka and Africa

Kapur
Indigenous to Malaysia

Queensland walnut
Indigenous to coastal areas of north-eastern Australia

Sapele
Indigenous to Cameroon, east Africa, Gold Coast, west Africa

Hardwoods 2

Entandrophragma utile

Eucalyptus spp.

Fagus sylvatica

Fraxinus excelsior

Utile
Indigenous to west and central Africa

Tasmanian oak
Indigenous to south-eastern Australia

European beech
Indigenous to Europe

European ash
Indigenous to Europe

Gonystylus bancanus

Gossweilerodendron balsamiferum

Juglans regia

Khaya ivorensis

Ramin
Indigenous to fresh-water swamps in Malaya, Sarawak

Agba
Indigenous to Angola, Nigeria

European walnut
Indigenous to Europe

African mahogany
Indigenous to Ghana, Ivory Coast, Nigeria

Lovoa trichilioides

Microberlinia brazzavillensis

Pericopsis elata

Platanus acerifolia

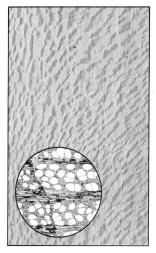

African walnut
Indigenous to the rain forests of Cameroon, Ghana, Ivory Coast, Nigeria

Zebrano
Indigenous to Cameroon

Afrormosia
Indigenous to Ghana, Ivory Coast, Zaire

European plane
Indigenous to Europe

Prunus avium

Pterocarpus macrocarpus

Quercus robur

Quercus rubra

European cherry
Indigenous throughout Europe to western Asia and the USSR, mountains of north Africa

Burma padauk
Indigenous to northern Burma

European oak
Indigenous to Europe and north Africa

American red oak
Indigenous to North America

Hardwoods 3

Shorea pauciflora

Swietenia macrophylla

Tectona grandis

Terminalia ivorensis

Dark red meranti
Indigenous to Malaysia

Honduras mahogany
Indigenous to Brazil, British Honduras, Costa Rica, Mexico, Nicaragua, Peru

Teak
Indigenous to India, south-eastern Asia

Idigbo
Indigenous to deciduous and rain forests of Cameroon, Ivory Coast, Nigeria

Tieghemella heckelii

Tilia × vulgaris

Triplochiton scleroxylon

Ulmus procera

Makore
Indigenous to the rain forests of Ghana, Ivory Coast, Nigeria, Sierra Leone

Lime
Indigenous to Europe

Obeche
Indigenous to Cameroon, Ivory Coast, Nigeria

European elm
Indigenous to Europe

Softwoods

Araucaria angustifolia

Cedrus spp.

Larix decidua

Pinus sylvestris

Parana pine
Indigenous to Argentina and Brazil

Cedar
Indigenous to the Himalayas, the Middle East and North America

European larch
Indigenous to the mountains of Europe

European redwood
Indigenous to Scandinavia, Scotland, the USSR and the mountains of Europe

Pseudotsuga menziesii

Sequoia sempervirens

Taxus baccata

Thuja plicata

Douglas fir
Indigenous to western North America

Californian redwood
Indigenous to western North America

Yew
Indigenous to Asia, Europe and north Africa

Western red cedar
Indigenous to western North America

Conversion and seasoning

The process of converting trees into marketable-sized boards takes place at a sawmill. The first stage, primary conversion, is when the log is cut, by a bandsaw or a circular saw. This is done in one of two ways: either plain sawing or quarter sawing.

Plain sawing, also referred to as "through-and-through" or slash sawing, is the simplest and most common way. The logs are gripped and sliced perpendicularly. It is a fast, economical process yielding the maximum number of usable boards. Quarter sawing requires greater skill on the part of the sawyer. The logs are first cut into quarters and then sawn into boards, using radial or approximately radial cuts. Wood cut in this way is more stable in use than plain-sawn boards and is therefore more suitable for structural work. The disadvantage with this method is cost as a higher percentage of wood is wasted when making truly radial cuts.

After primary conversion the boards are usually fed into the chipper canter — a machine developed to remove the waney edges — although some timber is left with the waney edges intact. The boards are usually dried or seasoned before re-sawing (secondary conversion) to specific dimensions. Before the boards are fit to use they must then be dried or seasoned to levels suitable for their required end use (*see* table opposite). Seasoning also minimizes subsequent shrinking and provides resistance to insect and fungal attack. Strength properties are improved and the wood is easier to work and more able to take a surface finish.

Water in the living tree is contained as free liquid in the cell cavities and bound liquid in the cell walls. Once the timber has been converted into boards, it will start to lose this moisture by evaporation until a level known as fibre saturation point (about 30 per cent moisture content for most wood) is reached, in which the cell cavities are comparatively dry but the cell walls are still saturated. Subsequent loss of moisture will be at a slower rate until the boards are in balance with the relative humidity of the surrounding atmosphere. At this stage the wood is said to be at its equilibrium moisture content.

One method of debarking (*above*) is to rotate the logs in a cylindrical drum, bombarding them with jets of water. Another method is to place the logs between spiked rollers that tear off the bark.

After debarking, the logs in this modern sawmill (*right*) pass under an electronic scanner that assesses the taper of the log and computes the best lengths for cross-cutting to ensure maximum timber yield.

Plain sawing

Quarter sawing

A vertical bandsaw (*above*) cuts the log to yield plain-sawn boards, which are then removed by a conveyor belt to be stacked. Quarter-sawn timber (*right*) is first cut into quarters and then converted by one of the four methods shown.

Converted boards piled in layers for air drying are said to be "in stick". Quarter-sawn boards may be sticked in neat stacks (*right*) and plain-sawn boards in "boules" — the order in which they were cut from the log (*above*).

If the humidity of the surrounding atmosphere changes so will the wood's equilibrium moisture content. The moisture content of boards stored in the open but protected from direct sun and rain will vary from approximately 17 per cent in dry weather to 23 per cent in wet weather in temperate countries.

The two most usual methods of seasoning wood are air drying, which uses the ambient heat from the sun, and kiln drying, which uses a combination of hot air and steam. For moisture levels below 17 per cent, kiln drying is necessary.

For natural seasoning (air drying), the unseasoned boards must be stacked exactly over each other on a firm, level base of concrete or creosoted timber with "stickers" of the same or neutral wood, such as poplar or fir, between each board. Spacing is crucial: the boards should be wide enough apart to allow adequate circulation of air but not so far apart that the boards will sag and warp; nor should they be so close that mould and fungal attack are encouraged. The top of the stack should be weighted with waste wood and the whole stack covered with a lean-to roof to protect the boards from rain and direct heat from the sun. To dry boards to their normal equilibrium moisture content of 17 to 23 per cent takes approximately one year for every 25 mm/1 in of wood thickness for hardwoods — less for softwoods.

Kiln drying has to be carefully monitored. To prevent too rapid drying, and therefore degradation in the timber, steam is injected into the kiln to temper the rate of moisture evaporation from the boards. The rate of kiln drying is controlled by many factors, such as the quality of the timber and the method of conversion. This type of drying is very much dependent on the skill of the operator. The advantage of kilning is that the drying time is reduced from years to weeks.

After seasoning the converted boards are usually planed. Other finishing processes available for specific purposes are mortising, spindle moulding, tenoning, drilling, routing and tongue and grooving. These latter processes, however, are normally done by the retailer or the woodworker rather than the timber merchant.

Grain direction
There are various ways of determining the grain direction on a board: by feeling or planing the surface for rough and smooth direction; and by examining the edges of the board to see in which direction the grain is slanting.

Across the grain
Against the grain
With the grain
Along the grain

Moisture content of timber for various purposes		
Air drying sufficient %	27%	Appreciable shrinkage starts at about this point
	25%	Suitable moisture content for creosoting
	20%	Decay safety line (wet rots)
	18%	Exterior joinery
Kiln drying necessary %	16%	Garden furniture
	14%	Woodwork for use in places only slightly or occasionally heated
	12%	Interior woodwork with regular intermittent heating
	11%	Woodwork in continuously heated buildings
	9%	Woodwork used in close proximity to sources of heat, e.g. radiator casings, mantlepieces

It is advisable to know the average moisture contents required for wood in various environments (*left*), as it is important not to vary these by more than 2 per cent if degradation is to be avoided. The moisture content of a piece of wood is first found by weighing an unseasoned sliver, drying it in an oven and re-weighing it. It is then calculated as: wet weight less dry weight over dry weight, multiplied by 100. Wood is not a homogenous material and the rate of shrinkage is unequal along the three main axes (*below*). Circumferential shrinkage along the length of the growth rings is roughly twice as much as that between the rings. Thus the shrinkage of plain-sawn boards across the width is almost exactly twice that of quarter-sawn boards.

Veneers and manufactured boards

Veneering is the term given to the method of laying thin slices of wood (veneers) on a groundwork of plain but structurally sound wood. There are two main uses for veneer: the first is as a decorative surface in traditional and fine cabinetmaking; the second is as a facing or base in the construction of manufactured boards, such as multi-ply, blockboard, battenboard and laminboard. Manufactured boards can be bought ready surfaced with veneer or unsurfaced, in which case a decorative veneer can be applied separately.

Selecting trees that will yield well-figured wood is extremely difficult. Apart from external signs such as burrs and stumps, there is little to indicate in the standing tree the extent of the figure contained within, until it is actually sawn. There are various methods of sawing that are suitable for revealing the figures in a particular tree. The main methods are flat, quarter and half-round slicing. Rotary-cut veneers are used mainly when making three-ply and multi-ply.

Manufactured boards are usually made of beech or birch. They are becoming increasingly popular as a substitute for solid wood. They can be categorized into plywoods (for example, multi-ply and blockboard), particle-boards (for example, chipboard) and fibreboards.

One of the most utilized and particularly versatile plywoods is obtainable in three-ply or multi-ply up to 19 layers; each layer is glued with the grain at right angles to the previous one. Alternating the plies in this way improves strength and stability by counteracting any tendency to distort through shrinkage or swelling. Having no natural line of cleavage, it also eliminates the possibility of splitting along the length or the width. This is a valuable quality when nailing, screwing or fastening on the outer veneer or face, but take care not to work near the edge of the wood or the surface will delaminate. It can also be cut and bent more easily than solid wood.

Three other types of plywoods are blockboard, battenboard and laminboard. They differ from three- and multi-ply in having a solid core made of strips of wood combined together to form a slab, which is then sandwiched between outer veneers. Blockboard has strips of wood up to 25 mm/1 in wide, but when faced with veneers there may be a tendency for the line of the strips to show through the facing; for this reason it is not normally used for high-quality work. A cheaper

Manufactured boards

modification of this type of board is battenboard, in which the core strips vary from 50 mm/2 in to 75 mm/3 in in width. Laminboard is of similar construction, but the strips making up the core are much narrower, between 1.5 mm/$\frac{1}{16}$ in and 6 mm/$\frac{1}{4}$ in thick. As it is usually made of hardwood and is generally used for higher quality work, it tends to be more expensive than any other type of manufactured board.

It is important to assess the end use when selecting plywoods. Different types of adhesives are used to bond plywoods, depending on whether the materials are to be used inside or outdoors. Standard plywoods are not bonded with a waterproof adhesive, but other grades of plywoods are available that will not only resist water but extremes of weather too.

Particle-board is not as strong as plywoods, but it is still of sufficient quality for a variety of non-structural uses such as in panels, ceilings and cladding for partitions. It can be made of flax-shives (flaxboard) or sugar cane (bagasse board), but the best quality board is manufactured from compressed wood particles (chipboard). All these boards are made from waste wood obtained from forest thinnings and shavings from other wood manufacturing processes, bonded together with a synthetic resin glue under heat and pressure. Various methods of processing provide three basic types of chipboard, including a special type of furniture board that has a gradation from coarse to fine chips towards the surface, giving a smooth close-textured finish. This can then be faced with quality veneers. The other types of particle-boards have either a single layer of chips all of a similar size, giving the board uniform density and strength, or a core of coarser chips between two outer layers of finer chips (sandwich board). As with plywoods movement is quite small compared to solid wood. Particle-board, however, is very absorbent so all its surfaces must be sealed if it is to be used in damp areas. It is available faced with a variety of veneers or plastic coatings.

A useful manufactured board for low-grade non-structural work is fibreboard. There are two basic types: insulation board and hardboard. Insulation board is usually made from bagasse, flax-shives or straw and has little application in furnituremaking. Hardboard is manufactured almost exclusively from wet wood fibres bonded together under extreme pressure to produce a dense finished board.

Multi-ply   Battenboard   Blockboard

Methods of obtaining veneers

Butt veneer
A highly decorative veneer found at the swollen base of trees such as walnut (*above*).

This veneer is obtained by halving the log longitudinally and converting it by using the half-round slicing method.

Curl veneer
This attractive veneer is found at the crown and the base of the branches. Walnut and

mahogany (*above*) are highly valued for this type of figure. Other variations of curl are feather and swirl.

Burr veneer
Irregular outgrowths called burrs are found on many trees and often yield a highly

ornamental figure. They are caused by injury to the tree and are commonly cut from oak, ash and walnut (*above*).

Oyster veneer
The striking pattern of this veneer is achieved by cutting transversely at an angle of 45°

from the branches of trees such as kingwood (*above*) and laburnum. It is used mainly on reproduction furniture.

Flat-sliced veneer
This is the most common method of cutting, in which the half log is sliced longitudinally,

producing landscape or cathedral figures. The rio rosewood sample (*above*) shows marbled heartwood.

Quarter-cut veneer
A quartered log is sliced at right angles to the tree's growth rings. This is the best

method to obtain the striped effects and ray figures that are a feature of some woods. The sample (*above*) is sapele.

Half-round sliced veneer
With this method, which is also known as semi-rotary, the log is mounted eccentrically on

a rotary lathe. This produces a pattern with a broad-grain figure. The sample illustrated (*above*) is yew.

Rotary-cut veneer
When the log is mounted centrally on a lathe and then rotated against the blade, a

continuous sheet of veneer is produced. This method is often used to obtain the "bird's-eye" effect in maple (*above*).

Laminboard   Chipboard   Flaxboard

Selecting and buying timber

Landscape

Ray or flame

"Bird's-eye" maple

Blister

Quilt

Stripe

Ribbon

Fiddleback

Burr

Masur birch

Mineral streaks

Gum veins

Landscape

Growth rings are one of two structural features that can produce an attractive figure, depending on the method of conversion. The elongated growth ring pattern known as landscape or cathedral figure is seen only on plain-sawn surfaces. Quarter-sawn surfaces will show the rings as parallel lines in the wood.

"Bird's-eye" maple

This figure is seen on the tangential surfaces of only a few species, the best known being Canadian rock maple. The pattern is caused by fungi, which attack the cambium. This retards the complete formation of the annual rings, leaving conical depressions that on conversion appear as circles resembling pin knots.

Quilt

This form of blister figure is caused by irregularities in the tree's growth rings. The pattern is most effectively seen on plain-sawn surfaces, where the incident light is reflected from the irregular grain at different angles, giving a three-dimensional appearance to wood such as African mahogany (*illustrated*).

Ribbon

A growth characteristic of many tropical hardwoods is interlocked grain. This produces a striped figure on quarter-sawn surfaces. If the wood is moved in relation to the light source the colour of the stripes will appear to alternate. This optical effect is not due to colour variation in the wood.

Burr

Burrs are the result of injury to trees such as common elm (*illustrated*). The highly irregular grain, which contains many small knots, also contributes to the pattern of the figure. Burr is extremely difficult to season and convert and for this reason the wood is best utilized as a veneer rather than as solid timber.

Mineral streaks

These are localized discolorations of timber, in the form of streaks or patches usually darker than the natural colour, which do not impair the strength of the piece. The colour of the streaks can vary from the dark red common in parana pine (*illustrated*) to yellow or white, as seen in red meranti and keruing.

Ray

The second structural feature that plays an important role in the production of figure is rays. As they occur radially throughout the tree they are best seen (if they are visible at all) on radial or quarter-sawn surfaces. Decorative figures of this type in woods such as oak and maple (*illustrated*) are used mainly as veneers.

Blister

This type of figure, in common with the "bird's-eye" figure in maple, is caused by injury to the cambium, with the result that large depressions are formed in the growth rings. The figure is seen in softwoods such as pitch pine and hardwoods such as kevazingo (*illustrated*) and American whitewood.

Stripe

This figure is most commonly seen in ebonies such as macassar (*illustrated*). The stripes are due entirely to colour variation within the wood, caused by alternation of the pale sapwood with the darker coloured heartwood. Where the colour is less evenly distributed the pattern is known as marblewood.

Fiddleback

This figure is seen on the quarter-sawn surfaces of woods such as sycamore (*illustrated*). This particular wood is often used in the manufacture of violins, hence the name of the figure. As with the ribbon figure the apparent colour changes occur because of the way in which the light is reflected from the grain.

Masur birch

This distinctive figure is found in the butt logs of birch from Finland and Norway. It is caused by the larvae of a gnat-like fly of the genus *Agromyza*, which tunnels into the wood. The tree heals the damage by producing resin to fill the bore channels. Masur birch is used mainly in the production of treen.

Gum veins

These are caused by traumatic incidents such as wounding or forest fires. They are normally considered to be a defect, but in Italian ancona walnut they are a natural characteristic that actually enhances the appearance of the wood. The gum veins can show as streaks as in paldao (*illustrated*) or as flecks.

When selecting wood from the 12,000 species commercially available, the worker will usually be considering two distinct uses — wood for decoration or wood for structural purposes. The appearance, or figure, of wood is determined by inherent colouring substances and the way in which the different tissues or grain grow. These characteristics are best seen in veneers that are bought purely as decoration, which are laid on a groundwork of structurally sound timber or manufactured boards. The direction of the grain is also a good indication of the structural properties of timber, that is, its bending and compressive strength (*see* pages 244–51). Any marked deviation of the grain from the vertical axis of the tree will affect the wood's strength. This may not matter for some uses.

There are five naturally occurring types of grain: straight, irregular, wavy, spiral and double spiral or interlocked. Straight-grained timbers usually have the greatest overall strength but may be least figured. Such wood, therefore, is best used for structural purposes. Diagonal grain can occur naturally, but it also frequently results from incorrect conversion. Grain that has been deflected from a straight course by, for example, a knot is described as irregular. Such timber still has many uses for the woodworker. Wood with a wavy grain has an attractive appearance that, used in joinery, outweighs any loss of strength. On quarter-sawn surfaces this distinctive figure sometimes shows as fiddleback. Spiral grain is the term applied to grain that follows either a left- or right-handed diagonal course up the tree. Such timber is not suitable for cabinetwork. Double spiral or interlocked grain inclines obliquely first one way, then the other. Workability is difficult and there is some loss in strength.

A combination of fiddleback and ribbon is sometimes found in interlocked grain, producing a mottled figure called roe. Interlocked grain and wavy grain combined can produce many beautiful figures.

Types of grain

Straight grain

Irregular grain

Wavy grain

Spiral grain

Interlocked grain

Defects

Defects in timber can be divided into two basic categories: man-made defects, caused by incorrect seasoning or conversion, and natural defects. The latter can be divided into biodegradation, which is the collective term for attack by living organisms, such as wood-borers, fungi and rots, and inherent defects, such as knots and pitch pockets, which occur as the tree is growing. Only experience will provide the knowledge to assess good-quality wood. A selection of the defects that may be encountered in furniture or when buying timber and storing it is outlined below.

A. Cupping   B. Springing   C. Diamonding

Man-made defects

The most common seasoning defects are caused by the wood warping as a result of too rapid drying. They include cupping (A), where the board hollows across the width; bowing (E), where it curves like a bow along its length; springing (B), where the board lies flat but bends along its edges; "in winding" (F), where the board is twisted along its length; and diamonding (C), where the squared material is distorted. Rapid drying can also cause case-hardening, where the outside of the wood dries more quickly than the inside, setting up stresses within. This may be remedied if the wood is steamed again and re-dried. If this defect is not remedied quickly the wood will set, forming interior splits known as honeycombing. The condition is unalterable and renders previously sound wood useless. If green wood is dried too quickly the wood cells flatten or collapse, resulting in a concave surface across the width of the board. Badly converted wood can result in diagonal grain, that is, grain that is inclined obliquely to the longitudinal axis of the tree. If the grain is very eccentric it can impair impact and bending strength. Roller check (D) and machine burn (H), depending on the severity of the fault, can be remedied by planing. Boards that have retained the natural trunk shape of the tree are known as waney edged (G).

Natural defects

Attack by wood-borers, such as the furniture beetle, is a common form of biodegradation. This pest, also known as woodworm, can attack and completely riddle all wood, seasoned or unseasoned. Marine borers (K, R), such as the shipworm and gribble, occur in temperate and tropical countries, devastating marine timbers. Termites (Q) are the most voracious wood predators in tropical and sub-tropical countries. The wood

D. Roller check   E. Bowing   F. "in winding"

G. Waney edge

H. Machine burn

J. Brown rot

K. Temperate water shipworm

L. Shakes

M. Pitch pockets

N. Live knot

P. Reaction wood

Q. Termites

has to be broken to reveal the extent of termite damage, as unlike most wood-boring insects they do not leave any external signs of attack. The most common species of brown rot (**J**) are dry rots. They are usually found indoors, where they attack the cellulose content of wood, leaving a brown friable residue. White rots usually occur out of doors and attack the cellulose and the lignin, leaving a white friable residue. The most common inherent defect in wood is knots, either live or dead. All knots distort the grain and can affect the strength properties of the wood. A live knot (**N**) occurs where a tree, in increasing its diameter, envelops the base of a living branch, which then becomes an integral part of the trunk. A dead knot occurs where the stump of a dead branch is enclosed by the living tissue of the trunk. Dead knots can fall out during conversion and seasoning or when the boards are being worked. Internal stresses in a growing tree or in wood being seasoned can cause large splits known as shakes (**L**). The splits tend to occur along the rays — the weakest tissue in the tree or at the end of boards dried too quickly in the sun. Lesser splits or cracks are called checks. Trees growing on a steep gradient or in areas of strong prevailing winds show an off-centre pith and uneven growth rings in cross-section; this is known as reaction wood (**P**). This distorted growth is called compression wood in softwoods and it is often brittle. In hardwoods this type of growth defect is known as tension wood and is subject to severe shakes and warping. Injury to a tree can result in pitch pockets (**M**), a serious defect as it is not usually visible until the timber is being converted.

R. Tropical water shipworm, also showing smaller holes made by the gribble

Selected world timbers 1

Wood	Natural characteristics	Technical qualities	Natural durability	Reaction to preservative	Seasoning qualities
Acacia melanoxylon **Blackwood** (page 230)	Medium even texture; straight to interlocked grain; fiddleback ray figure; pronounced growth ring; a natural lustre	Strong; good impact properties; pliable	Fair	Very resistant	Good; stable when dry
Acer pseudoplatanus **Sycamore** (page 230)	Smooth texture; the grain may be close and wavy but is more usually straight; fiddleback ray figure; shows a satiny sheen	Quite strong; good bending strength	Poor	Resistant	Stable when dried slowly
Afzelia spp. **Doussié** (page 230)	Medium texture; straight grain with some irregularity; yellow deposits may cause surface flecks	Moderately good bending and compressive strength; resistant to splitting; very stiff	Good	Very resistant	Dries slowly; prone to slight distortion and checking
Araucaria angustifolia **Parana pine** (page 235)	Fine even texture; straight grain; fairly knot free	Varies from soft to hard	Poor	Fairly resistant	Good; but dry carefully to avoid distortion and splitting
Aucoumea klaineana **Gaboon** (page 230)	Medium coarse texture; often irregular grain; few figures; nondescript appearance	A weak wood in all properties	Poor	Poor	Fair; slight tendency to distort
Buxus sempervirens **European boxwood** (page 230)	A very fine even texture; straight and irregular grain	A hard timber; excellent compressive strength; fair bending properties	Fair	Resistant	Dry slowly; a tendency to surface checks; splits badly if dried in the round
Cardwellia sublimis **Silky oak** (page 230)	Coarse but even texture; fairly straight grain; good silver grain ray figure on quarter-sawn surfaces; occasional dark lines	Strong and stiff; fair bending strength	Fair	Poor	Fair, if dried slowly; some checking and distortion
Carya spp. **Hickory** (page 230)	Coarse texture; straight grain but can be wavy; well-defined growth rings	Good steam-bending properties; very strong; hardness varies according to growth rate	Poor	Fairly resistant	Dry very slowly due to high rate of shrinkage
Castanea sativa **European chestnut** (page 230)	Coarse texture; some straight but often spiral grain; growth rings prominent; tannin content	Reasonable bending strength and shear; stiff but not as good as oak; splits easily	Good	Very resistant	Dry very slowly; prone to collapse, internal cracking and distortion
Castanospermum australe **Black bean** (page 231)	Medium texture, somewhat greasy; straight to slight interlocked grain	Stiff and strong but inclined to be brittle; hard	Fair to good	Poor	Dry carefully; prone to distortion, collapse, checking and internal cracking
Cedrus spp. **Cedar** (page 235)	Fine even texture; conspicuous growth rings; aromatic when freshly sawn	Medium strength; brittle	Very good; resistant to fungi	Poor	Fair; prone to distortion
Ceratopetalum apetalum **Australian coachwood** (page 231)	Fine texture; fairly straight grain; decorative growth ring figure	Good bending strength	Poor	Poor	Good; stable when dry
Chlorophora excelsa **Iroko** (page 231)	Fairly coarse texture; interlocked grain gives typical ribbon figure on quarter-sawn surfaces; white flecks caused by calcareous deposits often present; good acid and fire resistance; Iroko is sometimes likened to teak	Good bending strength; hard; resistant to shock loading	Excellent if the grain is straight	Fairly resistant	Quite good; minimal checking and distortion

Air dried weight	Working qualities	Fixing qualities	Finishing qualities	Relevant uses	Woods with similar qualities	General comments
656 kg/m³	Reasonable but some hard patches; tends to crumble on the end grain	Good	Excellent	Cabinetmaking; furniture; fine interior joinery; woodwind instruments; gun-stocks	Black bean	An excellent multi-purpose wood
640 kg/m³	Fair	Care needed with nails and screws; good with glue	Excellent	Fine interior joinery and veneers; string instrument backing; fine furniture; turning; an excellent flooring wood	Rock maple (weight 800 kg/m³) has a distinctive "bird's-eye" figure	Susceptible to stains when being kilned; stack vertically for air drying; never put in stick formation
816 kg/m³	Fairly hard to work; keep cutting angle low	Poor with nails and glue; fair with screws, pre-boring required	Fair but may need filling	Fine interior joinery; staircases; flooring; sills; doors etc.	None	Not suitable for domestic use as it stains yellow in damp conditions
544 kg/m³	Good	Good	Good	Fine interior joinery; framework; drawer sides; mouldings	Western yellow pine	Prone to movement so ensure stable humidity conditions. It is also used as a general purpose plywood
432 kg/m³	Abrasive to saws and tools, caused by silica content	Poor with nails and screws; good with glue	Fair	Door skins; drawer sides; partition work	Red meranti	Used to face three-ply, multi-ply, blockboard and laminboard
912 kg/m³	Fairly resistant to saws but cuts cleanly; fairly hard to work; tendency to tear on irregular grain so keep cutting angle low; tendency to machine burn	May split with nails; pre-boring required with screws; fair with glue	Excellent	Tool handles; mallet heads; croquet heads; skittles; rulers; chessmen; draughts; fancy carvings	Species of boxwood from central America, South and North Africa, western Asia, Iran	A good wood for carving and turning
528 kg/m³	Good; some grain pick-up on quarter-sawn surfaces caused by wide rays; lower cutting angle by 20° for best results	Good	Fairly good	Furniture; interior joinery; panelling; flooring	American red oak	A good, lightweight, decorative wood, similar to oak in appearance
816 kg/m³	Fair; some grain pick-up; inclined to blunt tools and saws	Difficult with nails and screws; good with glue	Fair	High impact strength makes it useful for pick and hammer handles; sports equipment	European ash	Now often replaced by metals and synthetic materials
544 kg/m³	Good; tendency to bind on saws	Good	Excellent but may need filling	Furniture; turning; kitchen ware; cleft fencing	Oak	Because of its resemblance to oak is often used as an oak substitute; stains in contact with ferrous metals
704 kg/m³	Fair; prone to hard and soft patches	Fair with nails and screws; good with glue	Good	Good all round cabinetmaking; fine interior joinery; doors; panels	Blackwood	A decorative wood
560 kg/m³	Good	Care needed with nails and screws; good with glue	Good	Fine interior joinery; non-structural parts of furniture		Has a decorative appearance. Cedar of Lebanon is the best-known commercial species.
640 kg/m³	Good	Good	Excellent	Interior joinery; cabinetmaking; furniture	Ash; hickory	One of Australia's first coach-building woods
640 kg/m³	Good but calcareous deposits may blunt saw and tool edges	Good	Good, but needs filling	Fine interior joinery; exterior joinery; boat building counter and bench tops; garden seats; parquet flooring, even with underfloor heating	Afrormosia; teak	Not so attractive a wood for furniture as teak but has a good combination of properties and is comparatively inexpensive

Selected world timbers 2

Wood	Natural characteristics	Technical qualities	Natural durability	Reaction to preservative	Seasoning qualities
Dalbergia latifolia **Indian rosewood** (page 231)	Coarse to very fine even texture; generally straight grain but some slight interlock; irregular black markings give an unusual appearance	Very strong and hard; good bending, compression and impact strength; stiff	Excellent	Poor	A tendency to surface checking; dry slowly
Diospyros spp. **Ebony** (page 231)	Very fine texture; straight grain; very hard; subspecies, e.g. macassar, have a pronounced figure	African spp. have good strength; the Asian spp. are variable	Good	Poor	African spp. season well if dried carefully, but Asian spp. have a tendency to fine surface checking
Dryobalanops spp. **Kapur** (page 231)	Coarse even texture; reasonably straight grain; whitish resin ducts show as lines mainly on plain-sawn surfaces; a distinct camphor smell when freshly sawn	Reasonably hard; good bending properties; stiff	Excellent	Very resistant	Dries well; has a slight tendency to check
Endiandra palmerstonii **Queensland walnut** (page 231)	Medium even texture; some interlocked grain producing chequered markings on quarter-sawn wood; lustrous surface; distasteful odour when freshly sawn	Stronger than European walnut; hard; stiff; good bending strength	Poor	Poor	Care needed; a tendency to surface and internal checking and distortion; surface collapse possible
Entandrophragma cylindricum **Sapele** (page 231)	Fine texture; interlocked grain; striped roe figure on quarter-sawn surfaces; growth rings pronounced on plain-sawn surfaces; cedar-like scent when freshly sawn	Good strength properties; equal to oak in bending, stiffness and shock resistance; hard; good splitting	Fair	Poor	Dry carefully; seasoning needed to avoid distortion
Entandrophragma utile **Utile** (page 231)	Rather coarse texture; interlocked grain shows a ribbon figure on quarter-sawn surfaces	Reasonably hard; fair shock resistance; poor bending strength	Fair	Very resistant	A tendency to check and distort; steady drying recommended
Eucalyptus spp. **Tasmanian oak** (page 232)	Coarse texture; straight grain; similar in appearance to ash or oak, but minus the characteristic silver grain of oak	About the same hardness as European oak; good bending properties; good stiffness; tough; excellent resistance to shock load	Fair	Resistant	Careful drying needed; a distinct tendency to surface and internal cracking, collapse and distortion
Fagus sylvatica **European beech** (page 232)	Fine, even texture; straight grained; a "seed pip" ray figure shows on tangential surfaces; a small flecked figure on quarter-sawn surfaces	Excellent bending and impact strength; stiff; shear; resistant to splitting	Poor	Good	Fairly good; dry carefully; inclined to check and distort; high shrinkage factor
Fraxinus excelsior **European ash** (page 232)	Coarse to medium fine texture; straight grain; conspicuous growth rings	Good strength; tough; excellent bending qualities; resistant to splitting	Poor	Fairly resistant	Fairly good but inclined to distortion and end grain splitting at high temperatures
Gonystylus bancanus **Ramin** (page 232)	Moderate to fine texture; straight to slightly interlocked grain; can cause skin irritation; prone to staining	Fairly good; nearly comparable to home-grown beech; good compressive strength but prone to splitting; not a good bending timber and rather weak in shear	Poor	Good	Prone to end-grain splitting but shows little distortion; care needed to prevent staining
Gossweilerodendron balsamiferum **Agba** (page 232)	Fine texture; generally straight grain; resinous; similar appearance to gaboon or light-coloured mahogany	Quite good, comparable to American mahogany; subject to brittle heart; moderately good bending strength	Quite good	Resistant	Quite good with little tendency to split or distort, but gum exudation can be a problem

Air dried weight	Working qualities	Fixing qualities	Finishing qualities	Relevant uses	Woods with similar qualities	General comments
848 kg/m³	Quite hard to work; calcareous deposits dull blades; turns well	Poor with nails; good with screws; fair with glue	Excellent	Fine furniture; solid veneer; interior joinery; shallow carving; knife and brush handles etc; musical instruments, e.g. guitars	Cocobolo kingwood; South American rosewood	Becoming more popular; a decorative wood
African spp. 1,008 kg/m³ Asian spp. 1,168 kg/m³	Difficult; inclined to be brittle; blunting effect on tools; use a low-angled plane blade	Very difficult with nails and screws; fair with glue	Excellent	Small work, e.g. door handles, knobs, cutlery handles, tool handles, chessmen, organ stops, decorative inlays, finger boards of stringed instruments; a good turning wood; domestic flooring	African blackwood	A good multi-purpose wood for small intricate work
704/768 kg/m³	Fairly easy to work; saws may be blunted; some grain pick-up when planing	Fair	Fair	Flooring; interior joinery	Keruing	Stains when wet if in contact with ferrous metals
672 kg/m³	A severe dulling effect on saws and tool cutting edges; keep well sharpened; use a low-angled plane blade	Poor with nails; good with screws and glue	Excellent	Fine interior joinery; cabinetmaking; furniture; decorative panelling	European walnut; paldao	Not botanically related to walnut, but similar in appearance, texture and weight
624 kg/m³	Good; some grain pick-up when planing quarter-sawn surfaces; keep cutting angle low	Good	Excellent	Furniture, solid and veneer; fine interior joinery; flooring	African mahogany; Honduras mahogany; utile	A well-utilized, decorative and sound timber
656 kg/m³	Works well; some tendency to grain pick-up during planing due to interlocked grain	Good	Good, but needs filling	Furniture, solid and veneer; cabinet-making; interior joinery	African mahogany; sapele	An attractive mahogany-type wood; for constructional and decorative work
Variable around 656 kg/m³	Moderate, similar to ash	Slight tendency to split with nails; good with screws and glue	Good	Furniture, solid and veneer; interior joinery; flooring; spade handles; ladder rungs	Ash; European oak	A good general-purpose timber
720 kg/m³	Variable; some wood tends to bind and burn when sawing or drilling; usually reasonable to work	Fair with nails and screws; good with glue	Good	Furniture, especially chairs; fine interior joinery; toys; small models; small turning	Chilean beech; silver beech; Southland beech from Australasia	A good multi-purpose timber in plentiful supply
688 kg/m³	Fair; tendency to wastage when planing flat-sawn wood due to distortion	Fair with nails and screws; good with glue	Excellent; may need filling	Furniture; fine interior joinery; tennis, squash, badminton frames; gymnasium equipment; drum frames; turning	Hickory; Japanese ash, North American ash	An excellent and attractive general-purpose wood
656 kg/m³	Tends to tear on quarter-sawn surfaces; keep cutting angle low; wear goggles and gloves when sawing unseasoned wood	Tends to split with nails; fair with screws and glue	Good	Interior joinery; turning; mouldings; handles; toys	None	A generally good utility wood; can be quite attractive
512 kg/m³	Good; gum can sometimes bind saw and tool blades; interlocked grain can tear so keep cutting angle low	Fair with nails and glue; good with screws	Fair; gum can affect finish	Interior joinery; furniture linings and backings	African mahogany (except for colour)	A good multi-purpose timber; do not use in damp areas, e.g. kitchens, bathrooms; can produce objectionable odours

Selected world timbers 3

Wood	Natural characteristics	Technical qualities	Natural durability	Reaction to preservative	Seasoning qualities
Juglans regia **European walnut** (page 232	Usually fine texture; a general naturally wavy grain; clear of knots except on burr veneers, which have pin knots	Hard, tough; good splitting and impact resistance; good bending properties and shock loading strength	Fair	Resistant	Dries slowly but well; tendency to checking and internal cracks with thick wood
Khaya ivorensis **African mahogany** (page 232)	Medium texture; shows a ribbon figure on quarter-sawn surfaces; subject to black gum line figure	Medium strength, but some heartwood is prone to brittleness; boards subject to hair-line cracks due to compression failure	Fair; subject to pin-hole and bark borer attack	Resistant	Good; stable when dry
Larix decidua **European larch** (page 235)	Coarse to medium texture; resinous; high contrast between early- and latewood; small knots; faintly aromatic	Strong; hard; not pliable	Fair	Fairly resistant	Good; stable when dry
Lovoa trichilioides **African walnut** (page 233)	Fairly coarse texture; interlocked grain produces fair ribbon figure on quarter-sawn surfaces; fairly clear of knots	Fairly hard and stiff; fair compressive strength; moderate bending and shock loading qualities; fairly resistant to splitting	Good	Very resistant	Good; dries fairly quickly without much checking or distortion; reasonably stable
Microberlinia brazzavillensis **Zebrano** (page 233)	Normally coarse texture; interlocked grain; striped figure on quarter-sawn surfaces; colour variations give an attractive figure	Strong; shock resistant	Good	Resistant	Prone to distortion so slow drying necessary
Pericopsis elata **Afrormosia** (page 233)	Fine texture; interlocked grain; good acid and alkali resistance	Strong and hard	Excellent	Very resistant	Dries well if slowly with little degradation
Pinus sylvestris **European redwood** (page 235)	Coarse texture; resinous; clear growth rings; knotty	Resilient; flexible; good bending and compressive strength	Poor; prone to insect and fungi attack	Good	Good; dries quickly
Platanus acerifolia **European plane** (page 233)	Smooth even texture; usually straight grain; on quarter-sawn surfaces the dark brown ray figure shows as flecks — it is then known as lacewood	Reasonably good properties in bending; hard; resistant to splitting, although the knots are inclined to split	Very poor	Fairly resistant	Seasons well but sometimes there is slight distortion
Prunus avium **European cherry** (page 233)	Fine even texture; straight grain; gum marks sometimes visible on surface	A tough wood; good bending and impact strength; stiff; resistant to splitting; knots are usually small	Fair but do not use externally unless treated	Poor	Tendency to distort so care needed; reasonably stable when dry
Pseudotsuga menziesii **Douglas fir** (page 235)	Coarse texture; resinous; conspicuous growth rings	Medium strength	Poor; fairly resistant to decay	Poor	Good; stable when dry
Pterocarpus macrocarpus **Burma padauk** (page 233)	Fine smooth texture; slightly interlocked grain; narrow ribbon figure on quarter-sawn surfaces; few knots	Very strong and hard	Good	Poor	Seasons slowly but well with little surface checking or distortion; very stable when dry
Quercus robur **European oak** (page 233)	Coarse texture; straight grain; well-defined growth rings; relatively knot-free timber; quality varies according to locality; wide rays very noticeable on quarter-sawn surfaces giving a silver grain figure.	Very strong, used as a yardstick for other hardwoods for this reason; bends well, but care must be taken to avoid rupture on inner face of curved wood	Fair; subject to lyctus attack	Very resistant. Do not treat with a salt chemical, which will turn the wood bluey black	Must be dried slowly; a tendency to distort; some collapse and inner checks

Air dried weight	Working qualities	Fixing qualities	Finishing qualities	Relevant uses	Woods with similar qualities	General comments
640 kg/m³	Good	Good	Excellent	Furniture, solid and veneer; fine interior joinery; good for carving and turning	African walnut; American black walnut; Australian walnut; Indian laurel	A highly desirable wood, often well figured, especially ancona Italian walnut; decorative work can be done using burr veneers
512 kg/m³	Good; some grain pick-up due to interlocked grain	Good	Mainly good	Furniture, solid and veneer, especially reproduction work; fine interior joinery; panelling; turning	Other mahoganies	A common African redwood; not a true mahogany but an excellent substitute. Used in the manufacture of plywoods
592 kg/m³	Good	Care needed with nails; good with screws and glue	Good	Fencing; boat building	All species of larch	Of limited use but excellent
544 kg/m³	Fair; some grain pick-up when planing quarter-sawn surfaces; keep cutting angle low	Good	Fair	Furniture solid and veneer; interior joinery; cabinet-making	African mahogany (except for colour)	A good all round decorative wood; in fairly good supply
Variable around 720 kg/m³	Good	Fair with nails and screws; good with glue	Good	Furniture mainly in veneer form; small items, e.g. tool handles	Berlinia	Used mainly as a veneering wood
688 kg/m³	Fairly good but inclined to blunt cutting edges; keep cutting angle low; some grain pick-up on quarter-sawn surfaces	Poor with nails; good with screws if pre-bored; good with glue	Excellent	Furniture, solid and veneer; fine interior joinery; boat superstructure	Iroko; teak	A first-class wood
528 kg/m³	Good	Good	Good	Interior joinery; furniture carcasses; flooring	Western yellow pine; pitch pine	Resinous knots can be troublesome; either pre-treat or drill out and plug. Also known as Scots pine
624 kg/m³	Saws well; tends to bind; keep cutting angle low on quarter-sawn surfaces	Good	Good	Decorative work, e.g. inlay; marquetry	White beech; planes indigenous to Iran, North America and Turkey	The Scots call their sycamores "plane"; the Americans call their plane trees "sycamore"; in America their species are more prolific and used for furniture and cabinetmaking
608 kg/m³	Very good	Good	Excellent	Furniture, solid and veneer; cabinetmaking; interior joinery	American black cherry; other fruitwoods, e.g. apple, pear, plum	The European wood is used mainly for veneering; American cherry is less heavy
544 kg/m³	Good; with care	Good	Poor	Interior joinery; laminated boards	None	Prone to windblow defects
848 kg/m³	Fair	Not easy with nails; fair with screws if pre-bored; good with glue	Excellent	Furniture; interior joinery; flooring	African padauk; Andaman padauk	Burma padauk is one of the heaviest, strongest and hardest of the South East Asian woods
704 kg/m³	Good; some grain pick-up on lowland oak timber	Good	Good but needs filling	Furniture, solid and veneer; fine interior joinery; Flooring, both strip and block	Other oaks, especially American white, Japanese, Turkish	German slavonia considered to be the finest oak; stains occur when in contact with ferrous metals in damp conditions; a well-utilized hardwood

Selected world timbers 4

Wood	Natural characteristics	Technical qualities	Natural durability	Reaction to preservative	Seasoning qualities
Quercus rubra **American red oak** (page 233)	Coarse but even texture; fairly straight grain; not usually a knotty timber; fairly fire and acid resistant; pronounced growth rings	Variable according to growth conditions; good bending qualities; quite strong	Poor	Poor	Reasonable; dries slowly; prone to checking and distortion
Sequoia sempervirens **Californian redwood** (page 235)	Texture varies from fine to coarse; straight grain; knot free; prominent growth ring figure; resistant to acid and alkali	Medium strength	Good	Fairly resistant	Good; stable when dry
Shorea pauciflora **Dark red meranti** (page 234)	Fairly coarse texture; grain tends to be slightly interlocked giving ribbon figure on quarter-sawn surfaces; often has conspicuous resin ducts	Good strength; used as a substitute mahogany; poor bending quality	Good	Poor	Fairly good but a tendency to slight checking and distortion
Swietenia macrophylla **Honduras mahogany** (page 234)	Reasonably fine, even texture; straight grain, but some interlocked grain shows a ribbon figure on quarter-sawn surfaces; growth rings clearly defined; natural surface lustre	Quite strong; good for bending and compression	Fair; subject to pin-hole wood borer attack	Fairly resistant	Good; dries well with little tendency to checking and distortion
Taxus baccata **Yew** (page 235)	Smooth fine texture; irregular grain	High strength; very hard	Excellent	Resistant	Good
Tectona grandis **Teak** (page 234)	Coarse greasy texture; prominent growth ring figure especially on plain-sawn surfaces; often smells like old leather; few knots; acid, alkali and fire resistant	Good impact and excellent bending strength; stiff	Excellent; resistant to insect and fungi attack	Very poor	Seasons well but slowly; otherwise prone to checking and distortion
Terminalia ivorensis **Idigbo** (page 234)	Medium to coarse texture; some interlocked grain but fairly straight with a few irregularities; distinct growth rings	Moderate strength properties; similar to African mahogany, but a tendency to brittleheart; subject to small knots; contains a yellow pigment that stains when wet	Fair, but prone to insect attack; fairly resistant to fungi and termites	Very poor	Seasons rapidly and well with little tendency to check or distort; stable when dry
Thuja plicata **Western red cedar** (page 235)	Soft texture; straight grain; prominent growth rings; subject to bruising; aromatic	Low strength	Excellent	Poor	Good; stable when dry, but thicker stock may collapse
Tieghemella heckelii **Makore** (page 234)	Fine texture and generally straight grain; some interlock grain; the roe figure gives a chequered appearance on quarter-sawn surfaces when interlocked grain is present; a lustrous sheen on plain-sawn surfaces	Medium strong; reasonable bending qualities	Excellent	Very poor	Stable when dry; some tendency to split around knots
Tilia × vulgaris **Lime** (page 234)	Fine even texture; good straight grain; rather soft	Good bending and compressive strength; stiffness	Poor	Good	Good; fairly stable when dry; but some tendency to distort
Triplochiton scleroxylon **Obeche** (page 234)	Moderately coarse but even texture; interlocked grain shows ribbon figure on quarter-sawn surfaces; lustrous surface; bad smell when freshly sawn; prone to blue stain	Good bending strength; resistant to shock loads	Poor	Poor	Seasons well, but may split around knots; prone to slight distortion
Ulmus procera **European elm** (page 234)	Coarse texture; often coarse grain	Good bending strength; resistant to splitting	Poor; subject to heart rot and insect attack	Poor	Variable; subject to checking and distortion

Air dried weight	Working qualities	Fixing qualities	Finishing qualities	Relevant uses	Woods with similar qualities	General comments
768 kg/m³	Fair	Good	Good but needs filling	Furniture, solid and veneer; interior joinery; flooring	American white; European; Japanese and Turkish oak	The other species listed are slightly better quality than the American red oak
416 kg/m³	Good; with care	Good	Good	Exterior joinery; window and door stock	None	A lightweight timber; not suitable for heavy structural work
688 kg/m³	Good; with care	Good with nails and screws; fair with glue	Fair but may need filling	Joinery (interior and exterior)	Light red meranti; white meranti; yellow meranti	A good multi-purpose wood that can be used as a substitute mahogany. Generally, dark red meranti is a better quality wood and is easier to work than the other merantis.
544 kg/m³	Good; some grain pick-up when planing	Tends to split with nails; good with screws and glue	Excellent	Fine interior joinery; panelling; furniture, solid and veneer; cabinetmaking; turning	Honduras and Cuban mahogany are the best-quality woods but other redwoods are similar, e.g. African mahogany	This wood replaced Cuban mahogany on the world market; Cuban mahogany is much darker and denser, but has been in short supply for many years
672 kg/m³	Good but high wastage	Care needed with nails and screws; good with glue	Good	Veneers; mallet heads; long bows; objets d'art; turning	None	Has a relatively low yield; the hardest known softwood
640 kg/m³	Slow machine speeds needed to prevent surface burning and tool edges blunting; care required with end-grain work	Fairly good with nails and screws; fair with glue	Fair	One of the best woods for furniture, solid and veneer; fine joinery (interior and exterior); sheds; gates; turning	Afrormosia, iroko and, for non-structural work, western red cedar	The best-known timber for exterior use, especially in marine work
544 kg/m³	Good; some tearing on quarter-sawn surfaces; keep cutting angle low	Fairly good with nails and screws; fair with glue	Fair; if filled, use teak oil	Fine interior joinery; exterior joinery; flooring; boat building	Indian laurel	Stains yellow in damp conditions; do not use for draining boards, kitchen utensils or tables
384 kg/m³	Good	Care needed with nails and screws; good with glue	Good; an oil base is best	External cladding; wooden shingles; interior panelling; gates; sheds	None	Not a true cedar, but one of the best and most durable exterior softwoods available for non-structural work.
624 kg/m³	Works well but tends to blunt saws and tools due to abrasive silica content; fine dust tends to irritate eyes and nose; use goggles and mask	Tends to split with nails; good with screws; fair with glue	Excellent; in a few cases filler required	Furniture, solid and veneer; fine interior joinery; exterior joinery; flooring	Cuban mahogany; sapele	A good timber for structural and decorative work
544 kg/m³	Good	Good	Good	Brush handles; toys; models; an excellent turning and carving wood	Obeche	A very good multi-purpose wood
384 kg/m³	Good; some tendency to crumble on end grain	Will not hold well in tough usage with nails and screws; fair with glue	Fair	Framing for cabinetmaking; drawer sides; cupboard linings	Meranti	A good wood – but not strong or hard enough for constructional use
560 kg/m³	Fair	Variable with nails and screws; fair with glue	Good but needs filling	Structural parts of furniture; veneers; turning; chopping blocks	Other elms e.g. American white, Dutch, rock, wych	Rock elm in particular is noted for its strength

Fixtures and Fittings

A detailed compendium of all the universal woodworking accessories

Screws, nails and adhesives

Screws are used for fastening wood to wood and for fitting hardware. They are also used to fix joints, particularly those made with knock-down fittings. Screws are ordered by length and gauge (thickness). The higher the gauge number, the thicker the screw. Screws are usually made from brass, steel or aluminium alloy. They may be coated with chromium plating, zinc, black japan, cadmium or bronze.

When joining wood to wood the threaded portion of the screw should penetrate the bottom piece. When joining two pieces of equal thickness, the screw length should be just less than the combined thickness. When joining very thick pieces, counterbore the top piece. Drill pilot holes when there is a danger of the wood splitting. Lubricate screws with grease or soap so they turn more easily, are protected against corrosion and can be withdrawn later. Always use brass screws in oak and sycamore, as steel is attacked by the acid in the wood and will corrode, staining the wood.

Both nails and screws are used in combination with glue when making permanent joints. Nails are made from steel, brass, aluminium alloy, iron and copper.

Screw parts

Shank Gauge Core Pitch
Head Thread
Length

Countersunk, round- and raised-head screws have straight and cross slots. Length is that part sunk into the wood. Add 3 to the gauge number for the drill size in $\frac{1}{64}$th of an inch.

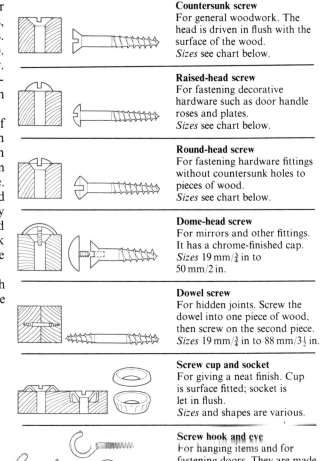

Countersunk screw
For general woodwork. The head is driven in flush with the surface of the wood.
Sizes see chart below.

Raised-head screw
For fastening decorative hardware such as door handle roses and plates.
Sizes see chart below.

Round-head screw
For fastening hardware fittings without countersunk holes to pieces of wood.
Sizes see chart below.

Dome-head screw
For mirrors and other fittings. It has a chrome-finished cap.
Sizes 19 mm/$\frac{3}{4}$ in to 50 mm/2 in.

Dowel screw
For hidden joints. Screw the dowel into one piece of wood, then screw on the second piece.
Sizes 19 mm/$\frac{3}{4}$ in to 88 mm/$3\frac{1}{2}$ in.

Screw cup and socket
For giving a neat finish. Cup is surface fitted; socket is let in flush.
Sizes and shapes are various.

Screw hook and eye
For hanging items and for fastening doors. They are made from brass and coated steel.
Sizes and shapes are various.

Screw lengths and gauges																	

Countersunk ⋎   Straight head ⊘
Round head ⊕   Cross head ⊕
Raised head ⋎   Straight and cross head ●

Gauge number	0	1	2	3	4	5	6	7	8	9	10	12	14	16	18	20
6 mm/$\frac{1}{4}$ in	⊘ ⊘	⊘	⊘ ⊘		⊘ ⊕											
10 mm/$\frac{3}{8}$ in		⊘	⊘ ⊘	● ●	● ● ⊘	⊕	● ●		⊘ ⊕							
13 mm/$\frac{1}{2}$ in			⊘	● ●	● ● ●	● ●	● ● ●	⊘	● ●		⊘					
16 mm/$\frac{5}{8}$ in				⊘	● ● ⊘	● ● ●	● ● ●	● ⊘	● ●		⊘ ●					
19 mm/$\frac{3}{4}$ in				⊘	● ● ●	● ● ⊘	● ● ●	● ⊘	● ●	⊘ ●	● ●	⊘ ⊘				
22 mm/$\frac{7}{8}$ in					⊘		● ⊕	●	● ⊕							
25 mm/1 in				⊘	● ● ●	⊘	● ● ●	● ⊘	● ● ●	● ●	● ● ⊘	● ●	⊘			
28 mm/$1\frac{1}{8}$ in							●		●							
31 mm/$1\frac{1}{4}$ in				⊘	⊘		● ● ●	● ⊘	● ● ●	● ●	● ● ⊘	● ⊘ ⊘				
38 mm/$1\frac{1}{2}$ in				⊘			● ● ●	●	● ● ●	● ●	● ● ●	● ⊘ ⊘	⊘	⊘		
44 mm/$1\frac{3}{4}$ in						⊘	●	⊘	● ● ⊕	● ●	● ● ●	● ⊘ ⊘	⊘	⊘		
50 mm/2 in						⊘	● ⊘	⊘	● ● ●	● ●	● ● ●	● ⊘ ⊘	⊘ ⊘	⊘	⊘	⊘
56 mm/$2\frac{1}{4}$ in							⊘		●		●	●	●			
63 mm/$2\frac{1}{2}$ in							⊘		● ⊘	⊘	● ●	● ⊘ ●	⊘			
69 mm/$2\frac{3}{4}$ in									⊘		⊘	⊘	⊘			
75 mm/3 in							⊘		●		● ⊘	● ⊘ ●		⊘ ⊘	⊘	
81 mm/$3\frac{1}{4}$ in											⊘	⊘				
88 mm/$3\frac{1}{2}$ in									⊘		⊘	⊘	⊘	⊘		
100 mm/4 in									⊘		⊘	⊘	⊘	⊘	⊘	⊘
113 mm/$4\frac{1}{2}$ in									⊘		⊘	⊘				⊘
125 mm/5 in									⊘		⊘	⊘	⊘	⊘		
150 mm/6 in											⊘	⊘	⊘			

Adhesives

Type	Uses	Description	Strength	Water resistance	Setting time	Requires clamping	Gap filling
Animal glue	interior woodwork; veneers; leather; paper	soften cake pieces in cold water overnight. Heat these pieces, powder or granules in cold water. Apply hot	good	very poor	12 hours	no	poor
Gummed paper tape	temporary fixing of veneers	obtained in rolls	good	poor	instant	no	no
Impact (contact)	sheet materials; wood; cork; metal, etc.	ready to use in syrup form. Is a flammable vapour. Not suitable for joints or veneer	very good	good	instant	no	poor
Synthetic resin (four types)	most materials except PVC	add epoxy resin to hardener in equal parts. Fast- and slow-setting types available	very good	very good	12 hours fast type; 3 days slow type	no	very good
	interior woodwork; glass; cork; hardboard	PVA (polyvinyl acetate) is a ready-to-use liquid. Does not stain. Unlimited shelf life	very good	poor	2–3 hours	yes	fair
	interior and exterior woodwork	add resorcinol syrup or powder to liquid hardener	very good	very good	4–8 hours	yes	fair
	interior and exterior woodwork	mix urea formaldehyde powder with water and add hardener	very good	good	4–8 hours	yes	very good

Nails

Round wire nail
For work where strength is more important than looks.
Sizes 19 mm/$\frac{3}{4}$ in to 150 mm/6 in.

Oval wire nail
For joinery. Its head will minimize splitting.
Sizes 13 mm/$\frac{1}{2}$ in to 150 mm/6 in.

Lost-head nail
For general use. The head is driven below the surface.
Sizes 13 mm/$\frac{1}{2}$ in to 150 mm/6 in.

Panel pin
For cabinetwork and mouldings. It is also available with a twisted shank.
Sizes 13 mm/$\frac{1}{2}$ in to 50 mm/2 in.

Veneer pin
For temporarily holding veneers in position on the ground before they are taped.
Sizes 13 mm/$\frac{1}{2}$ in to 50 mm/2 in.

Hardboard pin
For hardboard. Its diamond-shaped head grips strongly.
Sizes 19 mm/$\frac{3}{4}$ in to 38 mm/1$\frac{1}{2}$ in.

Masonry pin
For fastening wood to masonry. It is made from hardened steel.
Sizes 19 mm/$\frac{3}{4}$ in to 100 mm/4 in.

Annular nail
For fastening manufactured boards especially three-ply. Its barbed surface aids grip.
Sizes 19 mm/$\frac{3}{4}$ in to 75 mm/3 in.

Twisted square-head nail
For general use. Its shank provides a screw-type grip.
Sizes 19 mm/$\frac{3}{4}$ in to 100 mm/4 in.

Corrugated fastener
For framing and batten joints.
Sizes 6 mm/$\frac{1}{4}$ in to 22 mm/$\frac{7}{8}$ in. deep; 22 mm/$\frac{7}{8}$ in to 31 mm/1$\frac{1}{4}$ in long.

Small brad
For carpentry. Used in place of round-head nails when extra holding power is required.
Sizes 13 mm/$\frac{1}{2}$ in to 19 mm/$\frac{3}{4}$ in.

Dowel nail
For fastening end to end and for hidden joints.
Sizes 38 mm/1$\frac{1}{2}$ in to 50 mm/2 in.

Needle point
For fastening small mouldings. The head is cut off flush. It has a very fine gauge.
Sizes 13 mm/$\frac{1}{2}$ in to 50 mm/2 in.

Chair nail
For upholstery. It is finished in copper, chrome and bronze.
Sizes 3 mm/$\frac{1}{8}$ in to 13 mm/$\frac{1}{2}$ in head.

Knock-down fittings

Knock-down fittings can be used to assemble furniture made from both solid wood and manufactured boards. The fittings, usually of plastic or of metal, are especially suitable for manufactured boards, such as plastic laminated and wood-veneered chipboard, that cannot be jointed in the traditional way. Furniture with these fittings is usually bought ready to be assembled by using a screwdriver or spanner. Such furniture can easily be assembled or dismantled. The best knock-down fittings remain firm and stable when correctly fitted and tightened, and they distribute the load evenly throughout the structure.

Knock-down fittings are of three basic types: those with threaded fittings, in which a bush lines the hole in the board and the other part is attached to it with a dowel or screw; those with interlocking fittings, in which both parts are surface mounted and locked by wedge action; and those with cam-action fittings, either onset or inset, in which a hook that is attached to one part engages in a cam-operated fitting on the other part and is tightened with a screwdriver.

Knock-down dowel fitting
For making a right-angled butt joint.
Fitting Surface.
It is made from hardened plastics. Drill a 10 mm/⅜ in hole in each piece of wood; then drive in the fitting. Tighten the joint with a dome-headed machine screw to give a strong rigid joint.
Size 19 mm/¾ in.

Bolt and cross dowel
For joining frames such as those on tables and chairs.
Fitting Sunk flush.
The steel bolt has an electro-brass finish and a solid brass collar. Use the bolt in conjunction with a cross dowel and two guide dowels. Tighten the joint with an Allen key.
Sizes 50 mm/2 in and 75 mm/3 in.

Cross dowel and guide dowel
For use with the bolt (*above*) when constructing frames.
Fitting Recessed.
The steel cross dowel has a tapered entry, allowing the bolt to engage more easily.
Sizes 13 mm/½ in and 19 mm/¾ in.
The brass guide dowel prevents the joint swivelling.
Size 10 mm/⅜ in diameter.

Cabinet connecting screw
For joining shelf units or cabinets together, especially kitchen fitments.
Fitting Recessed.
It is designed for use where the overall thickness of the two boards to be joined is between 31 mm/1¼ in and 38 mm/1½ in. Once the screw is in position cover with a plastic cap.
Size 50 mm/2 in.

Pronged T nut and bolt
For fastening frames.
Fitting Recessed.
Drill a hole through both pieces of wood and press the nut home through one piece. The prongs will bite into the wood, providing a firm anchor for the nut. Place the bolt through the other hole. Screw it into the nut.
Size 6 mm/¼ in.

Panel butting connector
For butt jointing panels edge to edge.
Fitting Recessed.
Made from steel, this fitting is particularly useful for anything that requires a tight joint such as a counter top. Once the nut is tightened, the panels will not twist and buckle. The connector is better concealed.
Size 63 mm/2½ in.

Hanger bolt and wing nut
For use with a corner bracket when constructing furniture.
Fitting Recessed.
The bolt is made of steel and has a 6 mm/¼ in machine screw thread on one end and a standard wood screw thread on the other. The joint is tightened with a wing nut on the machine screw end.
Size 50 mm/2 in.

Chipboard dowel rivet
For fastening manufactured boards, especially chipboard, of a greater thickness than 16 mm/⅝ in.
Fitting Recessed.
The barbs on the dowel are in opposite directions to hold both pieces together. The fitting is strong and permanent.
Size 38 mm/1½ in when fastened.

Hollow door fitting
For anchoring hooks and other fittings to doors with cavities, such as those faced with hardboard or five-ply.
Fitting Sunk flush.
Pass the anchor through a pre-drilled hole in the door. As the screw is driven in, the anchor arms grip the inside of the cavity.
Size 16 mm/⅝ in long.

Plastic bush
For preventing chipboard from crumbling when a screw is driven in.
Fitting Recessed.
As the screw is inserted, the outer threads of the bush expand and grip the board, ensuring a tight fit. It may be used for end or face fastening.
Sizes 13 mm/½ in and 25 mm/1 in.

Chipboard screw

For joining frames and panels.
Fitting Recessed.
A pilot hole the thickness of the core is required to sink the bolt. Countersinking is necessary. The thread is designed to fasten chipboard without it crumbling. It is made from steel, with a cross-head that can be covered.
Size 50 mm/2 in.

Metal covered block joint

For making a right-angled butt joint with all types of manufactured board.
Fitting Surface.
The hardened plastic block is composed of two parts, which are screwed into the panels. The whole joint is then covered by a metal fastening plate, to conceal the method of fitting.
Size 31 mm/1¼ in.

Keyhole plate

For concealed hanging of wall cabinets or removable frame components, such as bedheads.
Fitting Surface.
The plate is fastened on to the cabinet and is hung from a No. 10 gauge wood screw driven into the surface to which the cabinet is to be attached.
Size 44 mm × 16 mm/1¾ in × ⅝ in.

Flushmount fitting

For hanging lightweight cabinets on to walls and other cabinets. It is made from zinc-plated steel.
Fitting Surface.
There are two identical parts, each with a slightly raised tongue. One part interlocks with the other.
Size 3 mm/⅛ in thick when assembled.

Right-angled bracket

For joining and supporting frame and furniture panels. The bracket, which is made of zinc-plated steel, is used where appearance is not important, for example, in greenhouses.
Fitting Surface.
Sizes 19 mm × 19 mm × 19 mm/¾ in × ¾ in × ¾ in and 38 mm × 38 mm × 16 mm/1½ in × 1½ in × ⅝ in.

Taper connector

For hanging wall cupboards and joining heavy framed components. Often used for bed frame constructions.
Fitting Surface.
The parts slide together and lock. It is made from heavy gauge, cold-rolled steel.
Sizes 100 mm/4 in and 150 mm/6 in long; 6 mm/¼ in deep.

Shrinkage plate

For edge or end fixing of solid wood. The screws should be fixed at the appropriate end of the slot to allow the wood to shrink across the grain. It can also be used as a fastener on furniture made of manufactured boards.
Fitting Surface.
Size 44 mm × 31 mm/1¾ in × 1¼ in.

Cabinet hanger

For hanging cabinets.
Fitting Surface.
Once fitted, the cabinet can be moved up to 13 mm/½ in from side to side, and up to 13 mm/½ in from back to front. To obtain vertical adjustment to within 10 mm/⅜ in, twist the nut on the nylon cam. It is a simple, effective device.
Size 44 mm/1¾ in square.

Block joint

For making a right-angled butt joint; ideal for 13 mm/½ in to 16 mm/⅝ in thick boards.
Fitting Surface.
Screw the plastic blocks to the panels. Join the two blocks with a machine screw. It is usually necessary to have two fittings per joint.
Size 28 mm × 38 mm × 16 mm/1⅛ in × 1½ in × ⅝ in.

Bolt and cam fitting

For joining panels.
Fitting Bolt is recessed; cam is sunk flush.
This fitting is composed of a plastic bush, a connecting bolt and a plastic or metal cam. Once in place, tighten the cam with a 90° turn of the screwdriver. Plastic caps are available to cover the cam.
Size 28 mm/1⅛ in bolt length.

Modesty block

For light construction work or for strengthening right-angled butt joints on long panels, shelves and frames. Made from hardened plastics, it is ideal where a neater, less obtrusive fitting than the block joint is required.
Fitting Surface.
Size 28 mm × 13 mm × 13 mm/1⅛ in × ½ in × ½ in.

Hooked cam fitting

For joining panels and attaching cabinets to walls and shelving.
Fitting Surface.
The cam action is operated by turning the central slot with a screwdriver. This draws the two parts together. It is made from various metal finishes.
Size 56 mm × 35 mm/2¼ in × 1⅜ in.

Hinges

The traditional butt hinge set into a hand-cut rectangular recess remains one of the most popular hinges for hanging cabinet and room doors. The development of rapid assembly furniture, however, has resulted in the introduction of many new types that are easier to fit. These are fitted as surface mounted hinges or as recessed hinges, which are set into holes that have been bored or routed out. On inset doors, hinges are positioned 150 mm/6 in from the top and 175 mm/7 in to 225 mm/9 in from the bottom. On framed doors hinges should line up with the rail lines. However, doors are usually hinged the hinge length from the top and bottom. It is the position of the centre of the knuckle that determines the throw of the door. Hinges that open 180° or more are often incorporated on kitchen units to save space.

Hinges are available in a range of finishes. Brass hinges tend to be used for fine cabinetwork and are of two types, solid or extruded brass being superior to folded or pressed brass. Steel and nylon hinges tend to be used with cabinets, such as kitchen units.

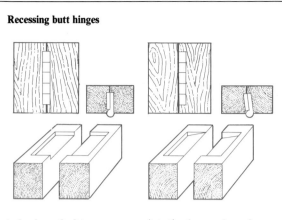

Recessing butt hinges

A simple method to recess a butt hinge is to let both flaps equally into the frame and carcass. Alternatively, the total thickness of the knuckle may be recessed into the door and one flap tapered into the carcass. If the swing of the door is restricted, move the hinge pivot point forward (*see also page 159*).

Common butt hinge
For all doors.
Fitting Surface and recessed.
Sizes Narrow suite, 25 mm × 16 mm/1 in × $\frac{5}{8}$ in to 75 mm × 35 mm/3 in × $1\frac{3}{8}$ in; broad, 38 mm × 22 mm/1$\frac{1}{2}$ in × $\frac{7}{8}$ in to 100 mm × 60 mm/4 in × $2\frac{3}{8}$ in; strong, 38 mm × 25 mm/1$\frac{1}{2}$ in × 1 in to 100 mm × 75 mm/4 in × 3 in; extra broad, 25 mm × 25 mm/1 in × 1 in to 75 mm × 63 mm/3 in × 2$\frac{1}{2}$ in.

Rising butt
For room doors. As the door is opened, the hinge rises and the door is lifted clear of the carpet. The hinges are either left- or right-handed. The top of the door should have a taper bevelled to prevent it from jamming against the frame.
Fitting Recessed.
Sizes 75 mm/3 in to 100 mm/4 in.

Lift-off hinge
For room and cabinet doors. This hinge, which can be left- or right-handed, is made in two parts so that one half can be removed yet still be attached to the door. The leaf with the pin must be fixed to the frame, countersunk side facing.
Fitting Recessed.
Sizes 38 mm/1$\frac{1}{2}$ in to 150 mm/6 in.

Loose-pin hinge
For cabinet and room doors. The whole of the knuckle protrudes to throw the door clear of the carcass. The ball tips may be unscrewed at one or both ends to remove the pin if the door has to be taken off.
Fitting Surface and recessed.
Sizes 25 mm × 16 mm/1 in × $\frac{5}{8}$ in to 75 mm × 41 mm/3 in × 1$\frac{5}{8}$ in.

Piano hinge
For supporting long lengths such as chest flaps, piano lids and table flaps. It is available either as a drilled and countersunk flap or as an undrilled flap.
Fitting Recessed.
Sizes 1,800 mm/72 in and 825 mm/33 in long (can be cut to the required length); 25 mm/1 in and 31 mm/1$\frac{1}{4}$ in wide

Back flap hinge
For table leaves and fall flaps on desks, bureaux and cabinets. Its wide flaps provide strong support.
Fitting Surface and recessed.
Sizes Light pattern, 25 mm × 41 mm/1 in × 1$\frac{5}{8}$ in to 75 mm × 125 mm/3 in × 5 in; heavy pattern, 31 mm × 75 mm/1$\frac{1}{4}$ in × 3 in to 75 mm × 150 mm/3 in to 6 in.

Rule joint hinge
For table extension flaps. The extra long flap is designed to clear the hollow in the cove of the rule joint. The knuckle is on the reverse side to a normal butt hinge to permit a full 90° drop. It has a bronzed finish.
Fitting Recessed.
Sizes 31 mm × 63 mm/1$\frac{1}{4}$ in × 2$\frac{1}{2}$ in to 38 mm × 63 mm/1$\frac{1}{2}$ in × 2$\frac{1}{2}$ in.

Counterflap hinge
For counters and tables with lift-up leaves. The hinge allows the flap to lie back flat along the counter. The most common type has a double pin connected by a smooth link let in flush with the hinge surface.
Fitting Recessed, knuckle down.
Sizes 31 mm × 75 mm/1$\frac{1}{4}$ in × 3 in to 38 mm × 113 mm/1$\frac{1}{2}$ in × 4$\frac{1}{2}$ in.

Flush hinge
For all types of door. This thin one-flap hinge has part cut away to act as a second flap. It is a weak hinge but has the advantage that it will support light doors without the need for recessing. It is made from coated steel.
Fitting Surface.
Sizes 38 mm/1½ in to 75 mm/3 in.

Flush fitting flap hinge
For fall flap bureaux and cocktail cabinets. The pivot action allows the open flap to finish flush with the inner surface of the cabinet. This hinge is often used instead of back flap and counterflap hinges. It is made from metal and plastics.
Fitting Recessed.
Size 35 mm/1⅜ in diameter.

Cranked hinge
For lay-on doors. This good-quality decorative hinge is available mainly in highly polished extruded brass. It gives an opening of 270°. It may be used on either a right- or left-handed door. It is also available double cranked and in a lift-off pattern.
Fitting Surface.
Size 38 mm/1½ in.

Oni semi-mortise hinge
For hanging two doors from a central division; for kitchen cabinets and storage units. The long flap is held by six wood screws. Double and single leaf hinges are available.
Fitting The long flap is mortised; the narrow flaps are recessed.
Size 50 mm/2 in and 75 mm/3 in.

Pivot hinge
For inset or lay-on doors, particularly suitable for kitchen cabinets. This hinge will throw the door clear of the carcass and through an angle of 270°, tucking it out of the way. A small angled cut is needed at the top and bottom of the door for a flush finish.
Fitting Recessed.
Size 16 mm/⅝ in.

Oni semi-invisible hinge
For all types of door, particularly those made from manufactured boards. The cabinet edge has to be hollowed slightly for the hinge to clear it. It is a strong hinge made from extruded brass.
Fitting Recessed.
Size Available in one size only for a minimum door thickness of 19 mm/¾ in.

Necked pivot hinge
For doors that need to be thrown clear of a carcass or through an angle of 270°; suitable for kitchen units. The hinges are fitted into the top and bottom of the door, the pivot plates being recessed into both the frame and the door.
Fitting Recessed.
Sizes 50 mm/2 in to 75 mm/3 in in the closed position.

Cylinder hinge
For inset and lay-on doors, fall flaps, flush tops and cabinet folding doors. It is designed to improve the appearance of furniture, as the hinge is completely concealed when the door is closed. It has an 180° angle of opening.
Fitting Recessed.
Sizes 13 mm/½ in to 16 mm/⅝ in diameter.

Lay-on concealed hinge
For cabinet and cupboard doors. The hinge, which opens at 90°, is available spring-loaded to ensure a secure hold in either the opened or closed position. It can also be used to hold small lift-up flaps in the horizontal position.
Fitting Surface.
Size 113 mm × 41 mm/4½ in × 1⅝ in.

Soss hinge
For all types of light door. It is the original invisible hinge and was the forerunner of the cylinder hinge. It operates through the interconnection of a number of scissor joints, which improves the load distribution of the door. It has an 180° angle of opening.
Fitting Recessed.
Size 44 mm/1¾ in.

Standard 170° opening hinge
For lay-on doors. This wide-angled hinge makes it possible to open the door without disturbing an adjoining closed door by projecting it outwards. The hinge, which is made from metal and plastics, is also available spring-loaded.
Fitting Surface.
Size 110 mm/4⅜ in along the straight edge.

Sepa hinge
For inset and lay-on doors, fall flaps, flush tops. This invisible hinge has a unique seven-pivoted action that allows an inset door to be thrown through an angle of 90° and a lay-on door through an angle of 180°. It is made from extruded brass.
Fitting Recessed.
Size 50 mm/2 in.

Stays, castors and handles

Stays are used to support the fall flaps of cabinets and bureaux, to restrict the swing of wardrobe doors and to support and hold lift-up flaps and box lids. Modern stays have plastic slides or stay housings, for a quiet action, and mechanisms that control the fall so that the flap is lowered smoothly. Some stays are handed, that is, they can only be used on either the left- or the right-hand side of the carcass. Most stays can be fitted on either side. The fitting of a stay is dependent on the carcass to which it will be attached, but as a rough guide a stay should be positioned at approximately 45° to a carcass or flap that is opened at 90°.

Castor wheels, balls or rollers are fitted to furniture to make it more manoeuvrable. Castor wheels are made from hard or soft rubber or plastics. The ball and roller types are made from hardened plastics, solid brass and coated steel. Less common are wooden rollers and porcelain wheels.

Glides have a greater bearing surface than castors, but create more friction. They are used to protect floor surfaces against scarring and are commonly made from nickel plated steel and plastics. Height adjusters, or levellers, similar in design to glides, are fitted on to legged furniture to obtain even floor contact.

Handles, knobs and pulls are available in a wide range of shapes and finishes to suit most types of furniture. The number and placing of handles on furniture is not critical as long as the door or drawer functions smoothly and efficiently. Handle styles should ideally be seen as an integral part of the furniture design. Once these considerations have been made, the final choice is a matter of personal taste.

Stays

Cranked stay
For fall flaps or doors. The steel arm is hinged at the centre, enabling the stay to fold into the cupboard when the flap is closed. It is made right- and left-handed in nickel-plate and electro-brass finishes.
Size 250 mm/10 in long.

Friction stay
For all fall flap applications. The movement of the arm is controlled by adjusting the screw, which responds to finger pressure, on the plastic stay housing. It is made left- or right-handed from nickel-plated steel.
Size 250 mm/10 in.

Quadrant stay
For fall flaps on bureaux and cabinets. A slotted bracket is attached to the carcass. A curved arm screwed to the flap slides through the bracket into a groove cut in the bottom of the carcass. It is made from steel and extruded brass.
Size 113 mm/4½ in.

Telescopic stay
For fall flaps of shallow carcasses in particular. Screwed to the carcass and flap, the supporting arm slides into a hollow metal rod. Once closed, the leaf is held tight; thus extra catches are not needed.
Sizes 125 mm/5 in and 200 mm/8 in.

Self-locking flap stay
For lift-up flaps. To open, lift the flap until it locks. To close, lift the flap slightly and then lower it. One stay is normally sufficient for the average-size flap. It can be adapted for left- or right-handed use by adjusting the plastic housing.
Size 150 mm/6 in arm length.

Cranked lift-up stay
For lift-up flaps on small storage units. The wide sturdy arm locks in the open position. To close, lift the flap slightly before lowering. Its friction mechanism prevents slamming. It is made left- and right-handed from nickel-plated steel.
Size 125 mm/5 in.

Heavy-duty flap support stay
For attaching fold-away tables, shelves and work tops to a wall. Made from steel, it locks automatically when fully opened. To fold, lift slightly and press the middle of the stay. Stays are sold in pairs.
Size 300 mm × 300 mm/12 in × 12 in.

Up and over door mechanism
For wide access to wall units. It comprises two telescopic stays and two straight stays. The mechanism moves the door out of the way — a useful safety feature. No hinges are required.
Size 160 mm/6⅜ in when stays extended but door closed.

Lid stay
For lids that need to be retained open, for example, on hi-fi cabinets. The controlled braking of this stay ensures smooth quiet closing of the lid. It is made left- and right-handed from nickel-plated steel with a plastic housing.
Size 169 mm/6¾ in arm.

Silent stay
For cupboard and wardrobe doors. The nylon slide gives a quiet action. It can be fitted to suit the chosen opening angle of the door and it is made from steel with an electro-brass finish.
Sizes 216 mm/8⅝ in and 253 mm/10⅛ in.

Castors

Methods of fixing castors

Plate   Peg and socket   Screw   Box castor

Castors may be fitted by: a plate made in various shapes, fastened to the base of furniture; a peg and socket driven into the leg; a screw; or a box castor cupped over the end of a tapered or splayed leg.

Ball castor
For all types of furniture. A heavy-duty ball-bearing castor capable of supporting loads up to 230 kg/500 lb.
Fitting Plate, peg and socket, screw-in.
Size 50 mm/2 in diameter.

Roller castor
For easy moving of furniture such as divans and bed frames. The roller is made from plastics and is sometimes slightly crowned to facilitate easy swivelling.
Fitting Plate, peg and socket.
Size 60 mm/$2\frac{3}{8}$ in roller width.

Wheel castor
For trolleys and beds. If the trolley is required to carry heavy loads, wheel castors should be used together with the ball castors.
Fitting Plate, peg and socket, screw-in.
Size 41 mm/$1\frac{5}{8}$ in diameter.

Adjustable swivel glide
For legged furniture. This combination of protective glider and leveller compensates for uneven floors or legs. The steel pin adjusts automatically to the leg angle.
Fitting Steel pin.
Size 6 mm/$\frac{1}{4}$ in pin length.

Handles

Open-pull handle
For doors, drawers and flap pulls. It is available in wood, plastics and metal with numerous finishes and patterns. It can be fitted horizontally or vertically.
Size 88 mm/$3\frac{1}{2}$ in.

Drawer pull handle
For drawers. It was originally designed for use on military chests but it can be equally effective on modern furniture. It is made from brass and steel.
Size 88 mm × 44 mm/$3\frac{1}{2}$ in × $1\frac{3}{4}$ in.

Swan-necked handle
For high-quality furniture, such as chests of drawers. It is commonly available in solid brass and steel with various finishes and patterns.
Sizes 88 mm/$3\frac{1}{2}$ in to 113 mm/$4\frac{1}{2}$ in.

Extruded aluminium pull handle
For doors and drawers, such as on built-in cupboards. It can be fitted vertically or horizontally.
Sizes It is supplied in multiples of 75 mm/3 in, up to a maximum of 900 mm/36 in.

Door handles

Lever handle

Knob set

Recessed pull handle
For sliding doors and drawers. On sliding doors, it is designed to give a convenient grip. It is made from wood, metal and plastics in numerous finishes.
Size 78 mm × 31 mm/$3\frac{1}{8}$ in × $1\frac{1}{4}$ in.

Knob
For cupboards, drawers and doors. It is available in many shapes — round, oval, cylindrical and polygonal. It is made from wood, metal and plastics in numerous finishes.
Size 50 mm/2 in.

Lever handle
For room doors. Most are available spring-loaded for automatic return; the door can then be opened with the elbow or the hand.
Size 100 mm/4 in.

Knob set
For room doors. The most popular type of handle for rim and mortise locks, it is usually sold in pairs and is made in various shapes.
Size 63 mm/$2\frac{1}{2}$ in diameter.

Ring handle
For cupboards and drawers. The handle and its round- or square-shaped surround are made from solid brass and coated steel.
Size 50 mm × 38 mm/2 in × $1\frac{1}{2}$ in.

Locks, bolts and catches

When fitting locks, bolts and catches for security, always fit the best quality available in each category. Locks made from solid brass are superior in quality to those made from folded or pressed brass or steel. Handed locks are also available. When viewed from the opening side, these are either left- or right-handed, according to the direction in which the bolt shoots when the key is turned.

Catches are required only to fasten doors or boxes and to hold them closed. Many are made from plastics or coated steel with plastic rollers for a smoother, quieter action on doors in constant use.

Unless specified below, the escutcheons for locks and striking plates for all the fittings are usually bought separately from the main fitting. They are available in a wide range of sizes and finishes.

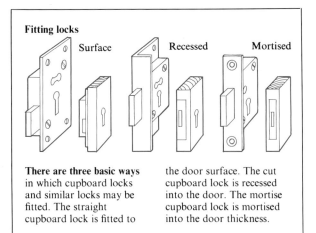

Fitting locks

Surface   Recessed   Mortised

There are three basic ways in which cupboard locks and similar locks may be fitted. The straight cupboard lock is fitted to the door surface. The cut cupboard lock is recessed into the door. The mortise cupboard lock is mortised into the door thickness.

Locks

Drawer lock
For flush-fitting drawers.
Fitting Recessed.
Some locks have two keyholes placed at right angles so that the lock can be used upright, in which case they are handed.
Sizes 38 mm × 31 mm/1½ in × 1¼ in to 75 mm × 47 mm/3 in × 1⅞ in.

Fall-flap lock
For fall-flap bureaux and cabinets; it can also be adapted for small cabinet doors.
Fitting Mortised.
The actual lock is made from hardened plastics but has a nickel-plated mechanism. Recessed locks are also made.
Size 19 mm/¾ in.

Piano lock
For securing lids of long lengths such as those on pianos.
Fitting Mortised.
The bolt shoots upwards and sideways to lock the lid. The mortise must be lengthened to accommodate the bolt.
Size 81 mm/3¼ in.

Box lock
For lift-up lids on boxes.
Fitting Recessed.
The striking plate has two projecting tabs that fall with the lid and are engaged sideways by a bolt in the main part of the lock.
Sizes 38 mm/1½ in to 75 mm/3 in.

Bird's-beak lock
For roll-top desks originally, but can be used on other furniture such as television cabinets.
Fitting Mortised.
The two bolts move upwards and sideways to lock. It is supplied with an escutcheon.
Size 81 mm/3¼ in.

Spring lock
For drawers and cupboards.
Fitting Recessed.
This spring-loaded lock can close without a key. It has a striking plate and is made left- and right-handed.
Sizes 75 mm × 38 mm/3 in × 1½ in to 75 mm × 47 mm/3 in × 1⅞ in.

Hook lock
For inset sliding room doors.
Fitting Recessed and mortised.
A back hook lock is also available for lay-on doors. Both are available as left- and right-handed locks.
Sizes 50 mm × 25 mm/2 in × 1 in to 75 mm × 38 mm/3 in × 1½ in.

Sliding door lock
For wooden sliding doors.
Fitting Sunk flush.
A socket set into the rear frame receives the bolt from the lock when the key is turned. This lock is supplied with an escutcheon. It is finished in nickel plate.
Size 19 mm/¾ in long.

Espagnolette lock
For tall cupboards and wardrobe doors.
Fitting Surface.
Top and bottom bolts are shot or withdrawn in one movement. It is supplied with an escutcheon.
Size 1,200 mm/48 in bar length (can be cut to any length).

Escutcheon
For protecting the wood against scarring by the key.
Fitting Pressing an open-based escutcheon into a hole (*left*); pressing a serrated escutcheon into a hole (*centre*); fixing a plate to the surface with escutcheon pins (*right*).
Sizes and finishes are various.

Bolts

Barrel bolt
For cabinet doors.
Fitting Surface.
Made from extruded brass with a steel shoot, the bolt is available either straight or necked for rebated doors.
Sizes 50 mm × 25 mm/2 in × 1 in to 150 mm × 25 mm/6 in × 1 in.

Flat bolt
For light cabinet doors.
Fitting Surface.
Made from solid brass, it is supplied with a catch plate.
Size 50 mm × 16 mm/2 in × ⅝ in.

Flush bolt
For cupboard doors.
Fitting Recessed.
The bolt can be operated by a knob or a concealed lever. It is made from brass or chromium-plated steel.
Sizes 150 mm × 19 mm/6 in × ¾ in to 900 mm × 25 mm/36 in × 1 in.

Spring bolt
For doors that require a safety catch.
Fitting Surface.
To open, pull out the knob.
Size 16 mm × 69 mm/⅝ in × 2¾ in.

Catches

Single ball catch
For cabinet doors.
Fitting Mortised.
It is made from brass and has a spring-loaded steel ball at the top. The edging gives a neat finish. It is supplied with striking plate.
Sizes 3 mm/⅛ in to 16 mm/⅝ in diameter.

Double ball catch
For high-quality furniture.
Fitting Surface.
The two spring-loaded steel balls are adjusted by turning an integral screw to vary the pull of the door. It is made from solid brass, steel or plastics with a variety of finishes.
Size 50 mm/2 in.

Single roller catch
For kitchen units.
Fitting Surface.
This spring-loaded catch and its striking plate are made from plastics or steel with a rubber roller. Both parts have elongated screw-holes for adjustment when fitting.
Size 35 mm/1⅜ in.

Double roller catch
For cabinet doors.
Fitting Surface
This catch is made from zinc-coated steel and has nylon rollers. It is also available in plated steel with rubber rollers.
Size 31 mm × 28 mm/1¼ in × 1⅛ in.

Peglock catch
For doors or flaps; can also be used to secure small detachable panels or plinths, when a panel that can be easily removed is required.
Fitting Surface.
This catch is made from nylon.
Size 38 mm × 31 mm/1½ in × 1¼ in.

Automatic latch
For opening cabinet doors automatically.
Fitting Surface.
Once fitted, light pressure on the door releases the spring-loaded roller clear of the hook.
It is made from steel and has a plastic roller.
Size 44 mm/1¾ in.

Magnetic catch
For cupboards and doors.
Fitting Surface and recessed.
It is made from hardened plastics and steel. Cylindrical recessed magnetic catches are suitable for lay-on doors.
Sizes 44 mm × 16 mm/1¾ in × ⅝ in to 60 mm × 16 mm/2⅜ in × ⅝ in.

Showcase catch
For display cabinets and cupboards generally.
Fitting Surface.
When fitting to a double door, fit a bolt to the inside of one of the doors. This catch is made from brass.
Sizes 50 mm/2 in to 63 mm/2½ in.

Elbow catch
For wood or metal cabinets.
Fitting Surface.
It has a simple spring action and is made from steel. The lock can be released with the elbow when neither hand is free.
Size 28 mm × 16 mm/1⅛ in × ⅝ in.

Toggle catch
For the lids of boxes and trunks where the catch presses the lid against the base.
Fitting Surface.
Both this catch and its fastening plate are available in brass- or zinc-plated steel.
Size 38 mm × 69 mm/1½ in × 2¾ in.

Shelves, drawers and storage fittings

With the advent of modern types of fittings and techniques, it has become possible for many woodworkers to build a piece of furniture, such as a chest of drawers or a bookshelf, that was perhaps too complicated or too time-consuming to attempt previously. With the availability of new extension fittings, it has also become feasible to construct built-in wardrobes in, for example, narrow recesses. Other modern fittings serve to utilize space more economically within the room. The extending table runner, for example, provides support for an extra work surface.

The construction of wooden drawers is, perhaps, one of the most difficult tasks for the woodworker. For certain applications such as bedroom, kitchen and bathroom furniture, which tend to be made from manufactured boards, this problem has been solved by the introduction of ready made, easy to assemble plastic drawers available in kit form. No drilling or routing is required to assemble them. They are supplied with four sides, or three sides if a drawer front of another type is required to match existing furniture.

There are a number of fittings available for supporting shelves made from solid wood and manufactured boards. These fittings range from small plastic studs, 19 mm/¾ in long that slide into sockets on the side of the carcass, to metal brackets 250 mm/10 in long that support the shelf from the back. As long as the shelves are sufficiently sturdy, that is, between 19 mm/¾ in and 25 mm/1 in thick, and there is no more than 750 mm/30 in between supports, sagging should be minimal. The advantage of adjustable shelving is that it can be readily adapted for most storage purposes.

Shelves

Heavy-duty shelving system
Comprises steel wall channels into which two-pronged brackets are inserted. The S-shaped bend between the prongs ensures that there is no lateral movement. Accessories include tilt brackets and bookends. Each bracket can support 40 kg/88 lb.
Size Channel 1,000 mm/40 in; bracket 150 mm/6 in and 250 mm/10 in.

Lightweight shelving system
Comprises aluminium wall channels into which PVC locking strips are inserted to provide anchorage for the shelf brackets. Press fit each bracket in the horizontal position, then twist it until vertical. Shelf heights can be adjusted by tilting bracket up and sliding it. Each bracket supports about 15 kg/33 lb.
Size Channel and brackets are cut to order.

Shelf bracket
For shelves in which the finish is secondary to strength, for example, in workshops and greenhouses. The bracket, which is made from zinc-plated or japanned steel, offers rigid support, the long vertical arm being capable of countering much leverage.
Size 31 mm × 19 mm/1¼ in × ¾ in.

Cantilevered bracket
For moderate shelf support. The bracket is simply fitted by pushing the pin at the back into a pre-drilled hole in the wall and reinforcing it with a screw driven through the rear upturned part of the bracket. Screw the shelf to the bracket, which is made from zinc-coated steel.
Size 113 mm/4½ in.

A

B

C

D

E

F

Stud shelf supports
For adjustable shelving in cabinets, bookcases and other fitted units. Fit the studs into holes about 150 mm/6 in apart along the length of the carcass sides, according to requirements. Four studs — two at each end — will support most shelves. Some of the various types of stud shelf support available are: a plastic stud with an integral nail (A); a coated steel or brass eye and socket for lightweight shelves (B); an angled, coated-steel stud and socket for supporting heavily-laden shelves (C); a plastic stud and bush (D); a moulded plastic bracket stud (E); and a two-piece shelf support (F). This last fitting comprises two plastic pegs. Fit the shelf between these two pegs so that the arms of the upper peg spread and grip the shelf. Once fitted, the shelf cannot be moved accidentally.

Magic wire
For fitting wooden shelves invisibly. Fit the ends of the wires into two holes positioned slightly closer than the length of the wire. Make stopped grooves in the ends of the shelf, which can then slide on to the wires. The shelf is given almost total support along its width.
Sizes 138 mm/5½ in to 219 mm/8¾ in.

Bookcase strip
For bookcases or fitted units. Screw the strip along the length of the carcass sides and clip the studs into the horizontal slots. Both the strip and the studs are made in two finishes — zinc- or bronze-coated steel.
Size 900 mm/36 in length (can be cut shorter with a hacksaw); 19 mm/¾ in width.

Drawers and runners

Roller
For heavily-laden drawers. Set the roller into the bottom of a drawer and fasten it with two wood screws. Form a small rebate beneath each roller to allow for free movement.
Size 25 mm/1 in diameter.

Drawer glide
For lightweight drawers. Attach the plastic glide to the inside of the carcass by inserting four wood screws into the push-in dowel supports.
Size 288 mm × 16 mm × 6 mm/11½ in × ⅜ in × ¼ in.

Drawer side saddle
For wooden and plastic drawers so they open and close smoothly. Fit into the drawer aperture and adjust it by means of its slotted screw-holes.
Size 19 mm × 31 mm/¾ in ×1¼ in.

Central drawer guide
For preventing the drawer from tipping when fully extended and for securing the drawer to the centre rail. Attach it to the drawer back at the top or the bottom.
Size 44 mm × 35 mm × 6 mm/1¾ in × 1⅜ in × ¼ in.

Ready to assemble drawers

Drawer sides made from plastics are bought cut to the required size. Assemble them with corner fittings that push into the drawer ends. A bottom made of 3 mm/⅛ in hardboard or three-ply is supplied separately, as are the drawer runners.
Sizes 100 mm/4 in and 119 mm/4¾ in depth.

Drawer runner
For chipboard-sided drawers or for providing existing cupboards with wooden drawers. Made from steel, it is fitted with nylon wheels for smooth and quiet running.
Sizes 450 mm/18 in and 550 mm/22 in.

Storage fittings

Extending table runner
For supporting a work-top extension up to 769 mm/30¾ in long. Attach this steel runner to a work top made in three sections so that it can slide down the back of the cabinet when not in use.
Size 800 mm/32 in.

Corner fitting
For providing easy access to items stored in corner cabinets. The doors help to support the shelves. It only fits inset doors as when one door is opened the other door automatically moves inside the cabinet.
Size 741 mm/29⅝ in of pole.

A. Rod and socket.

C. Extending rail.

B. Guide rail.

D. Sliding rail.

E. Pull-down rail.

Wardrobe fittings
Storage space for clothes needs to be at least 600 mm/24 in deep to allow for the coat hangers. The conventional rod and socket (**A**) is made from plastic-covered steel or brass. The plastic guide rail (**B**) runs on an aluminium track. Mounted directly on the underside of the carcass, this type of fixing prevents the sagging sometimes encountered with the rod and socket. The extending wardrobe rail (**C**) is used when there is insufficient depth to hang clothes sideways. The sliding wardrobe rail (**D**) is an alternative space-saving fitting to the extending wardrobe rail. The pull-down rail (**E**) utilizes the space in a floor to ceiling wardrobe, the pull-down rail giving easy access to clothes.

Glossary

Abrasive paper A general term used for paper such as garnet paper and glasspaper. It is sometimes referred to as sandpaper.
Adze A tool similar to an axe on a long shaft but with the blade turned at a right angle to the shaft axis.
Allen key A cranked hexagonal iron rod used for turning bolts and screws with hexagonal recessed heads.
Annual ring *see* Growth ring.
Apron rail The long rail fixed at right angles under or against a horizontal board or rail.
Arbor A spigot that is integral with an accessory for fixing into the chuck of a power tool.

Banding Strips of veneer set around central veneer panels, comprising borders and sometimes stringing.
Barefaced Employing only one shoulder.
Batten A narrow strip of wood used for making or stiffening light frames.
Bead in To insert beading into a rebate by gluing and occasionally pinning.
Beading A moulding with a curved profile, usually semicircular.
Bearer Anything that supports and/or spreads a load.
Bevel An edge fully formed at an angle other than 90° to the face side.
Bleeding The process in which some of the substances in wood, such as soluble salts and resin, are removed, either naturally or during the manufacturing process.
Blister A defect found in laid veneer, in which the veneer is raised from the ground because there is no adhesion.
Blooming A defect resulting from a surface coating taking in moisture from the air while drying. It shows as a whitish film or mist on the surface.
Boat A piece of abrasive paper or card folded into a container shape to hold spirit stain when colouring.
Bodying The second stage of french polishing, using a rubber.
Bolster The shoulder of a chisel blade where it meets the handle.
Bucked Cross-cut.
Buff To rub with a soft absorbent cloth by hand or machine in the final stages of polishing.
Bull-nose work Planing into corners and stopped rebates as done by the bull-nose plane.
Burnish *see* Buff.
Burnisher A cylindrical silver steel rod with a wooden handle for turning over the edges of a cabinet scraper.
Burr edge A wire edge such as that left on a tool after grinding or the finish on a hardboard edge after planing.
Burr, of a tree An irregular outgrowth on a tree caused by injury to the tree and often yielding a highly ornamental figure.
Bush A metal or plastic lining inserted in a hole in chipboard for gripping a screw; it can be smooth or threaded. Also, a lining for a hole reducing the diameter to a required size.
Butt joint Two boards that meet side edge to side edge or side edge to end.

Calcareous deposit A chalky white stony deposit.
Capping A finishing strip of wood, often a moulding.
Carpentry The structural use of wood in the building trade.
Catch plate A receiving plate on a frame for bolts or catches.
Caul Flat wood used to distribute the pressure evenly on to the veneer and ground. A double caul is two flat pieces of wood placed on either side of counter-veneered ground to distribute the pressure evenly on to the two veneers.
Chamfer That part of an edge that is angled.
Cheeks, of a carcass The outer vertical sides of a carcass.
Cheeks, of a saw The upright pieces of a bowsaw.
Chilling A surface defect in which the coating has taken in moisture from the air resulting from a solvent evaporating too quickly.
Chisel plane A bull-nose plane with the front removed leaving the blade completely exposed and projecting beyond the front of the plane.
Chuck A device for holding wood for turning, or for gripping a bit in a handbrace or a drill in a hand drill or power drill.
Cleat A batten fastened to an accessory for holding and reinforcement purposes.
Cock beading A thin decorative beading surrounding a drawer front.
Cockle A defect, usually with dry veneer leaves, in which the material bends into ripples.
Core The centre material. Blockboard, for example, has a solid wood core.
Core, of a screw The central part of the threaded portion of a screw.
Counterbore To bore a hole the diameter of the screw-head for deep sinking of the screw. This allows a shorter screw to be used.
Countersink To shape a screw-hole to allow the head of a countersunk screw to finish flush with the wood surface.
Counter veneer To veneer both sides of a ground, so balancing its tendency to warp.
Crest rail The top back rail of a chair.
Crossbeam An intermediate horizontal support.
Crosshatch To draw diagonal lines at right angles to hatch lines to distinguish one area from another.
Cross member Any member or component that crosses another or others.

Dado A groove cut across the wood grain. When the end of a second board is fitted into the dado, a housing joint is formed.
Datum line A reference line on a flat straight surface from which all measurements can be taken, for example, face side, face edge.
Depth The measurement from front to back or the recess measurement in from a surface.
Dowel plug A wood plug filling a cylindrical hole with its grain running perpendicular to the surrounding area.
Draw bore To insert a dowel through a mortise and tenon joint

with the hole in the tenon slightly offset towards the shoulder to draw the joint up tightly.
Drawfile To draw a file horizontally backwards and forwards at right angles to a metal edge, to remove some of the marks made by filing, when the file was held at an angle with its teeth at right angles to the metal edge.
Drying in the round Drying wood in such a way as to allow air to circulate around all its surfaces.
Dulling A process in which a surface coating is rubbed with a very fine abrasive to diminish its original gloss.
Durability (seasoning) The length of time over which wood remains stable.
Dustboard A board, usually made from three-ply or hardboard, inserted between drawers to cushion their movement.

Ebonize A process in which wood is blackened to resemble ebony.
Edge The narrow surface at right angles to the sides. In this book, where it has been necessary to distinguish between the various edges of a board, the edges that run along the grain are referred to as side edges and the other two as ends.
End The cheek of a carcass or the edge that runs across the grain.

Face edge An edge planed perfectly straight and at right angles to the face side.
Face mark A mark on the face side that reaches over to the face edge to distinguish them from the other surfaces during working.
Face side The better of the two wide surfaces that is chosen to be exposed on the finished work. It must have been planed absolutely flat.
Face veneer Veneer laid on the uppermost side of the ground.
Fadding The initial stage of french polishing, using a fad or a rubber.
Feather To taper to a thin edge.
Fence A fixed or adjustable stop against which the work can be held or guided.
Ferrule A metal band around the handle base of a tool to prevent splitting where the shank is fitted.
Fibres The strengthening tissues in wood.
Fielded panel A panel tapered and sometimes shouldered towards its edges so it will fit into grooves in the frame.
Figure The surface appearance of the wood caused by inherent colouring substances and the arrangement of the wood tissues.
Fillet A narrow sliver of wood.
Fillister plane A general term for rebating planes fitted with fences.
Fishtail blade A blade with a fanned out shape.
Flush Level. When two adjacent surfaces are level with one another, they are said to be flush.
Fluting Concave grooves used for decoration.
Former The mould against which wood is held to bend it to shape. The male former is the convex mould; and the female, the concave mould.

Full-grained finish A surface finish in which the pores between the grain are filled.

Gauge To score or mark with the spur of a gauge.
Gauged line A line marked by the spur of a marking or mortise gauge parallel with an edge of the wood.
Glue block A block of wood glued to the inside corner of a joint for additional strength.
Grain The arrangement and direction of the wood tissues. Wood may be worked in one of four ways: *with the grain*, meaning in the direction of the grain; *across the grain*, meaning at right angles to the grain; *against the grain*, meaning in the opposite direction to the grain; and *along the grain*, meaning up and down the grain.
Grain, end At the end of a piece of wood where it has been cross-cut.
Grain, interlocked Grain that inclines obliquely up the tree, first in one direction and then in the other.
Grain, silver A distinctive ray figure that shows in quarter-sawn oak.
Grain, spiral Grain that follows either a left- or right-handed diagonal course up the tree.
Groove A channel worked along the grain.
Ground The base, either of solid wood or of manufactured boards, on to which veneers are laid.
Growth ring A ring produced by a layer of open earlywood followed by a layer of dense latewood.
Guide A general term for a fence or a jig.
Guide, drawer A square strip of wood glued and pinned to a drawer runner to guide the drawer in square with the carcass front.

Handed A term applied to rising butt and lift-off hinges, locks and stays. Where a door opens towards the operator, a hinge on the left side of that door is said to be left-handed; conversely, a hinge on the right side is said to be right-handed.
Hanger A piece of wood dovetailed into a carcass top rail to support a lower component, such as a drawer runner, when there is no upright running centrally from the top to the bottom of the carcass.
Hardwood A botanical term used for broad-leafed trees. The wood is not necessarily hard.
Hatch To draw diagonal lines; used to indicate waste to be cut away.
Haunch A shortened portion of a tenon to keep the joint locked at the corner.
Hinge knuckle The spine of a hinge.
Hone To sharpen a tool edge on a stone.
Horn The excess wood left on a mortise piece to prevent the mortise from splitting while the joint is being cut. The horn is sawn off after the joint is assembled.
Housing A groove cut across the grain to house the end of a board.

In-cannel Where the blade of a gouge has a grinding bevel on the inside.
Inlay The insertion of wood, metal or other material into a veneered or solid wood surface to give a

decorative appearance. The inlay is flush with the surface.

Inset door A door that fits in the sides, top and bottom of a carcass or frame.

"In winding" A defect in which a board is twisted along its length as a result of faulty drying or storage.

Jig A device for holding wood or a tool enabling work to be done quickly and accurately.

Joinery Fine woodwork in the building trade.

Kerf The cut made in wood by a saw blade.

Key To roughen, usually with an abrasive paper or a toothing plane, to give a surface stronger adhesive properties.

Keying The reinforcement of a mitred corner with $2\,\mathrm{mm}/\frac{3}{32}$ in three-ply or veneer.

Kickback The action of a portable power saw when it jumps out of the wood towards the worker or wood when it shoots from a fixed power saw towards the worker. This occurs when the blade cannot cut forwards either because the kerf closes around the blade, the blade hits a nail or knot, or, in the case of portable power saws, because the blade has twisted in the wood.

Kicker A device—usually a small strip of wood—fitted to a carcass rail above the drawer to prevent the drawer tipping upwards when it is withdrawn.

Knock-down fitting A modern fitting designed to assemble and dismantle components easily. It is often suitable for manufactured boards, where traditional jointing or fixing is not practical.

Knot, pin A small knot.

Laminated board Solid wood or manufactured board faced with smooth hard plastic on both sides.

Lath A flexible strip of wood, thinner than a batten. It can be used for panel infilling.

Lay-on door A door that shuts against the front of a carcass rather than being framed by the carcass.

Length The measurement along the wood grain.

Loper A horizontal arm that slides out of a bureau or an extending table to support a flap.

Louvre door A door frame with horizontal sloping wooden slats to provide both cover and air circulation.

Magic wire A wire shelf support.

Mating pieces Two pieces of wood with shaped surfaces, which when brought together fit closely.

Mitre joint A joint in which the junction bisects the angle of the mating pieces, usually at 45°.

Mortise A rectangular hole. On a workbench, a bench-dog fits into a mortise. On a joint, a tenon fits into a mortise.

Moulding A shaped wooden edge used as decoration. It can be integral (stuck) or planted on in strip form with pins and glue.

Moulding, half-round A moulding of semicircular section.

Moulding, ogee A reverse-curved moulding.

Moulding, ovolo A convex moulding.

Moulding, quarter-round A moulding of quarter-circular section.

Muntin The dividing piece of wood between two stiles or two panels, to provide extra support to the frame or drawer bottom.

Out-cannel Where the blade of a gouge has a grinding bevel on the outside.

Oversailing A top that is planted on to the carcass cheeks and that projects on one or more sides, front and back.

Overset To set the blade of a plane or the teeth of a saw too coarsely.

Pack A bundle, especially of veneers.

Panel A thin infilling board in a frame.

Parcel A bundle, of veneers or mixed solid wood boards and manufactured boards.

Patina The valued surface finish on old furniture produced naturally by time and aided by repeated burnishing.

Pellet A slightly tapered wood plug filling a round hole with its grain running in line with the surface grain.

Pilaster A vertical piece of wood with a rectangular section applied to the front of a carcass.

Pilot hole A small hole drilled into wood to act as a guide for a larger drill bit; it is usually made with a bradawl or a small drill bit.

Pitch The angle at which a sloping surface meets a horizontal surface.

Pitch, of a screw The ratio of screw-thread turns in relation to the distance travelled along the axis of a screw; for example, eight turns to $25\,\mathrm{mm}/1$ in.

Plain sawing The commonest method of slicing logs, in which they are sliced perpendicular to the growth rings. It is also called through-and-through and slash sawing.

Planted Not built into the structure but added later.

Plinth A base for a piece of furniture or ornament usually constructed separately from the rest of the carcass.

Plumb Vertical. When a component stands absolutely vertically, it is said to be plumb.

Ply A single thin sheet of veneer. An odd number of plies laid and bonded at right angles to the adjacent ply or plies is known as three-ply, five-ply or multi-ply, according to the number of plies.

Pocket screw To screw through an angled slot or hole on the inside of a rail.

Post The vertical corner member in carcass construction.

Proud Uneven. Two adjacent surfaces at different levels. The surface that projects is said to be proud.

PTFE Polytetrafluoroethylene. A plastic used as a non-stick coating on saws and other tools.

PVA Polyvinyl acetate. It is the basis of many cold glues.

PVC Polyvinyl chloride. It is a plastic sheet material.

Quarter sawing Logs first cut longitudinally into quarters, then cut into boards.

Quirk stick A small pared piece of wood shaped to remove excess woodfiller and glue from recesses and corners.

Radial cut A cut from the bark towards the pith, along the rays.

Rail A horizontal piece of wood between two vertical components in a carcass or frame.

Rays Storage tissues radiating in thin lines from the pith to the phloem of a tree.

Rebate A right-angled recess or step along the edge of a piece of wood.

Recess An area at a lower level than the surface.

Reeds A series of small beadings worked closely together.

Relief line A line drawn around the base of a relief carving to indicate the lowest depth to which to carve.

Resin glue A chemical, vegetable or mineral glue, usually in two parts, resin and hardener, mixed together before use.

Resin, in a tree An inherent sticky substance characteristic of certain woods, particularly pines.

Reverse curve A concave curve followed by a convex curve, or vice versa.

Reviver A solution made from equal parts linseed oil, household vinegar and methylated spirit used for removing dirt, grease and wax from wood surfaces.

Ricking The distortion of a carcass out of square, usually leading to a loosening of the joints.

Rod A full-size model or sectional drawing showing constructional detail.

Roe A combination of fiddleback and ribbon figure on wood with interlocked grain.

Rubbing compound An abrasive paste rubbed on to surface coatings to dull a gloss finish.

Runner A channel or support along which the side or bottom edge of a drawer slides.

Saddle A nylon plate fitted into a drawer aperture and used in conjunction with a drawer guide. The saddle induces smooth action and alignment of the drawer.

Saddle seat The slotted part of the saddle that encompasses the drawer guide.

Scratch bead Beading formed by a scraping tool such as a scratch stock.

Screw, machine A screw with a blunt end that is unsuitable for driving into wood without pre-drilling a hole.

Screw, wood A screw with a tapered end for easy driving into wood.

Scribe To mark out against a profile with a sharp point.

Section The true shape of a piece of wood shown when cut at right angles to its length.

Set down To position below the surface.

Set in To outline features in a design by cutting vertically around them into the wood when carving.

Shank, of a bit That part of a bit or drill held in the jaws of a brace or hand drill.

Shank, of a screw That part of a screw between the head and the first thread.

Shear To break across the axis of a bolt or a screw.

Shellac A substance produced by masses of small tree insects in India. "Lakh" in Urdu means a hundred thousand. It is the basic ingredient in french polish.

Shoulder The end-grain surface perpendicular to the tenon.

Side The wide surface at right angles to the edges.

Side edge The narrow surface of a board that runs parallel with the grain.

Silver sand Fine sand.

Size A dilute glue used for sealing a porous surface.

Slab construction A carcass made from manufactured boards.

Slab form The form in which manufactured boards are available, that is, sheets.

Slat A wood component that has a width far greater than its thickness.

Slot screw To drive a screw through a slot instead of a hole to allow for wood shrinkage.

Slow-schedule wood Wood that takes a long time to season.

Softwood A botanical term used for cone-bearing trees with needle-like leaves. The wood is not necessarily soft.

Spacer A piece of wood or metal, either collar or block shaped, used in pairs to position the work a certain distance from the fence.

Spigot A peg or peg-like protrusion, usually integral with the work, that enters a mating socket for locating or pivoting.

Spindle, in a drill press A vertical rotating shaft in a stationary housing.

Spindle, on a chair A thin, often tapered, turned piece of wood, commonly used in chair backs.

Spindle, on a lathe A small rotating hollow shaft on which stock is turned; one is at the tailstock and a second is at the headstock where it protrudes on both sides.

Spur, on a gauge The vertical pointed pin on a marking or mortise gauge used for marking and scoring measurement lines parallel to an edge.

Spur, on a plane The vertical cutting blade on a combination plane or multi-plane used for severing the fibres when cross-cutting.

Squared line A line marked with a pencil or marking knife and a try square, the stock of which rests against a datum line or face side.

Square off To cut or plane ends or side edges at right angles to each other.

Square round To mark a continuous line around a piece of wood, using a pencil or a marking knife and a try square.

Squaring rod A device, taking many forms, for checking if two edges form a right angle.

Stable wood Wood that has been efficiently seasoned for its intended environment and is therefore liable to shrink or distort only minimally.

Steel wool Strands of very tough fine steel, used in pads for smoothing wood or surface coatings; also for removing surface

Glossary

coatings. It is available from grade 4, which is the coarsest, to grade 0000, which is the finest. Steel wool is also known as wire wool.

Stem, of a gauge The rod along which the stock of a marking, cutting or mortise gauge slides.

Stepping off To mark off a measurement, usually with dividers, along a continuous line.

Sticking and stacking A method of piling boards so air circulates around them while they are seasoning.

Stile The vertical sides in the frame of a door or a window.

Stock The body of a plane gauge, T-square or mitre square.

Stock, on a lathe A roughly shaped piece of wood ready to be formed more fully on the lathe.

Stop-block, on a table saw A block of wood clamped in the required position to act as a stop and datum point when cross-cutting a number of pieces of wood to the same length.

Stopped Not cut through. When a rebate, housing or chamfer does not run to the end of the work.

Stopping The process of filling holes and cracks; also, the waxy material or resin compound used to fill the holes in wood surfaces. It is available in coloured blocks or hard sticks.

Stretcher rail The horizontal crosspiece or rail connecting the lower parts of the legs of a chair, table, etc.

Striking plate A metal plate used to protect the wood surface against the bolts of locks and catches and to provide more security.

Stringing Narrow straight-grained veneer strips laid between central veneer panel(s) and borders. They should be of contrasting colour to the borders. They can be bought or made.

Strop A strip of stiff leather dressed with a fine abrasive used for perfecting the cutting edges of tools after they have been sharpened on an oilstone or slipstone.

Strop To perfect the cutting edge of a tool by rubbing on a leather strop or on the palm of the hand.

Stumpwood Wood cut from the base of a tree.

Sub-base A plinth. The base that raises the unit from the floor to show the design in the round and to prevent bruising the carcass when floor cleaning.

Sub-frame A subsidiary frame that is assembled separately and connected to a carcass frame.

Substrate The lower layer or layers.

Surform A brand name for a range of rasp planes. They have rasp-like blades fitted into shaped holders.

Sweep The curved cross-section of a gouge.

Take off (dimension) To transfer measurements from a drawing to the work.

Tang, of a bit That part of a bit that fits into the chuck of a brace.

Tang, of a chisel The pointed end of a chisel blade that drives into the wooden handle, to hold the two parts together.

Tangential cut A cut made by plain sawing wood longitudinally.

Tannin An astringent substance found in oak and other trees that has the capacity to rust ferrous metals.

Tempered, of a tool Heat-treated to change the natural physical properties. Tempered cutting edges on tools have been treated to hold their sharp edges.

Tempered, of hardboard Hardboard soaked in oil to make it water resistant.

Template A shape or pattern cut to act as a guide in the repeat work on a design.

Thickness The sectional measurement between the two wide surfaces.

Thread, of a screw The spiral part of a screw.

Three-leaf top An extending table top in which the outside leaves can be pulled apart, allowing for the insertion of a third section.

Through From end to end; when a rebate, housing or chamfer runs the length of the work.

Transverse cut A cross-sectional cut across the trunk of the tree.

True Accurately shaped. When work is perfectly shaped it is said to be true.

True up To check that edges are straight and corners are square.

Truss The end supports for a refectory table; also, a framed structure for roof support.

Undercut To cut inside the line of the vertical.

Underframe A frame beneath a top or main frame.

Underside The opposite side to the face side.

Veneer, constructional Plain-figured veneer, usually thicker than decorative veneer.

Veneer, decorative Finely-figured veneer used for laying on the face of the ground.

Waney edge The natural edge of a tree trunk that has been retained after conversion.

Warping A general term used for cupping, bowing, "in winding" and diamonding in wood. Warping can be caused by underseasoning or careless storage.

Wedges, folding Pairs of wedges used as a basis for exerting pressure. As the tapered surfaces are slid together their combined thickness increases. The force generated can be applied to cramps.

Width The measurement across the grain.

Window An opening cut in a piece of veneer when doing marquetry.

Wire wool *see* Steel wool.

Yellow deposits Stony deposits in wood.

Credits

The publishers wish to thank the following individuals and organizations for their assistance in the preparation of this book:
Bob Adsett; E.P. Barrus Limited, Bicester, Oxfordshire; Black and Decker Limited, Maidenhead, Berkshire; Robert Brant, Hawkhurst, Kent; John Brazier, Princes Risborough, Buckinghamshire; Brine Veneer Mills Limited, London; Burgess and Galer, London; Ceka Works Limited, Pwllheli, Gwynedd; Christies South Kensington; Copydex, London; Craft Supplies, Buxton, Derbyshire; Craftsman Division, Hagemeyer (London) Limited; Geffrye Museum, London; General Woodworking Supplies, London; GKN Wood Screws, West Midlands; Harvey's Auctions Limited, London; Kity Tools UK, Leeds; James Latham Limited, London; Ledbury Antiques, London; Jack Maynard; Peter Metcalfe, London College of Furniture; Steve Newton; Terence Morse and Son, London; Neill Tools Limited, Sheffield; Quailcraft, Working Wood magazine, Surrey; Record Ridgeway Tools Limited, Sheffield; Michael Rock; Roger's, Hertfordshire; John Sainsbury; Sandvik UK Limited, Sotheby Parke Bernet and Company; Spear and Jackson Tools Limited, Sheffield; Stanley Tools Limited, Sheffield; Statton Engineering Company, Stone, Staffordshire; TMT Design Limited, Warwick; H. G. Triggs; Victoria and Albert Museum, London; Wolf Electric Tools Limited, London.

Particular thanks are due to the following shops for the loan of tools for artists' references: E. Amette and Company Limited, London; Buck and Ryan Limited, London; Old Woodworking Tools, London; Alec Tiranti Limited, Theale, Berkshire; S. Tyzack and Son Limited, London.

Photographs 227 top left Building Research Establishment; 227 top right Bill Hallworth; 228 top International Paper Company; 228 bottom G.R. Roberts; 228/229 centre National Film Board of Canada; 229 top left Malcolm Kirk, The Daily Telegraph Colour Library; 229 top right Frank Prazak, The Image Bank of Canada; 229 bottom The Commonwealth Institute; 230/235 microphotographs Building Research Establishment, Princes Risborough; 230/235 wood photographs Mike Busselle, Mitchell Beazley; 236 top left G.R. Roberts; 236/237 centre Bryan and Cherry Alexander; 236 bottom left Canadian Pacific; 236 bottom right Ernest Scott; 237 G.R. Roberts; 239 top centre left, top right, bottom centre left, bottom centre right and bottom right Mike Busselle, Mitchell Beazley.

Principal artists
Mick Gillah, Kevin Maddison, Peter Morter, Coral Mula.

Additional artwork by
Kai Choi, Harry Clow, Chris Forsey, Nigel Osborne, Charles Pickard, Mike Saunders, Del Tolton.

Title pages and section openers photographed by Clive Corless and tools loaned by Old Woodworking Tools, London.

Additional photography by Frances Eveleigh and Angelo Hornak.

Picture research by Brigitte Arora assisted by Meg Price Whitlock.

Index

Index

Index